The Faith
of the Old Testament

WERNER H. SCHMIDT

The Faith
of the Old Testament
A History

Translated by John Sturdy

THE WESTMINSTER PRESS
PHILADELPHIA

English translation ©1983 Basil Blackwell Publisher Limited

Published in German as
Alttestamentlicher Glaube in seiner Geschichte
(Neukirchener Studienbücher Band 6)
©1968, fourth edition 1982, Neukirchener Verlag des
Erziehungsvereins GmbH, Neukirchen-Vluyn

Published by The Westminster Press®
Philadelphia, Pennsylvania

PRINTED IN THE UNITED STATES OF AMERICA
9 8 7 6 5 4 3 2 1

Library of Congress Cataloging in Publication Data

Schmidt, Werner H.
  The faith of the Old Testament.

  Translation of: Alttestamentlicher Glaube in
seiner Geschichte.
  Bibliography: p.
  Includes index.
  1. God—Biblical teaching. 2. Bible. O.T.—Theology.
3. Bible. O.T.—History of contemporary events.
I. Title.
BS1192.6.S3513   1983   221.6′7   82-21780
ISBN 0-664-21826-1
ISBN 0-664-24456-4 (pbk.)

Contents

Foreword

Werner H. Schmidt has characterized his book, now in its fourth edition in German, as standing midway between a 'history of Israelite religion' and a 'theology of the Old Testament'. So the faith of the Old Testament is depicted in terms of its historical development in its widest context, not only through the history of the nation of Israel and its antecedent elements, but also in relation to the social, political and religious situation in the contemporary peoples and cultures of the ancient Near East. Indeed, not the least valuable feature of this book is the way in which the influences of the surrounding world on the Israelite religious sphere are set out, comprehensively yet succinctly and with a sober assessment both of the likely resemblances and of the ultimate differences.

The overall theme is structured in four great historical epochs from the beginnings through to the post-exilic period. Within each, the main concerns that occupy modern Old Testament scholars are clearly explained and fairly discussed. As the author has himself noted – and others have commented similarly – Old Testament studies are today in a transitional phase, where earlier, and even comparatively recent, reconstructions of Israel's religious development have been demolished to a greater or lesser degree, without anything comparable emerging in their stead. They are dying the death of a thousand cuts but no new living synthesis has yet replaced the mangled corpses. Hence the student or the general reader, for whom this work is intended, more than ever needs authoritative guidance through the mass of specialized investigations and the constant emergence of new issues that will confront him. Werner H. Schmidt provides this in a way that no other available textbook quite does. He distils the viewpoints found in a vast body of literature into short, but tightly-packed, sections that enable the reader to come to grips with the present state of knowledge about the main problems. The author certainly indicates his own conclusions, where he feels able to do so, on many hotly disputed questions but he is always careful to provide the evidence on which he relies and a reader will profit most from this book if he has his Bible at hand and looks up the frequent references to it which are given in the text. Equally, however, Schmidt is careful to indicate where even relative certainty cannot be achieved and where, as particularly in the area with which the first main section of the work is concerned, all we can do is to choose between various possibilities.

But he does not leave the reader with just a collection of loose ends. An Old Testament theology does emerge, if by that we mean the depiction of a faith with a basic unity, individuality and distinctive character. The very conjunction of the beliefs of Israel with the religions of its environment only serves to emphasize their particularity. Schmidt sees the distinctive nature of Israelite religion as emerging very early, specifically in the important tenets that were to be embodied in the first two commandments of the Decalogue. Here is the acorn from which grew the mighty oak of Old Testament religion in the monarchical period, the account of which comprises the major section of the work. The abiding value of the Old Testament's understanding of God is brought out continually and not simply in the final pages. So, while this book is, in a completely scholarly and critical way, *about* the faith of ancient Israel and the Old Testament, it can also speak *to* faith in the present.

J. R. PORTER

§1   The Problem

1   It has recently been recognized how important it is to determine the nature of the relationship between the faith portrayed in the Old Testament and neighbouring faiths. The ancient Near East (the more distant great powers of Egypt and Mesopotamia, but particularly neighbouring Canaan and at a later date Iran) influenced Israel deeply not only in its political, legal and economic systems, but also in worship and religion. Fresh links are constantly being discovered; they indicate how closely the history of Israel is tied in with that of its neighbours. The borrowings made by Israel involve more than marginal matters, such as parts of the cult, its sacrifices and feasts, its rituals and equipment.

From Egypt it borrowed particularly certain formal elements in kingship, and wisdom concepts. Mesopotamia provided models for mythical narratives of primeval history, the patterns of particular psalms, legal traditions and the Book of Job. Such influences from the cultures of the great powers came only in part directly, and were more often mediated through the Canaanites (§10, below). The apocalyptic concepts of resurrection and universal judgement which appear in the post-exilic period were probably not actually initiated by Iranian eschatological concepts, but these did perhaps play a part in their development.

Israel did not make use of foreign forms simply in order to give expression by means of them to its own faith. Its various encounters with the religions of its neighbours altered even central concepts about God himself. These too have a history; so that the conclusion has been drawn that the 'distinctive and particular character of Israel was not given from the start and unalterable, but was one that developed' (R. Rendtorff, 'Die Entstehung der israelitischen Religion als religiongeschichtliches und theologisches Problem', *TLZ* 88 (1963), col. 744).

Israel borrowed much, but equally the converse is true; it also rejected much, and by no means shared all its ideas about God with its neighbours. But even what was borrowed did not remain unaltered; for the most part a different understanding was extracted from it or imposed upon it. Borrowing means reinterpretation. In what is common to Israel and the ancient Near East what is distinctive comes out too. What is this distinctive approach which made it possible for Israel to choose from among the varied concepts of God and to recast those that it made its own? What norm did Israel apply, consciously or unconsciously, in encountering its neighbours? An answer will have at the least to refer to the first (and second) commandment, which divided Israel from the ancient Near East. It is precisely when contrasted with its immediate neighbours, the Canaanites, that the distinctiveness of Israel is particularly striking. When Israel is set in its environment, it is seen to differentiate itself from it:

> Yet in spite of all these historical connections and possibilities for comparison, 'Israel' still appears a stranger in the world of its own time . . .; not merely in the sense that every historical reality has its own individual character, and therefore an element of uniqueness, but rather that at the very centre of the history of 'Israel'·we encounter phenomena for which there is no parallel at all elsewhere, not because the material for comparison has not yet come to light but because, so far as we know, such things have simply never happened elsewhere. (M. Noth, *History of Israel,* 2nd edn., London, 1960, pp. 2f.)

The recognition that Israel is a 'stranger' in its world demands that we should inquire into its distinctive character. This is undoubtedly connected with its understanding of God, and therefore with its historical consciousness. Although there are certain parallels no similar faith can be found anywhere in the ancient Near East. The characteristic features of the faith of the Old Testament (especially the first and second commandments and its special relationship to history) only allow to an extremely limited degree the judgement that 'Israelite religion gradually worked its way up out of paganism; this is the actual content of its history' (J. Wellhausen, *Israelitische und jüdische Geschichte,* 9th edn., Berlin, 1958, p. 32).

2   This faith did not of course remain unchanged with the passing of time, for it is related to the situation in which it is placed. It not only appeals to history, but is itself history, and is included in the movement of history. The question is whether there is any firmly fixed element in this process which resists all change. History always contains both elements, the traditional and the new, the enduring and the changing, continuity and discontinuity. However this distinction is really inappropriate. In the strict sense there is nothing permanent in history which avoids change altogether; even what is constant is subject to variation, and affected by the radical changes of history. Everything that appears in history is itself history. So in historical events an unimportant shell cannot be separated from an important core, nor a universally valid, lasting content be distinguished from a particular changing form. The one does not exist without the other; in fact such a distinction simply cannot be made. For the same reason caution is essential in respect of the concept of 'development' if it is taken literally and not in a completely emptied sense as 'becoming'. The event-filled character of history is neglected if it is interpreted as the unfolding of a sketch-plan given beforehand in embryo.

If however it is unhistorical to look for what is unchanging among all the changing elements, is it inappropriate to ask what it is in Israel's faith that is constant through the centuries? Israel's distinctive character at the end is only explicable from the forces that were at work from the beginning. Among them are undoubtedly the first and second commandments. These posed a duty to the following periods, and we can look at the history of Israel's faith from the point of view of the question whether Israel succeeded in maintaining this demand in constantly changing situations. The demands of these two commandments link the earlier and later periods. To this extent the degree of continuity in the history of Israel is also the criterion by which Israel conducted its argument with the surrounding world.

3   Old Testament scholarship owes to the nineteenth century the realization 'that the religion of Israel really had a history, and was not complete from the beginning as if fallen from heaven' (K. Marti, *Geschichte der Israelitischen Religion*, 5th edn., Strasbourg, 1907, p. 3). This led to permanent gains in our insights into the individuality of the Old Testament, of its different periods and books, of the difference between the pre-exilic and post-exilic period, the distinctive character of prophecy, etc. But the recognition of the strangeness and the historically bound character of the individual features too easily allowed the total phenomenon of the Old Testament, its distinctive character and its unity, to disappear from sight.

The so-called 'History of Religions' School learnt 'to understand religion as history, that is, as a living phenomenon in constant change, and in close contact and constant interaction with its time and its environment'. (W. Baumgartner, *Zum alten Testament und seiner Umwelt*, 1959, p. 375). Gressmann, like Gunkel before him, saw this problem in sharp definition:

> The historical task which is set the Old Testament scholar [demands] of him not only that he should draw out the threads which lead from the Old Testament to the ancient Near East and vice versa, but also at the same time that he should understand the originality of Israel, of its literature and of its religion, in distinction from the ancient Near East. When this happens, the distinctive experiences of Israel are not at all diminished; on the contrary they appear all the more sharply through the contrast drawn. For this reason we should confidently place Israel within the history of the development of the ancient Near East, and to a greater extent than previously quote and compare material which is ready to hand among related and neighbouring nations, in the firm confidence that the Old Testament and its religion will not lose by this, but can only gain.
>
> [From this grows a desire for an Old Testament history of religion] which does not aim to be complete and to present all the Old Testament material, but which restricts itself to the main themes, works out clearly the characteristic lines of development, and at the same time points out clearly the essential character and the dynamic forces of Israelite religion. Then attention would have to be paid less to the positive influences, and much more to the negative reaction of Israel and of Judaism to alien influences.

The religion of the Old Testament would then stand out sharply from the background of the ancient Near Eastern cultures, which it was constantly confronting and dissenting from. ('Die Aufgaben der alttestamentlichen Forschung', *ZAW* 42 (1924), pp. 10, 30)

As modern scholarship takes up again the religio-historical problem at the same time it takes over the objective of the 'History of Religions' School. The 'question which thrusts itself into the centre' is directed towards the 'distinctive character of Israel within the world of ancient Near Eastern religions' (R. Rendtorff, 'Die Entstehung', col. 738); 'the unmistakable uniqueness of Israel among the religions of antiquity' (K. Koch, 'Der Tod des Religionsstifters', *KuD* 8 (1962), p. 106). But this question of the distinctive character of Israel is forced upon us in a new and more difficult form: by what criteria does the faith of the Old Testament choose from the multiplicity of foreign religious phenomena, change what it has taken over, and reject what cannot be reconciled to its essential character? Research into the history of the religion thus comes to have a theological task as well. According to G. von Rad every concern for the unity of the Old Testament must first pose the question 'anew what is the typical element in Israel's faith' (*Old Testament Theology*, vol. 2, Edinburgh, 1965, p. 415). This challenge to seek what is typical of Old Testament faith places upon religio-historical research an obligation to work out the standards which determine Israel's relationship to its environment.

A history of Old Testament religion has therefore not simply to portray the development of Israelite religion as one religion among others, but also to emphasize the special features which distinguish it from other religions, and which mark it distinctively in the course of time. In this way a history of religion contains at the same time two themes of the criticism of religion: they are seen first in the debate with the surrounding religions and with the ideas taken over from them, secondly in the self-criticism which Old Testament faith exercises upon itself. It comes to expression not only, but to a special degree, in prophecy.

A history of religion cannot in any case proceed in a neutral way in relation to values, not even in the selection and presentation of material. The distinctiveness of each particular object of study in relation to the comparable material and the basic nature of this phenomenon within its history cannot be determined without interpretation.

I NOMADIC PREHISTORY

The beginnings of the history and religion of Israel remain in obscurity. Earlier scholarship sought to illuminate them by reconstructing Israel's prehistory on the basis of particular original features. Certain survivals of the cultic worship of ancestors, of the dead or even of animals, of the worship of trees or of stones, formed the clue. Scholars referred to belief in spirits and demons, to totemism or fetishism. The superstition of a later period was regarded as the faith of the early period. But such 'primitive' features, which certainly occurred, do not give us 'the religion of the patriarchs'. What seems alien in a later period is not necessarily constitutive for the early period. The ancient Near East, in the developed cultures of Egypt and Mesopotamia as well as in the city cultures of Syria-Palestine, had long since advanced to belief in personal deities, and so to the mythological state of religion (cf. §6a, 1). In this respect too Israel did not come to be itself through an increasing separation from paganism, while the opposite assumption, that in the beginning there was a pure relationship to God, but that the subsequent ages brought apostasy to the religion of the settled lands and the hardening into Judaism, is no less of an oversimplification.

§2 The Individual Traditions

1   When the Old Testament itself tells of Israel's origins, it refers to quite specific historical events, as for instance in Ps. 136. This song seems to come from a setting of worship. It can easily be imagined that a cantor recites each first half-verse, which tells of the deeds of God, while the community sings the unchanging refrain 'for his mercy endures for ever'. It thanks God for the 'great wonders, which he alone accomplishes'. Among them the psalm includes creation:

> Who by understanding made the heavens,
> who spread out the earth upon the waters . . . (vv. 5–9)

The Exodus from Egypt:

> who smote the first-born of Egypt,
> and brought out Israel from among them . . . (vv. 10–15)

and the leading through the wilderness into the cultivated lands:

> who led his people through the wilderness,
> who smote great kings . . .
> and gave their land as a heritage,
> a heritage to Israel his servant . . . (vv. 16–24)

The conclusion of this comprehensive listing of the works of God in creation and history is strange:

> who gives food to all flesh. (v. 25)

This final confession shows us the purpose and goal of the statements made. The psalm is not intended to record historical facts; the events are used to display God as the giver of food. The nourishment which man now takes for himself is a gift of the God who has led him hitherto. The past was retold because of its connection with the present; it has consequences which determine the character of daily life.

The farmer according to Deut. 26: 5–11 similarly utters a prayer when he is delivering the first fruits of the field, which contrasts past and present: 'a wandering Aramaean was my father . . . And now I bring the first of the fruit of the ground, which thou, O Lord, hast given me.' A historical outline has apparently secondarily been inserted into the prayer, which (with a change of person from singular to plural) recalls the sojourn in Egypt, the development into a nation, the Exodus and the entry. Here past and present are again strikingly interwoven: 'The Egyptians treated us harshly; we cried to Yahweh . . .' This 'short historical creed' (as G. von Rad calls it) presupposes the Pentateuchal narrative, probably including the late Priestly writing (cf. 'hard service' v. 6b with Exod. 1: 14P), and represents therefore a later composition.

Surprisingly the thanksgiving for the gift of bread is not found in direct connection with declarations about creation. The beliefs about creation and preservation are clearly not identical; we hear an echo of the fact that, from a religio-historical point of view, the two ideas are of different origins (below, §10a, 2). The thanksgiving for harvest is grounded rather in God's guidance in history: Israel interprets its present life in the land with the help of the time long past before the entry. Ps. 136 is probably to be dated to a later period of Israelite history. Its reference to the early period is all the more astonishing. Israel according to its own tradition had decisive experiences of God before it settled in the land. In contrast to the neighbouring nations it has not forgotten its origins, but has preserved its nomadic heritage in the cultivated land, in seeking to relate its new experiences to its earlier ones. Its closest ties of kinship were in fact not with the Canaanites. The shepherd became a farmer in the land of Canaan, but he saw in his fields a gift of the nomadic period. The man who prays Ps. 136 is aware that he stands in a line of history, and understands himself on the basis of it. It has assigned to him the place in which he lives. Particular events of the past are held on to in their once-for-all character, and (in contrast to mythical events) are not 'repeated' in the cult, but rather remembered (Exod. 12: 14; Deut. 16: 3, 12; Ps. 111: 4 et al.; cf. below, §9b). In the family too they are passed on from generation to generation (Exod. 12: 26f.; 13: 8, 14; Deut. 4: 9f.; 6: 7, 20ff.; Josh. 4: 6ff., 20ff.).

2   Since the reference to the wilderness period is fundamental to Israel's historical self-understanding, a religio-historical examination will have likewise to make a distinction: where are nomadic traditions still preserved in the Old Testament, and where is the influence from the lands of civilization to be found? Definite limits are set to scholarship by the problem of sources. The recollections from Israel's early periods which are deposited in the Pentateuch have been deeply penetrated by later material after a long time of oral transmission, and have become interwoven with one another. Before any historical evaluation is made the relevant texts must be examined to establish their character.

The Pentateuch falls apart into different individual complexes; for the joins between the great blocks of tradition, the promises to the patriarchs (Gen. 12–50), Exodus from Egypt (Exod. 1–15) and revelation at Sinai (Exod. 18 or 19-Num. 10), do not stand up to critical examination. The weakest is the connection of the period of the patriarchs with the sojourn in Egypt; here only two verses, which tell of the growth of the family of Joseph into the nation of Israel (Exod. 1: 6–7), form the connecting link. The conquest narratives of Joshua probably do not form the original conclusion of the story of the Exodus. The most disputed, however, is the extensive middle section. It has long been recognized (by Wellhausen, Gressmann and others) that the Exodus and Sinai traditions do not form an original unity, but at first existed independently of one another. Successive attempts to demonstrate that there was an original connection have hitherto failed, or at least have not won general agreement. Even in their statements about God the two traditions differ substantially: is the 'God of war' who casts the pursuers into the sea the same God who reveals himself in nature on Sinai? So the continuous historical outline from the time of the patriarchs to the conquest is a later formation. It is the individual narratives that are original. Their linking together took place so early that it is attested by all the three sources of the Pentateuch. Nevertheless the different traditions only grew together into a complete unity at a late date. The prophets can still appeal to certain strands of tradition in isolation, and in lists of the acts of God, such as Ps. 136 (cited above) offers, their original independence can perhaps still be heard.

If the basic encounters with God clearly happened independently of one another, they did not happen to Israel as a whole either. The later tradents of the tradition are a much bigger group than those originally involved. This explains many alterations and expansions of the early traditions. The people of the twelve tribes developed only after the settlement in Canaan from individual tribes or even smaller units and clans, who apparently migrated into the land at widely separated dates and from different directions. Instead of a continuous history with an internally linked sequence of events history has before it for examination only the individual traditions of certain nomadic groups. 'It is impossible to produce a historical continuity out of these disparate saga complexes' (M. Buber, *Moses*, Oxford, 1946, p. 6). So the first section of a 'history of Israel' is better entitled 'prehistory'.

From the beginning of the monarchy on, the course of history is basically firm, for from this time Israel's own tradition has developed into the writing of history. The older literary remains down to the book of Judges do not have a similarly strong evidential force, so that the origins of the twelve tribes down to the period of the judges or even to the beginning of the monarchy are generally a matter of more or less probable conjectures. We cannot expect to discover archaeological remains from the nomadic period. It is therefore precisely the events from the period before the settlement, to which the faith of Israel appeals, that are historically difficult to take hold of, although they are not simply 'mythological'. They certainly have a historical basis, but anything more precise than that is generally disputed.

3   The Old Testament itself indicates that the prehistory of Israel is not a religio-historical unity either. The three sources of the Pentateuch do not give the same picture of the early period, or at least make the worship of Yahweh begin

at different periods. These sources are already a late development in the history of transmission, separated by three or more centuries from the events which they narrate. Furthermore they each express their theological viewpoints by expansions and reinterpretations of the traditions. Nevertheless their differences are significant.

According to the Elohist (E, from *c*.800 BC) Yahweh first reveals his name in the revelation to Moses (Exod. 3: 6, 9–14), and only indirectly through the interpretation of the name 'I will be' (below §6a, 2, 4). In the preceding period of the patriarchs God remains without a proper name, and is instead called *'elōhīm*, 'god' (hence the name of this source).

The Priestly writing (P, *c*.550 BC) also makes the worship of Yahweh begin with Moses (Exod. 6: 2–8; but in Egypt, not at Horeb). In the primeval history (Gen. 1: 1ff.) the Priestly writing too employs the term *'elōhīm* in order to designate the God of Israel as a God of all mankind. However it calls the God of the patriarchs (from Gen. 17: 1 to Exod. 6: 3) El Shaddai. The change in the name indicates that both sources inherited a separation between the periods of the patriarchs and of Moses.

Only the Yahwist (J, *c*.950 BC; but this dating is particularly disputed) sees 'Yahweh' as active as God of the nations in the whole of history from creation on (Gen. 2: 4bff.), and after Gen. 4: 26, 'at that time men began to call upon the name of Yahweh', he is expressly worshipped under this name. In the revelation to Moses God does not introduce himself with a new name; nevertheless it is hinted (Exod. 3: 16) that the name of Yahweh is new to Israel. (In this oldest source some traditions are so unconnected and so unassimilated to one another that a fourth source has sometimes been distinguished to explain this).

If historically faithful recollection is to be found hidden in the individual pictures, the question must arise when a faith in Yahweh originated. Is its universal availability, as portrayed in the Yahwistic tradition, later? In which tradition is Yahweh original? Do the other traditions perhaps know of another deity? Perhaps both the pictures of the sources, basically different though they are, are correct: there was a worship of Yahweh before Moses, as the Yahwist indicates, but Israel itself first learnt to know Yahweh at Sinai, as the Elohist and the Priestly writer tell us.

§3 The God of the Fathers

Israel came to see its origin as the people of God more and more in the revelation at Sinai. But it also distinguished from this event an earlier time, characterized by another relationship with God, in which he is the ancestor of the people. So we are following the Old Testament itself if we start with the question of the faith of the patriarchs. One source, the Elohist, actually makes its narrative begin with the period of the patriarchs, while the further information in the other sources for the primeval period applies not to Israel alone but to mankind as a whole. In the end Abraham becomes the chosen ancestor of the nation and father of faith for Judaism (cf. Matt. 3: 9; Rom. 4), just because he is seen as the inaugurator of a new faith.

1 Josh. 24 reminds its hearers in a speech by God that Israel's ancestors did not yet worship the one God, but foreign gods:

> Your fathers lived of old beyond the Euphrates, Terah the father of Abraham and of Nahor, and they served other gods. (v. 2; cf. vv. 14f.)

This statement is unique in the Old Testament; it is all the more unfortunate that it is expressed in such general terms. Polytheism is ascribed to the ancestors – though only in the time before Abraham (cf. Jubilees 11f.). But which gods are meant? The Old Testament knows nothing otherwise of a borrowing of Mesopotamian religion with its pantheon, for example the moon god Sin. Is there any historical recollection here, or is the statement intended just to give a dogmatic basis for the demand to remove in principle all other foreign deities, in a warning with contemporary application against Babylonian and Assyrian influences? In any case the exclusivity of the relationship to God, which is very unusual for the thought of the ancient Near East, is here even accentuated: the relationship with the ancestors beyond the river is stressed, but a community of faith with them is denied. Similarly the narrative of the burial of the foreign gods (Gen. 35: 2–4) does not explicitly state whether this operation applies particularly to the deities of the land. For both traditions it is more important to stress the separation from the past than to give more details about the nature of the earlier religion. In this way the accounts leave the religio-historical problem unanswered, but acquire thereby more comprehensive significance: they give an example of the realization of the first commandment.

2   The recollection of Josh. 24: 2, according to which the ancestors of the patriarchs of Israel 'served other deities' has been transferred by scholarship to the patriarchs themselves. But with what justification? Can we gather from the Old Testament even by way of hints which deities the patriarchs of Israel worshipped before Yahweh? At the call of Moses the Elohist makes God say: 'I am the God of your father, the God of Abraham, the God of Isaac, and the God of Jacob' (Exod. 3: 6), and according to the Yahwist Moses told the elders: 'Yahweh the God of your fathers... has appeared to me' (v. 16). While these words only let us guess at the different stages of the revelation of God, the later Priestly writing makes the distinction quite explicitly, 'I appeared to Abraham, Isaac, and to Jacob, as El Shaddai (God Almighty), but by my name Yahweh I did not make myself known to them' (Exod. 6: 2). Before God turned to Moses, and through him to Israel, there was a time in which he encountered the patriarchs in other forms, whether it be under the name of 'god of your father', 'God of Abraham' or of El.

What religio-historical facts are concealed behind these names for God, and how do they relate to one another? The different names in the Old Testament, in accordance with the first commandment, are all names of the one God Yahweh; the God of Abraham and the God of Moses are the same. Israel, according to its (later) self-understanding, did not worship different deities, not even one after another. But the identification of the gods of the fathers, or of El gods, with Yahweh only took place in the course of a historical development. It is running counter to the sense of the texts we have to draw conclusions on the basis of the types of names and individual fragments of tradition about early independent religious patterns which preceded the identification with the Yahwistic faith. Because the evidence for this reconstruction comes from a later period, however, and is found in Genesis in very varied contexts, it is often difficult to decide in detail whether in any instance we have the tradition in its early stage, or whether the following period has affected it, putting its stamp upon it and altering it from the point of view of its own faith. So the worship of God of the patriarchal period can only be described with reservations, and in broad, ideal or typical outlines.

Nevertheless the patriarchal traditions cannot as a whole be derived from a later period; Genesis in no way reflects only the worship (within the family) of the period of the monarchy. On the one hand important elements of tradition which characterize the course of the later history of Israel are lacking in the patriarchal period: Jerusalem and the Zion tradition play no part here. (An exception to this is the scene of the encounter of Abraham and Melchizedek in Gen. 14: 18ff., which appears to go back to the beginnings of the monarchy.) Nor are there any indications yet of the sharp dispute with the Ba'al cult, which dominated the period of the monarchy, especially in the northern kingdom. On the other hand quite apart from personal names (like Abraham or Isaac) and place names (like Beth-el) other old elements of tradition have been preserved:

(1) The patriarchs had relations of kinship with the Aramaeans (Gen. 25: 20; 28: 5 etc.); the credo preserved in Deut. 26: 5 even states specifically, 'a wandering Aramaean was my father.' Possibly Israel's ancestors originally spoke Aramaic (cf. §6a, 2).

(2) The patriarchs led a semi-nomadic life with a gradual transition to sedentariness. With their herds of sheep and goats they were compelled to change over every half year between the winter pastures in the steppe or wilderness, and the summer pastures of the cultivated lands, which were accessible after the harvest. (It is the Midianites who seem to have been the first camel-nomads, and so more mobile and warlike; cf. Judg. 6f.; Gen. 37: 25.)

(3) Forms analogous to the term 'God of Abraham' are rare at later dates (Gen. 9: 26; 2 Kgs. 2: 14; 20: 5, etc.). In particular in the Exodus and Sinai traditions a form like 'God of Moses' is not found (cf. Exodus. 3: 6). So the family and tribal milieu of the patriarchal narratives is certainly not a later development.

(4) Titles for God like 'God of Abraham' are strikingly found also in the Yahwist (e.g. Gen. 28: 13) although he uses the name Yahweh from the beginning.

(5) Finally such a story as that in Gen. 31: 53, which with its plural formulation has an almost offensive sound (see below), is difficult to account for from a later period.

a THE NAME OF THE DEITY

It is noteworthy how many varied terms there are for the gods of the patriarchs. We must first distinguish between 'God of Abraham, Isaac, Jacob' on the one hand and 'God of the fathers' on the other hand. But even the latter expression as a collective term must be divided up further. Only the singular expression 'God of my/your father' seems to be ancient (e.g. Gen. 31: 5, 29, 42; 43: 23) while the plural 'God of our/your fathers' is found primarily in later writings, apart from Exod. 3f. It already presupposes the combination of the individual gods of the fathers, originally worshipped by different clans, to be one God of the fathers. In fact our heading 'the God of the Fathers' represents a late stage in the history of the tradition. Similarly among the titles which include a proper name the form with one name 'God of Abraham' is older than the combination 'God of Abraham', Isaac, Jacob' (Exod. 3: 6, 15f.), which was only possible after the genealogical combination of the patriarchs.

Is it necessary also to make a choice between the two early possibilities of 'God + Father' and 'God + proper name'? It is a plausible conjecture that the first form 'God of my father' originally meant the actual father of the family (cf. Gen. 26: 24; 46: 1). A name like 'God of Abraham' would then have been introduced only after a longer interval of the third or following generations, perhaps to distinguish one God of the fathers from another. But the form 'God + proper name' does in fact appear in a particularly early and trustworthy passage (31: 44ff.).

The narrative of the treaty between Jacob and Laban probably goes back to a frontier delimitation between Transjordanian Israelites and Aramaeans. Mount Gilead is to divide the pasturing lands of the two nations. A heap of stones and a pillar serve as indicators of the border or as witnesses of the treaty, and a common meal before the invisibly present deity confirms the agreement. Each partner calls upon his God as judge (cf. Gen. 16: 5;

1 Sam. 24: 13, 16). He is to protect the treaty and to avenge breaches of it. In the oath they take (Gen. 31: 53) it can still be seen that each group has its own 'god of the fathers':

The God of Abraham and the God of Nahor
judge between us!

It is a later addition, 'the God of their father', that seems explicitly to have understood both deities as one – unless this addition is to be understood as distributive ('of each's father'), the distinction between the deities being thus preserved.

Apparently therefore both forms of the names, 'God of Abraham' as well as 'God of my father', etc., go back to firm tradition. (The mixed form 'God of my father Abraham', Gen. 32: 9 [Heb 32: 10]; 26: 24 et al., is to be explained from the joining together of the two.)

It is possible that apart from the occurrence of the form 'God of Abraham' (Gen. 31: 53; Ps. 47: 9 [Heb. 47: 10]) the Old Testament has preserved a yet older form of the divine name: 'Fear' (or kinsman?) of Isaac' (Gen. 31: 42, 53 et al.), 'mighty one (or bull?) of Jacob' (49: 24; Ps. 132: 2, 5 et al.). But these expressions remain rather ambiguous.

Yet more uncertain are 'shield of Abraham' (cf. Gen. 15: 1) or 'Shepherd, rock of Israel' (?: Gen. 49: 24). The name 'God of Israel' (33: 20 et al.) probably does not belong in this context.

Furthermore the inscriptions of the Nabataeans and Palmyrenes offer parallels to the usage of 'god + proper name'. These tribes made the transition from a nomadic existence to the cultivated lands much later than Israel. Did they retain the names of gods from their nomadic period even after they became sedentary? Comparable titles, such as 'god of my/our father' are found also in for instance ancient Assyrian religion: they indicated a personal tutelary deity, 'to whom an individual or a family turned in invocations, asseverations and petitions' (H. Hirsch, 'Gott der Väter', *AfO* 21 (1966)). In these and other parallel formations we often have epithets of deities which are known by name.

b   THE CHARACTER OF THE DEITY

The name of the deity reveals his true nature. This general insight could be demonstrated precisely from the expression 'god of the fathers'. If the different forms of the name are not epithets, but proper names, this god is characterized by his relationship to a man, while for example the Canaanite deities 'El Beth-El' or 'Ba'al of Tyre' bear the name of the place at which they have appeared. What does this signify?

For this deity the type of religion is 'characterized not by a firm link with one place, but by a continuous connection with one group of people.' . . . Here an essential feature of later Yahwistic faith can be seen already: 'it stressed above all the relationship between God and man, and between God and whole groups of men, without any fixed association with one place. This made it all the more adaptable to the changing fortunes of the worshippers.' (A. Alt, 'The God of the fathers' [1929],' *Essays on Old Testament History and Religion*, Oxford, 1966, pp. 22f., 61)

So in this religion man has the decisive significance: for revelation is only possible to and through man. Because the God of the fathers does not reveal himself in natural phenomena at a fixed place, he does not need to be 'sought' there either (cf. Amos. 5: 5). No pilgrimage needs to be undertaken to him, he does not 'dwell' anywhere; for he is already present with man. He needs no special priests, to mediate in dealings with the deity; the head of the clan himself exercises priestly (and prophetic) functions. Perhaps the God of the fathers was even worshipped without image or statue. However sacrifice seems to have been offered to him (Gen. 31: 54; 46: 1; cf. Exod. 18: 12), as was likewise customary in the cultivated lands. It was precisely the lack of a local tie that made it possible for the God of the fathers to share the life of nomads; he journeyed around with them, led the group upon their way, protected them from dangers (Gen. 28: 15; 31: 3, 5; 35: 3; 46: 4) and so is 'with' them as their kindly helper (26: 3, 24, 28 et al.; cf. on the kinship relationship below §12b, 3). Care and provision for the clan seems to be his area of activity. So the gods of the fathers protect their worshippers in the treaty between Jacob and Laban, and stand up for their rights (31: 53). The saga of Cain too is aware of a protective sign which God gives Cain (4: 15).

The deity did first appear to one individual, and was named after him, but this person does not stand alone; he represents a larger number. It must be asked whether he became the head of the clan and the remembered first ancestor through his reception of the revelation, or whether he receives the revelation as being already leader of the wandering group. It is not possible to give a clear answer. In any case the belief in the God of the fathers, in distinction from the later Yahwistic religion, which embraced the whole nation of Israel, is a clan religion, which includes only the family circle with its dependants. So the narratives of Genesis can in general be correctly termed 'family narratives' (so C. Westermann, *BK* I/12, and others); for they take the material of their stories substantially from this area of life, and tell of birth, famine, disputes and the like.

In this sort of world faith is particularly something which is transferred, 'inherited from the fathers'; men do not need to abandon what is their own in order to take over foreign institutions. But the content of the tradition is concerned not so much with the past as with the future. The words of God in the patriarchal narratives are for the most part promises: an assurance of guidance (28: 15), but also the promise of descendants (15: 4f.; 16: 11f.; cf. 28: 14; 17: 5f.)

and of possession of the land (12: 7; 13: 15, 17; 28: 13 et al.). The wandering group follows its leader in obedience to the word of God which he received. Accordingly belief in the God of the fathers is shown in trust in his guidance in the future. 'A God whom men trust because they have been addressed by him. He is a God who says to a man that he is guiding him' (M. Buber, *Werke* II, p. 273).

Historians have however certain reservations to make about the originality of the promise of increase and of possession of land; for the promise was seen in the light of later circumstances and so expanded. The promise of a son is interpreted to refer to Israel's becoming a nation, and the promise of land is regarded as fulfilled by Israel's taking possession of Palestine (cf. Deut. 1: 8 et saep.). The words of promise of the patriarchal narratives have therefore been influenced by the later position of Israel in relation to land, but are surely not derived entirely from a latter period. The promise of numerous descendants may be secondary, but the promise of a son is surely old. Probably the earliest form of the tradition came to be expanded more and more on the basis of the circumstances of the following period. The protective guidance of the tribe by the deity is an old element in the belief in the God of the fathers, and the promise of land and the promise of a son are readily understood from the life of wandering shepherds. With their change of pasturage between steppe and cultivated land a complete transition to the sedentary life was tempting.

c THE GODS OF THE FATHERS AND THE GOD EL

Although the gods of the fathers did not appear at fixed places but to particular men, and guided them upon their way, in Genesis they are almost always associated with particular places, usually famous Palestinian sanctuaries. How is this contradiction to be explained? Already in the reconstruction of the faith of the patriarchs we stumble upon the problem which is important in the history of Israel: how are traditions from the nomadic period and those from the cultivated land to be distinguished?

1 The nomadic groups around Abraham, Isaac and Jacob gave up their wandering existence early, and settled in various regions of Palestine. In this way the promise of the land to them was originally fulfilled. They did not settle in uninhabited territories, but in the neighbourhood of Canaanite local sanctuaries. Perhaps the change in pasturelands had already led them there; they had gone on pilgrimage to the holy places to offer sacrifice.

In which areas belonging to which tribes of the later people of Israel did these sanctuaries and thus the areas of settlement of the groups around the patriarchs, lie? If this question can be answered, it can be conjectured into which tribes the patriarchal groups were absorbed.

The group of	settled at	belonged probably to the tribe of
Abraham	tree sanctuary of Mamre near Hebron (Gen. 18J; cf. 13: 18; 14: 13; 23P; further to the south: 12: 9; 13: 1; 20: 1 Negeb)	Caleb (cf. Num. 13; Josh. 15: 13ff.) or later Judah
Isaac	Beersheba (Gen. 26: 23ff.; cf. 21: 14, 31ff.; 22: 19) and the well of Beer-Lahai-Roi in the south (Gen. 24: 62; 25: 11; cf. 16: 13ff.)	Simeon in the south or the house of Joseph in the north (which has connections with Beersheba, cf. Amos. 5: 5 et al.)
Jacob	(a) Transjordan: Penuel, Mahanaim and Succoth (Gen. 31f.; esp. 32: 1, 22ff. [Heb. 32: 2, 23ff.]; 33: 17; cf. 50: 10f.) (b) the West Bank: Shechem (Gen. 33: 18ff.; 35: 4; cf. 12: 6; 48: 22; Josh. 24: 32) and Bethel (Gen. 28: 10ff.; cf. 35: 1ff., 6f., 14f.; 12: 8; also Jer. 31: 15)	Reuben (whose settlement area perhaps expanded from east to west); later Ephraim and Manasseh

So the 'Abraham group' seems to have settled primarily around the tree sanctuary of Mamre near Hebron (Gen. 18: 7; 23P), while the area of Isaac lay further to the south in and around Beersheba (26: 23–33). Jacob is connected both with the West Bank, Bethel (28: 10ff.) and Shechem (33: 18ff.; 35: 2ff.) and with the Transjordan, Penuel and other places (Gen. 31–32). This double localization must be connected with a later expansion of the area of settlement. It remains uncertain however where Jacob's descendants settled first, in which direction they spread out – most probably from east to west – and therefore to which tribe they were originally attached.

The Isaac tradition is perhaps owed to the house of Joseph; for the northern kingdom with the house of Joseph for centuries preserved links with Beersheba in the south (cf. Amos. 5: 5; 'Isaac' in Amos. 7: 9 et al.). On the other hand the tradition about Abraham must originally have been located in the tribe of Caleb, which lived around Hebron (Num. 13), and then been transferred to the larger tribe of Judah, to which none of the three patriarchal figures originally belonged. In this way the increasing importance of Abraham can be explained; narratives about Isaac and Jacob were transferred to him, so that he came to be connected with their sites too (and so with Shechem and Bethel: Gen. 12: 6, 8; 13: 3). Is there an indication in the predominance of Abraham of the preeminence of the tribe of Judah at the time of David (2 Sam. 2: 4)? Or were there early connections between the south and central Palestine? When and for what reasons the patriarchal traditions reached the form in which we have them in the Old Testament remains a difficult question to answer.

2   In any case the patriarchal groups settled separately from one another, and were not therefore closely connected from the beginning, and apparently they were associated with different tribes. Their settlement around the ancient Palestinian sanctuaries has great traditio-historical importance, since the traditions of the patriarchs were cultivated at just these places; it has yet greater religio-historical significance when the 'gods of the fathers' of the immigrants were merged with the local deities. The first encounter of nomadic and settled religion in Israel's prehistory led to the gods of the clans and the gods of the land being equated with one another. At the beginning we do not yet have a contrast with the world around, but a combination to form a unity. To put it another way, the holy places were taken over for the incoming faith; it was not a strange god, but their own, that had appeared here. But this identification also altered their own faith. So the 'sanctuary legends' or 'cult aetiologies' which account for the sacral character of the site (below, §3e) were transferred to the patriarchs and their gods. The 'god of the father' revealed himself each time to the particular group alone, so that this religion could with qualification be described as an early form of monotheism, or rather as monolatry. When the individual gods of the fathers were later united, they were not juxtaposed in a pantheon, but identified, so that the unity was preserved. A cultivated land religion by contrast is polytheistic.

In the local saga of Mamre, which now tells of an experience of Abraham, three 'men' appear (Gen. 18). But at least in the Old Testament the polytheistic element has been driven into the background: the three divine figures retire behind the one speaker, Yahweh (vv. 1, 10, 13; cf. 19: 1).

Such sagas of the foundation or discovery of a cult (e.g. Gen. 28: 10ff. of Bethel) do not come into the reconstruction of the faith in the 'god of the fathers', since by their nature they are connected with one particular place. The nomads went on pilgrimage to the sanctuaries; they did not found them but came across them there. In the present narrative context it looks as if the shepherds had stopped on their migrations in order to plant a tree, to erect a standing stone or to build an altar. But the places at which the patriarchs founded such cults had long been holy places with a well-known deity. Even the brief accounts of the construction of altars at Shechem, Bethel or Mamre (Gen. 12: 7f.; 13: 18; 35: 1, 7) are only intended to attribute the already existing Canaanite sanctuaries to the patriarchs. The great majority of stories of the patriarchs in fact come from the lands of cultivation.

3   As a result of the transfer of the cult aetiologies to the patriarchs, acts which the inhabitants of the land had originally attributed to their deities came to be ascribed to the gods of the fathers, and ultimately to Yahweh. Who were these deities? The place-names of the sanctuaries themselves point to the answer: Beth-el, 'house of El', or Penu-el, 'face of El'. This god El appears several times

with an expanded name; an El Olam is known from Beersheba (Gen. 21: 33), an El Roi (16: 13f.) from another place in the south; and an El Beth El (31: 13; 35: 7) from Bethel. The vision of heaven which (according to Gen. 28: 10ff.) Jacob had in a dream, and which was interpreted as of Yahweh (vv. 13, 16) was originally no doubt a theophany of this local god of Bethel.

On the other hand another El deity, El Elyon of Jerusalem (Gen. 14: 18ff.) is not identified with the God of the patriarchs; the connection is looser (see below, §10a, 1).

What sort of a deity is this El? The individual epithets and the his localized character could mislead us into seeing in him only an insignificant local deity of the various sanctuaries. But this view is inadequate. The name El Olam 'God of eternity' for a start does not fit this assumption. Strikingly, El in the texts from Ugarit that have become known since 1930 is the king and head of the pantheon (below, §10a, 3). How are the El deities of Genesis, which appear without an accompanying heavenly court (but cf. Gen. 28: 12; 32: 1 [Heb. 32: 2]) related to this high god? There are no real criteria for answering this question. Probably however the local deities are to be understood as the local manifestations of the one god El (so O. Eissfeldt); this would certainly explain the multiplicity as well as the unity. El would have been worshipped at different places with different epithets and different emphases. Perhaps it was just this juxtaposition and intermingling of local and universal deity that made possible the identification of the god of the fathers with El; for over and above the local connection a measure of transcendence is preserved to the deity.

Although the patriarchal narratives often allude to the El cult, they never mention the other leading Canaanite deity Ba'al; they neither point to a worship of Ba'al nor open up a contrast with this religion, as later Old Testament passages do. Nor do the El deities of Genesis themselves display any features of a storm or fertility deity such as Ba'al is. Massebas, holy standing stones erected to represent the deity as present, are certainly attested both in the patriarchal period (Gen. 28: 18ff.; 35: 14) and in the epoch of the contest with Canaanite religion; but the asheras are not yet found (although Gen. 12: 6; 13: 18; 18: 1; 35: 4 et al. suggest a tree cult). These symbols of a female deity, holy stakes or trees, are only later regularly mentioned together with the massebas (Judg. 6: 26f.). The stories of Genesis apparently do not yet know anything of a strongly sexual deity, whether male or female.

Do the patriarchs belong therefore to a period which did not yet know the juxtaposition of El and Ba'al? Certainly Ba'al was already worshipped from the second millennium BC in Syria. It is a likely conjecture therefore that the nomads did not first get to know the god El in the cultivated land, but already called their 'god of the fathers' El. Then the equation of their god with the El deities would be readily understandable. In the present state of our sources we must try to distinguish between the belief of the semi-nomads and the religion of the cultivated land, a cult practised by priests at fixed sanctuaries; but it remains very hard to determine what there is in common between the god of the fathers and El, for the identification to have been made. It would seem easiest to see the unity in the name. If the gods of the fathers were already called El (cf. Gen. 49: 25 'the El of your father'; also 46: 3; Exod. 18: 4, and the disputed expression 'El the god of Israel', Gen. 33: 20), a connection with the local deities would follow naturally. El is not only the proper name of a particular deity but at the same time a general expression for 'god'. In fact the word is also found in personal names from the patriarchal period such as Isra-el or Ishma-el, while in Jacob, Isaac et al. the name 'El' is probably to be supplied (Jacob-el). Such names (verb in the imperfect with name of god) are characteristic of the great proto-Aramaean, Amoritic, etc., movement of peoples which in the course of the second millennium broke in from the Arabian wilderness from the east into the civilized lands of the ancient Near East; Israel's ancestors also belonged to this wave of peoples.

The name Abra(ha)m is also attested early (cf. below, §12b, 3). Furthermore parallels of language and of the legal position have been discovered through the finds at Mari and Nuzi; the legal usages of the patriarchal narratives are however in part at least also attested at a much later date. For this reason the period of the patriarchs can only be dated very roughly (cf. Gen. 15: 16). Historically exact statements are not a possibility; the tradition placed no value upon them. Certain connections with the political and social situation of the second millennium can be demonstrated, but no individual events determined. The only exception, the account of the war of Abraham with some ancient Near Eastern kings (Gen. 14) does not help to make an unambiguous dating possible.

Was El already the chief god of the west Semitic nomads, who were striving everywhere to become sedentary in the period before the thirteenth to the twelfth centuries? In that case 'God of Abraham' or 'fear, or kinsman of Isaac' would only be epithets of this polymorphic El. However the Genesis narratives, apart from the personal names mentioned, do not support this conjecture. Here the El deities first appear at the local sanctuaries; El does not appear in the older passages on its own (e.g. Gen. 35: 1, 3; 46: 3) but only with a following more precise determination as a proper name. Is it therefore better to assume that the gods of the fathers were first called El in the encounter with the religion of the cultivated lands? It is in any case very improbable that the patriarchs worshipped El Olam or El Shaddai any earlier.

This impression is first given by the later Priestly writing, which strongly identifies the God of the fathers with El Shaddai (the translation remains uncertain). With this one name P on the one hand summarizes the different names of the gods of the fathers and the El gods, and on the other hand maintains the distinctive character of the patriarchal period (from Gen. 17: 1 to Exod. 6: 3) over against the preceding primeval period and the following period of Moses, in which the regulations for the cult were given. So even here the memory that the El deities are at home in the cultivated land has its effect: El Shaddai first reveals himself to Abraham in Canaan (Gen. 17: 1; 28: 3; 35: 11). Before this P gives us no command to emigrate, in order to avoid having to mention God by name. It has been conjectured that El Shaddai too was once a local version of the god El (in Hebron), but in the Old Testament, unlike the instances of El Elyon or El Olam, there is no sign of a local connection. This peculiarity of itself suggests that this divine name does not come from old tradition. Only the element Shaddai is attested from an early date (Num. 24: 4, 16; Gen. 49: 25 – most translations here assimilate it to the usual title; cf. Gen. 43: 14), while the combination 'El Shaddai' is not attested before the exile (Ezek. 10: 5 and P). Perhaps therefore the double name was formed only later on the analogy of the compound names of the tradition, because in the title Shaddai (which is also popular in Job – and is there translated in the Greek version as *pantokratōr*, the almighty) an expression of God's transcendence and might was seen.

The divine names preserved in Genesis, whether formed with El or formed on the pattern of the gods of the fathers, cannot all be derived in the same way, but have different origins. If the El deities sometimes appear in Genesis without a local connection this peculiarity depends on the later influence of Israelite faith, and does not permit inferences about the earlier period. El Shaddai basically became a 'god of a father'. Beyond this, reservations about too confident conclusions from the titles of El attested in the Old Testament are appropriate.

By contrast with the address 'you are El Roi', the 'God who sees me (?)' (Gen. 16: 13J) the probably older name of a well, Beer-lahai-roi, 'Well of the living one, who sees me (?)' (16: 14; 24: 62; 25: 11), does not contain the element El, so that the spirit thought of as living in the well was perhaps originally not regarded as an El deity at all (cf. below, §3e).

The name attested from Beersheba, El Olam 'God of eternity' (Gen. 21: 33J), is to some degree supported by the 'sun-god of eternity' attested from Ugarit and Karatepe, the divine title attested in Ugarit 'king of eternity' (cf. Jer. 10: 10) and also by the Ulomos mentioned in the cosmogony of Mochus.

In Gen. 35: 7E El-Beth-el is strikingly the name of a place. In the world around Israel (Elephantine papyri, etc.) Bet-El is found both as a name of a place or a stone, and as a divine name (cf. Jer. 48: 13). The formula of self-introduction 'I am the God (of) Bethel' (Gen. 31: 13E) does not go back to old tradition.

So none of these composite divine names is attested in its present form outside the Old Testament; only individual elements can be found in the surrounding world. Perhaps however the religio-historical position in pre-Israelite Palestine is only reflected very partially in the Old Testament, because the tradition has apparently altered it more strongly than is usually assumed.

d   THE GODS OF THE FATHERS AND YAHWEH

1   While the nomads as they settled identified their 'gods of the fathers' with the El deities of the sanctuaries of the cultivated land, the identification of the gods of the fathers with Yahweh, which the tradition of the call of Moses shows happening (Exod. 3: 6, 13ff.; 6: 2f.), represents a third stage in the course of the history of the religion. Since the tradition of the patriarchs had already been enriched by Canaanite elements before Israel borrowed them, Yahweh did not simply drive out the gods of the local sanctuaries. He continues to bear both names, both 'God of Abraham' and El. In spite of Yahweh's demand for exclusiveness, as it is proclaimed in the first commandment, both the alien tribal religion and in part

the Canaanite El cult were absorbed by the faith of Israel. But the Old Testament does not understand the word El as a proper name, but as a general expression. El Olam loses his distinctive character, and is understood as 'god of eternity' or 'eternal god'. The foreign deity becomes an epithet of Yahweh; otherwise it would be inexplicable why the Old Testament never shows signs of any polemic against the god El. But only concepts that were capable of being united with Israel's own faith (although it is difficult to state in detail what they are) were taken over; for by no means all the features characteristic of the worship of El, as they are known from the world around Israel, are found also in Genesis.

By taking over the cult legends of the local sanctuaries the immigrant tribes could give a basis for their claims to a particular area over against the settled Canaanites. The individual sagas state now that Yahweh has invested Israel with the land; here a hidden contrast with the world around can be detected. The promise of offspring and of conquest had come true long before Israel's entry into the land! The whole of the past from creation on was thus understood as the history of the one God.

In this new context the aetiologies acquire a different sense: they are no longer intended to guarantee the cultic holiness of a place, but are drawn more strongly into history, and associated with the history of the nation (below, §3e). With this release from local connections an impulse from the nomadic period wins the day against the laws of the civilized land. Israel's ancestors did not leave alien sagas unaltered, but incorporated them into their own faith, permeated them with their spirit and so reshaped them.

It was especially the encounter with the Exodus tradition that demanded a far-reaching reinterpretation of the patriarchal one. While the promise to the patriarchs had in the first instance been fulfilled with their move into the cultivated lands, it now appeared to be in tension with the faith of Israel which attributed the conquest of the land to Yahweh, who had led them out of Egypt. This contradiction was removed by the realization of the promises in effect being taken away from the patriarchs; the real fulfilment was experienced by the nation, after a protracted detour by way of Egypt. According to Deuteronomy (6: 10, 23; 8: 1 et al.) God gives the land which he has 'sworn to the fathers' to Israel. P finds an expression for the new situation: Abraham obtains the cave of Machpelah (Gen. 23) as an earnest, a sort of sign serving as an assurance of the future 'in the land of sojourning' (Gen. 17: 8 et al.); the patriarchs do not yet have their lasting place in Palestine.

2   Although the Old Testament is still aware of the difference between the faith of the patriarchs and the worship of Yahweh, it asserts a continuity. In spite of the sharp historical change it holds fast to the theological unity. What made the incorporation of this foreign tribal religion from the period before the appearance or spread of the worship of Yahweh possible for Israel's faith? On the one hand the God of the fathers was concerned for man; he revealed himself alone, and was perhaps even worshipped without images. On the other hand the area of activity

of the God of the fathers was the area of history. He journeyed with the wandering band, in order to lead them into the future. The group responded by setting out on its way in trust in the leadership of its God and in obedience to his command. This interest in what is new, this pressing after a longed-for future, is a dominant feature of the faith of the patriarchs.

This tradition is further developed and intensified by the experiences in faith and the hopes of the later period. Abraham no longer remains the head of the clan, but becomes the model of obedient faith (Gen. 15: 6) and an example of God's guidance, holding fast to God's promise even in strong temptation (Gen. 22). The future character of the narratives is thematically emphasized and placed independently before the whole patriarchal narrative (Gen. 12: 1–3J). Abraham is to pass on the blessing which he has received: 'by you all the families of the earth shall bless themselves' (v. 3b). In this statement of principle only slight traces are left of the traditional themes of the promise of possession of the land and of offspring; with the word 'blessing' the gift is deliberately formulated in a more all-embracing fashion. In this way a later period can refind its own present in this saying and associate itself with this blessing. As the material of the promise was expanded, so the circle of those affected grew. The blessing not only left the area of the clan, and was connected with Israel as a whole, but was meant to go yet further to determine the life of the nations. When the different cultic legends gained in importance outside their own areas when they lost their local ties, the concrete was generalized, the specific and historical situation was given up, because it had obtained universal significance. It is no longer stated where, when and how God speaks (Gen. 12: 1); what is decisive is the power of the word over the future.

The tradition of the patriarchs is at first markedly unimportant for the prophets. Hosea (12) uses the Jacob tradition as evidence for the sin of the nation. It is only after the exile that the promise is taken up emphatically and proclaimed anew. Deutero-Isaiah declares it to the nation in exile: because Abraham was one single man and the blessing of Yahweh made of him a great nation, the despairing exiles too can have hope (Isa. 51: 1–3; cf. 41: 8; 44: 3–5; 54: 1–3; Ezek. 33: 24; but Isa. 63: 15f.). In his wake the motif of the blessing of the patriarchs influences the later prophets too (Zech. 8: 13; 10: 8, 10; cf. Hos. 2: 1 et al.). The word of God from the nomadic period is not yet completely fulfilled with Israel's residence in Palestine. The prophets detach it again from realization, and change the 'now already' of fulfilment into a 'not yet'. What was already realized becomes future again, in order to retain its present significance for later generations.

e   APPENDIX: THE SANCTUARY LEGENDS

The complex of patriarchal sagas which we now have grew out of a large number of individual sagas, which developed into cycles of sagas when mixed up with other materials, and then obtained a place within a historical sequence of events from Abraham to Israel's emergence as a nation. The individual sagas are related either more to particular people, figures like Abraham, Lot, Jacob, Esau Laban, etc., or more strongly to particular places. Included in this second form of saga are the sanctuary legends, also called cultic aetiologies or *hieros logos*, a group which is not numerically significant but is important in content. It tells of the origin, and more particularly of the discovery and naming, of a holy place. The expression sometimes used, 'foundation narrative', is to this extent liable to misunderstanding, that a holy place is not 'founded' but discovered. At a prominent place, for instance at a tree (Gen. 18; cf. 21: 15; Exod. 3: 1–5; Judg. 6: 11ff.; 1 Kgs. 19: 5; Josh. 24: 26), stone (Gen. 28: 10ff.), river (32: 22ff [Heb. 32: 23ff.]) or spring (16: 7) a deity appears unexpectedly. Man responds to the presence of God, which is expressed always in 'an uttered revelation of salvation' (C. A. Keller, 'Über einige alttestamentliche Heiligtumslegenden', *ZAW* 68 (1956), p. 94), with the erection of an altar and the establishment of a cult. The theophany is therefore the centre of the saga.

Typical elements of the narrative are e.g. that someone come accidentally upon the place (Gen. 28: 11; Exod. 3: 1), explicitly states the peculiar character of the place in a word (Gen. 28: 16f.; Exod. 3: 5; cf. Josh. 5: 15), gives it its name (Gen. 16: 13f.; 22: 14; 28: 19; 32: 2, 30 [Heb 32: 3, 31]; 35: 7; Josh. 5: 9 et al.) and builds an altar or something similar (Judg. 6: 24; Gen. 12: 7f.; 28: 18 et al.).

Such a narrative does not however have to tell of the inauguration of a cult, but can tell, for example, of the reshaping of one. The subject of the (still recoverable) original version of Gen. 22: 1–14 was the replacement of human sacrifice by the sacrifice of an animal (v. 13). Compared with this the present narrative has a completely different intention: 'God tested Abraham' (v. 1) and he proved to be god-fearing (v. 12).

Every sanctuary requires a legitimation which points to just this place as the site of divine revelation. The sanctuary legend answers for the visitor the question 'why should I journey to this place?', and so justifies the pilgrimages and at the same time champions the claim of the cultic place in question over against other sanctuaries. The question 'why' is answered by stating 'whence', in the form of a narrative from the past. However the Old Testament does not preserve any aetiology in its original version. In particular two far-reaching alterations took place.

On the one hand the narrative lost its local ties. After its transfer to the patriarch it recounts an important event in the life of the tribal ancestor, and so grows beyond the former narrow circle and obtains significance for all Israel (cf. Gen. 32; 28), until finally it finds its ultimate setting in the framework of the Pentateuch. Originally independent, the saga becomes a part of a greater whole. In the process its primary purpose, to demonstrate the holiness of a place, is completely displaced or even lost. The person comes into the foreground. On the other hand through the reinterpretation of the old content and the incorporation of new purposes, the narrative acquires future aspects to a much greater degree (Gen. 28: 14f.; Exod. 3: 7ff.). In this way even the cultic legends come to take part in the total sense which seems to be almost all that the Old Testament leaves to the patriarchal narratives. This is to point to the future, that is beyond themselves. How extensive this process of reinterpretation was can be demonstrated from two particular examples.

1   The sanctuary legend of Bethel (or Bet-el) (Gen. 28: 10–22) answers several questions of interest to the pilgrim: why is Bet-el a holy place, why is it called 'house of God'? Why do we offer the tithes there, and how has the ritual of the anointing of a stone come about? The narrative is furthermore preserved in two different versions: one is substantially older in its individual features, but has only later literary attestation, with the silent vision of the ladder to heaven (approx. vv. 11b, 12, 17f., 20–22E, without 21b), and a version which traditio-historically is later, but fixed earlier in literary form, with a conversation between Yahweh and Jacob (vv. 10, 11a, 13–16J; also 19a?). Both accounts, which in each instance stand in larger literary contexts (cf. 31: 13; 35: 1ff.E, and 12: 3, 13: 15f.J) presuppose the transference of the narrative to the patriarch Jacob, and therewith the all-Israelite interpretation. But an older tradition can with caution be conjectured, which itself has in turn undergone several different stages.

(a) The holiness of Bethel seems in the early stage to have been only accounted for by the fact that a masseba (i.e. holy stone) was found there, in which according to the general belief a divine being dwelt. At a late period Philo of Byblos still knows of 'animate stones', which he calls Baitylia. This is a term in which we can hear echoes of the word Bet-el, house of God. This old idea may be traced also in the ritual action (v. 18; cf. 35: 14) which Jacob performs at the stone – independently of the later certainly differently interpreted sense of the anointing.

(b) Not only the patriarchs, but also the Canaanites before them did not think of their God El (cf. 35: 7) as living in a stone (or in a river, Gen. 32), but understood him as a sky-god. So the stone became the place where the heavenly 'ladder' (more exactly a staircase or slope) stands. It represents in mythological terms the bridge between the heavenly and the earthly world; by this way God's messengers come to earth and return again to heaven.

Just as an earthly lord makes use of messengers, so the deity too sends his messengers to earth. These messengers or angels (in Hebrew, as in Greek, the same word), who were no doubt thought of as being in human form, need a slope to go up and down, since unlike the mixed beings in the form of animals, like sphinxes, cherubim or seraphim, they have no wings.

Probably Israel inherited the concept of a multiplicity of messengers (Gen. 28: 12; 32: 2f.; also attested in Ugarit), while the Old Testament itself prefers to speak of one messenger (16: 7ff.; 21: 17; 22: 11, 15; Exod. 3: 2 et al.). In him God is near to man, while remaining himself at the same time distant (cf. §6c, 6).

Here at Bethel is the place of the link between heaven and earth, 'the gate of heaven' (v. 17)! The myth thus makes a basic distinction (much more than did the assumed earlier stage at which the demon lived in the stone) between heavenly and earthly realms, but allows the one to be open to the other.

(c) From this basis Israel, and specifically the Elohist, can take over the idea (vv. 11f.). It preserves God's transcendence as such (God in heaven) and is simply understood as a dream, so that the mythological element has a place now only in the appearance by night. Further through the insertion of the narrative in the story of Jacob the stone loses its original character. It becomes at first a sort of pillow (v. 11), then a monument (vv. 18, 22) which Jacob erects in order to remind himself in the future of the revelation he has experienced, and to realize his vow to build a house of God: the stone no longer is a house of God, but is to become a house of God, that is, a temple.

> Even the old saga no longer understands the originally very close connection of stone and deity, and motivates it by the story, according to which the stone is erected . . . as a reminder of a divine revelation. (H. Gunkel, *Genesis*, 3rd edn., Göttingen, 1910)

While the Elohist contents himself with the soundless vision of the gate of heaven, the Yahwist says nothing of this scene nor of the stone; he thus seems to avoid the mythological and instead lets the word of Yahweh, who stands 'before him' be uttered directly to Jacob: 'I am with you, and will keep you wherever you go' (v. 15; cf. Hos. 12: 4, 6 [Heb. 12: 5, 7]; in Gen. 28: 20E as a vow). While the cultic legend has as its goal the recognition of the holiness of the place, now the God who makes the promise is no longer 'with' the place, but 'with' the man who is on a journey and wants to return with good fortune. This relationship of protection and trust between God and man is extended beyond the situation and the man immediately affected: the promise of land and offspring already made is reaffirmed, now as a blessing for 'all the families of the earth'.

2   The saga preserved in Gen. 32: 22ff. [Heb. 32: 23ff.] which is extremely peculiar within Old Testament faith, answers in the first place the question of the peculiar character of a place: why is there in Transjordan on the river Jabbok a place which is called Penu-el or Peni-el, 'face of God'? In this case it is less certain that a sanctuary existed there; for corresponding recollections, like the account of the building of an altar (Gen. 12: 7f. et al.) have not been preserved. Further the story explains the name Israel (v. 28 [Heb. v. 29] and the sacrificial custom of not eating the sciatic nerve (v. 32 [Heb. v. 33]). The mixture of such very varied motifs and all sorts of unevennesses in the text allow us to deduce a lengthy oral stage of transmission, since it is no longer possible to reach a satisfactory literary analysis; in this all three aetiological motifs accrued only subsequently. Here the different and interlocking layers of tradition will only be roughly separated from one another.

(a) The oldest recoverable tradition tells of an unusual event: a divine being, probably a river demon, attacks by night a passer-by, who is crossing the river at a ford, but, in the course of life and death wrestling cannot prevail over the man (cf. Hos. 12: 4a [Heb. 12: 5a]). Details of the story are less clear: does the man originally give the demon the blow on the hip (Gen. 32: 25b [Heb. 32: 26b] as a correction of v. 25a [Heb. 26a])? Does the man attacked succeed in holding fast the demon, so that in fear that he will not be able to flee before the dawn he blesses him (vv. 24b, 26 [Heb. 25b, 27])?

It is a typical mark of a demon that his capacities are limited, in time as well as in space: he works only at night (cf. Exod. 4: 24–26; 12: 12, 22ff.; Num. 22: 21ff.; 2 Kgs. 19: 35), and only at one particular place, so that one has to run into him (Num. 22). A demon has therefore to observe certain 'laws', without which his power would be unrestrained, and he would be equal to a god. Further a positive result belongs with this sort of story: the demon is defeated at the end – whether through the strength of a man (Gen. 32), the protective act of circumcision (Exod. 4) or the cleverness of an animal (Num. 22).

(b) As the name Penu-el 'face of God' indicates, the river demon is identified, even if not explicitly, with the God of El. The features of the demon do not originally fit in with the character of a high god (although O. Eissfeldt, for example, disagrees, see 'Non dimittam te, nisi benedixeris mihi' [1957], in *Kleine Schriften* III, Tübingen, 1966). So as in the case of the saga of the foundation of the cult at Bethel at least two pre-Israelite stages of transmission (which can be broadly characterized as 'demonic' and 'mythological') can be distinguished.

H. J. Hermisson ('Jakobs Kampf am Jabbok', *ZTK* 71 (1974)) looks for the origin of the story in the experience the nomads had of God, especially in the encounter of their ancestor Jacob with a god of the fathers, such as the 'mighty one of Jacob'. But Hermisson has to regard the local connection, and perhaps even the wrestling, as later features of the narrative. But surely it is in them that the inner core of the narrative is found.

(c) During the (in the broader sense) Israelite stage of the story, different aims are found together. Jacob becomes the hero of the narrative, instead of an unnamed figure, and his name is replaced by 'Israel'.

Just as in the interpretation of the place-name 'face (i.e. appearance) of God' God becomes the object, 'I have seen God' (v. 30 [Heb. v. 31]), so Israel (really 'God strives' or something similar; cf. Ishma-el, 'God hears') is explained as 'he who strives with God' (v. 27 [Heb. v. 28]).

In this way the strange story of the demon comes to have significance for the nation as a whole; the aetiology for Israel surpasses the aetiology for Penuel. As a result of the transference of the action to Jacob the former river demon or the Canaanite deity El, whichever it is, is brought into relationship with Yahweh. However the identification is not stated explicitly; clearly the narrative was too strange or even offensive for this to be done.

So in the last resort it is not clear whether the being, 'the man' (v. 24 [Heb. v. 25]) is understood as God himself (cf. v. 28 [Heb. v. 29]) or as the angel of Yahweh (Hos. 12: 4 [Heb. 12: 5]) (cf. Gen. 18; Judg. 13). In any case important features of the narrative are reshaped in consequence of their association with Yahweh. The being refuses his name (v. 29 [Heb. v. 30]) – and perhaps has always done so from the beginning of the story; and the man cannot overcome this God. His superiority is turned into inferiority. Hos. 12: 3 [Heb. 12: 4]) interprets Jacob's 'victory' by saying 'he wept and sought his favour'. Similarly in the present form of the story in Genesis Jacob leaves the field vanquished; he could only 'preserve his life' (vv. 30f. [Heb. vv. 31f.]) and becomes the recipient instead of the giver of the blessing. Probably it is deliberately left unclear who the participant in the fight is (v. 25a [Heb. v. 26a]), and originally only the attacking demon was perhaps asked for his name. The story, which previously told of the direct encounter of a man with a divine being in tangible form, is now treated from the point of view of the theological principle that 'he who sees God dies' (v. 30 [Heb. v. 31]; cf. Judg. 6: 22; Exod. 33: 20 et al.).

Finally in its context in Genesis the story acquires a meaning which is reminiscent of the testing of Abraham (Gen. 22): Jacob, who deceives his brother but receives God's promise (28: 13–15), returns from foreign lands, richly blessed in family, goods and chattels, but immediately before his return home, in spite of his prayer for God's gracious preservation (32: 9–12 [Heb. 32: 10–13]), falls into a danger which threatens to destroy everything again. The blessing which he has experienced is put in question and thus, in temptation, given anew; the *deus revelatus* can at the same time be a *deus absconditus*. It can be seen that the Old Testament does not take over pre-Israelite sanctuary legends without reinterpreting them profoundly, even to the extent of altering the sense.

§4   The Exodus from Egypt

The 'God of the fathers' was a God of promise. Does the Old Testament succeed in preserving the inheritance of this nomadic tradition? Those who came out of Egypt and wandered in the wilderness were also recipients of the divine guidance which the patriarchs experienced. In fact the patriarchal tradition seems to have passed on its distinctive character to the Exodus tradition. This knows the same God of the future, who precedes his people on the way, and cares for his charges, until he leads them into the promised land. Just as the word of God promised offspring and possession of the land to the patriarchs, so the Exodus was later interpreted from the viewpoint of the promise (Exod. 3J and E; 6P).

Moses is first promised guidance from Egypt to Canaan at his call (Exod. 3: 8, 17D), and this assurance is taken up again and again in the Old Testament because of its importance (Deut. 6: 3; Josh. 5, 6 et al.) until it is possible to make the confession 'all came to pass' (Josh. 21: 43–5).

For this reason the Exodus to a far greater degree than the emigration of Abraham from his native country became a symbol of setting out into a better future, a symbol of liberation from vassalage, and of departure from a foreign land for one's home.

In spite of this thematic kinship however it is hard to decide how the God of the patriarchs and the God of the Exodus are originally related. The way the transition from the one to the other tradition took place was not that the group which stayed in Egypt originally worshipped the 'God of Abraham, Isaac and Jacob'. The whole interrelated patriarchal tradition was scarcely known; for not all of the tribes of the later Israel were in Egypt. Fundamentally therefore we have two originally different strands of tradition, which were first united in Canaan, when the tradents of both traditions joined together to form a tribal confederacy. Were there nevertheless already some early connections between the two?

Certain indications suggest that the Exodus tradition was cultivated especially in the 'house of Joseph' (cf. Josh. 17: 17f.; Judg. 1: 22, 35), that is, in the later northern kingdom; for Hosea, the prophet of the northern kingdom (12: 9 [Heb. 12: 10]; 13: 4 et al.; but also Amos. 9: 7), and (perhaps following him) Deuteronomy mention it often, while it is actually lacking in Isaiah of Jerusalem. Joshua, the first certain bearer of a name compounded with Yahweh, comes from the tribe of Ephraim in the house of Joseph. It is surely no accident that it is the Joseph narrative (Gen. 37–50) that unites the traditions of patriarchs and Exodus. In addition the sons of Joseph, Ephraim and Manasseh (according to Gen. 41:

50–2; 46: 20; 48: 5ff.) had an Egyptian mother and were born in Egypt; while people living in the area of Ephraim have Egyptian names (Josh. 24: 33; 1 Sam. 2: 34). Finally, by comparison with the temple in Jerusalem, the close connection of the northern Israelite bull symbol with the Exodus tradition (1 Kgs. 12: 28; Exod. 32: 4) is striking. It has therefore been assumed that parts of the tribe of Ephraim, from the 'house of Joseph', were led by hunger into the fertile Nile valley, had to serve there as vassals, but by good fortune returned home. If the Exodus tradition was cultivated in the heartland of Israel in particular, and the patriarch Jacob-Israel was connected with Egypt (Gen. 46: 1ff.; cf. Deut. 26: 5), this could explain how it came to have such fundamental significance for the faith of Israel.

If these considerations are correct, the group in Egypt perhaps worshipped 'the God of Isaac' (cf. Gen. 46: 1), the tradition about whom is equally to be ascribed to the 'house of Joseph'. However this conjecture rests upon assumptions which must remain uncertain. No really cogent arguments can be derived from the Old Testament for the conjecture that the Exodus was at one time ascribed to a God of the fathers and not to Yahweh (Exod. 15: 2 is a later passage). So it remains in the end unexplained what connection gave rise to the common fundamental features in the understanding of God in the patriarchal and Exodus traditions. Is it possible to think specifically of Moses (cf. below, §6a, 4)?

There are no extra-biblical witnesses which directly attest the sojourn of the ancestors of Israel in the land of the Nile, but Egyptian sources confirm the general indications of the situation that we have in the Old Testament.

What led nomadic groups to move into Egypt? Israel's ancestors were certainly not deported forcibly as prisoners of war to Egypt, and probably did not attempt of their own to become permanently sedentary in the eastern Delta. When the Old Testament mentions a reason for the journey to Egypt, it is simply the pressure for self-preservation. A report contemporary with the Exodus made by an Egyptian frontier official confirms that the threat of famine compelled such a move (Gen. 12: 10; 26: 1; 41: 57; 42: 1ff.; 43: 1ff.): the frontier guards allowed the nomads, who wanted to move into Egyptian territory, to pass in order to keep them and their cattle alive through the good will of Pharaoh (cf. *ANET*, p. 40). Furthermore historical inquiry finds more or less firm support for the tradition in three recollections in the book of Exodus (1: 11; 14: 5a; 15: 21), although opinions differ very much about their value.

The pharaoh in Exod. 1–15 is never mentioned by name, but Raamses is once attested as a place-name. Exod. 1: 11J with its account of the obligation to perform forced labour in the building of the 'store-cities' of Pithom and Raamses gives the one concrete basis for the dating and localization of the stay of the Israelites in Egypt. Rameses II (or already his father Sethos I) transferred his residence in the thirteenth century BC to the northeastern corner of the empire, and named the newly founded capital 'house of Rameses'. Pithom, literally 'house of (the god) Atum' lay further to the south, but also in the area of eastern Delta, which is called in the Old Testament 'the land of Goshen' (Gen. 45: 10 et al.). Since the name of the city of Raamses later fell into disuse and was replaced by Zoan or Tanis (Num. 13: 22 et al.) the tradition of the building of Pithom and

Raamses reaches back exactly to the thirteenth century BC or to the immediately following period. During their stay in the Delta area the ancestors of Israel had to perform forced labour – as did later aliens in Israel during Solomon's building activity (1 Kgs. 9: 15, 19 et al.). However the Old Testament does not understand these apparently customary obligations politically, as the performance of service to the Egyptian state, but theologically, as a plot of the Egyptians to 'oppress' Israel, and so to hinder the multiplication of the nation, and therewith the realization of the promise (Exod. 1: 10f.).

In a letter from the time of Rameses II (*c.*1290–1224 BC), in whom the 'pharaoh of the oppression' has often been seen, we hear of ' *'pr*, who drag stones . . . for the great pylon of . . . Rameses'. This term, which is likewise attested in Mesopotamia and Syria in the form of *Khabiru* (*hab/piru*) is probably connected with the term Hebrew. It appears at the beginning of Exodus (1: 15ff. et al.; cf. already Gen. 39: 14ff.) of the relationship between Israelites and Egyptians, and later of the relationship to the Philistines (Sam. 4: 6ff.) as a designation for Israel by others or by themselves. But does the term refer to a social stratum with lower legal status (e.g. economic failures or foreign immigrants) or to an ethnic unit? Probably there was a change of meaning in the course of the long time in which the term is used in the ancient Near East, especially in such far separated regions. In the Old Testament, at least in its later instances, the expression refers most probably to Israel (cf. Deut. 15: 12ff. with Exod. 21: 2ff.).

In contrast to the main stream of tradition, according to which the Pharaoh, compelled by all sorts of plagues, had to 'let Israel go' against his will (Exod. 5: 2; 12: 31; 13: 17 et al.), Exod. 14: 5a (E?) tells that the Israelites fled. Does this historical fragment give us a genuine recollection? In that case the nomadic group will have escaped from forced labour through flight into the wilderness.

a   THE DELIVERANCE AT THE SEA

The decisive event in the flight is the miraculous deliverance of the Israelites from their pursuers at the sea. The Old Testament tradition of this unique event is found in four main versions: the prose version of Exod. 14, in which (as the repetitions indicate) at least two different literary sources (J, P, and partially too E) are united, and the two hymns of Exod. 15. Of these the long Song of Moses (15: 1–18) is probably only a later expansion of the brief Song of Miriam (15: 21). Numerous allusions to the Exodus and the miracle at the sea are also found in the psalter and in passages in the prophets.

According to the first version (J) a strong east wind drives the sea together by night. The Egyptians, thrown into confusion by a terror sent from God, plunge into the sea as it streams back (14: 21a, 24, 27); there is no mention of a march of Israel through the water. According to the other description (P) Israel marches through the divided sea, while the masses of water crash together over pharaoh's host (14: 16, 21b–23, 26, 28f.; according to 15: 8ff. the pile-up of the water is caused by wind; cf. also Josh. 2: 10; Isa. 43: 16; 51: 10 et al.). The divergences come therefore not only in the details (in the one version God terrifies the enemy only through the pillar of cloud, in the other he places his power in the 'hand' of his representative Moses) but are very substantial in the course of events itself. As the recollection is kept alive new features are added; the presentation increasingly acquires miraculous traits. But the theological motifs remain important: as in the creation narrative (Gen. 1) in this later presentation too God's word and the event correspond with one another.

While the later accounts differ, it is no longer possible to recover the detailed course of events even from the oldest tradition. The victory song of Miriam (Exod. 15: 21) may stand very close to the event; the fact that the defeated enemy army consisted in war-chariots seems to be something unusual for the (unnamed) giver of thanks (cf. 14: 6f.). Later Israel suffered under the superior strength of the 'iron chariots' of the Canaanites (Judg. 1: 19 et al.). Can it be accidental that a journey of Israel through the sea is not (yet) mentioned, and indeed that Israel itself, like the Egyptians, is not even named? Israel as a whole was as we know not in Egypt. The conjecture has even been made that the hymn represents the earliest answer to the experience, and therefore expresses the event for the first time in words:

> Sing to Yahweh, for he has exalted himself (or, is exalted),
> Horse and (chariot) rider he has thrown into the sea.

Here nothing is said about how the event happened; the bare fact of it is acknowledged. In the same way, while the fact of the event seems probable, how it happened must remain open. But this brevity demands expansion; a later age wishes to know how it happened. But this expansion takes place within the context of the history of Israel, into which the event is later incorporated.

b   THE GOD OF THE EXODUS

1   The miracle at the sea was never treated 'purely naturally', for example, as a natural event or as a victory for Israel. The early song of Miriam is already a confession of faith. Similarly the older detailed narrative of the Yahwist does not give a historical account, but interprets the event simply as the action of God. When the Israelites caught sight of the pursuing Egyptians and fearfully upbraided Moses, he made them a speech (rather like the later charismatic leaders of the period of the judges):

> Stand firm and see the salvation of Yahweh! . . . Yahweh will fight for you,
> and you have only to be still. (Exod. 14: 13f.; cf. Deut. 20)

The assurance which here comforts the anxious Israelites anticipates the future. Any action of their own by Israel or assistance is completely excluded; they are not to move. Even the pursuers have to acknowledge the effectiveness of Yahweh's action alone: 'Yahweh fights for them against the Egyptians!' (v. 25). The goal of the story is Israel's faith in God; the action follows the faith (v. 31, in a probably later addition; cf. 4: 1 et al.). Since the miracle at the Red Sea is acknowledged as a 'War of Yahweh' (below, §7), something new appears here compared with the understanding of God of the patriarchal period, and this points forward to the early history of Israel in Palestine. Does this feature depend on later adaptation, or does it appear from the beginning, and is simply emphasized by the Yahwist in Exod. 14? The core of the Exodus tradition does seem always to have been the destruction of the pursuers: 'Yahweh threw' (15: 21; cf. 15: 4) or 'poured the Egyptians into the midst of the sea' (14: 27), and so a warlike event. A later period still expressly says in the song of Moses: 'Yahweh is a man of war' (Exod. 15: 3), and Deutero-Isaiah in his preaching of a new Exodus picks up this confession (Isa. 40: 10; 42: 13).

The God of war of whom the Exodus tradition tells is Yahweh. The rescue is owed to him; the flight was already undertaken in his name. Did the later Israel then first meet its God at the deliverance from Egypt, hear his promise, experience his guidance and believe in him (cf. Exod. 14: 31)? This question is not an easy one to answer (below, §5d)

2   Or does the Exodus tradition in some way indicate to which God the miracle of the sea was at first ascribed, as the tradition of the patriarchs has preserved a recollection of the previously worshipped patriarchal gods? O. Eissfeldt (*Baal Zaphon, Zeus Kasios und der Durchzug der Israeliten durchs Meer*, Halle, 1932) has attempted such a reconstruction on the basis of the mention of a place-name. According to Exod. 14: 2, 9 Israel, before the Egyptians caught up with them, encamped 'in front of Ba'al Zephon'. This place can be identified with a sanctuary of Zeus Kasios at the west end of the Sirbonian Lake (on the coast of the Mediterranean to the east of the Nile delta). This God was worshipped in later antiquity as a deliverer in distress at sea and in the wilderness. So it is fully conceivable that the Israelites too gave thanks for their deliverance to his predecessor at the same place, Ba'al Zephon. If this is so we have not only a geographical but also a religio-historical solution. The sanctuary legends of Genesis, the stories of creation and flood, were also originally ascribed to other deities. On this conjecture Israel's 'earliest confession', the deliverance at the sea, would be really the work of a deity against whom the Old Testament later directed a bitter and sharp polemic. Hosea's threat (ch. 2) that the nation would be led back out of the land of Ba'al to Yahweh in the wilderness would then in fact bring Israel precisely back into the dominion of Ba'al.

But the geographical details of Exod. 14: 2, 9 are not really reliable (cf. M. Noth, 'Der Schauplatz des Meerwunders', in J. Fück (ed.), *Festschrift O. Eissfeldt*, Halle, 1947). They depend upon a later localization of the event on the much used trade-route which led from Egypt to Palestine. For the same reason the religio-historical conclusions too are not compelling. Other, probably older, sources contain much less exact indications. Exod. 13: 20 speaks only generally of 'the edge of the wilderness'. The term later frequently used, 'the Sea of Reeds', is not unambiguous; it usually indicates the Gulf of Akaba at the east of the Sinai peninsula, but this region lies too far from Egypt. The most likely candidates for the site of the miracle at the sea would be the Gulf of Suez, the Bitter Lakes, or the Sirbonian Lake. But the old passages (14: 21, 27) and the Song of Miriam (15: 21) speak only very generally of 'the sea'. Perhaps the deliverance from the persecutors was at first narrated without any firm localization.

The various attempts to find another deity than Yahweh to whom those concerned owed their deliverance at the sea (whether Ba'al Zephon, a patriarchal god (cf. Exod. 15: 2; 18: 4) or even the 'God of the Hebrews' (5: 3 et al.)) have so far adduced no convincing results.

3 While the earliest witness to the miracle at the sea gives no more precise details of the events, it already shows a peculiarity of Israel's belief and thought. The brief hymn takes this one event as the action of God; it calls upon its hearers to sing, and bases its praise upon the 'saving' (3: 8; 18: 4, 8f.) intervention of Yahweh. So the Old Testament comes to know God by his action, especially by his action towards man. It acquires its understanding of history because it understands God from the event; when it speaks of God it narrates history. The general statement 'he is high exalted' is expanded by saying, 'the horse and his rider he has thrown into the sea'. The later song is constructed upon the same pattern, developing the general confession 'Yahweh is a man of war' (Exod. 15: 3) into a comprehensive historical retrospect from the destruction of the pursuers down to the conquest. So it does not stop at recollection of a situation. Later history can be added to it as a continuation, because the event was not complete for later listeners. The confession of God's being is from now on understood as an account of God's action.

4 The Exodus from Egypt was for Israel straightforwardly Yahweh's act of election, the beginning and (throughout its history) the lasting foundation of its relationship to God. Here men had experienced who it is that is called Yahweh, and in what way he helps even the unworthy (Ps. 106: 7f.). So the event came to have a general significance far beyond the individual group affected by it, which outstrips the promise to the patriarchs:

When Israel went forth from Egypt,
    the house of Jacob from a people of strange language,
Judah became his sanctuary,
    Israel his dominion. (Ps. 114: 1f.)

'I am your God from the land of Egypt', Hosea makes Yahweh say (12: 9 [Heb. 12: 10]), in order to show the motivation of the exclusiveness of the love of God (13: 4; cf. 3: 1). To the prophet the time in the wilderness, after the Exodus and before the entry, appears as a time of undisturbed communion with God; Jeremiah (ch. 2) and to a heightened degree Ezekiel (20; cf. 23) take up the idea in a developed form. Year by year the Passover feast is to remind them of the Exodus (below, §9b, 1). It is interpreted in new and changing concepts: God 'buys out, sets free' (in Deut. 7: 8; 9: 26 et al.), 'redeems' (Exod. 6, P et al., see below, Excursus 1).

There are strata of the Old Testament which know this tradition of faith only slightly or not at all, for example, the wisdom literature or the Jerusalem traditions, the psalms of Zion and the royal psalms on the one hand and the prophecy of Isaiah on the other. Nevertheless the declaration that God led them out from Egypt is 'to judge by the frequency of its occurrence, the most important theological statement of the Old Testament', according to E. Zenger (*ZDMG* Supp.1 (1969), 334: 42; (cf. W. Gross, *ZAW* 86 (1974)).

If one wants to find the theologically most important event for the whole Old Testament it would have to be the Exodus. Later writers love to portray the miraculous deliverance at the sea (Ps. 78: 13; 136: 13ff.; Isa. 63: 12f.; Neh. 9: 11), to draw parallels with the crossing of the Jordan (Josh. 4: 23) or to expand with mythological motifs from the fight with the sea or with the chaos monster (Isa. 51: 9f.; below, §11e).

The Exodus tradition is encountered scattered about the Old Testament, and often hardened into a stereotyped form: 'Yahweh who brought Israel out of the land of Egypt' becomes a fixed confessional statement, for example, in the introduction to the Decalogue (Exod. 20: 2; Deut. 5: 6; Ps. 81: 10 [Heb. 81: 11]). Here the commandments are connected with the act of God; similarly social consequences are drawn from the deliverance from servitude (Deut. 15: 12ff.; 24: 17f.; Lev. 19: 33f.; 25: 42). Does the northern kingdom seek to legitimate the bull cult by means of the Exodus tradition after the separation from the dynasty of David (1 Kgs. 12: 28; Exod. 32: 4)? In Deuteronomy and the Deuteronomic school its significance increases even more; the past is drawn together in retro-spect to form a 'uniform picture of history' (H. Lubsczyk, *Der Auszug Israels aus Ägypten*, Leipzig, 1963), and so actualized in particular credal formulations (Deut. 6: 20ff.; 26: 5ff.; Josh. 24: 2ff. et al.). This reference to salvation history becomes so important that it is secondarily inserted into the sayings of the prophets in the process of redaction of their books when it is found to be missing (Amos 2: 10; 3: 1; 5: 25 et al.).

The prophets themselves can deduce the responsibility of the nation from God's act of election (Amos 3: 2) or can so relativize the tradition of the Exodus that they take away from Israel the possibility of basing on it any real advantage for themselves:

> Are you not like the Ethiopians to me,
>   O people of Israel?
> Did I not bring up Israel from the land of Egypt,
>   and the Philistines from Caphtor and the Syrians from Kir? (Amos 9: 7)

Hosea looks forward to the imminent judgement as a return to Egypt (8: 13; 9: 3, 6; 11: 5) and the new beginning as a return from foreign lands (11: 11; cf. 2: 14f. [Heb. 2: 16f.]).

A future saying in Jeremiah completely sets aside the old confession of faith and sets up a new one in its place.

Therefore, behold, the days are coming, says Yahweh, when men shall no longer say: 'As Yahweh lives who brought up the people of Israel out of the land of Egypt,' but 'As Yahweh lives, who brought up and led the descendants of the house of Israel out of the north country and out of all the countries where I had driven them.' Then they shall dwell in their own land. (Jer. 23: 7f.; 16: 14f.)

The message of Deutero-Isaiah even demands that they should forget the earlier history of Israel in order to understand the coming time (Isa. 43: 18f.). But tradition gives him the language in which to proclaim the promised release from alien dominion as surpassing the first Exodus. The second, future Exodus is no longer to take place in haste (Isa. 52: 12 against Exod. 12: 11P); the wilderness is to change into fertile land, the mountains into plains, and Yahweh himself will lead the march (Isa. 40: 3f., 10; 41: 18f.; 43: 19f.; 49: 10 et al.). Thus the Exodus becomes expectation again, and it appears again as a future event in the sayings of the later prophets (Mic. 2: 12; Zech. 10: 11 et al.).

EXCURSUS 1: 'REDEMPTION'

The older period describes the deliverance from Egypt as 'bringing up or out', or 'rescuing' (Exod. 3: 8, 10; Amos. 9: 7 et al.), later times interpret it as 'redeeming' (*pādāh*: Deut. 7: 8; 13: 6; Mic. 6: 4; Ps. 78: 42) and as 'releasing, delivering' (*gā'al*: Exod. 6: 6P; Ps. 74: 2; 77: 15 [Heb. 77: 16] et al.). The connection with servanthood seems to the nation in retrospect so strong 'that it could not have set itself free' (A. Jepsen, 'Die Begriffe des "Erlösens" im Alten Testament' [1957] in *Der Herr ist Gott*, Berlin, 1978).

1 'Redemption' is a very characteristic legal usage for the Old Testament, which is regulated by law (Lev. 25: 24ff.). An Israelite has both the right and the duty to assist a member of his family who has fallen into distress, in a quite particular way: if anyone has to dispose of his house and lands because of poverty, his nearest relation (who is called the 'redeemer') has the right of purchase (Jer. 32: 7) and also the duty of recovering the land. Thus it remains in the hands of the family; for inherited lands, being the basis for life, may not be alienated (cf. 1 Kgs. 22). If however a free Israelite is so impoverished that he has to sell himself (to a foreigner) as a slave, his relative is under a duty to buy him back. The 'redemption', that is, the repurchase, therefore presupposes family ties. The book of Ruth (2: 20ff.) and Jeremiah's purchase of a field in Anathoth (Jer. 32: 6ff.) attest that the custom really was put into practice in fact.

In each case the property of the clan in land and persons must be preserved unharmed (J.J. Stamm, *Erlösen und Vergeben im Alten Testament*, Bern, 1940, p. 28). If a member of the family is murdered, the relative gets the task of the 'redeemer' or avenger of blood; if any one becomes a killer by accident, he can find refuge in the cities of asylum (Num. 35: 10ff.; cf. Exod. 21: 13; Deut. 19: 4ff.; 2 Sam. 3: 27). If a member of the family dies childless his brother is under a duty to marry the widow; the first son is then regarded as the heir of the dead man (brother-in-law or levirate marriage: Deut. 25: 5ff.; Gen. 38: 8; Ruth 4: 5, 10).

On the other hand *pādāh* does not necessarily presuppose blood ties, and seems to have a weaker sense, to 'free, deliver' from slavery (Exod. 21: 7–11; Lev. 19: 20; Job 6: 23), to 'redeem' by a substitute the first-born that belongs to God (Exod. 34: 19f.; 13: 11ff.; Lev. 27: 26ff.; cf. 1 Sam. 14: 45 et al).

2   As a relation takes care of the needy man, so God 'redeems' man from distress, be it enemy action or sickness (Gen. 48: 16; 2 Sam. 4: 9; 1 Kgs. 1: 29; Jer. 15: 21 et al.). The individual can pray for deliverance from distress (Ps. 26: 11; 69: 18 [Heb. 69: 19]; 119: 154), and give thanks for deliverance when it has happened: 'Thou hast redeemed me, O faithful God' (31: 5 [Heb. 31: 6]; 107: 1; Lam. 3: 58). The man who because of his social position has no legal helper finds one in God himself; he takes over the duty of the nearest relative:

Do not remove the landmark of the widow,
   nor enter the fields of the fatherless.
For their redeemer is strong,
   he will plead their cause against you.

(Prov. 23: 10f.; cf. 22: 23; Jer. 50: 34)

Because God protects the socially weak and has set Israel free, Israel's faith has ethical consequences (Deut. 24: 17f.; 15: 12ff.).

God's redemption applies to the individual as well as to the nation as a whole. The prophet Deutero-Isaiah addresses the exiles as a single person, and declares to them the impending, indeed present, deliverance: 'Fear not! for I have redeemed you!' (Isa. 43: 1). Those returning from the captivity in Babylon are to confess 'Yahweh has redeemed his servant Jacob' (48: 20; cf. 52: 9). In fact 'redeemer' becomes a fixed epithet of God (44: 6, 24; cf. 63: 16; also 1: 27 et al.).

An appendix to Ps. 130 gives this individual lamentation a place in the worship of the community:

O Israel, hope in Yahweh;
   for with Yahweh there is steadfast love,
   and with him is plenteous redemption.
And he will redeem Israel
   from all his iniquities. (Ps. 130: 7f.; cf. 25: 22; 34: 22 [Heb. 34: 23])

While redemption means here (for the only time in the Old Testament) forgiveness of sins, it means ultimately deliverance from death (Ps. 103: 4) or even in death (49: 15 [Heb. 49: 16]; 73: 24; cf. Job 19: 24; and below, Excursus 8, 6). With this the faith in God's 'redemption' reaches out beyond the area of history and of human experience.

§5   The Revelation at Sinai

In the Exodus tradition Yahweh appears as a God of war, who protects his people from their pursuers. Like the gods of the patriarchs he is at the same time a God of promise, who announces deliverance beforehand and leads men to freedom. By contrast the Sinai tradition opens up a quite different area of Yahwistic faith; several completely new features are found in its utterances about God. Hitherto God has been encountered primarily as the God accompanying men, and leading them in their wanderings. On the other hand a connection with a particular place, which in the patriarchal traditions is only secondary, is here present from the beginning. The Sinai pericope attests Yahweh as a mountain God. Was Yahweh originally a local deity? Did men have to go on pilgrimage to a holy mountain in order to worship him?

1. The appearance of this God, the theophany, is achieved in natural events, in thunderstorm and in volcanic eruption. It leads to the making of a covenant, at which the law of God is proclaimed. While the words of God to the patriarchs convey promise, the words of God at Sinai are almost exclusively commandment.

To the extent that the Old Testament has a legal character this impression depends primarily upon the Sinai pericope (Exod. 19–Num. 10: 10). In the course of time the most varied legal ordinances have accumulated here, so much that they almost overwhelm the narratives of the appearance of God and of the making of the covenant. Legal instructions for daily life in the community in the Decalogue (Exod. 20; 34) and the Book of the Covenant (Exod. 20: 22–23: 33) were inserted into the older sources, the Yahwist and the Elohist (Exod. 19–24; 32–34); and in the later Priestly writing a place was found for extensive cultic ordinances as being authoritative words of Moses (Exod. 25–31; Lev. 1–Num. 10). So most of the legal collections, including the Decalogue, were only subsequently included in the narrative of the revelation at Sinai.

To go beyond the literary division, the question arises whether the current understanding, by which the revelation at Sinai is the origin of the Old Testament giving of the law, is really correct? The proclamation of the law of God upon Sinai is clearly not all that firmly traditio-historically anchored here.

Wellhausen could pointedly write, 'the true and original significance of Sinai is quite independent of the legislation. It was the seat of the Deity, the sacred mountain, doubtless not only for the Israelites, but generally for all the Hebrew and Cainite (Kenite) tribes of the surrounding region' (*Prolegomena to the History of Ancient Israel*, London, 1885, pp. 343f.). On the other hand it is according to G. von Rad 'the basic datum to which all the individual traditions in one way or another go back' that 'at Sinai Yahweh revealed to his people binding ordinances, on the basis of which life with its God was made possible' (*Old Testament Theology*, vol. 1, Edinburgh, 1962, p. 188).

The oldest stratum of tradition did not perhaps yet know the now dominant combination of covenant and announcement of God's will. Our understanding of the Sinai revelation is too strongly influenced by the picture which a later age has developed.

2   While the Exodus was the fundamental act of God for Israel, the Sinai event acquired the significance of the revelation of Yahweh without qualifications. After the preceding appearance of God to Moses (Exod. 3; 6) the relationship of God and nation is grounded in it. The account of the Sinai revelation takes the biggest space in the Pentateuch, but outside this historical work it is surprisingly little mentioned; it is insignificant by comparison with the confession of the delivery from Egypt. Even the names Sinai or Horeb are scarcely found elsewhere in the Old Testament (cf. below, §5d). For example Hosea, who frequently refers back to the Exodus tradition, does not mention Sinai, even if he alludes to the Decalogue (Hos. 4: 2 et al.). Even in Deutero-Isaiah the Exodus and Sinai traditions are not, or not yet, connected together; he promises the new Exodus and pure future salvation, without instruction and declaration of commandments (the Torah appears in Isa. 42: 21, 24 as the gift of God in the past, which was not heeded; a different view comes in 42: 4; 51: 4, 7). We thus hear echoes of the separate status of the two great blocks of tradition until far into the prophetic period.

In its present form the Sinai account is a confusion of extremely different traditions from the individual sources. Just as we began from the individual instances in the case of the patriarchal tradition, it is best here to deal briefly with the most important older passages.

a   THE THEOPHANY ACCORDING TO EXOD. 19

1   God's appearance on Sinai has its climax in the brief account of Exod. 19: 16–20:

16. On the morning of the third day there were thunders and lightnings, and a thick cloud upon the mountain, and a very loud trumpet blast, so that all the people who were in the camp trembled. 17. Then Moses brought the people out of the camp to meet God; and they took their stand at the foot of the mountain.
18. And Mount Sinai was wrapped in smoke, because Yahweh descended upon it in fire; and the smoke of it went up like the smoke of a kiln, and the whole mountain (LXX the whole people) quaked greatly.

19. And as the sound of the trumpet grew louder and louder, Moses spoke, and God answered him in the trumpet blast (i.e. in thunder, or in an audible voice?).

20. And Yahweh came down upon Mount Sinai, to the top of the mountain; and Yahweh called Moses to the top of the mountain, and Moses went up.

In these few sentences the duality of the statements is striking. Through the different terms for God, 'Elohim' ('God', vv. 17, 19) and 'Yahweh' (vv. 18, 20), but also through the other expressions ('trumpet blast', 'Mount Sinai') the passage divides roughly into Elohistic (vv. 16–17, 19) and Yahwistic (vv. 18, 20) sections.

There is a measure of uncertainty only over the assignment of v. 18b, the text of which is not entirely clear, to one of the two older sources J or E (or to a later redaction).

Both have the appearance of Yahweh accompanied by natural phenomena, but make completely different statements about the nature of the event. The Yahwist mentions the natural elements, the smoking of the mountain as of a kiln, fire and perhaps earthquake (v. 18; cf. 1 Kgs. 19: 11f.), and so probably presupposes volcanic phenomena. The 'pillar of cloud and of fire' which journeys with the people as a sign of the presence of God (Exod. 13: 21f.; 14: 19b, 24J) would fit this well. Only Yahweh's 'coming down' (cf. Gen. 11: 5, 7; 18: 21J et al.) fails to fit the otherwise uniform picture, and is to be understood as a theological correction, to the effect that Yahweh does not dwell continuously upon the mount and that he causes the natural phenomenon.

Similarly the later accounts of Deuteronomy (4: 11ff.; 5: 23f.; 9: 15: 'the mountain burned with fire, to the heart of heaven, wrapped in darkness, cloud and gloom') and the still later Priestly writing (Exod. 24: 17: 'the appearance of the glory of Yahweh was like a devouring fire on the top of the mountain') remind us of a volcanic eruption, although a rain of ashes or a stream of lava are never mentioned.

On the other hand the Elohist, with the natural phenomena of thunder, lightning and heavy cloud (Exod. 19: 16, 19; cf. 19: 9; 34: 5), points to a thunderstorm. But again it is not a mere spectacle of nature that is offered: the people, led by Moses (v. 17; cf. 3: 10ff. E) tremble before the blast of a ram's horn (vv. 16, 19), such as was blown before worship to summon the congregation. Here therefore a later cultic practice seems to have influenced the presentation. It has indeed frequently been conjectured that cultic factors have influenced the Sinai narrative; but it is impossible to establish anything more definite about this.

While in the section vv. 16–20 the two versions are juxtaposed, they can also be completely interwoven. Exod 20: 18, 'When all the people perceived the thunderings and the lightnings and the sound of the trumpet and the mountain smoking', combines thunder and smoke with a storm and volcano; this assimilation is an attempt at mediation, inserted in what is from a literary viewpoint an inappropriate place between Decalogue and Book of the Covenant (20: 18–21 if not as a whole later, has at least been redactionally reworked). In addition material as well as linguistic contacts can be seen with the secondary sections Exod. 24: 1b–2. Only Moses may 'come near', 'the people' stands 'afar off'. So here too we have in place of the directness of revelation a mediation through Moses.

2   The representations which were made later of the Sinai event are therefore very different one from another. The question is whether we have genuine recollections here at all. Are the natural occurrences only a means of representing God's revelation? Do we have to content ourselves with the recognition that the original event remains totally obscure, or is there a possibility of a choice between the thunderstorm and the volcanic phenomena? The second version is much more strongly attested (i.e. by the three sources J, D and P), from the point of view of their later residence in Palestine is much more unusual, and finally is necessarily associated with a mountain, while thunderstorms occur everywhere. So a cautious conjecture could be made that the volcanic features are traditions inherited from the nomadic period, while the thunderstorm elements were only added in Canaan. Canaanite religion had much to say of appearances of God in a thunderstorm; are there possibly influences of the storm god (Ba'al) in this depiction of the Sinai event?

If the volcanic phenomena are to be regarded as original expressions of the theophany, the so-called 'Mount of Moses' on the southern tip of the Sinai peninsula is ruled out as the site of the divine revelation, since it is not a volcano. The identification of Sinai with this mountain range is in any case only attested in the post-Christian period. However the area was a centre of pilgrimage about the time of Christ; Nabataean pilgrim inscriptions attest the holiness of the spot. Had the same 'holy mountain' already been visited for centuries before (cf. the ritual rules of Exod. 19: 10–15; 21–5)?
    In the historical period the nearest volcanoes are far away in northwestern Arabia, on the far side of the gulf of Akaba. The Sinai event has often therefore been located in this (at that time perhaps Midianite) area. In fact a number of other indications point to early connections with the Midianites (see below, §6a, 3).
    Against the placing of Sinai in the volcanic area to the south of Tebuk, about 200 km. to the south-east of Akaba, 'cannot be urged the fact of the great distance of this area from Egypt as well as from Palestine; for for pilgrimages . . . distances are not of real importance', as the Nabataean pilgrimages to the Sinai peninsula and the journeys of Islamic pilgrims to Mecca at a later date show (M. Noth, *Aufsätze zur biblischen Landes- und Altertumskunde*, Neukirchen-Vluyn, 1971, vol. I, p. 73, n. 61). But to what extent was it the domestication of the camel that made it possible to cover such great distances?

In the end the event was in all probability volcanic in character. However this conclusion is not entirely compelling, since it is not possible beyond all doubt to make a decision between the two different old presentations. Like the miracle at the sea, the revelation at Sinai too can no longer be located with certainty. The site of the mountain remains in the last resort no longer capable of determination. Here too a more precise description of the manner of the event is impossible; only the fact of it is certain. A historical event set the tradition in motion; the later period has in many different ways developed it and changed it.

3   The different names 'Sinai' (J, P) and the (probably later) 'mount of God' (E) and Horeb (D, and insertion into E) of themselves indicate something of the complicated course that the tradition later took. In Palestine the connection to the mountain of revelation was apparently almost lost, and only persisted in memory. Only in 1 Kgs. 19 does the Old Testament tell of a pilgrimage to the mount of God, Horeb. Elijah (as successor of Moses?) returns at a time of apostasy from Yahweh 'to the origin and to the sources' (G. Fohrer, *Elia*, 2nd edn, Zürich, 1968, p. 95). God's appearance on the mountain is again accompanied by volcanic phenomena, storm, earthquake and fire. But now the older tradition is explicitly corrected: 'But Yahweh was not in them' (vv. 11f.). Then follows 'a still small voice' – God's transcendence is represented metaphorically, or at least thus indicated in this world. Even the stilling of the wind does not as such represent God's presence; rather in the quiet God's voice is heard (cf. Job 4: 12f.). So God's appearance on Sinai leaves its traces in the time of the monarchy. Elsewhere too the Old Testament adopts similar conceptions of a coming of God seen in nature (below, §11d).

b   THE MAKING OF THE COVENANT ACCORDING TO EXOD. 24

The revelation on Mount Sinai has for its goal the creation or confirmation of a fellowship between God and people. So the theophany (Exod. 19), after which the commandments (Exod. 20–23) have been inserted later, is followed by the conclusion of the covenant (Exod. 24 and 34). The first narrative falls apart in turn into two accounts (Exod. 24: 1–2 + 9–11 and 3–8). The division into sources is admittedly disputed, but it is basically more important to recognize the difference between sources than to place them in a broader context.

1   The more original narrative creates a central scene: seventy unnamed 'elders', the representatives of Israel by tribe and clan, have an encounter with God.

The named individuals, Moses and Aaron, Nadab and Abihu, were probably added only later to this group, which was itself differentiated more precisely. In the introductory verses (24: 1–2, and in part too v. 9) which traditio-historically if not literarily are later, a theological interest can be perceived.

   The addition of vv. 1b–2, which are reminiscent of Exod. 20: 18–21, sharply reduces the significance of the other characters. Moses alone is to come near to God, the others may only 'worship afar off'. Only one is allowed what was originally given to all, and the demand 'to cast themselves down (with their faces to the earth)' introduces an alien note into the scene: distance from God is placed higher than fellowship with him (v. 11). So the introduction directly contradicts the older tradition, according to which a larger group is able to see God. At a later time, reaching right down to the legends of Judaism, an

increasingly special position is reserved for Moses (cf. also Exod. 19: 3, 21; 20: 21; 34: 3f., 27). He lives in unique closeness to God; it was only to Moses that God spoke 'face to face' (Exod. 33: 11; Num. 12: 6–8; Deut. 34: 10).
The same tendency marks vv. 1a and 9, though in less acute form. Moses receives the command to go up, and thereby gains an advantage, which he does not have in the main narrative (vv. 10f.). Furthermore the priests (Aaron, Nadab and Abihu) surely do not originally belong to the group of the 'chief men' (v. 11; similarly Exod. 18: 22). The circle of participants was therefore probably originally anonymous.
The heart of the narrative (at least vv. 10f.) may well be Elohistic (cf. *'elōhīm*, 'God', and 'God of Israel' Gen. 33: 20E).

In various respects (a–f) the narrative gives an extremely unusual, even strange, effect. (a) Moses does not yet have an exclusive role as mediator, and seems therefore not originally to have been the towering founder figure who mediated fellowship with the Yahweh of Sinai. (b) In the theophany (Exod. 19: 16–20) God was not visible, but only audible (although it is not said what the words were that he uttered) and traceable in the effects of his appearance. Now Israel's representatives 'see' God himself, without the experience having any evil consequences for them. That so many people were found worthy of seeing God is unique in the Old Testament (cf. Num. 14: 14) and is later looked forward to at God's future revelation (Isa. 40: 5; 52: 7f., 10). While for Greek thought God is regarded as invisible, in the Old Testament the principle holds that 'the man who sees God dies' (Exod. 33: 20; cf. 19: 21; below §6c, 6). Not even the mount of God may be touched by man or beast (19: 12; 34: 3). However in this case it is stated with a note of wonder, 'God did not stretch out his hand', that is, he did not exploit his power and majesty, and spared those with whom he sought fellowship.

9. Then Moses and Aaron, Nadab, and Abihu, and seventy of the elders of Israel went up, and they saw the God of Israel; and there was under his feet as it were a pavement of sapphire stone, like the very heaven for clearness. And he did not lay his hands on the chief men of the people of Israel; they beheld God, and ate and drank.

In other ways too the scene preserves (c) God's transcendence. God himself is not described, although he is 'seen'. Only the ground is described; it is clear as a pavement like the blue of the lapis lazuli stone and the clearness of the heaven. Is God then already in this apparently primitive scene thought of as dwelling in heaven? The narrative contents itself with describing the place with a reserved comparison ('as') and so indicates through an image that God remains transcendent even in his appearance to man (cf. Ezek. 1: 25f.). (d) The sight of God is the centre, but not the climax of the encounter. The common meal, which the representatives of the people take upon the mountain in the sight of God, is meant to settle and confirm the fellowship that has been established (but not to realize it for the first time), as a sacrificial meal too can establish a fellowship (cf.

Exod. 18: 12; 32: 6; Gen. 26: 30; 31: 46, 54 et al.). It is not however said that God himself participates in the meal; as when he lets the elders see him, so here too he gives proof of his grace (cf. 2 Kgs. 25: 29). (e) The term 'covenant' is noticeably absent it was probably not yet current at the earlier period (cf. below, Excursus 4). Accordingly any cultic or ritual character is in the background here. (f) Finally there is no mention of a proclamation of law. The fellowship between God and people is concluded, without being based on specific rules, without any particular commitment being expressed, without God even speaking. The scene is strangely silent.

It has recently been interpreted (on the analogy of later passages like Isa. 6; Ezek. 1: 22ff.) as a banquet for the God who is enthroned as king upon a mountain reaching up into heaven. Then the tradition would have been formed upon Canaanite models. But is it probable that a scene which in so strong and even unique form expresses the will of the transcendent God for fellowship with Israel should have only secondarily been transferred to Sinai? It is surely not accidental that the title king is not found here, and that the throne of God and his heavenly court are not mentioned. Even the action of falling down is only found in the later form of the narrative (v. 1b). The fact that the presentation was only assimilated with difficulty to Israel's later understanding of its early period through the insertion of vv. 1f., 9, argues for the great antiquity of the tradition.

2   Into this narrative setting (Exod. 24: 1–2, 9–11) another account has been inserted (the source of which is uncertain), according to which the conclusion of the covenant was not accomplished without a commitment to a law in the course of a cultic act. Moses now functions as mediator, and in place of the elders the people appear, without it becoming really clear where the participants come from and where they are. Moses tells the people 'all the words of Yahweh and all the ordinances', and writes them down, after the people has declared itself ready 'to do all the words which Yahweh has spoken' (vv. 3–4a said at first for the spoken word, in v. 7 for the written form). This later ceremony of commitment (already attested in similar form in 19: 3ff.) forms the interpretative framework for two apparently older elements of tradition, a scene of sacrifice (vv. 4b, 5) and a blood ritual (vv. 6, 8a).

In this version fellowship is not established through a meal upon the mountain, but through a sacrifice at the foot of the mountain:

And he [Moses] rose up early in the morning and built an altar at the foot of the mountain . . . And he sent young men of the people of Israel, to offer burnt offerings and sacrifice peace offerings . . .

Are these 'young men' really people who are not entitled to offer sacrifice, or only cultic servants (cf. 1 Sam. 2: 11, 13; Exod. 33: 11)? In any case they only act at Moses' command; and he reserves for himself the decisive action of the sprinkling of blood:

THE REVELATION AT SINAI 45

6. Moses took half of the blood and put it in basins, while he threw the other half of the blood upon the altar. 8a. Moses took the blood and threw it upon the people . . .

An interpretation of this controversial text is made more difficult by the fact that while it leaves important elements unmentioned, it tears apart the two acts of the blood ritual by the declaration of assent of the people (v. 7) and thus to some extent blunts it. Only when the people have committed themselves to obedience are they sprinkled. It is most natural that the two acts of the blood ritual belong originally to one single cultic action (v. 8a repeats v. 6 verbally). Since the blood of the sacrificial animals was used for it, the sacrificial ceremony and the blood ritual form a single uniform sequence of events. The peace offerings of themselves establish the fellowship. In addition, contrary to the usual custom, only half of the blood is sprinkled upon the altar; with the other half the people is sprinkled. So both partners, God and people, seem to be bound together by the blood of the sacrificial animals; only the newly erected altar appears in place of God. This early ritual is not attested again in the Old Testament, but is comparable with the application of blood at the ordination of the priests (Exod. 29: 20; Lev. 8: 23f.), attested also in similar form among the pre-Islamic Arabs.

The presentation given is not uninfluenced by later cultic usages. But it is an argument for the antiquity of the tradition that in certain places it has clearly been expanded and so reinterpreted. The twelve massebas or pillars (v. 4b) represent the twelve tribes of Israel (cf. Josh. 3: 12; 4: 3f., 8f.). The term 'communion sacrifice' (*zᵉbāḥīm*) is apparently explained by 'peace offering' (*shᵉlāmīm*); for the sprinkling of the altar is usual in this type of sacrifice (2 Kgs. 16: 13; Lev. 7: 14; 3: 2ff.).

Blood ritual and self-commitment of the people, which traditio-historically (or even literarily) do not from the beginning belong together, are linked together in the concluding remark which interprets the event and draws it together into a unity. In it Moses states the achievement of fellowship:

This is the blood of the covenant which Yahweh made with you in accordance with all these words. (v. 8b, taken up in the communion saying in Mark 14: 24; Matt. 26: 28; cf. Heb. 9: 19f.).

Here the expression 'covenant', which was missing in the scene on the mountain (24: 9–11) is noteworthy. Since a 'book of the covenant' is mentioned, the narrative is to be regarded as the conclusion of the preceding collection of laws, in fact of the so-called Book of the Covenant (Exod. 20: 22–23: 33, with its core in 21: 1–23: 9). Does 'these words' to which the people consent (24: 3f.) refer to the Decalogue (20: 1) and the 'ordinances' (24: 3) to the Book of the Covenant (21: 1)? Probably the older tradition of sacrifice and blood ritual was expanded by the later declaration of consent of the people, when the Book of the

Covenant, perhaps together with the Decalogue, was inserted into the Sinai event. In any case a later framework which works with a theology of covenant includes both collections of commandments (19: 3ff.; 24: 3f., 7f., cf. 20: 19). There may too be connections with other later developed stories of commitment to the covenant (like Josh. 24; 2 Kgs. 23: 7f.). The older tradition elements of this complex narrative (24: 3–8) seems then to know nothing yet of legal demands which the other partner had to acknowledge.

3   The two different accounts (vv. 9–11, 3–8) cannot simply be understood as recollections from the time of the Sinai event. According to the early portrayal the 'elders of Israel' saw 'the God of Israel'; a historical reconstruction of the events would have to go back on this all-Israelite interpretation. The other narrative too presupposes Israel, or the people of the twelve tribes (esp. v. 4).

Like the account of the journey through the sea, the rendering of the Sinai event in the texts varies. Later elements have too strongly influenced the presentation for us to be able to get back to the historical facts. This critical restriction holds good also for the last great representation of a covenant making – Exod. 34.

Between the narratives of covenant making of Exod. 24 and 34 many cultic ordinances from the Priestly writer (Exod. 24: 15–31: 18) are inserted. P has a covenant with Noah and Abraham (Gen. 9; 17), but no Sinai covenant; for him the revelation at Sinai has become basically the giving of commandments about right worship. When God's 'glory' (i.e. his presence) 'came down' upon Sinai, it appeared to Israel like a consuming fire. Only Moses climbs the mountain and receives the cultic instructions (Exod. 24: 15–18) in the cloud, especially for the building of the tabernacle. After Israel has carried out the instructions, God's 'glory' fills the newly erected sanctuary (40: 34–8; cf. Lev. 9: 23f.). The taking up of the cloud gives the sign for the departure from Sinai (Num. 10: 11f.).

c   THE MAKING OF THE COVENANT ACCORDING TO EXOD. 34

In this section of the Sinai narrative the motif of God's proclamation of commandments is so firmly anchored that we can no longer discover any tradition of a revelation without a giving of commandments. According to the present form of the story, which has been strongly influenced by later expansions, Moses receives the tablets of stone with the ten commandments, destroys them in anger at the people's breaking of the covenant and renews them (Exod. 32–4). This last scene of covenant making was once an independent story, but has been modified and reshaped by the insertion before it of the narrative of the Golden Calf to become a picture of a covenant renewal (34: 1). The text has been so extensively expanded that it is hardly possible now to delimit with certainty the oldest state of the tradition.

Moses receives the commission to cut himself tablets of stone and to climb to the top of the mountain. As in the theophany (Exod. 19: 18, 20J) Yahweh 'descends'. When Moses calls upon the name of Yahweh and falls down (vv. 5, 8),

God passes by, without himself becoming visible. (This corresponds in substance to 19: 20, although the elders according to 24: 10 'saw God'.) But God is audible:

Behold, I will make a covenant! (v. 10)

In the following Ritual Decalogue (vv. 14–26) again extensive reworking and insertions can be established, including the introduction, 'Observe exactly what I command you today'. Whether an original core can be extracted from them (not in any case the 'ten commandments' mentioned in v. 28) is disputed. In any case the short apodictic laws in their present form and arrangement presuppose Israel's domicile in the cultivated land. Nevertheless these laws are regarded as the basic words of the Sinai covenant, which (as in 24; 4, 7f.) are explicitly fixed in writing:

27. And Yahweh said to Moses: 'Write these words; in accordance with these words I have made a covenant with you and with Israel.' 28. And he was there with Yahweh forty days and forty nights; he neither ate bread nor drank water. And he wrote upon the tables the words of the covenant, the ten commandments.

God formally declares the making of the covenant to be binding and valid. His partner is originally not Israel, nor the elders, but (as in the late passage 24: 1f.) Moses alone, who functions as representative of the people. Similarly fellowship is established not through a meal (24: 9–11) nor through sacrifice (24: 3–8) but simply through God's unilateral declaration. The theophany is directed towards the word, and is to be understood from it, while Moses is no more than the man addressed.

In such a statement theological formulation is clearly at work; the presentation given cannot be directly transferred to the early period, whether parts of Exod. 34 are assigned to an older source (J) or not. Just as the laws of the 'cultic Decalogue' are a non-uniform mixture, so apparently the whole chapter has been composed out of what were originally separate motifs, theophany and covenant making, tablets of stone and ordinances. Some particular features point to a later date. It is not possible to exclude the later (mostly Deuteronomistic) redaction with such certainty that a reliable tradition of the Sinai event itself emerges. The declaration of the making of the covenant (v. 27) is not conceivable without the preceding laws (vv. 10–26); if their juxtaposition only takes place in the settled land, the account of the making of the covenant can hardly be earlier than this. Further Israel seems not yet to have understood its relationship to God in the oldest traditions as a 'covenant' (cf. below, Excursus 4), so that it is only with reservations that the Sinai event can be described as a 'making of a covenant' at all. The account of the 'tablets', which are mentioned again only in the later books of the Old Testament, does not belong to the original material of the Sinai account. In any case Exod. 34 does not offer a reliable possibility of regarding a combination of Sinai covenant and divine law as the original state of the tradition. This tentative result can also be supported from some quite different passages.

d THE GOD OF SINAI

1   Although the Old Testament only alludes very infrequently to the Sinai covenant, the relationship of Sinai to Yahweh is attested already in some very ancient passages from outside the Pentateuch too. The Song of Deborah, which must go back to the time of the judges, proclaims Yahweh's departure from Sinai to theophany and to battle:

> Yahweh, when thou didst go forth from Seir,
>   when thou didst march from the region of Edom,
>   the earth trembled. . . . (Judg. 5: 4)

The introduction to the Blessing of Moses is worded similarly:

> Yahweh came from Sinai,
>   and dawned from Seir upon us;
>   he shone forth from Mount Paran. (Deut. 33: 2)

These passages are apparently not influenced by one another nor by the Pentateuchal narratives, so that they independently attest Yahweh's connection with Sinai at a very early date. Both times the nearer or further surroundings of Sinai are described with different geographical expressions. Since these place-names point to the area of the Edomites or also of the Midianites, there is additional support here for the conjecture that Sinai was located in the territory of the Midianites. However these early poetical texts do not establish the tradition of a theophany *at* Sinai, but describe a theophany as the consequence of Yahweh's journey *from* Sinai (below, §11d): God 'journeys' or 'comes from' the mountain in order to help his people. This portrayal is taken up even at a late date:

> God came from Teman,
>   and the Holy One from Mount Paran.
>   (Hab. 3: 3; cf. 3: 13; Ps 68: 7f. [Heb. 68: 8f.])

Apart from these scattered attestations one strange expression probably brings us to a yet earlier stage of the tradition. In two descriptions of a theophany, in the Song of Deborah (Judg. 5: 5) and in Ps. 68: 8 (Heb. 68: 9), a title of God is preserved, which stands outside the metre 'the one (or the God) of Sinai'. The pronoun here used ('the') is no longer found elsewhere in the Old Testament.

Similar expressions are however current in the ancient Near East. For example the chief deity of the Nabataeans Du-shara (in Greek or Latin Dusares) is called 'the (God) of (the region) Shara' (between the Dead Sea and the Red Sea).

So the whole expression gives an impression of being genuine. Further, since the title is found in this fixed form already in the Song of Deborah from the early period of the judges, it must be of great antiquity.

2   This reliable attestation of Yahweh as the God of Sinai can be contrasted to the brief Song of Miriam, which praises Yahweh (at a time close to the event) as the deliverer in the Exodus from Egypt:

Sing to Yahweh, for he has triumphed gloriously;
    the horse and his rider he has thrown into the sea. (Exod. 15: 21)

In both cases we are dealing with old tradition. Certainly the frequent confessional formula 'Yahweh who brought Israel out of Egypt' is a later formation which backdates the people of the twelve tribes, Israel, to the early nomadic period, and identifies it with the fugitives from the Nile delta. But perhaps it is not accidental that this short Song of the Sea mentions Yahweh but not Israel; it may go back to a time before the foundation of the tribal confederacy called Israel.

The introduction to the Decalogue, which reminds the people at Sinai of the Exodus, 'I am Yahweh your God, who has led you out of 'Egypt' does connect the two traditions, but the Decalogue is probably a later insertion into the Sinai pericope, and its date remains uncertain. So there remains a choice between two possibilities, of seeing in Yahweh originally the God of the Exodus or of the Sinai covenant. Which statement, Judg. 5: 4f. or Exod. 15: 21, can claim to be more correct, if the two events are not really historically connected? If it is assumed that the Sinai tradition is later, and that the name of Yahweh was transferred at a later date from the experiences at the crossing of the sea to the revelation at Sinai, an almost irremediable difficulty appears: the events at the sea do not give the impression of being revelatory events, which establish a new relationship with God. The God who delivers them never reveals his name, but those affected give thanks to a God already known to them. If however the Sinai event is recognized as the older tradition, from which Yahweh has penetrated into the Exodus tradition, then the Old Testament picture has inverted the sequence of events. Furthermore there are no traces preserved of any memory that the miracle of the sea was originally ascribed to another God. Certainly it cannot be shown that the event was ever understood as only 'secular', not as the action of God.

Neither of the two exclusive solutions is satisfactory. If one or the other has to be chosen, the importance of the Sinai tradition offers more occasion for the assumption that it was at this mountain of God that the relationship between Yahweh and his worshippers was established. But can the strict choice of an alternative be avoided, since the tradition of the Exodus too is not conceivable without the invocation of Yahweh? Can there be a still hidden connection between the two strands of tradition, which removes the difficulties and satisfies all the critical considerations? Perhaps at this point in the discussion a reference to the cross-links which exist between the worship of Yahweh and the area of the Midianites may be of help (below, §6a, 3 and 4). Possibly the group which had stayed in Egypt, in its migration from the east into the Nile valley, travelled through the area of the Midianites and the Sinai peninsula, and learnt there the name of Yahweh. This sequence of events could still be reflected in the narratives of Moses' flight to Midian and return to Egypt (Exod. 2–4). This assumption cannot however be more than a conjecture, even if it makes sense of both the original connection of Yahweh with Sinai and the early occurrence of his name in the tradition of Exodus. But it cannot be right to connect the two narratives together too closely either, if it is not to be inexplicable why they diverge so much in the Old Testament.

3   If the Sinai tradition is treated on its own, a whole series of questions remains unanswered. The earliest texts strictly speaking contain no revelation of the name Yahweh. The self-introduction 'I am Yahweh' is not firmly rooted in any old passage (below, §6a, 1). The 'I' of God is lacking in the theophany (Exod. 19) as well as in the scene of the making of the covenant (Exod. 24). It is furthermore striking that the different encounters with God at Sinai, theophany and covenant making, stand side by side quite unconnected, without internal links. When the elders of Israel are allowed to see God, he does not speak; when he displays his power in nature, he speaks 'in the trumpet blast' – in the thunder, or with an audible voice (Exod. 19: 19). The two events can hardly have happened at the same time at the same place; it is however a common feature of both narratives that they do not describe God.

Finally the most original forms of theophany and of covenant making as yet say nothing of the third element, which dominates the Sinai pericope in its final form, the giving of the law. Neither the old title 'the one (the God) of Sinai' nor the witnesses to Yahweh's 'coming' from Sinai (Judg. 5: 4f.; Deut. 33: 2) point to a lawgiving. Apparently the Sinai tradition itself originally contained no divine law. Perhaps however at some time there occurred a proclamation of law at places which have a loose connection with the Sinai event (Exod. 18: 13ff. et al., below, §6a, 3); then the combination of these originally independent elements of tradition would be easy to understand. In any case events in the land of civilization (cf. Josh. 24; Deut. 27 et al.) had a retrospective effect on the portrayal of the Sinai event. A later period emphasized more the sequence of proclamation of law and commitment to obedience of the people; the theophany became a revelation of divine will, and conversely the law which gives the framework for human society became a consequence of the relationship with God (cf. below, §6a, 1). A general objection can be raised to such a reconstruction. When a relationship with God is established somewhere, a law must be given there which directs life in this relationship. On the other hand we may perhaps be reminded of the faith of the patriarchs, which apparently also had no legal regulations. In any case the core of the tradition is not the proclamation of the law, but the appearance of God upon the mountain, which has as its consequence fellowship between God and man.

4   On the basis of the old accounts of a theophany in nature some have wished to see in Yahweh originally a volcano or storm deity. Appeal has also been made to the revelation of God to Abraham (Gen. 15: 17), 'a smoking fire pot and a flaming torch'; cf. Exod. 3: 2) and to the saga of the destruction of Sodom and Gomorrah by fire and brimstone (Gen. 19: 24); but both narratives were only secondarily applied to Yahweh. The relationship of God to the phenomena of nature is perhaps most clearly indicated by the widely scattered descriptions of a theophany in the Old Testament (below, §11d); they connect the two closely, but are able to distinguish: the natural phenomena do not show Yahweh himself, but are effects which accompany his coming. (Canaanite religion too did not by any means identify God and nature.) The effects may appear or they may be missing. Yahweh is not bound to manifest himself in storm or volcanic eruption. Not every storm as such is a revelation. 'Yahweh was not God of one single natural phenomenon . . . One particular natural phenomenon is not in itself a theophany of Yahweh, nor is Yahweh in his theophany bound to one particular phenomenon. Yahweh was never a 'storm god', 'fire god' or 'light god' (J. Jeremias, *Theophanie*, 2nd edn., Neukirchen, 1977, p. 38). According to the evidence of the Old Testament the activity of God has always extended far beyond the realm of nature into the world of men. Perhaps the natural phenomena have at the same time the task of hiding the deity when he is manifested. In any case they are intended to express the fact that God is a power which breaks into the world, and is able to alter it. God 'is' because he 'appears'.

The distance of Yahweh from the natural phenomena is also true in relationship to local connections. The early divine name 'he of Sinai' presupposes that Yahweh is a mountain deity. Other passages support this conclusion.

Elijah undertakes a pilgrimage to the 'mountain of God' (1 Kgs. 19; cf. Exod. 3: 1 et al.). Moses 'went up to God', and led the people 'to meet God' (Exod. 19: 3, 17; 24: 12f.). He 'drew near to the thick darkness where God was' (20: 21), or appeared in the place alongside Yahweh to let the glory of God pass by him (33: 18ff.). Finally Moses raises the question how the presence of God can be preserved for the people when they leave the mountain at God's behest (33: 12ff.). Egyptian sources too seem to hint at these associations of traditions (below, §6a2, 2).

The Yahwist is already weakening the old tradition of Yahweh's residence upon Sinai: 'Yahweh came down upon Mount Sinai' (Exod. 19: 18, 20; 34: 5). The mountain is only the place of his appearance, Yahweh dwells in heaven. Here a sharper distinction is made between the place upon earth, and the transcendent God. P emphasizes God's transcendence yet more strongly. His 'glory' does not rest continuously upon Sinai, but only 'settles' upon it from time to time (24: 16f.; cf. 29: 45f. et al.); for the presence of Yahweh is not a permanently present circumstance. It is attractive to regard the transfer of God's dwelling place to heaven as a later stage of religious thinking (cf. §17, 4). But perhaps the two different statements are not simply mutually exclusive. Already according to the early scene of the conclusion of the covenant (Exod. 24: 9–1) blue tiles lie at God's feet (i.e. no doubt, the sky). Either therefore the mountain reaches up into the sky, or the sky represents Yahweh's footstool, as later visions see Yahweh upon a throne (Isa. 6: 1, Ezek. 1: 26; cf. Ps. 29: 10). In any case the God who appears upon earth remains transcendent. Even in the oldest period therefore God is not simply linked with a phenomenon of this world, the mountain, but is at the same time transcendent. The concept of a dwelling place of God does not thereby put God at man's disposal. With one exception (1 Kgs. 19) the Old Testament does not even tell of a pilgrimage to Sinai, because men do not need to seek God there.

Yahweh does not in any case remain a God of a place. Already according to the old descriptions of theophanies (Judg. 5: 4f.; Deut. 33: 2). he sets out from Sinai in order to intervene on behalf of his people elsewhere. The God of the patriarchs passes on to the God of the mountain his essential nature: 'the one from Sinai' journeys with men guiding and helping them. So the nomadic spirit has penetrated this once locally tied concept too. 'Here something that was historically and phenomenologically crucial for the Old Testament idea of God stands out clearly, that the Biblical God can in principle be delocalized, that he is capable of transcending local restrictions' (K. Goldammer).

At a later time the process of interpretation was taken further upon another level, when the Sinai event too was understood eschatologically. The fellowship meal (Exod. 24: 11) will take place anew upon Zion 'at that day', but then all the nations will take part (Isa. 25: 6). When the lawgiving takes place again, forgiveness will be its lasting basis, and the knowledge of God will be achieved without any mediation, so that rule by God and self-rule become identical (Jer. 31: 31ff.).

§6 The characteristic features of Yahwistic faith

For a large part of the Old Testament tradition the worship of Yahweh begins in the course of the Sinai event with the revelation to Moses (above, §2, 3). But it cannot be clearly established what are the origins, traditio-historically speaking, of the first commandment, with its exclusion of the worship of foreign gods, of the prohibition of images, or of the less important sabbath commandment. Nevertheless the Israel of which the Old Testament speaks is inconceivable without a Yahwistic faith with these characteristics. This is so whether or not the first and second commandments were. actually enunciated very early, that is, whether they were verbally in force or only in substance. In any case it is impossible to conceive of an Israel at any time or place in which other gods were generally and in principle worshipped alongside Yahweh or in his place. Nor can a particular event be singled out in the history of Israel, when the basic demand of the Yahwistic faith appeared and was generally introduced. The worship of Yahweh, the relationship to history typical of it, and the first and second commandments are therefore both in time and in substance 'given' for Israel. For this reason they must be placed before the description of the religion of Israel after the entry into the land. They can therefore (in agreement with the later tradition of Israel) be appended here to the Sinai event.

a THE NAME OF YAHWEH

1 'I am Yahweh'

1 The self-revelation of God in his word is a basic characteristic of the Old Testament understanding of God. It catches distinctively the difference between God and man: God speaks, man hears. Because God makes himself known by name, man is able to call upon him. With his self-introduction God gives man a commission, and the one addressed obeys (Exod. 3 et al.). The prophets, who are still waiting for the decisive revelation, can promise the knowledge 'that I am Yahweh' for the future (Isa. 43: 10; 45: 6 et al.).

This interpretation of the relationship of God and man is by no means inevitable in the history of religions. In the neighbouring Egyptian religion for example God appears not so much in the word which man hears, as in the image which he sees, and in the cultic rites which he performs. In the ancient cultic religions 'the gods were made present or simply worshipped in holy actions, without the word, still less a word attributed to God himself, playing more than a subsidiary part' (S. Morenz, *Gott und Mensch im alten Ägypten*, Leipzig, 1964, pp. 20ff.). The cult is performed predominantly in the delimited area of the sanctuary by the priesthood (cf. below, §6c, 4). Accordingly the written tradition of such a religion primarily concerns rules about ritual actions. 'In particular the listing of laws by which the deity undertakes to regulate the life of society and of the individual is completely lacking.' By comparison with the Old Testament the word of revelation was not a constitutive element for Egyptian religion.

2   While the 'I am Yahweh' that is so frequent in the Old Testament is characteristic of it, the form of speech as such comes in fact from polytheism. The deity introduces himself by name, so that the one addressed may know who he is meeting (cf. Gen. 17: 1; Exod. 6: 2 with Gen. 45: 3). In the ancient Near East the deity generally bears a name which characterizes him or her and distinguishes him from others. This first makes it possible that men can speak with the deity and of him; for it is only because they have names and appear as persons so named that the myths can tell of the gods and their deeds. Perhaps in the course of the history of religion this mythological stage was preceded by a magical one, in which the divine power as yet had no personal existence. 'For to religion 'God' is a late comer' (G. van der Leeuw, *Religion in Essence and Manifestation*, London, 1938, p. 48). If there ever was such a development, by the time Israel entered into history, the ancient Near East had long moved on to the age of the myth.

The deity introduces himself by name. Probably the most frequently quoted example from Israel's neighbours is the oracle which the Assyrian king Esarhaddon received from the goddess Ishtar:

I am Ishtar of Arbela, O Esarhaddon, King of Assyria! ...
'Fear not, O king', I said to you. (*ANET*, p. 450)

In a much older Sumerian song the goddess Inanna says of herself:

My father has given me the sky,
has given me the earth:
I am the mistress of heaven,
Is any, a god, a match for me?
(*Sumerische und akkadische Hymnen und Gebete*, ed. A. Falkenstein
and W. von Soden, p. 67)

Through such expansions the self-introduction can easily turn into boastful self-glorification, by which one God vaunts himself before another. Since his own deeds and properties are added to the name, in place of an introduction we have boasting. Deutero-Isaiah uses similar formulations in debate, in which God refers to his deeds, to creation:

I am Yahweh, who made all things,
who stretched out the heavens alone,
who spread out the earth – Who was with me?
    (Isa. 44: 24; cf. 41: 4; 45: 7; Ps. 46: 10 [Heb. 46: 11] et al.)

The formula for self-introduction changes its sense by such expansions. So it is found in different forms and with changing meaning throughout antiquity.

3 In the Old Testament the formula is not really intended any longer to introduce someone completely unknown. Frequently it refers explicitly to the history which God has experienced together with Israel. So God's 'I am' begins the Decalogue with 'I am Yahweh, your God, who brought you out of Egypt, out of the house of bondage' (similarly Hos. 12: 9 [Heb. 12: 10]; 13: 4; Ps. 81: 10 [Heb. 81: 11]; Gen. 15: 7). The self-introduction is expanded by the assurance 'your God', and this statement of concern is confirmed by the reference to God's act of liberation. Who God is and what he is like is shown by his actions. Only for one to whom God has so revealed himself is the following law in force; the prologue is like a 'basic law', from which the individual commandments follow (cf. Gen. 17: 1; Lev. 19: 10, 14, 18; Ps. 50: 7 et al.). The obedient Israelite responds to God's action by his own action, and gives thanks for what he receives. Because of its importance the solemn first-person address of God is repeated after the second commandment (Exod. 20: 5; cf. Lev. 19: 2–4).

This association of divine self-introduction and giving of commandments appears to be unknown to Israel's neighbours. Only the king can prefix his 'I' to the proclamation of the law; so Hammurabi introduces his collection of laws (the Code of Hammurabi) by 'Hammurabi, the shepherd, called by Enlil, am I' (*ANET*, p. 164). Do we then have in the 'connection of the proclamation of the law with the epiphany of Yahweh' a distinctive feature of the Old Testament (W. Zimmerli, 'Ich bin Jahwe', in *Gottes Offenbarung*, 2nd edn., Munich, 1969, p. 40).

The association of divine self-introduction and commandments however is surely not original. The difference between the two is already seen formally in the fact that only the prologue to the Decalogue and the first and second commandments are given in the 'I' form, while from the third commandment onwards God appears in the third person. In this change of person a trace is seen of the fact that the ethical instructions of the second table of the law (from the fifth commandment on) were only secondarily altered to be words of Yahweh. So the Decalogue in its present form is a composition from different old elements, which had already come together in sequences of laws (e.g. the first and the second commandments), and later expansions.

The two versions, Exod. 20 and Deut. 5, while they agree verbally in large measure, do not do so completely. Deut. 5 with its greater fulness represents a later stage. The most significant addition is that the command to rest on the sabbath is explicitly extended to slaves, while the sabbath commandment in Exod. 20: 11 is explained by God's rest in creation, and accordingly presupposes Gen. 1, which is from P, in the exilic period. A similar reworking must also be assumed however for the older version, Exod. 20. It too already contains a mass of explanations and expansions. The Decalogue has been constantly expanded, as the difference in length of the commandments still suggests. However the earlier additions are harder to detach. The date of the original composition too is disputed. Do prophetic quotations like Hos. 4: 2 or Jer. 7: 9 only show us antecedents of the Decalogue, or do they select material from an already completed whole?

In any case all such series of laws in apodictic style (like Exod. 34; Deut. 27), first among them the extensive Book of the Covenant, presuppose Israel's settlement in the cultivated land, and indeed closer contact with the Canaanite environment. The same must be true also of the Decalogue; it too does not come from the nomadic period, but from Palestine. This conclusion is true only for the collections of laws, not for the individual laws, which could well come from the nomadic period. As a whole the Decalogue shows a tendency to formulate the commandments in general terms, in order to indicate the relationship of God and man in a basic form. This almost timeless version, which no longer gives specific points of reference for dating, and the well-arranged structure of the whole suggest that we should regard the Decalogue as a later construction. In that case the Ten Commandments will have only gradually in the course of time obtained the dominant position which they now have in the Pentateuch.

4   The address of God in the theophany 'I am Yahweh' was therefore not from the beginning connected with the proclamation of the law, even if this connection is earlier than the Decalogue. But it is still more surprising that the oldest Sinai tradition (Exod. 19; 24 and also 34), unlike the patriarchal tradition (Gen. 28: 13J; 31: 13; 46: 3; Exod. 3: 6E) does not contain a revelation of the divine name. The formula is therefore never attested at such an early date that Yahweh is presenting himself as one previously unknown and unnamed to a group by revelation of his name. Rather the 'self-introduction' of God seems only later to have become more and more the real centre of the Sinai event, until finally the revelation was understood as self-revelation. The acknowledgement of the divine 'I' was regarded as the goal of the story (Exod. 6: 7 et saep.), and the laws were, as in the Decalogue, explicitly associated with this 'I' (Lev. 18: 2 et saep.). The 'formula of self-introduction' is at first found only rarely. The older prophets scarcely employ it at all; it is first used frequently by Ezekiel and Deutero-Isaiah and is then predominantly found in the priestly material from the time of the exile. Since the Old Testament instances of the address 'I am' do not, in spite of Gen. 46: 3, reach back indisputably into the early period, while on the other hand there are many parallels to it from the surrounding world, the formula of self-introduction may be assumed to have developed first in Canaan under foreign influence (cf. Gen. 31: 13?). In that case Israel took over a formula from other religions, in order however by means of it, by associating it with historical retrospect and with the first and second commandments (Exod. 20: 2–5; Lev. 19: 2–4; Hos. 13: 4; Ps. 81: 10f.) to distinguish its God from the gods of other nations and so to express the distinctive character of its faith.

2 *The name Yahweh*

1   Just as a deity is portrayed in his image as having particular characteristics, similarly he is characterized by his name and distinguished from others. The name betrays something of the essential character of the deity, and declares his characteristics or the place of his appearance. In his personal name the deity is made present in such a way that man knows him and can call upon him. Does the name Yahweh therefore indicate something of the essential character of the God of Israel? The original meaning of the name perhaps still indicates the origin of God, but does not necessarily have something to say of the activity which he comes to show in history. Origin and essence are not simply the same. 'The important thing theologically in the matter of a divine name is not what its essential and original meaning is, but only what realm of ideas and confession and revelation the worshippers associate with their god's name. . . . The gods too have their history and their divinity has its changes of form, and even in those cases where originally the name of the god accurately and clearly describes his nature, the name can fall into utter insignificance. Yet the nature of the god can develop and even grow into something quite different' (L. Koehler, *Old Testament Theology*, London, 1957, p. 40). Yet it is probably too hasty a conclusion that the philological explanation of the name Yahweh is theologically indifferent, especially since the Old Testament itself undertakes such an attempt at explanation (Exod. 3: 14). Even if we are wary of speculation, the name does not have to remain simply mysterious.

The Canaanite divine names El or Ba'al are at once general terms for God or Lord, and personal names of a particular god. On the other hand Yahweh is only a name. 'Yahweh is his name' is the formulation of, for example, Hosea (12: 5 [Heb. 12: 6]; Exod. 15: 3 et al.), or God introduces himself by saying 'I am Yahweh, that is my name' (Isa. 42: 8). It is not until we come to Judaism that the utterance of the personal name for God is strictly avoided (below, §17, 4).

2   Beside the full name Yahweh shorter forms too appear, mostly in personal names, like Yahu (in the Elephantine papyri), Jah (Exod. 15: 2; and in Halleluyah) or at the beginning of a name as Jo- (cf. Jo-nathan). It has long been disputed whether the longer form is original, or a later expansion. The first of these solutions is the more probable: 'Yah' is an abbreviation of 'Yahweh', which itself is attested at an early date, not only in the Old Testament, but also upon inscriptions.

The name Yahweh is attested on newly discovered inscriptions from Kuntillet Ajrud, 50 km. south of Kadesh-Barnea, from the ninth to eighth centuries BC, from the victory inscription of King Mesha of Moab (c. 840 BC; below, §7, 13), and later on the ostraca from Arad and Lachish. The tetragram on the stele of Mesha has been interpreted as Yhw with a suffix ('his Yahweh') (so L. Delekat, in G. Jeremias et al. (ed.) *Tradition und Glaube,*

Göttingen, 1972; M. Rose, *Jahwe*, Zurich, 1978), but the divine name given on the parallel column, 'his Dod', unlike Yahweh, can also be interpreted as an epithet ('his uncle, or beloved'). In the Old Testament certainly Yahweh is not attested with a suffix.

Texts like the stele of Mesha (the Moabite stone) from roughly the period of the Old Testament which attest the name Yahweh refer it to the God of Israel. They therefore have nothing important to contribute to the investigation of the origin of the name; they provide no evidence for a historical derivation. For this reason the view was very seriously supported until recently that the name was genuinely Israelite.

In personal names from Syria, Ya is attested already at an early date as a theophorous element (Ebla, third millennium BC; Ugarit), and later 'Ya'u is also attested (Assyrian inscriptions from the eighth century).

In the mythological texts from Ugarit a god Yaw, son of the god El, is mentioned once. The passage is however so obscure that it contributes little to our understanding of the name. Yaw is here probably only another name for the sea-god Yam, of whom the myths have much to tell (cf. below, §10b). It can certainly not be concluded from this single instance that 'Yahweh' was earlier a Canaanite god, a son of El (cf. above, §3c).

From Mari Amorite personal names are known, which contain a verb element *yawi* similar to the name Yahweh. They are however interpreted in different ways: '(God) is/shows himself (to the child as his helper)' or causatively '(God) brings into being'. The translation '(God) lives' or 'brings to life' is also possible. We are dealing in any case with names of thanksgiving or trust, which acknowledge or pray for the protection and support of the deity for the child. There could be a connection with the name Yahweh 'in so far as the action which the namegiver desires from the deity in these ... names could in the name Yahweh have become the description of the character of a particular god and so a personal name for him' (M. Noth, *Die israelitischen Personennamen . . .*, 1928 (repr. 1980), p. 11).

Of the extra-biblical material some Egyptian lists from pre-Israelite times (from Soleb in Nubia and Amara west, fourteenth and thirteenth centuries) probably have the highest claim to be taken into consideration. They mention alongside a 'land of the Shasu (bedouin) of Seir' a 'land of the Shasu-Yhw' '. This name probably refers to an area, or to a mountain range in particular. So the information fits the early evidence in the Old Testament, in which Yahweh appears as a mountain God, and further leads us again to the area to the southeast of Palestine (on Seir cf. Judg. 5: 4 et al.; above, §5d). Is this the original home of the name Yahweh? In any case some old conjectures seem to be confirmed: the name Yahweh is not restricted to Israel, and furthermore is older than the Old Testament, that is, it is quite probably originally not Israelite.

3   If the name Yahweh was already in existence and taken over by the Old Testament, its basic meaning may have been unintelligible for a long time back. Its origin has been sought in different languages and in different parts of speech. Yahweh can be taken as a noun or as a verb form in the imperfect, and can be

derived from the root 'fall' (*hāwāh*) or 'be' (*hāyāh*, Aramaic *hᵉwāh*). Depending upon which possibilities are chosen and combined, quite different senses can be obtained: the 'one who blows away, or causes to fall' (i.e. the hurler of lightning) would characterize Yahweh as a weather-god. But similar deities from the lands around Israel, like Ba'al or Hadad, never have names of this form. An interpretation as a cultic cry *ya-huwa* 'O he!', or the translation 'the one who loves passionately' have been suggested. The most likely solution is a derivation from the verb 'to be'. For a god's name a causative understanding, 'he makes to be', 'calls into being', 'the creator' looks at first most likely. But such a form (in the causative form, the hiphil) is not otherwise attested for the verb 'to be'. Further it then remains a puzzle why the Old Testament in general only speaks at a really late date of Yahweh 'creating'. Israel seems only to have attained its belief in creation in the course of time (below, §11f.). In the end the simplest solution seems the most likely: 'he is, shows himself, is at work'.

In the name Yahweh the older verbal form in the history of the language (*a* in the prefix, *hāwāh* as in Aramaic instead of *hāyāh*) seems to have been preserved. The same form (third person singular imperfect) is found in personal names like Jacob or Joseph. Divine names of comparable form and meaning are also known from pre-Islamic Arabia: Yagūt, 'he will help' or Ya'ūq, 'he will protect(?)'. The form of the name seems therefore to be possible for the nomadic period.

If this etymology is correct, it helps us a little bit further, almost against our expectation, towards the understanding of Yahweh. Strictly Yahweh is not a personal name but a statement about God in the third person. A proper name of this God is not found. It may therefore be asked whether 'the constantly recurrent striving to avoid the divine name because of its great holiness, and to use substitute expressions like '(my) Lord', the 'holy one', 'the name', appeared much earlier than we have hitherto assumed' (W. von Soden, 'Jahwe 'Er ist, Er erweist sich' ', *WO* 3 (1966), p. 184). Was the third commandment, which forbids the misuse, or, on the later stricter understanding, even the use of the divine name, already given with the name 'Yahweh', or at least applied to it?

If further our explanation of the word Yahweh is correct, we can see here to a special extent a unity of name and being. What God 'is' appears in the name he is called. 'To be' means in the Old Testament not an absolute 'being on one's own', but specifically 'to be active in the present', or even 'to appear as a helper'. So the name 'he is' on the one hand expresses both man's thankfulness that God has intervened, and his hope and trust that God will again show himself favourable. On the other hand this God shows himself as he wishes to be understood, through his deeds. The reality of this God is (even in his very name) his activity.

4   The Old Testament itself offers the same etymological derivation of the word 'Yahweh' from the root 'to be' in the one place at which it gives a meaning for the name of God (Exod. 3: 14E; cf. Hos. 1: 9). It has frequently been conjectured that

we have here, as in many other cases (like Babel, Gen. 11: 9, or Moses, Exod. 2: 10) a popular folk etymology, which at a later date sought to elicit a new sense from a word the meaning of which had been lost. Certainly the interpretation has a theological purpose; and for this reason this passage is only brought into the discussion at this late stage. But it may in fact be correct in its procedure. It places the utterance of the name 'he is' in a first person address in a divine word of revelation, and changes it over from Aramaic to Hebrew; in this way the considerable linguistic difference between the name and its interpretation (*yahweh* and *'ehyeh*) becomes understandable.

When Moses asks for information about the name of God, God replies: 'I will be who I will be', or 'I am who I am' (or, 'I am the one who is'?). When it is repeated the periphrasis is abbreviated, and Moses is told to say, ' "I am" has sent me to you'. With such an answer God can hardly intend to be moving into the realm of the unnamable, the indeterminable and intangible in order to preserve his independence, or to be refusing his name; he is revealing it with an explanation. The sense of the sentence does not lie however in the statement that God is indubitably real; for the possibility of denying God's being was hardly open at this early date. Finally God should not be characterized as 'the only one who is', the one who exists on his own (cf. Mic. 4: 5) or 'the unchanging, the eternal' in a monotheistic way. This statement about God also defines being as acting. God assures men of his powerful helping presence (cf. Exod. 3: 12 'I am with you', and the denial of this in Hos. 1: 9). Here the thought may in context have been especially of the release from vassalage to the Egyptians. But the statement sounds much more general, much more basic, than the situation demands: 'I will be, or will act'. The saying includes not just the event, but also those that are to come. The name itself points to a future in which God will be active.

3   Was Yahweh God of the Midianites?

1   Probably the name of Yahweh is earlier than the Israelites and taken over by them (cf. Gen. 4: 26; 9: 26 et al.). Where could it have come from? Different indications have already suggested an original connection of Yahweh with the area to the south of Palestine, in which the Midianites also dwell:

(a) if the features accompanying the theophany (Exod. 19) were volcanic, 'Sinai' is to be located to the east of the Gulf of Akaba.
(b) according to the old descriptions of theophany (Judg. 5: 4f.; Deut. 33: 2f. et al.) Yahweh sets out from a mountain in the territory of the Edomites.
(c) the name Yahweh seems according to the non-biblical (Egyptian) sources to have been at home in this area in the pre-Israelite period.

Quite independently of these arguments the Old Testament itself gives further grounds for the reconstruction of such a line of tradition. According to a number of passages Moses' father-in-law was a Midianite (Exod. 2: 16; 3: 1; 4: 18f.; 18:

1ff.; Num. 10: 29), according to another tradition, however, a Kenite (Judg. 1: 16; 4: 11).

Like Moses' parents (Exod. 2: 1), his father-in-law, 'the priest of Midian', perhaps originally appears in the story without a name. In the Old Testament he bears a number of different names, Reuel (2: 18), Jethro (3: 1; 18: 1f.), Jether (4: 18), Hobab (Judg. 4: 11; cf. 1: 16) and, probably reconciling two traditions, Hobab the son of Reuel (Num. 10: 29).

Since Moses' father-in-law is also called a Kenite, it can be conjectured that the tribes of the Midianites and the Kenites stood in a relationship of kinship (cf. Enoch as a son or sub-group of Kain in Gen: 4: 17 and of Midian in 25: 4), that is, ultimately we have a single tradition. If however a distinction must be made between the two traditions, the connection with the Midianites must be regarded as the older. Israel's connections with them were, unlike those with the Kenites, tense at a later date (see below). The evidence of Judg. 1: 16; 4: 11 is not of the same value as the different accounts in the Pentateuch. Further the late Priestly Writing is silent about Moses' contacts with the Midianites (Exod. 1: 13f.; 2: 23–5; 6: 2ff.), and this is hardly accidental.

Num 12: 1 refers further to a Cushite wife of Moses. Probably however this is not an Ethiopian woman, but a member of the tribe called Cushan, which is mentioned in Hab. 3: 7 in parallel to Midian. So this separate tradition leads to the same area, that of Midian.

In addition the revelation of God in which Moses received his call took place according to Exod. 3: 1 in Midian. Taken on their own, each of these very different facts certainly tells us little. But if all these individual features are brought together, the general agreement can hardly be regarded as accidental. Too many clues point to the land of the Midianites.

2   In the light of these remarks a very specific Old Testament story which perhaps still reflects Israel's link in faith with this tribe is of significance. Directly before the Sinai pericope there is an account of a common sacrifice of the Midianites and Israelites (Exod. 18). This story, which is basically old, but has been subsequently expanded, is an isolated story (of the Elohist, with certain expansions). It is prepared for by Moses' flight from Egypt to Midian (2: 15ff.), but has no continuation. 'Moses' father-in-law' comes to meet Moses 'in the wilderness, at the mount of God' to bring back to him his wife after his successful deliverance from Egypt (vv. 5f.). But the occasion for this visit has no part to play in the encounter itself; from this awkwardness it becomes clear that the story unites different motifs, and has grown only gradually. After a formal greeting the Midianite learns what Yahweh has done for Israel in Egypt, and praises his might for it: 'now I know that Yahweh is greater than all gods' (v. 11). Does this imply that the Midianite 'now' becomes converted to Yahweh for the first time? In the following scene however he appears in a dominant position as the officiating priest. So this confession of the superiority of Yahweh over all gods is not part of the original tradition, but brings out subsequently the truth of the faith itself, and prefaces it to the action that follows; the original climax at the end (v. 12) is in some tension with what precedes. But it is only in the narrative section (vv. 8–11), which looks like an expansion, that the name Yahweh is mentioned. The original story did not therefore say directly which God was worshipped on the 'mount of

God'. At least the final verse is completely silent about who the sacrifice is offered to, although Yahweh is certainly meant by 'God':

And Jethro, Moses' father-in-law, offered a burnt offering and sacrifices to God; and Aaron came with all the elders of Israel to eat bread with Moses' father-in-law before God. (v. 12).

The first surprising thing is the meal, which concludes and confirms a fellow-ship between Israelites and Midianites 'before God' (cf. Gen. 31: 54 et al.). The Sinai story too, which does not mention the Midianites, likewise tells of a meal upon a holy mountain, in which also 'the elders of Israel' took part (Exod. 24: 11), and of sacrifices at the foot of the mountain in the wilderness (24: 5). There is however no mention of a covenant here; but the oldest form of the Sinai tradition too does not have this concept. What is still more surprising is that Moses' father-in-law, who as 'priest of Midian' (v. 1; cf. 2: 16; 3: 1) has an official position, offers the sacrifice, while 'all the elders' as representatives of Israel at the meal are only invited as guests, and take part therefore in the sacrifice of another people.

Aaron has probably been added later, as in Exod. 24: 1, 9, as a representative of the priesthood; similarly the formal burnt offering, which is not for consumption, is an addition.

Finally Moses is not mentioned again – perhaps because the meeting for a common meal was more than a family occasion? Was Israel brought into the worship at a Midianite pilgrimage sanctuary, so that both nations or tribes could have just one God? Chapter 18 on its own is too weak to prove the borrowing of the worship of Yahweh from the Midianites, but it is one link in a chain of arguments. Since the Midianite priest sacrifices to his own god, it seems a probable conjecture that the Midianites were originally worshippers of Yahweh.

The dependence of the Israelites upon the Midianites is also hinted at by the following story of the organization of the giving of judgement (Exod. 18: 13–17). In order to reduce the burden upon Moses, his father-in-law advises him to appoint subordinate judges, so as to distinguish between everyday law and the more important (sacral?) law which was ·reserved for himself. 'Moses gave heed to the voice of his father-in-law and did all that he had said' (v. 24). The connection between this story of the Midianites assisting in the arrangement of the legal system and the preceding sacrificial scene is only very loose. Does this story help however to explain why Sinai came to be the place of the proclamation of the law?

Elsewhere too the tradition tells of oases at which judgement was given (Gen. 14: 7; Exod. 15: 25; 17: 7; Num. 20: 13, 24 et al.). The tribes wandering in the wilderness are supposed at least according to later tradition to have stayed some time in Kadesh (13: 26; Deut. 1: 46; Judg. 11: 16 et al.).

3   Several motifs therefore connect the tradition of the 'mountain of God', not more exactly localized (Exod. 3: 1; 18: 5; 1 Kgs. 19: 8), and that of Sinai. Nevertheless the two are distinguished. The mountain of God is not called at the same time Sinai; in the Sinai pericope on the other hand the term 'mountain of God' is rare (only Exod. 24: 13) and the Midianites are not mentioned. Do the two names refer to different localities, so that the Sinai and the Midianite traditions fall into two separate groups? There are many mountains of God in the extensive lands of Canaan and Syria. Nevertheless it would be strange if the mountain of God at which the encounter with the Midianites took place were not the Sinai which supposedly lay in Midianite territory. In the older texts the use of the term 'mountain of God' could reflect the preference of the Elohist for the expression God. If the references in the Old Testament originally concern the same holy mountain in the wilderness, then the event only appears in various scattered forms in all sorts of single stories, which can be divided up into the two great strands of tradition of Sinai (Exod. 19; 24) and of the mountain of God (Exod. 18; cf. Exod. 3).

If the different accounts go back to one event, the revelation of God on the mountain in the wilderness may have been mentioned to the Israelites by the Midianites. But this reconstruction is not proof against objections. The Sinai tradition is dominated by the theophany, of which the meeting on the 'mountain of god' knows nothing. On the other hand the appearance of God in the burning bush takes place 'at the mountain of God' (Exod. 3: 1JE). Does this event correspond to the occurrences (of Exod. 19) in which God's presence is revealed in natural phenomena?

Exod. 3 contains two themes: an older 'discovery saga' only transmitted by the Yahwist, which tells of a theophany at a particular place in the wilderness, and so accounts for the sacral character of the locality (3: 1–5; cf. above, §3e) and a later 'call saga' (3: 6ff.) in which Moses is given the task of leading the Israelites out of Egypt. Just as the gods of the fathers are identified with the local El deities, so here Yahweh seems to be identified with 'him that dwelt in the bush' (this name for a deity is preserved in Deut. 33: 16). In the same way a former foreign saga might be hidden in this story, just as the sanctuary legends of Genesis go back to Canaanite narratives. In any case it remains dubious whether the narrative of a holy place in the wilderness referred from the first to Yahweh, and to Moses as the recipient of the appearance. Or does the revelation of the name of Yahweh, which is offered by only one of the two sources (vv. 12ff. E), but is hinted at in the other (v. 16J; cf. Exod. 6: 2P), belong to the original tradition? Finally the 'flame of fire' (in a sort of heading in Exod. 3: 2a; cf. Gen. 18: 1) as an accompaniment of the theophany is reminiscent of the revelation on Sinai; whether however the thornbush actually was on Mount Sinai (the word s^{e}nēh/thornbush is probably an allusion to Sinai) is hard to decide. Very varied motifs are found together in the account: the revelation of God and the commission of Moses, the identification of Yahweh with the gods of the fathers, the promise of delivery from Egypt, etc. So traditio-historically the chapter remains enigmatic, and it is difficult to draw historical conclusions from it. Caution is needed therefore in arguing for the hypothesis that a recollection that Israel borrowed the worship of Yahweh in the land of Midian is still to be seen showing through in the narrative of the call of Moses.

4   The accounts in the Old Testament (in Exod. 2f.; 18) of connections with Midian are less directly productive, but indirectly allow certain conclusions. In particular there is old tradition present in the account of a shared act of worship by the Israelites and Midianites (18: 12). However conjectures about the origins of the worship of Yahweh are made more difficult by the fact that the Old Testament also tells of early connections of Yahweh with the Kenites. Cain, the ancestor of the Kenites, bore a mark of Yahweh for protection (Gen. 4: 15); in general the saga in Gen. 4 presupposes a long-established close connection between Yahweh and Cain. Furthermore the Rechabites, who were passionate servants of Yahweh (Jer. 35; 2 Kgs. 10: 15ff.) were regarded at least later as Kenites (1 Chr. 2: 55).

Does this explain the use of the name Yahweh from the beginnings in the work of the Yahwist, which (unlike the Elohist) originated in the southern kingdom? Did he know the Kenites who dwelt in the south, and so could see that there was a worship of Yahweh outside Israel too, and perhaps had been from early times?

In broad outline, the Old Testament still preserves dim recollections first that Israelite tribes borrowed belief in Yahweh in the land of Midian, and secondly that the Kenites may have been worshippers of Yahweh. On the other hand the Old Testament contains no direct reports that the Midianites were believers in Yahweh, or that Israel took over the god of the Kenites. Can the two traditions nevertheless be linked, because the two tribes were closely connected with one another? Moses' foreign kinship can be determined to be Midianite as well as Kenite. Is is often therefore concluded that the Kenites were a part of the Midianites; but the Old Testament gives no basis for such an identification of the two tribes. The identity of the two cannot therefore be concluded from the narratives mentioned about the worship of Yahweh without arguing in a circle.

The so-called Midianite or Kenite hypothesis cannot therefore be proved unambiguously; other arguments that can be produced are not compelling either. Nevertheless there is some justification for the conjecture that the pre-Israelite nomadic groups took over belief in Yahweh from the Midianites or the Kenites, because it is supported by such very varied items of evidence. Israel's relationship to the Kenites was one of friendship (Judg. 1: 16; 1 Sam. 15: 5f.; 30: 29); as early as the battle of Deborah in the time of the judges Jael the Kenite decided Israel's battle against Canaan by murdering Sisera (Judg. 5: 24ff.). On the other hand at a later period the Midianites were Israel's bitter enemies, who pressed into Palestine to plunder (Judg. 6f.; Isa. 9: 3; 10: 26; Hab. 3: 7; Num. 25: 6ff.; 31). All the more noteworthy therefore are the links with this beduin people in the early period (cf. Gen. 25: 1–4). All things considered, the hypothesis which can so well explain the connection between Yahweh, Sinai and Midian has considerable probability but no certainty.

In any case Yahwistic faith became historically significant in Israel. Whatever any possible worship of Yahweh among the Kenites or the Midianites may have been like, we do not know what these tribes associated with the name Yahweh. Was he their tutelary deity (Gen. 4: 15)? Were they already supposed to worship exclusively a god without images? This is not likely. Neither from non-biblical sources nor from the Old Testament do we know anything more specific about the nature of faith in God among these nomads. The Midianites or Kenites have vanished, while Israel through its faith endured all the ups and downs of history, and so made history through its faith. To this extent C. H. Ratschow's general religio-historical statement is true also of Yahweh: 'the problem of the origin of the gods does not lead to any answer about the essential nature of the gods' (*Magie und Religion*, Gütersloh, 1947, p. 127).

4   Was Yahweh the God of Moses?

Can the beginnings of the Yahwistic faith be connected with a particular person? For a large part of earlier and later scholarship Moses is regarded as the founder of the Old Testament understanding of God; the religion is based upon the creative experience of an individual, which already contains within itself some important elements of the later development.

According to F. Baumgärtel, it is characteristic of founder religions that 'a person, stirred by his experience of revelation, that is, in the view of these religions called by God, must have developed once for all the basic conception in their understanding of God'. Because of the problem of sources we do not know what the beginning of the religion of Israel 'may have looked like; we do not even know whether this founder of a religion lived at all, and if he did whether he was indeed a founder of a religion'. But a religio-historical comparison 'leads one to postulate the existence of a founder', since 'the religion of the Old Testament cannot have developed out of its environment . . . but represents a discontinuity over against its environment' (*ZTK* 64 (1967), pp. 396, 398).

The complicated traditio-historical situation does not however permit such a recourse to an individual figure. When critical scholarship with its awkward questions gets involved in this situation Moses proves to have no distinctive 'face'. No personal attitude which could not have been invented can be recovered from the traditions, on the basis of which Moses as a specific individual could have reshaped what came to him or opposed to it what was his own, and thus proclaimed a new God. If the tradents of the different traditions are unknown to us, the figure of an individual is very difficult for us to see clearly. The later age which collected the traditions and filled them out greatly obscured the far distant past. Several possible ways of portraying the beginnings therefore remain open to us.

Egyptian documents have nothing to say of Moses, any more than they do of Israel's stay in Egypt. Even in the Old Testament itself Moses is mentioned outside the Pentateuch with remarkable infrequency (Jer. 15: 1; Ps. 90 heading [Heb. 90: 1]; 103: 7; Mic. 6: 4; cf. Hos. 6: 5 et al.), so that historical inquiry is in practice confined to the Pentateuch alone.

The tasks which Moses is given are very varied: according to the Yahwist he promises God's saving act (Exod. 3: 16f.; cf. 14: 13f) for the Elohist he is active as a deliverer (3: 10ff.), in the legal collections he is the proclaimer of the law (Exod. 21: 1; cf. 20: 19; 24: 3f., 7; Deut.), according to P he regulates the worshipping life of the community by cultic ordinances (Exod. 25ff.). Was he the founder of a religion, the founder and deliverer of the people, the mediator of the covenant, or, as he appears increasingly to a later period, the giver of the law? To whom is he to be compared? To the patriarchs as the recipient of revelation, to the heroes of the period of the judges as charismatic leader, or as promulgator of the word of God to the prophets who declare the future? He could in each case be termed a mediator; but this title remains unspecific in content.

The person of Moses stands at the point of intersection of the early traditions of Israel, since it connects together the tradition complexes of the Exodus, the revelation at Sinai, the leading through the wilderness, and (initially) the conquest. The course of Moses' life leads from Egypt (Exod. 2) through Midian (2: 15–4: 18), back to Egypt (4: 19ff.), from there through the wilderness (13: 17ff.; 15: 22ff.; Num. 10: 11ff.), by way of Sinai as the decisive stopping point on the way (Exod. 19–Num. 10: 10) to the edge of the cultivated land, in sight of which he dies (Deut. 34). So Moses experiences in anticipation the Sinai revelation, which is given to Israel generally only after the Exodus (Exod. 3). This movement back and forth of itself evokes critical questions.

The problem becomes acute if these great tradition complexes were originally independent of one another. Where was Moses originally at home, in the Exodus, Sinai, wilderness or conquest traditions, or even in the one area which stands apart from the four mentioned, and nevertheless markedly overlaps with them, the Midianite tradition (Exod. 2–4; 18)?

The traditions of Exodus, wilderness and conquest stand in a relationship given by history; but were the Exodus and Sinai traditions with their extremely different characters connected with one another from earliest times, or did they grow together only in the course of time? Problems appear again here similar to those in the inquiry into the origin of faith in Yahweh (above, §5d).

Did Moses live in Egypt, or did he alternatively experience or act as mediator in the Sinai theophany? Did he perhaps originally belong to neither of these traditions? Noth, who takes over and refines the analyses of E. Meyer (1906) and of Gressmann (1913) comes to the conclusion that the only indubitable element is the tradition of the death and burial of Moses in Transjordan. It is the 'foundation of a no longer derivable historical situation'. From this region 'Moses as a leader-figure initially gained entrance into the narrative elaboration of the theme 'guidance into the arable land', and then he came to assume this role in the remaining Pentateuchal themes as well' (M. Noth, *A History of Pentateuchal*

Traditions, Englewood Cliffs, NJ, 1972, p. 173). Critical doubts can hardly go further than this view, which understands the whole of the tradition about Moses preserved in the books of Exodus and Numbers as a later development; for the theoretically possible extreme, that Moses is entirely unhistorical, is totally improbable.

In fact the tradition that Moses died outside the area settled by Israel and was buried at a place which was not precisely known by Israel (Deut. 34: 5f.) must be historically reliable.

Later the fact that Moses, the mediator of the faith, was buried outside the promised land was interpreted as a punishment for sin, for his lack of trust in God: he was not allowed to enter the land for this reason (Num. 20: 12; 27: 12ff.; Deut. 3: 25ff.; 32: 48ff.).

However this burial tradition cannot explain the high status which Moses has in the Pentateuch. Some statements, even if not very many, can be made about Moses with confidence or even certainty.

The name Moses (Hebrew *mōše*) is undoubtedly not of Hebrew but of Egyptian origin. Well-known personal names like Thutmoses or Rameses have the meaning 'the god . . . is born, or has born (him)'. Moses is an abbreviated form (attested also occasionally in Egyptian) of a type of name with the sense roughly of 'son'; the theophorous element, that is, the divine name, has fallen out. It can furthermore be shown from Egyptian sources (cf. *ANET*, 3rd edn., pp. 553f.) that Semites who lived in a dependent position in Egypt received Egyptian names, as the Old Testament says happened to Joseph too (Gen. 41: 45).

The origin and original meaning of Moses' name is however no longer of importance to the Old Testament itself. An echo of the Egyptian origin may still be heard in the fact that it is the daughter of Pharaoh who gives the name (Exod. 2: 10), but it is there (erroneously) derived from Hebrew ('to draw out of the water').

A name does not permit a quite certain decision over the place of origin of its holder, since persons with Egyptian names who had not been in Egypt are found too in Israel (e.g. 1 Sam. 1: 3). But if a name were being given secondarily to the man who saved the Israelites from distress and mediated the word of God to them it would certainly have been an Israelite name, and indeed one compounded with Yahweh. So we may trust the tradition when it says that Moses, the bearer of an Egyptian name, also lived in the land of the Nile.

Is it possible to add any other fragments of old tradition? The trustworthy report that Moses married a Midianite woman deserves all the more attention in that Sinai, the original home of the name Yahweh, must have lain in the area of penetration of the Midianites (above, §5d, 2; 6a, 3). Independently of the Exodus tradition the Joseph story attests that the Midianites traded by caravan with the Egyptians, and so at least occasionally penetrated as far as Egypt (Gen. 37: 28, 36; cf. also 1 Kgs. 11: 18). Is it not then a likely conclusion that Moses, through the mediation of the Midianites, and perhaps especially of his father-in-law, who is a priest (Exod. 18: 12), came to know the Yahwistic faith, and brought it to the Israelites doing forced labour in Egypt? The Old Testament tradition does actually claim this (Exod. 3f.), and there are serious arguments in its favour.

Could the tradition also be right in claiming that Moses was convinced of the identity of Yahweh with the God of the patriarchs (Exod. 3: 16J, 13f.E)? Certainly Israel's ancestors in Egypt could have known the (or, a) God of the patriarchs (cf. Gen. 46: 1–4; above, §4).

According to the older source Moses promised the oppressed Israelites the help of Yahweh; the deliverance remains the act of God (Exod. 3: 8, 16f.J; cf. 14: 13ff.). The statement that Moses himself brings them out, and so has a political role as leader (Exod. 3: 10–12E), can be understood as a development of the earlier and more widespread tradition, occasioned by the theological purpose of the Elohist (which can be seen elsewhere too) to emphasize the transcendence of God.

When Moses in the further course of events appears as the leader and spokesman of the people in their dealings with Pharaoh, we have what is largely a sagalike or legendary expansion of the tradition.

Was Moses able to convince his countrymen, so that they trusted in his word and risked leaving, and then were indebted for deliverance from their pursuers to the same God Yahweh (Exod. 15: 21)? If such possibilities have any basis of its reality, it is more understandable how Moses takes a constitutive role for Yahwistic faith in the later form of the tradition; it was not only assigned to him later, even if it was then portrayed broadly and colourfully, but had been his role historically.

A further question which must not be taken lightly might find an answer in this same manner: how did it come about that faith in Yahweh of Sinai came to be accepted in all the different Israelite tribes in Palestine? Was not a God who had delivered men pursued by a band of chariots bound to commend himself in a situation in which the Israelites had to stand up for themselves against the superior might of the Canaanites with their 'iron chariots' (Josh. 17: 16 et al.)?

So Moses is with justification to be regarded as the connecting link between the areas of Egypt, Midian and the Transjordan; here there is, we must allow, a historical link. It is however much more difficult to decide whether Moses was personally present on the mountain of God, or Sinai.

Certainly it is possible to assign greater correctness to the tradition, and to expect that it will be confirmed to a greater degree than at present by the work of future scholarship; but the study of Moses at this point hardly gets beyond weighing up the different possibilities. It cannot be proved that the essential element in Yahwism, which can be paraphrased by the first commandment, can be assigned to the religious experiences of this one man. So the historicity of Moses is incontestable; his person is not in dispute, but by contrast his work is.

b   THE FIRST COMMANDMENT

Israel may have taken over the worship of Yahweh from other nomadic tribes, the Midianites or the Kenites. Israel is however separated from its environment by the first and second commandments. The ancient Near East can show no comparable prohibition which excludes the worship of foreign gods, and allows no image of God.

1   In the great empires of the ancient Near East there are here and there tendencies which lead to the worship of only one God. The multifarious polytheism of Egypt seems to move towards a solar monotheism. This tendency is to be seen at its purest in the worship of Aton by Amenophis IV, Akhnaton (c. 1350 BC), who in his hymn to the sun, which anticipates Ps. 104, sings of Aton as 'the only god' – but with the king as the vital mediator, which is the reason why Israel can hardly be dependent on this development. In any case the violent imposition of the cult of Aton, which also had a political purpose – to deprive the priesthood of Amon at Thebes of their power – remained only an interlude. After the death of the heretic king Egypt returned to the old deities. This attempt to attain a unity in the concept of God was no doubt unEgyptian; for it sought to attain this by the exclusion of other deities, not by subordination and amalgamation. A later period preferred to find unity in plurality; so, for example, the trinity Amon-Re-Ptah draws together the deities Amon, Re and Ptah into a single figure, without depriving them of their individual existences.

In Mesopotamia monotheistic tendencies were expressed in some measure in a similar form. Comprehensive lists of gods enumerated a large number of deities, and subordinated them one to another in different ways. Gods whose natures were similar were identified, others linked in families, others again demoted to be servants of more high-ranking gods, or even reduced to being hypostases (forms of appearance) and epithets of them. 'In fact the religious development which caused the power of certain gods to increase ever more in the eyes of their priests and worshippers, pressed towards constantly diminishing the number of the gods, since it seemed to many impossible that for example Marduk of Babylon, or the god of the Assyrian empire, Ashur could be restricted in their power in any way by other gods . . . The ultimate intellectual consequence of this latest stage of the Babylonian theology of identification would be monotheism; the Babylonian theologians did not however achieve this, since their "knowledge" did not go beyond an often strongly reinterpretative explanation of the tradition and of its development' (W. von Soden, *Leistung und Grenze sumerischer und babylonischer Wissenschaft*, Darmstadt, 1965, pp. 58f.). Moves towards monotheism are not however only seen in theological speculation. Prayers often do not address a particular deity by name, but simply invoke 'god'. Similarly Egyptian wisdom, which challenges men to right behaviour within an ordering of the world given by God, can speak quite generally of 'God', without referring to a particular form of God.

Usually the tolerance of alien deities and of their cults was taken for granted in the ancient Near East. It is true that for instance the last Babylonian king Nabonidus stayed away from the New Year festivals in honour of Marduk, and preferred the moon-god Sin, but as a rule syncretism was practised. Polytheism and syncretism go together. Because there was no strict exclusiveness in belief, there could not strictly speaking be such a thing as apostasy to alien deities. A man who moved to another country worshipped the gods of that land; and this is attested also in the early parts of the Old Testament (Ruth 1: 15ff.; 1 Sam. 26: 19; 2 Kgs. 5: 17f.; Deut. 4. 27f.; also Judg. 11: 24; cf. below, IV, I).

2   If the prohibition upon acknowledging other gods (especially in association with the prohibition of images) is not found in the countries around Israel, something specific to the Old Testament must be present in it. There is no real model for it, and it cannot be derived from the neighbouring religions, but is opposed to their essential nature. History looks for analogies for all phenomena, but so far as we know at present it is impossible to show that the first and second commandments were borrowed from elsewhere. Exclusiveness of creed is unique to Israel.

Perhaps the belief in the god of the fathers, who revealed himself on his own to lead and to protect the group, offered certain patterns for the sole worship or imagelessness of a god, although this will not have taken the form of a demand. When several 'gods of the fathers' came into relationship with one another through the amalgamation of tribes, they were not juxtaposed in the polytheistic way, but identified with one another as the one 'God of Abraham, Isaac and Jacob' and further identified with Yahweh (Exod. 3: 6ff.). So the faith of the patriarchs, at least in the form in which it is transmitted in the Old Testament, fulfils the first commandment. This basically characterizes the relationship to God at a time when it was not yet known literally. If finally it were to be conjectured that Israel took over these basic commandments from other nomadic tribes, it remains an unanswered problem why these nations, with a faith which was unique in the ancient Near East, disappeared so completely that they left no memory of themselves.

Quite independently of the religio-historical comparison, which indicates intolerance in creed as a peculiarity of Yahwistic faith, the first commandment appears in the Old Testament itself as a programmatic utterance; it summarizes God's demand upon Israel. Together with the prohibition upon images it stands at the head of the Decalogue (Exod. 20: 3ff.; Deut. 5: 7ff.; also Exod. 34: 14–17), although originally it stood on its own. Far more strongly than all the following ethical demands it forms in substance the basis for the relationship between God and the man addressed. So the prophet Hosea addressed the first commandment to his listeners not as a demand, but as an assurance:

I am Yahweh your God,
   from the land of Egypt;
you know no God but me,
   and besides me there is no saviour.
                              (Hos. 13: 4; cf. Isa. 43: 11; also Deut. 32: 12, 39)

The frequent repetition of the commandment indicates its importance. In changing situations apparently different, varying formulations were needed. So it is found in almost all the older collections of law, as in the Ritual Decalogue:

You shall worship no other God. (Exod. 34: 14; cf. Ps. 81: 9 [Heb. 81: 10])

and similarly twice between laws which refer to the cultivated lands, in the Book of the Covenant:

Make no mention of the names of other gods. (Exod. 23: 13)
Whoever sacrifices to any god, save to Yahweh only, shall be utterly destroyed. (Exod. 22: 20 [Heb. 22: 19])

The first version here, which prohibits the worship of a foreign deity in the cult, and the last, which links closely act and consequence, give an impression of antiquity. On the other hand the more generally expressed commandment in the Decalogue, which has the form of an address by God, and simply excludes 'other gods', represents no doubt a later concentration of the demands. To whom does the broad formulation originally refer, to the gods of Canaan (so Hos. 3: 1), the local deities of the surrounding nations, or the national gods of the empires of the ancient Near East? 'You shall have no other gods before my face' was perhaps originally intended to be understood quite literally: foreign deities might not be set up, worshipped or invoked (Exod. 23: 13, 24; Isa. 26: 13) before Yahweh's 'face', that is, in his presence. But the sphere of validity of the first commandment is not restricted to the cult; it is directed also against behaviour in daily life, for instance, against a prayer which 'over against' God, or even 'in spite of' God (as it could be also translated) entreats others to help. The language is in every respect basically and deliberately timeless, and was able for this reason to remain in force for so long; for it is freshly applicable to every situation.

3   No form of the commandment can be attributed with confidence to the nomadic period; in turn it cannot be clearly established that the God of Sinai had from the beginning made the demand for worship of himself alone. Was the first commandment only formulated in words after the entry into Canaan? Perhaps it presupposes the historical experience of the Yahwistic faith being exposed to foreign cults. The delimitation of their own beliefs from polytheism, and the

contrast of unity and multiplicity, would then have come about in the encounter with the Canaanite pantheon. But the uniqueness of the concern of God for man was certainly a basic element from the beginning; to this extent the Yahwistic faith laid claim to exclusiveness from the very beginning in Israel. There is no period of which it can be conceived that other deities stood fundamentally upon the same footing as the God of Israel, or in which Yahweh was associated with a goddess, although there were certainly house and family 'deities' (Gen. 31: 19, 30ff.; Exod. 21: 6; 22: 7f.; Judg. 17: 5; 18: 14ff., 24).

In any case the first commandment had at first a practical and not a theoretical aim. It is not intended to teach that there is one and only one God, creator and upholder of righteousness. The fundamental demand that they should acknowledge Yahweh alone is not monotheistic in its presuppositions, just as the god 'Yahweh' is already by his name distinguished from other gods.

So Wellhausen can put it emphatically: 'Monotheism was unknown to ancient Israel . . . Yahweh only came into consideration for them as the founder of Israel . . . Certainly they believed that the power of Yahweh extended far beyond Israel; this was why he was God, to help his own people if their own strengths were not sufficient. But this faith was not theoretically generalized. It was sufficient in any given instance that Yahweh was a match for every real distress and danger which threatened Israel . . . The God of Israel was not the Almighty, but only the mightiest among the gods. He stood alongside them and had to fight with them; Chemosh and Dagan and Hadad were entirely comparable to him, less powerful, but not less real than himself' (*Israelitische und jüdische Geschichte*, 9th edn., Berlin, 1958, p. 29).

The gods are therefore not denied in their essential being, but in their being in relation to Israel. They exist, or may exist, but they are of no significance for those addressed; for they can bring no assistance (Hos. 13: 4; Jer. 2: 13; below, §17, 1). To this extent the existence of other deities is, not believed in, but assumed (cf. Mic. 4: 5). The uniqueness of God depends not upon his being God alone, but on his concern and demands; he demands to be the only one for those who belong to him. It is the relationship to God that is exclusive at first (internally), later men draw the consequence (externally). It may be characterized by the not entirely unambiguous religio-historical terms henotheism or monolatry (temporary or permanent cultic preference for or sole worship of a god). But such general expressions are not sufficient to give an exact description of the historical phenomenon. In particular the contrast of the one Yahweh to the other gods is not fixed once for all in a particular way, but presses beyond all our static attempts to define it.

The first commandment was by no means everywhere and always a reality. The Old Testament tells from early times (Gen. 35; Num. 25; Judg. 6: 25ff. et al.) down to a late date (Jer. 44; Ezek. 8; Isa. 57: 3ff.; 65: 2ff.; 66: 17 et al.) of Israel's being attracted in different ways to the worship of idols. In order to ensure the life together of Canaanite and Israelite elements in the population in one state, the monarchy often, especially in the northern kingdom, supported syncretism. It was especially the prophets, from Elijah (1 Kgs. 17f.; 2 Kgs. 1) and later especially Hosea (2f.; 8), Jeremiah (2–3; 44) and Ezekiel (8; 16; 20; 23) who fought for the acceptance of the first commandment and expected its actualization in the future (Isa. 2: 17; 45: 6, 23 et al.). Deuteronomy too (6: 14; 7: 4ff.; 8: 19; 13: 2ff.; 17: 2ff. et al.) and its school, in the Deuteronomistic history, made it a basic demand (Josh. 23: 6ff.; Judg. 6: 8–10; 2 Kgs. 17: 7, 16, 35). Here the harsh demand to choose between alternatives was opposed to any possible compromise; turning to other deities as such meant apostasy from Yahweh. Did the period of the judges already see action on behalf of the exclusiveness of faith in Yahweh (Judg. 6: 25–32, the struggle of Gideon)? The public abandonment of foreign deities that the Israelites had brought with them (Gen. 35: 2–4; Josh. 24: 14f., 20) can be understood as amounting to the putting into practice of the first commandment. But it was undoubtedly in the struggle of Israel with Canaanite religion that the prohibition on foreign gods came to have its full force.

4   The subject matter of the first commandment (as of the second) is not primarily God himself, but man's relationship to God. But Israel later on directly inferred a property of Yahweh from the demand for exclusiveness, and interpreted the demand in turn by means of it: 'For I Yahweh your God am a jealous God' is the wording of the reason given for the first commandment (Exod. 20: 5; 34: 14; Deut. 6: 14f.; 32: 16ff.; Josh. 24: 19 et al.). This confession of God as a 'jealous God' is the more striking in that the Old Testament ascribes few epithets to God himself. The declaration of the fundamental character of God's grace and mercy is similar (Exod. 34: 6f.; Ps. 103: 8f. et al.). The first commandment cannot be understood historically on the basis of Yahweh's 'jealous holiness'; for even the instances in the Decalogue are first found in the later (Deuteronomistic) additions to the old laws. But like the commandment itself, the jealousy of a God against other gods is unknown in the world around Israel. It is only with this addition of *qannā* 'jealous' that the divine name El is fully reinterpreted in an Israelite sense, and directed now against its Canaanite origin. The neighbouring religions are familiar with the dominance of one god over the others, but not with exclusiveness; and there is a gap between the two which serves to separate Israel from the ancient Near East. Strictly speaking however, Yahweh's jealousy is directed not against the foreign gods, as if he were distrustfully persecuting his rivals, but against Israel for entrusting itself to foreign gods. Yahweh's 'jealousy' too therefore is connected with his relationship to men; he demands that their faith be exclusive, and punishes their transgressions (Exod. 20: 5; Deut. 6: 15). Deuteronomy even infers from the demand for worship of Yahweh alone the oneness or uniqueness of God:

Hear, O Israel: Yahweh our God, Yahweh is one (or, alone, unique). (Deut. 6: 4; cf. Zech. 14: 9; Mal. 2: 10; Job 31: 15)

Undivided commitment is owed to him (Deut. 6: 5; cf. 1 Kgs. 8: 61; 11: 4 et al.). The unity of God is matched by the completeness of the devotion of man: 'You shall be wholly devoted to Yahweh your God' (Deut. 18: 13; cf. Gen. 17: 1P).

5   The exclusiveness of their relationship to God had consequences which separated Israel substantially from the world around. With the belief in one God there was lost in the first place (and this is quite unusual for the ancient world) the sexual differentiation between god and goddess. Yahweh does seem to have been associated here and there with female deities.

> Syncretistic forms of Yahwism developed, especially on the fringes. Was the goddess Anat-yahu or Anat-Betel worshipped in the Jewish colony on the island of Elephantine as the consort of Yahweh? An inscription from Kuntillet Ajrud, deep in the south of Palestine, speaks of the 'blessing of Yahweh and of his Ashera'.

But in consequence of the first commandment exceptions were again and again set aside in favour of the exclusiveness of Yahweh. A substantial part of the ancient Near Eastern myths were thereby eliminated; for Israel was not in a position to tell stories of the marriage of the gods. It did not work back from Yahweh's being to ask questions about his origin, in order to represent the birth of the God in a theogony. The one God was not born and did not die (Hab. 1: 12; Ps. 90: 1 [Heb. 90: 2] et al.), just as he did not need to fight for dominion over the gods (cf. below, §11e). If the relationship of Yahweh to other gods needed to be stated, a juxtaposition of beings of equal importance was excluded. Their unification to form a pantheon was not possible, only at best an identification. So the name El, and at a later time the Persian title 'God of heaven', could be transferred to Yahweh. As a rule however Yahweh was seen in contrast to the other gods, or his superior might was recognized (Exod. 18: 11; Ps. 96: 4f. et al.) until the 'sons of God' were reduced in status to being his heavenly court (below, §11a).

As well as the worship of the dead (below, Excursus 8) the cult of the stars too was attacked (Deut. 4: 19; 17: 3; 2 Kgs. 17: 16; 21: 3, 5; 23: 5, 11 et al.). The stars are created by God, and therefore are not mythical and numinous entities (cf. Ezek. 8: 16), but are this-worldly phenomena, 'lamps' (Gen. 1: 14ff.; Ps. 136: 7ff.). The host of heaven, originally stars or personifications of them, is also created (Gen. 2: 1; Ps. 33: 6; Isa. 40: 26; 45: 12); its task is to praise God (Ps. 148: 2) and to fulfil his will (103: 21), and it forms his court (1 Kgs. 22: 19ff.).

No doubt as a consequence of the demand by Yahweh for exclusiveness, belief in demons, especially by comparison with the popular belief of the post-Old Testament period) is not of significance. Prophetic declarations of judgement may portray fallen ruins as the dwelling place of restlessness demonic figures (Isa. 13: 21; 34: 12, 14; Jer. 50: 39; a different view in Lev. 16: 5ff.). It is however prohibited to offer sacrifice to such demons; for they are not God (Deut. 32: 17; Lev. 17: 7; Hos. 12: 11 [Heb. 12: 12]; Ps. 106: 37; 2 Kgs. 23: 8). Demonic powers can be integrated into God (Gen. 32: 22ff. [Heb. 32: 23ff.]; Exod. 4: 24ff.) or subordinated to him! The wilderness demon of the night of the Passover (Exod. 12: 23; cf. Heb. 11, 28), like the angel of death (2 Sam. 24: 17; cf. 2 Kgs. 19: 35;

Num. 22: 22ff.), acts at Yahweh's bidding. The serpent (Gen. 3: 1; cf. Amos 9: 3) and the sea-monster (Gen. 1: 21; cf. Ps. 104: 26) are his creatures. Even the power of the earth to bring forth plants is not simply its own, but is assigned to it by the word of God (Gen. 1: 11, 24; cf. below, §11f, 3).

The third commandment is intended to exclude conjuration or magic (Exod. 20: 7; cf. 22: 17; Num. 23: 23 et al.). Indeed the law about prophecy (Deut. 18: 9ff.) contrasts cultic and magical practices, such as are customary among Israel's neighbours, with the prophetic word (cf. Exod. 7: 8ff.). The blessing, originally, like the curse, a word of power acting of its own might, changes because God is understood as its originator into a wish or prayer (cf. Num. 6: 24ff.; Deut. 7: 13f.; Mal. 2: 2 et al.).

Things which in the ancient Near Eastern and classical world could be ascribed to the workings of evil powers, are regarded in the Old Testament as the work of the one God who kills and makes alive, who creates darkness and light, sends disaster and prosperity (1 Sam. 2: 6; 16: 13f.; Amos 3: 6; Isa. 45: 7; Lam. 3: 37f. et al.). So man cannot turn from the evil spirit or the deity who is persecuting him to another deity who is well disposed to him; he receives joy and sorrow, good and evil from the same hand, meets the same God in both wrath and grace.

Shall we receive good at the hand of God, and shall we not receive evil? Yahweh gave, and Yahweh has taken away; blessed be the name of Yahweh. (Job 2: 10; 1: 21; cf. Prov. 16: 4; Eccles. 7: 14; Ruth 1: 13, 21; also Lev. 26; Deut. 28 et al.)

How far then is 'chance' still at work (Exod. 21: 13; Gen. 16: 2; cf. Ruth 2: 3 with 2: 20)? In spite of the complexity and even ambivalence of experience, life as a whole is understood from the oneness of the faith.

Perhaps the exclusive worship of one God also had social consequences, although this aspect of the faith of Israel has hardly been examined and is also difficult to prove. A mythological self-understanding presupposes an internal connection between society, the world, and religious concepts. In the hierarchy of gods of ancient Near Eastern religions the structure of society was reflected; the heavenly order paralleled the social structure upon earth. Deut. 32: 8 alludes to this correspondence at least in the existence of a like number of gods and of nations:

When the Most High gave to the nations their inheritance,
when he separated the sons of men,
he fixed the bounds of the peoples
according to the number of the sons of God.

The most high God divided up his realm and ruled over his subjects; this division continued down to lower levels. But not only the vertical but also the horizontal divisions of human society recurred in the coexistence of different professions among the gods.

There were not only gods of war and of fertility, but individual deities representing special areas of life. So the Egyptian Ptah and the Ugaritic Kosher-wa-Ḥasis, 'skilled and clever' were regarded as artist deities, who were both architects and craftsmen in one. Another was the inventor of writing and so lord of the scribes (Thoth). The particular professions in each case owed their activity or the creation of their tools to a particular god (cf. Gen. 3: 21; not so 4: 17ff.). He may at first have been responsible for the whole life of his worshippers, and only later restricted to particular functions for a wider circle of men. So it can be observed in Egypt: 'to begin with God means everything to a small group, but later comes to mean part of a greater whole to a larger number of faithful' (S. Morenz, *Egyptian Religion*, London, 1973, p. 28).

Certainly the structure and specialization by profession of society were not simply projected into heaven in order to form the divine world on the model of the human. It was the other way round; the ordering of nature and of society were felt to be a divine gift, and therefore a copy of the situation in heaven. Nevertheless in this way the social structure was rooted in tradition, and given a firm basis; for it was legitimated and kept stable by its heavenly counterpart. This structured mythological world, which supported and gave security to the earthly world, was absent from the faith of Yahwism. This meant that the relationship to God was the more capable of adaptation to changes in the form of society, or rather the reverse – that the social structure was capable of being criticized. There is no doubt an internal link here, when the prophets of Israel were able to reproach the highest levels of society (Amos 4: 1 et al.) with their unjust deeds, indeed to oppose critically even the monarchy (Hos. 1: 4 et al.; below, §12a, 4; 14b, 2). Influences from the early period which scarcely knew such a stratification of human society at all are also at work here. It is in this way too that we should understand the fact that the Yahwistic faith was able to reassert itself in the completely altered circumstances of the exile and post-exilic period, and even to make new demands?

So the first commandment had far-reaching consequences both in word and in substance in history; its voice was heard anew in each period. Because it was the basis of and preserved the distinctiveness of Israel, it justifiably determines the character of the Old Testament to a large degree. History certainly does not simply display Israel's development of the first commandment, but the various new beginnings of history can be connected with this commandment, because it posed a task (above, §1, 2). The history of Israel could be written as a history of the first commandment. The effective element in it is its character as a demand. It is not an actualized reality simply as such – and in the history of Israel it frequently was not a reality – but it sets a task of relating Israel's changing new experiences to the basic insight of faith, and so puts reality in motion. So the first commandment is not a doctrine uttered once for all and of timeless validity, but requires exposition and appropriation in changing circumstances. The same is true of the second commandment. Faith in the one God is not a situation attained by Israel on a single definitive occasion, which is laid down by the past for succeeding generations, but is a permanent challenge looking to the future.

c THE SECOND COMMANDMENT

To the Hellenistic and Roman world of late antiquity the absence of images in the Jewish faith was the really strange and indeed even offensive feature of it. It distinguished the synagogue from all temples, and excluded any shared community in religion and common life. The prohibition of idols therefore represents something that is characteristic for Israel, although in the history of religions as a whole the worship of God without images was by no means unique. However Israel's neighbours in time and immediately in space in the early period had nothing comparable. Since once again any real analogy is lacking, the prohibition of idols cannot be derived from the surrounding world. Religio-historical inquiry keeps on running up against the first and second commandments in the Old Testament, but the two also form the boundary beyond which historical research has not hitherto been able to pass.

Judaism extended the prohibition of images (in spite of the presence of representations in synagogues of the third to sixth centuries AD, as at Dura-Europus and Beth-Alpha) to the representation of animals and men. The Old Testament was concerned with the image man makes of God. The second commandment was not originally and in principle directed against art. Although Israel did not indeed attain to high levels in this area (the most beautiful pottery and ivory carvings found in excavations are imported) it was only an image worshipped by man that was forbidden, the image of God. A deity who could not be represented was however inconceivable for the ancient Near East, as for the classical world, or at least unusual, for God was thought to be present in the images which men served with holy rituals. While therefore in the surrounding world the destruction of images of god was regarded as blasphemy towards the deity, in Israel the creation and worship of an image were strictly forbidden. With this the Old Testament excluded precisely what for other religions represented the most worshipful thing possible, the presence of God. The second commandment, just as much as the first, separates the God of Israel from other gods; it takes him out of the ordinary religious world. It is that very God who guides men in history who in this way is withdrawn from ordinary reality.

The essence of the relationship of God and man in the Old Testament must be affected by this distinctive character of the Yahwistic faith. The most probable explanation of the second commandment is that man may not portray God in an image, because man is the image of God. God creates an image of himself in man, but man may not create an image of God. The Old Testament however is unaware of such a connection, or at least nowhere draws a connecting line between the two statements. Only in a few much later passages does the Old

Testament speak of man's being made in the image of God (below, §12c), and it uses other terms for 'image' than those in the different versions of the second commandment. Its significance must therefore be expressed in a different way, if it can be clearly indicated at all; and probably it has changed in the course of time.

1 Israel must have regarded the second commandment as fundamental already at an early date. For this reason it is often linked with the first commandment outside the Decalogue (Exod. 20: 2–6) too (Exod. 34: 14, 17; Lev. 19: 4; 26: 1; Deut. 4: 16ff.; cf. Hos. 11: 2, Jer. 1: 16 et al.), and appears in all the old legal collections. When the prohibition of strange gods is once strikingly absent, the prohibition of images can itself open the series (Deut. 27: 15, in a later formulation). The Book of the Covenant (Exod. 20: 23) prohibits the making of gods of gold and silver, the cultic Decalogue prohibits gods cast of iron ore (Exod. 34: 17; similarly the Code of Holiness, Lev. 19: 4) and finally the series of twelve curses (Deut. 27: 15) further prohibits the making of images carved of wood (possibly coated with metal) (cf. Judg. 17: 3f.; Isa. 44: 10ff.). So the various kinds of image employed in the Canaanite world are successively listed. The expression for image in the commandment in the Decalogue (Exod. 20: 4; Deut. 5: 8) means primarily an image of carved wood or hewn stone, and only later also one cast from metal (Isa. 40: 19; 44: 10). Does the commandment go back to a time for which molten images had no significance – and so back to the period in the wilderness? Perhaps however the Decalogue here too chooses a broadly expressed formulation, which avoids all specific details, because it is intended to have universal validity.

Probably the prohibition of images is of great antiquity, although no more precise statement of its date can be given. It was probably not developed only in opposition to the Canaanite cult, though it did come to show its force here. But why is it Hosea who first combats the worship of images, and not Elijah or even Amos?

An attempt has been made to derive the second commandment from the wilderness period, and to connect it with the Ark of the Covenant, which on this view as an imageless symbol was the only legitimate location of God's presence (K. H. Bernhardt, *Gott und Bild*, Berlin, 1956). In fact during the wandering in the wilderness we hear no mention of any image apart from the rejected golden calf (Exod. 32) and the bronze serpent (Num. 21: 4ff.; 2 Kgs. 18: 4). But this theory requires too many uncertain assumptions; not only is it disputed whether the Ark comes from the wilderness period, but it is still more dubious whether the prohibition of images can be ascribed to the same nomadic group to which the ark belonged.

Perhaps the worship of Yahweh was from the beginning without images, but this distinctive feature only assumed the character of a commandment in the dispute with the religion of Canaan.

2 Is the prohibition on creating an image of God and worshipping it connected exclusively with the portrayal of Yahweh, and not with the image of a foreign God? The actual wording does not allow a clear decision. It has even been conjectured that the second commandment was originally only directed against

other, perhaps Canaanite, idols, and was later reinterpreted to refer to an image of Yahweh. The parallel version in Exod. 20: 23, 'You shall not make gods of silver to be with me, nor shall you make for yourselves gods of gold' makes us think rather of foreign deities than of images of Yahweh (like Lev. 19: 4; 26: 1; Hos. 11: 2 et al.). Or is the prohibition aimed in two directions? If it excluded images completely in the worship of Yahweh, it could at the same time be directed against the introduction of foreign images as representations of Yahweh. This facing in both directions arises therefore from the actual situation: since Israel's neighbours worship their gods in images, the creation of any image means taking over of foreign examples, and so a measure of assimilation to their understanding of God. It is along these lines that Hosea and Jeremiah campaign against the Baalization of Yahweh.

The expansions of the second commandment interpret it in connection with the first. The original short version 'You shall not make for yourself a graven image' (Exod. 20: 4a) was later expanded and explained in a broader, awkward style; the increasing elaboration of this commandment is an example of the gradual growth of the Decalogue as a whole into its present final form.

The demand 'You shall not bow down to them or serve them' (20: 5) is usually associated with foreign deities (Deut. 8: 19 et al.), not with images of Yahweh or of idols. Correspondingly the added explanatory clause introduced by 'for', which serves to reinforce the commandment (v. 5b; similarly vv. 7, 11) reminds us in its first part 'I, Yahweh, your god, am a jealous God' of the demand for exclusiveness of the first commandment. Yahweh's jealousy will not permit the worship of other deities (cf. Exod. 34: 14). The placing of these explanations is only understandable if they do not just go back to the more distant prohibition of alien deities, but also apply to the immediately preceding prohibition of idols, that is, both are treated as a unity. Then however both commandments have the same purpose in the view of the interpretative additions; the second carries the first further; images too are rejected along with foreign deities.

Since the first commandment already prohibits the worship of foreign gods, the second would only repeat the prohibition for the images of these gods, if representations of Yahweh were not at least included. Further there is no indication that the worship of Yahweh once did officially have images, and that it only underwent this fundamental change in the course of its history; so far-reaching an alteration is nowhere hinted at, and is historically not probable either. On the other hand particular formulations of the prohibition of idols are unintelligible if it is restricted to images of Yahweh. Apart from 'make *images*' in the version in the Decalogue (Exod. 20: 4; Deut. 5: 8; 27: 15; Hos. 13: 2) it is found also in a form with a different object, 'to make (silver, golden, molten, etc.) gods' (Exod. 34: 17; Lev. 19: 4 et al.). This second formulation appears however to be later, since in it the first and second commandments have already come to form a unity.

When at a later time the foreign gods became unimportant to Israel or were even completely denied, the more narrowly formulated prohibition of images came to the fore as a distinguishing mark over against the world around.

3   The exclusive worship of Yahweh was not a reality everywhere and at all times, but remained a demand upon Israel; and the same was true with the absence of images from the cult of Yahweh. Several times we are told of the making of images of Yahweh, although it remains unclear how exactly they were understood. The story of Micah's shrine and the transfer of it to Dan (Judg. 17–18) appears to be thinking of a private image of Yahweh; it is referred to with quiet irony, but without polemic. As a rule the Old Testament mentions images of Yahweh polemically. The story of the golden calf (Exod. 32), the story of the introduction of calf images in Bethel and in Dan (1 Kgs. 12: 26ff.) and still more the accusations of Hosea (8: 4–6; 10: 5f.; 11: 2; 13: 2) are directed against endangering faith in Yahweh through the worship of images.

Gideon's ephod (Judg. 8: 24ff.) could have been a garment for an image of God; such a garment is later part of the vestments of the High Priest (Exod. 28f.).

The teraphim (whether they are representations of the gods of the family (Gen. 31: 19, 34f.), or a cultic mask (1 Sam. 19: 13; cf. Judg. 17: 5; 18: 14ff.) or are used to obtain an oracle (Ezek. 21: 26; Zech. 10: 2) come under the prohibition (1 Sam. 15: 23; 2 Kgs. 23: 14; cf. Hos. 3: 4).

The erection of massebas (Gen. 28: 18; cf. above, §3e; cf. Exod. 24: 4; Josh. 4), large cultic stones, is later prohibited (Deut. 16: 22; cf. 7: 5; 12: 3; Lev. 26: 1; Hos. 3: 4; 10: 1; 2 Kgs. 18: 4; 23: 24; also Exod. 34: 13 et al.).

The bronze sea (1 Kgs. 7: 24ff.; Jer. 27: 19), possibly once a representation of the primeval sea, becomes a basin for ritual washings (Exod. 30: 17ff.; 40: 11P).

The bronze serpent, Nehushtan, originally perhaps a representation of a chthonic goddess of prosperity or of life, becomes a symbol of salvation erected at the command of Yahweh and subordinated to him (Num. 21: 8f.; cf. Joh. 3: 14f.), and is then destroyed (2 Kgs. 18: 3f.).

Finally mention must be made of the many little statuettes and pottery figures found in excavations, intended for private use. To what extent were they also understood as representations of Yahweh?

Certainly the cherubim, although they are strictly representations taken over from other religions (cf. below, §9a, 2), are not images of Yahweh. Neither the older temple of Shiloh, nor the Jerusalem sanctuary (for all its syncretism, cf. Ezek. 8) ever housed an image of Yahweh in the strict sense (1 Sam. 3; 1 Kgs. 8). In the pre-exilic period only the Ark that had been brought by David to Jerusalem, which made the invisible god present, stood in the Holy of Holies, and the Holy of Holies of the second, post-exilic temple was empty.

4   Since there is no analogy for the prohibition of images, and its origin remains unknown, it is basically not capable of explanation. The numerous explanations

which it has received must be regarded as unsatisfactory, but in the end it cannot be stated with certainty what intention it originally had.

The Marburg philosopher H. Cohen gives the interpretation that 'the opposition between the unique God and the gods is not limited to *number*, it becomes prominent in the distinction between the unseen *idea* and a perceptible *image*. And the immediate share reason has in the concept of the unique God is verified in this opposition to the image.' 'The image has to be a likeness. Of God, however, there can be no likeness, he is absolutely the archetype for the mind, for the love of reason, but not an object for imitation' (*Religion of Reason out of the Sources of Judaism* [1929], New York, 1972, pp. 53f.). More broadly the view has often been expressed that the second commandment raises man's relationship to God to a higher level, and an intellectual worship of God replaces material worship. But this distinction of mind and body is not an Old Testament distinction. 'Spirit' is not as a rule understood in contrast to flesh, but as the power that is at work in flesh (below, Excursus 3). Further the prohibition of images is not primarily justified by the argument that God is invisible, or that it is dangerous to see him.

It is most likely that the second commandment was intended to prevent man from getting control of the deity in an image and using magic to make him do his will. He compels him to be present in the image, and can control him then, because he has him tangibly before him; he can do him good by clothing and feeding him, or harm him by refusing sacrifices and by punishments. But this understanding does not quite do justice to the way the cult of images understands itself. Perhaps image and deity were originally seen as a unity, but in the ancient Near East of the Old Testament period the two had for a long time not been regarded as identical. Worship was given not to the image, but to the deity in the image. Since the image does not hold the deity he is not capable of being grasped materially in the image. The image really does preserve the uncontrollability of the deity; for he transcends his image. What happens to his image does indeed happen to him, and the man who takes hold of the image is threatened with the death penalty, but the deity is not himself destroyed if the image is destroyed.

According to the so-called Memphitic theology, the Egyptian God Ptah first created the gods, then their bodies, that is, their corporeal form: 'So the gods entered into their bodies of every kind of wood, of every kind of stone, of every kind of clay, or anything (else).' For other witnesses the difference between god and image remains permanent: 'the god of this land is the sun which is on the horizon, and only his images are upon earth' (S. Morenz, *Egyptian Religion*, London, 1973, p. 154). An Assyrian inscription reports the destruction of city and temple, and continues: 'the god and goddesses which dwell in it mounted up to heaven' (Bernhardt, *Gott und Bild*, p. 49).
According to the systematic theology of the (Egyptian) New Kingdom . . . the deity is in heaven, his body rests in the underworld, and on earth among men the images of the deity bear witness to his presence. These images can also be regarded as the 'body' of the gods, into which they 'enter' . . . Usually the cultic image shared in the invisibility of the deity; erected in the dark Holy of Holies, it was only accessible to the priest of the temple in course, who daily celebrated the ritual to and before the

image. At the great feasts the portable image of God was carried out on the shoulders of the priests into public view . . . Even in these processions however, to judge from the pictorial representations, it remained invisible in a veiled shrine. To see God even in his image remained a special grace, which is only granted each day to the priest in course, when he opens the shrine of the image.(E. Hornung, *Der Eine und die Vielen*, Darmstadt, 1973, p. 125)

So the worship of images does not signify control of the deity by man, as happens in magic and sorcery. What the image offers is the powerful and salvific presence of the deity. For this reason it does not need either to be a strict representation of the transcendent deity; the important thing is that it embodies the deity, and so reveals him. It is not the appearance of the image that is basic, but its power. Because however the appearance of the deity becomes a continuing presence in the image, there is a danger that the image will no longer be understood as the place at which God dwells, but as God himself. This must have been the understanding of many participants in the cult. This perhaps is the justification of the polemic of the Old Testament, which (incorrectly in terms of the history of religions) regards God and image completely as a unity.

A workman made it;
    it is not God.
Men kiss calves! (Hos. 8: 6; 13: 2; cf. Jer. 2: 28; Exod. 32: 4 et al.).

It is only a later more enlightened era which thinks that in the image it has the deity himself (Isa. 41: 6f.; 44: 14ff.; inf. §17, 1), and a time which doubts the divinity of the image which is able to mock at the fact that the powerless deity leaves the sinner unharmed.

5   While the purpose of the prohibition of images is at first difficult to determine unambiguously, it appears all the more clearly later in the explanations of the second commandment and in the introduction to Deuteronomy. The more precise definition in the Decalogue (Exod. 20: 4b), 'any likeness of anything that is in heaven above, or that is in the earth beneath, or that is in the water under the earth' lists the areas from which an image may not be taken, and so expressly extends the prohibition of images to all parts of the world, for this threefold division embraces the totality of the world. While the neighbouring religions have gods of heaven, earth and the underworld, each with their own representations, the Old Testament declares that not only the earth but heaven too contains nothing comparable to God, because nothing in this world corresponds to him. Thus what is implied in the prohibition of images is made explicit; and this is the distinction between God and world. If nothing this-worldly is sufficient to represent God, we have the paradox that the God of the Old Testament is not invisible, but is nevertheless not able to be portrayed.

Along the same lines the Deuteronomic preaching (Deut. 4: 12–20) only tightens up the commandment explicitly by saying that no male, female or animal representation is to be made, and warning men against the seduction of star-worship. Here the prohibition on images clearly rejects any portrayal of Yahweh; but it is still connected with resistance to the worship of foreign deities. The first and the second commandments serve to interpret one another: the deities of the other nations can be represented in this world, since they are in the form of earthly beings, or are identified with the stars. Because there are no analogies in this world to the God of Israel, he remains unable to be portrayed; for representations are only possible in so far as there is something able to be compared. But this interpretation of the prohibition of images does not fundamentally draw a line between God and the world of the senses, and does not ground the distinction undertaken on creation (created things cannot represent the creator) but on the revelation at Sinai:

> And Yahweh spoke with you out of the midst of the fire; you heard the sound of words, but saw no form; there was only a voice. (Deut. 4: 12; cf. 5: 23f.)

Even when appearing, God himself was not visible but only audible. This explanation not only gives precedence in the understanding of God to hearing over seeing, but among the senses makes a distinction between hearing and seeing, word and image, even though immediately previously the features accompanying the theophany in nature have been mentioned. While these effects of Yahweh's appearance are perceptible, God himself remains imageless, impossible to portray; he comes near to men only through his voice. Seeing (in spite of Exod. 24: 11) gives too close a contact. The impossibility of representing God and so the distinction between God and world is here made the criterion of faith and the touchstone for the contrast between Israel and the nations. The encounter with God is not meant to lead to a portrayal of God.

6   Similar intentions of excluding the possibility of portraying God can be found elsewhere too.

Even stories with a mythical stamp, in which God intervenes directly in earthly events, can withdraw him from human sight when he is in action (Gen. 2: 21; 15: 12; Exod. 12: 22; cf. 2 Kgs. 4: 4, 33). Lot's wife, who disobeyed the prohibition on looking back at God's punishment of Sodom, is turned into a pillar of salt (Gen. 19: 17, 26). What is left unspoken here is formulated elsewhere as a principle, that 'man shall not see me and live' (Exod. 33: 20; cf. 19: 21; Judg. 6: 22f.; 13: 22; Isa. 6: 5; Jer. 30: 21 et al.). Not only Moses (Exod. 3: 6) and Elijah (1 Kgs. 19: 13) but even the seraphim (Isa. 6: 2) veil their faces before God.

Stories which say of God's revelation that 'he let himself be seen, or appeared', remain silent about the manner and form of the appearance, though they render the words of God (Gen. 12: 7J; 17: 1P; cf. 35: 1E et al.). Similarly, prophets in their vision can 'see' God, although they do not describe his form (1 Kgs. 22: 19; Amos 9: 1; Isa. 6: 1; also Ezek. 1). In each case a reserve about seeing or portraying can be perceived, which does not apply to hearing.

In other accounts of theophanies God is represented in the realm of the visible, or more generally of the perceptible, by angelic beings (Gen. 16; 21f.; 31; Exod. 3: Judg. 2; 6; 13 et al., cf. below, §17, 4). According to Exod. 33: 12ff. the distant God is only present in his 'face', according to Deuteronomy (12: 5, 11, 21 et al.) and the Deuteronomistic history (1 Kgs. 8: 16, 29 et al.) in his name, according to P (Exod. 16: 10; Lev. 9: 4ff, 23; Num. 14: 10 ff. et al.) in his 'glory'. In different ways a distinction is made between God in his holiness and his presence upon earth, between God's essential existence and his concern for man. God is at work in history, but is not completely to be found in it.

Linguistic images do not fall under the prohibition. The Old Testament permits to hearing what it forbids to seeing. When prophets and psalmists use the harshest of comparisons ('I am like pus, like decay, like a lion', Hosea makes God say, 5: 12, 14; cf. Lam. 3: 10; Isa. 7: 20 et al.), the word is allowed what the representational arts are forbidden. Such linguistic images do not describe properties or circumstances, but represent an event, and declare the God who intervenes in the fate of man.

d   THE RELATIONSHIP TO HISTORY

1   Apart from its exclusiveness and the absence of images from its worship no element of the faith of the Old Testament is so striking (especially in comparison with the surrounding world) as the relationship to history. Perhaps the demand for exclusiveness and the relationship to history should indeed be closely connected, because by contrast with mythological thought, which tells of a relationship of the gods among themselves, the assumption of a multiplicity of deities disappears, all talk of an act of God becomes almost necessarily historical, and every action of God directly a relationship to the world and to man.

> Where God as the only God has no counterpart other than man and his world, and where therefore all movement and drama in the area of the divine, love and war, birth and death, rise and fall are totally lacking, there must be a heightened significance in God's one counterpart, man and the history of man in his world. (C. Westermann, *BK*, I/1, p. 95)

The Decalogue too sees a connection between the reference to history and the first and second commandments; God first says what he has done for his hearers, and only then what the relationship with him should be like (God's words in Exod. 20: 2–6). Was the relationship to history a starting point for the demand for exclusiveness, and the first commandment a consequence of historical experience? Whatever the case here the faith of the Old Testament has appealed from the earliest times to a historical act of God (Exod. 15: 21; Amos 9: 7; Hos. 13: 4; also Gen. 15: 7; Judg. 5: 11 et al. cf. §4b, 3). Israel is conscious that a place has been assigned to it in history, the place where it lives; it knows that it has a place in a continuing history, and this helps it to understand the present (above, §2, 1). Indeed the Old Testament preserves a recollection that faith too has its history; the relationship of the patriarchs to God was different from that of the people (Exod. 6:2; cf. §17, 3). If historical study shows that the Old Testament originated in history, this recognition does not stand in contradiction to what it says itself (although the picture of history handed down by the Bible and the picture reconstructed through historical methods are not identical).

2   While the stele of King Mesha of Moab (below §7, 1b) declares of an Israelite tribe that 'the people of Gad had always dwelt in the land of Atarot', that is, from the beginning of time, for Israel's self-understanding the recollection of the period of the patriarchs was basic, a period in which Israel did not yet exist, but other ancient Near Eastern nations did already exist (Gen. 10); and it told of its entry into the land. While the Babylonian king-list reaches back to a mythical beginning, 'when kingship came down from heaven' (*ANET*, p. 265), Israel was able to tell how the institution of kingship was taken over at a particular time from the nations round about (1 Sam. 8: 5, 20; Deut. 17: 14). The crudest statement is a declaration of an Egyptian priest reported by Herodotus (II, 142), that the Egyptian empire had existed for more than ten thousand years: 'in all this time nothing had altered in Egypt.' By contrast the Old Testament is conscious of the changeableness of history.

The ancient Near East is not elsewhere familiar with so intensive a hold upon the past for the sake of faith and of the relationship with the present, and at the same time so far-reaching a concern for the future, as are to be found in the Old Testament. Israel's interpretation of the history of the world is the 'earliest known to us' (A. Alt, 'Die Deutung der Weltgeschichte im Alten Testament' *ZTK* 56 (1959), p. 130). Accordingly works of history proper appeared so far as can be seen first in Israel; they were still unfamiliar to the ancient Near East in this form.

In a statement which has often been quoted the historian E. Meyer expresses the view that 'a real historical literature was created fully independently in the area of the ancient Near Eastern and European culture only in Israel and in Greece. Among the Israelites, who in this too have a special position among all the advanced people of the Near East, it appeared at an astonishingly early date, and begins with some extremely important works', in fact a century before Hesiod (*Geschichte des Altertums*, I/1, 6th edn., 1963, p. 227). 'So the heyday of the kingdom of Judah created real history. No other advanced nation was able to do this; even the Greeks only achieved this at the height of their development in the fifth century, although they then immediately went still further. With Israel on the other hand we are dealing with a nation which has just entered upon true civilization' (ibid. II/2, 3rd edn., 1953, p. 285).

Both Mesopotamia and Egypt have however left us a mass of historical accounts. Building inscriptions tell of the construction of a temple, royal inscriptions of an important campaign. Lists were made of officials, priests and kings (cf.

1 Kgs. 4: 2ff.). Annals preserved the chronology of the most important particular events, after which too the years were named (cf. Amos 1: 1, 'two years before the earthquake'). (cf. 1 Kgs. 14: 19, 29), or regnal years were used for dating (14: 15 et al.). So the writing of history was to a large extent determined either by the king or by the cult. Not infrequently it is characterized by a given pattern, which lays down what ought to happen.

History itself could be interpreted in different way. An alternation of times of prosperity and of disaster, or the incalculable working of the gods towards good or ill made the course of history intelligible. The close connection of action and consequence ('a blow is to be repaid with its like. That is the application of that has been done,' says the instruction of Merikare (E. Otto, 'Geschichtsbild und Geschichtsschreibung im Ägypten', *WO* 3 (1966), p. 176; *ANET*, p. 417, cf. §15, 3) could make history appear to be the direct consequence of man's action. Like the return of day and night, of seasons and of stars, as well as the uniformity of the cult, which by its regular feasts bestowed life, history too was understood from the point of view not of singularity and contingency but more strongly of the repetitive and the typical (cf. E. Hornung, *Geschichte als Fest*, Darmstadt, 1966). It is disputed however how far the ancient Near East thought of a constant return of the same events (cf. Eccles. 1: 4ff.). In any case history remains embedded in myth in many ways; its origins and with them its continuing foundation remain in the world of the gods.

3   Because of the strikingly close connection of faith and history in Israel the view might be put forward with J. L. Seeligmann that 'for man in the Old Testament history is the mode of thought of faith' (*ThZ* 19 (1963), p. 385).

However R. Smend has rejoined, 'In this sentence one need only question the definite article: history is by no means *the* mode of thought of Old Testament faith, but one among several; there are besides it worship, law and wisdom' (*Elemente alttestamentlichen Geschichtsdenken*, Zurich, 1968, p. 4; cf. also the critical objections of J. Barr, *Old and New in Interpretation*, London, 1966, pp. 65ff.).

Certainly there are these other areas as well as history in the narrow sense; but law and cult, and to a lesser extent also wisdom, are integrated into history. What originally has no firm historical anchorage is at least subsequently given in the Old Testament a historical link. All significant occurrences are assigned to a particular place in the history of Israel and so to a situation in which they could have originated, and from which in turn they can be explained. So the laws as words of Moses are attributed to the revelation at Sinai (Exod. 20ff.), a large part of the psalms are regarded as songs of David (e.g. Ps. 51), and the proverbs (and also Ps. 72 and 127) are attributed to Solomon. A custom such as circumcision is connected with Abraham (Gen. 17); the attempt is made to insert even mythological concepts into historical thought (§10b, 3; §11g). The agrarian festivals which Israel took over after it became sedentary were also given a new task, of reminding

Israel of decisive events from its early history (Exod. 23: 15; 12: 14; Lev. 23: 42f. et al.; cf. below, §9b). This reinterpretation has the consequence that the feasts, while they are characterized by regular recurrence, serve to make present a once-for-all event.

Even B. Albrektson, who tries to show that the thought of a divine revelation in history is not specifically Israelite, but is familiar to the ancient Near East, comes to the conclusion 'that the idea of historical events as divine manifestations has marked the Israelite cult in a way that lacks real parallels among Israel's neighbours . . . Nevertheless it appears evident that the deity's saving acts in history are nowhere afforded so central a position in the cult as in Israel, where they dominate the Passover and other ancient feasts. This, then, is a field where we may be entitled to speak of something distinctive' (*History and the Gods*, Lund, 1967, pp. 115f.).

4   However the Old Testament does not have an actual concept of history.

The lack of an appropriate term for an (admittedly important) state of affairs is however by no means unique. It is characteristic of the Old Testament that it is familiar with phenomena which it does not yet comprehend in a word. It thinks in terms of achievement, not of concepts.

There is for instance no word for 'conscience', although the story of the garden of Eden (Gen. 3. 8ff.) describes the behaviour of a man whose 'heart smote him' (1 Sam. 24: 6), that is, who is driven by his conscience. Similarly the Old Testament apparently has particular expressions for the 'released' slave or for 'free from guilt, guiltless', but no general expression for 'freedom'. But Israel looks for its origin in the deliverance from slavery in Egypt, and so believes in a God who delivers from oppression (Ps. 146: 7) and hopes for freedom again in the future (Isa. 42: 7; 49: 9; 61: 1 et al.).

The position is similar with the phenomenon of history. Different expressions from different groups of traditions and areas of literature only describe it incompletely. The Hebrew term for word (*dābār*) includes not only speech but also 'thing'; rather as the word history means both the event in the past and also the report of it, the narrative. The account of the making of the covenant with Abraham in Gen. 15: 1 makes the transition from one scene to the next with the formula 'After these words (i.e. events) it happened . . .' Similarly behind the title 'the book of the words of Solomon' we have a work which contains the events of the time of Solomon, so a chronicle (1 Kgs. 11: 41) or annals (14: 29 et al.). The word 'generations' (Gen. 5: 1 et al.) can contain the meaning 'history of origins' (Gen. 2: 4a). Isaiah announces the future as God's 'work' or 'counsel' (5: 12, 19; 28: 21, 29; cf. 10: 12; 14: 26; also Ps. 44: 1 [Heb. 44: 2]; 33: 10f.; Prov. 19: 21 et al.). Finally Deutero-Isaiah creates a new terminology which depends on a strict separation of past and future, 'the former' and the 'latter', to announce deliverance from the pressure of the past, and to call men to look for what is to come (Isa. 41: 22f.; 42: 9, 43: 9, 18f.; 46: 9; 48: 3, 6). The prophet exhorts men to forget the former things, that is, the past, and to look only to the future. This pair of words in effect embraces the whole of history, just as the double expression 'heaven and earth' means the world.

5   Apart from the period of King David, Israel more often suffered in history than made history itself. Nevertheless the writing of history in Israel did not originate from its experiences of evil and of suffering, but started at the beginning of the new millennium, in the Golden Age of David and Solomon, after the material basis for it had been created by the formation of the state, and the neighbouring nations been drawn more strongly into Israel's horizon. The first historical works, telling of the rise of David (1 Sam. 16–2 Sam. 5 or 8) and of the succession (2 Sam. 9–20; 1 Kgs. 1f.) have only a limited circle of characters in view, but set out 'the internal connections of the forces that are at work of themselves and naturally in history' (G. von Rad). In a few scattered sentences the tangle of guilt and suffering at the royal court is evaluated as the providence of God (2 Sam. 11: 27; 12: 24; 14: 14). The writing of history in Israel begins apparently as a description of contemporary political history at the court. But this is still a consequence of faith; for it is the interpretation of the events that leads to their being written down. A little later we have the grand design of the Yahwist, who reworks theologically the narrative material from the creation to the conquest which he has inherited.

Ultimately it is only the difference in the relationship to God that explains why Israel unlike its neighbours came to develop historical thought. It no longer understood God's activity (at least in wide areas of the Old Testament), as did the myth and also the sagas of the early period, as a direct, miraculous intervention. Human and divine action are no longer thought of in a mythological way as being both upon the same plain. We see history in the givenness of the ordinary, and it is portrayed with all its cross-links and complexities; but the decisions taken and the events happening in it are regarded as the providence of God. Human freedom and responsibility on the one hand, God's activity on the other, human initiative and divine plan are not mutually exclusive. Both are true at the same time, entirely secular history and entirely God's work (cf. e.g. Gen. 50: 20; 2 Sam. 7: 14; Isa. 1: 9; 5: 26ff. et al.).

The oldest historical works have only a particular narrow aim and are not at first eschatologically directed (cf. however Gen. 12: 1ff.; above, §3d, 2). Prophecy and apocalyptic draw the future into historical thought, and at the same time extend the realm of history beyond the nation and its surroundings to the whole world. When the superior force of the ancient Near Eastern empires threatens and subjugates Israel, the one God assigns dominion not to the king of Israel, but to the foreigner (e.g. Jer. 25: 9; 27: 6; 43: 10; Isa. 44: 28f.).

EXCURSUS 2: THE SABBATH COMMANDMENT

1   The sabbath was observed in Israel from an early date. In the time of the

patriarchs there is, no doubt correctly, no mention of it; belief in the 'god of the fathers' does not seem to be connected with a fixed rest from work. But the early prophets of the eighth century mention the sabbath in both the northern and the southern kingdom (Amos 8: 5; Hos. 2: 11 [Heb. 2: 13]; Isa. 1: 13), the work of the Yahwist tells of a seventh day of rest in the gathering of the manna (Exod. 16: 29f.) and the legal collections of the Decalogue (20: 8ff.), of the Ritual Decalogue (34: 21), of the Book of the Covenant (23: 12) and of the Code of Holiness (Lev. 19: 3; 23: 3; 26: 2) all contain in different forms a sabbath commandment. However nowhere is there a statement about the institution and origin of this day. Non-Israelite origins have therefore been sought.

(a) The sabbath occurs several times in connection with the new moon (in the oldest period in Amos 8: 5; 2 Kgs. 4: 23 et al.; later Ezek. 46: 1; Isa. 66: 23 et al.), and in Babylonia the fifteenth day of the month, or day of the full moon, is called *shabattu*. It has therefore often been assumed that the sabbath was originally the day of the full moon. The Babylonian *shabattu* is not however attested as a day of rest. If however the sabbath is derived from the well-known unlucky days of the moon, it remains unexplained why (probably very early) it became independent of the course of the moon. Since the lunar cycle differs substantially from 28 days (it is 29½ days), the week would need constantly to be corrected, so that the sequence of six working days and one day of rest would be destroyed. The similarity with the Babylonian name does point to an early connection, but the derivation of the sabbath from the phases of the moon is not really convincing; and at least in the later period the sabbath in Israel was not a day of the full moon.

(b) A group of number sayings are known from Mesopotamia and Ugarit, which have a particular course of events or an action last for six days, to end on the seventh day as the climax and turning point (similarly Josh. 6). The number seven is in such cases only intended to indicate a short round period of time, not to give an exact time for a particular event. The regular recurrence of the week can certainly not be explained from such number sayings.

(c) Almost everywhere in the world particular days for certain forms of work, and also days without work, are known. Among the Romans, for instance, there were particular market days as days of rest. Since however they did not occur in a seven-day rhythm, and are not attested among Israel's neighbours, they are ruled out as the origin of the sabbath.

(d) Finally the derivation of the week, which recurs throughout the year, from a seven day New Year Feast (with the sabbath as the climax) is extremely dubious, especially since the duration of the autumn feast for seven days in Israel does not perhaps go back to the earliest period (cf. below, §9b, 3).

So the origin of the sabbath remains obscure, in spite of numerous theories. If it had an antecedent which Israel took over or changed, this has not yet been ascertained with certainty. There are no really sound reasons for the assumption that the sabbath was borrowed together with the name of Yahweh from other tribes, the Kenites or the Midianites. No instances are attested either from the surrounding nomadic world. But the commandment of Exod. 34: 21,

Six days you shall work,
but on the seventh day you shall rest;
(even) in ploughing time and in harvest you shall rest,

explicitly extends the commandment to rest to the agricultural work of the cultivated lands (M. Noth). If conclusions may be drawn from this fact, the sabbath extends back at least to the nomadic period. Apparently the alternation of six days' work and one day of rest, with the regular recurrence of the sabbath independently of the course of the moon, is a distinctive feature of ancient Israel. It has even been conjectured that Israel derived it from nature.

2   The essential characteristic of the sabbath is the rest. 'The sabbath mentioned in the Decalogue was from its origin characterized only by the prohibition of all work, and at the earliest period of Israelite history . . . had nothing to do with the positive cult of Yahweh' (A. Alt, *Essays on Old Testament History and Religion*, Oxford, 1966, p. 132, n. 135).

It is noticeable that the fourth commandment, 'remember the sabbath day to keep it holy!' (Exod. 20: 8) in this short form, without the following detailed explanation (20: 9f.) does not indicate how the day is to be observed, in what the remembering or keeping (Deut. 5: 12) consists. Accordingly the version in the Decalogue presupposes an older formulation, which is most probably preserved in the law in Exod. 34: 21 (and similarly 23: 12): 'six days shall you work, but on the seventh day you shall rest.'

Just as the second commandment originally gave no reason for the prohibition of the portrayal of God the demand for an interruption of work was also made at first without explanation. It is not possible therefore to look for a motive, if later considerations are not to be brought in. Perhaps the interruption of work may not even *a priori* be understood as an exemption of this day from human profit making. The many sorts of taboos which are familiar from the history of religion are not based on the rejection of a practical concern for usefulness; they are valid simply as such, and are preserved therefore in an altered situation. ' "Thou shalt" – what one should do is a secondary issue; why one should do it is not a question at all' (G. van der Leeuw, *Religion in Essence and Manifestation*, London, 1938, p. 49).

The sabbath is not primarily a feast; for the fourth commandment is not (at least originally) directed towards the observance of cultic occasions at particular places, but holds good outside pilgrimage areas too for ordinary life at all periods. Neither priest nor altar is necessary to observe the seventh day rest. For this reason the sabbath is not mentioned in the various calendar of feasts (Deut. 16; Lev. 23). Nor does the Decalogue appoint any feast days. The sabbath becomes however even at an early date a day 'for Yahweh', a time which is to be 'hallowed' (Exod. 20: 10, 8; 31: 14f.), that is, it is associated with the God of Israel and dedicated to him, because it belongs to him. So a form of worship is connected with the day of rest (cf. Hos. 2: 11 [Heb. 2: 13]; Isa. 1: 13); later sacrifices are ordained (Ezek. 46: 4f.; Num. 28: 9f.; Neh. 10: 31 [Heb. 10: 32]). In this way the rest from labour becomes a confession of faith.

This process of reinterpretation of the day as a feast day is already presupposed by the sabbath commandment of the Decalogue. In its more general form 'remember (or keep) the sabbath day...!' it may include particular cultic actions as well as the command to rest, and allow for the later intensification of the keeping of the sabbath.

On the pattern of a rest on every seventh day, Israel knew at least as a demand made upon it a rest each seventh year (Exod. 23: 10f.; cf. Neh. 10: 31 [Heb. 10: 32]). For this institution of a sabbath year too no real parallel is known either from the nomadic period or from the lands of civilization, from which this usage could be derived. After six years of sowing and harvest the whole arable land is to remain untilled and be left untouched. This should be understood as originally neither an attempt to raise the return (a fallow period for the land to recover) nor as the exclusion of it (a relinquishment of profits). But just as the rest from work is interpreted as a holy day 'for Yahweh', so too the year of release (Lev. 25: 2, 4) is understood as a proclamation 'to recognize the ultimate ownership by God of the land, which he gave to the tribes as a fief of his own free will' (A. Alt, *Kleine Schriften* I, 1953, p. 151).

In Lev. 25 the year of Jubilee is connected with the sabbath year; this is to be proclaimed after seven years of weeks, that is, in each 49th or 50th year. In it property and houses which have been sold are to be restored, and debt-slaves are to be released (cf. older regulations in Exod. 21: 2; Deut. 15; Jer. 32; 34; Ruth 4).

3   The addition 'for Yahweh' is therefore itself an interpretation. The categorical demand for a seventh day of rest also requires however detailed justification; and this is given in different forms in the two versions of the Decalogue. As with the second commandment later explanations come to be appended here too.

Deuteronomy (5: 14f.), which desires to preserve or recover 'rest' for the whole people of God, sees in the sabbath a social measure. The day of rest is available to all who belong to the family, even to the slave or household animals: 'Remember that you were a slave in the land of Egypt!' As the annual feasts come to have a setting in history (below, §9b), so here the sabbath is connected with the Exodus, the deliverance from slavery. Similarly the sabbath year is to be of benefit to the poor and the debtors of the nation (Exod. 23: 10ff.; Deut. 15).

The other explanation of the sabbath commandment (Exod. 20: 11; 31: 17) refers to the mention of God's rest after the creation:

for in six days Yahweh made heaven and earth, the sea, and all that is in them, and rested the seventh day.

The creation narrative, according to which God blesses the seventh day (Gen. 2: 2f.P) already attempts to give a motive for the observance of the sabbath. The word sabbath does not occur, and there is no order to observe the day. There is no idea therefore of a divine 'order of creation', with an alternation of work and rest. The rest is, rather like the creation, God's action alone, and it at most anticipates exemplarily what man later (cf. Exod. 16) follows by doing. What underlies this explanation of the sabbath from creation rather than from history, which is so unusual for the Old Testament? The alteration is understandable from the time at which the Priestly work was written: the exile marked an end to the primeval promises of possession of the land, of the temple and the covenant with David, so that commandments can no longer be connected with a historical event. So a connection is made not with a particular event, but with the history of the world at the beginning.

4   The exile brought a decisive change in the understanding of the sabbath: since the sacrificial cult was impossible for the deportees in exile, those customs in the Yahwistic faith which could also be practised at a distance from the temple acquired increased significance. The observance of the sabbath was raised to the level of a confessional indicator. Like circumcision (Gen. 17: 10–13P) the sabbath is seen as an 'eternal covenant', as God's permanently valid promise and obligation, and as a sign that indicates the unity of God and nation, and at the same time gives an assurance of it (Exod. 31: 13–17P; Ezek. 20: 12, 20).

This increasing significance of the sabbath law is matched in the course of history by an intensification of its demand. The bitter quotation of Amos 8: 5 already indicates that the break in work included trade as well; a command first attested in a stratum of P (Exod. 35: 3) prohibits the kindling of fire and the gathering of wood. In the late period we see an ever more precise and strict insistence on the sabbath rest (31: 14f.; Num. 15: 32ff.; Jer. 17: 21ff; Isa. 56: 2, 6; 58: 13f.; Neh. 13: 15ff.), while on the other hand the Christian Church proclaims the freedom of mankind from the sabbath commandment (Mark 2: 27f.).

II THE EARLY PERIOD AFTER THE CONQUEST

Having the great traditions of the nomadic period, the promise to the patriarchs, the Exodus from Egypt and the revelation at Sinai, the individual groups began their journey into the promised land. They will also have been familiar with particular ordinances for life, or legal rules, as well as the usages governing the practice of circumcision, observing the Passover and keeping the sabbath. Perhaps even before the settlement in Palestine they gathered around the tent or the Ark for religious observances. Finally the immigrants brought with them from the past a will for freedom, which in extreme difficulties gives rise to the holy war. But their decisive inheritance was the Yahwistic faith, connected with those pressures which led to the formulation of the first and second commandments; for it was this which led the different groups in the land itself to grow together into a nation. 'Historically, the people of Israel came into existence because their tribes united in the worship of the god Yahweh' (A. Alt, *Essays on Old Testament History and Religion,* Oxford, 1966, p. 3). Perhaps this unity is made easier, or even made possible at all, by the similarity of the traditions of the patriarchs and of the Exodus, since both tell of a God who protects his worshippers and leads them into the future. Certainly the consciousness of community and of kinship was substantially produced by the exclusive commitment to Yahweh, which formed and preserved the distinctive character of Israel. The self-understanding of the nation depends on its faith in this God.

To express it in the well-known words of Wellhausen, 'Yahweh the God of Israel, and Israel the people of Yahweh: this is the beginning and the lasting principle of the following political and religious history. Before Israel was, Yahweh was not; on the other hand the prophets are justified in saying that it was Yahweh who begat and gave birth to Israel. The two were bound to one another as indissolubly as body and soul. The life of Israel was the life of Yahweh' (*Israelitische und jüdische Geschichte,* 9th edn., Berlin, 1958, p. 23).

1   Since Israel as an entity first came into existence in Palestine, the land was not conquered in one single great campaign under Joshua, in spite of the picture given in the Book of Joshua. Probably the individual groups and tribes settled only gradually and successively in the hill country; they came from different directions, and in the course of a substantial period of time. Not only did their territory not include the whole land; it was not even a connected area. The coast, the plains and various city states remained for a long time in the possession of the Canaanites. The native population did not at that time have a uniform political organization; the land was divided up into numerous different units. The two empires

which in opposition to each other or together had dominated Palestine, were either weakened in power (Egypt in the south) or had collapsed altogether (the Hittites in the north). The statements of Judg. 1, (esp. vv. 27ff.) still represent the entry as an undertaking of the individual tribes, which in each case struggled with the natives for their own territory; there is no mention of a leader figure who is responsible for all the campaigns. So we read in summary of the house of Judah:

And Yahweh was with Judah, and he took possession of the hill country, but he could not drive out the inhabitants of the plain, because they had chariots of iron. (v. 19; cf. v. 21; Josh. 15: 63; 16: 10; 17: 11ff.)

Similarly the tribe of Benjamin did not succeed in taking Jerusalem from the Jebusites (Judg. 1: 21; cf. below, §13, 1); this was reserved for David centuries later. The entry as a whole had therefore more a peaceful than a warlike character, though with particular exceptions. Archaeology has shown for the period about 1200 BC many new settlements of previously abandoned sites or refoundations, but not violent destructions carried out by the invading Israelites. Jericho and Ai (Josh. 6–8), according to the excavations, had for a long time not been properly settled at the time of the entry. The high level of culture in Palestine had declined with the end of the middle Bronze Age, while Israel entered the land at the cultural change from the Bronze Age to the Iron Age.

2   If this picture is in general correct, the new tribes did not at the outset live in close contact with the native inhabitants, but at first maintained a measure of independence.

On another understanding an alteration in the Canaanite class system was an element in the origins of Israel, that is, some autochthonous groups also joined Israel.

The transition from nomadic to agricultural life-style removed a contrast between Israelites and Canaanites, and so made contact easier. In the course of time the physical division between Israel in the hill country and the Canaanite city-states also declined, so that there came to be closer contact with the culture of the cities (cf. Josh. 9).

In places an attempt was made to create a symbiosis between Israel and Canaan. Abimelech hoped to unite under his lordship the city state of Shechem and the tribe of Manasseh, but came to grief on the conflict between the two (Judg. 9; cf. already Gen. 34). In the Canaanite city of Gibeon there was an Israelite sanctuary at the time of Solomon (Josh. 9; 1 Kgs. 3), and the temple at Shiloh (1 Sam. 1ff.) must originally have been a Canaanite cultic site.

The closer the juxtaposition of the two peoples was, the stronger were the contacts in religion too. Israel took to a new style of life. It took over Canaanite local sanctuaries and their cultic usages. The same forms of sacrifices with which the Canaanites had honoured their gods, were offered at the same sites, and the same harvest festivals were observed. The transition to agriculture brought with it a gradual change in the economic and social structure; an association of tribes turned into a village society, and later into a yet more sharply stratified city class structure. Probably the immigrants changed their language too; they abandoned their Aramaic or a related dialect (above, §3c, 3 and 6a, 2 and 4) and took over the language of the land – Hebrew. Language in particular creates common links. It is in detail difficult to delimit how far the influence of the Canaanites went. The contacts were varied in kind and took different forms in different places.

Assimilation and syncretism undoubtedly also occurred. Were not the gods of the land directly responsible for agriculture? So a danger arose that not only would the people take possession of the land, but the land would take possession of the people; but Israel did not succumb to it entirely. It was not simply absorbed in the new culture, as was the fate of many ancient Near Eastern peoples who merged with the native population. Apparently opposition to the Canaanites also grew with time. After the entry into the land the foreign religious influence was stronger according to many indications, but in the long run it was less the unity than the difference, indeed the opposition, that was felt. There was conflict as well as borrowing, in which Israel came to recognize its own distinctive character or realized its possibilities. Finally the external threat actually drew the nation together internally.

The relations between Israel and Canaan in the early period of the judges cannot be distinguished from the relations in the time of the monarchy so as to show significant differences in real terms. In many respects we just see more clearly in the later period what was happening in much the same form earlier. So the encounter between Canaanite religion and Yahwistic faith is here only surveyed when the traditions of Jerusalem too can be brought into the picture. Reference must be made at first just to the most important religio-historical phenomena of the early period.

§7   The 'Wars of Yahweh'

There was a group in Israel strictly faithful to Yahweh which either never gave up the nomadic way of life, or at a later period took it up again in contrast to the life of the settled land. The Rechabites rejected fixed settlements, agriculture and viticulture (Jer. 35: 6f.), and so reminded Israel of its nomadic origins. But settled Israel too has not forgotten its past; this remained a lively memory and set off new life situations.

1   This impetus left a strong effect on the so-called holy wars of the period of the judges. The tradition comes with a high degree of probability from the early nomadic period, but first received its fixed form in the land.

(a) The Old Testament still preserves a recollection of wars which Yahweh conducted on behalf of Israel in the time before the settlement in Palestine (Exod. 14f.; 17: 8ff.). The group which sojourned in Egypt must have given thanks for its deliverance to the helping intervention of Yahweh (above, §4b). So the experiences which the ancestors had with Yahweh are repeated in the land; in spite of all the changes there is a measure of continuity.

(b) Ancient Near Eastern parallels for the form in which Israel carried out these wars are known above all from Assyria (see M. Weippert ' "Heiliger Krieg" in Israel und Assyrien', *ZAW* 84 (1972)). It is often reported that gods join in battle on behalf of their nation, and the victors owed their success to their god. Rameses III assigns all power to his God Amun-Re alone: 'You make the victory of the land of Egypt, your own land, without the hand of a soldier or of any man being involved, but only your great strength, which delivers it' (S. Morenz, *Gott und Mensch im alten Ägypten*, Leipzig, 1964, cf. pp. 18, 66).
The inscription of King Mesha of Moab (*c.* 840 BC) is nearest to the Old Testament accounts. The king at the bidding of his god Chemosh conducts war against Israel, achieves victory, puts everything living including women and children under a ban, and dedicates the conquered cultic equipment to his god. Certain exaggerations in detail serve to increase his own fame and to terrify the enemy: 'the people of Gad had lived in the land of Atarot from eternity, and the King of Israel had built Atarot for himself. I attacked the city and took it. I killed all the people of the city for a feast for the eyes (?) for Chemosh and Moab.... And Chemosh said to me: Go, take Nebo (in battle) from Israel! Then I went by night and fought against them from break of day to midday. I conquered them and killed all: seven thousand men, boys, women, girls and female slaves, because I had dedicated them to Ashtar-Chemosh. I took from there the vessels of Yahweh and dragged them before Chemosh' (*KAI* No. 181; *NERT*, pp. 238f.; *ANET*, pp. 320f.). As in Israel the divine command stands at the beginning and the surrender of the booty to God at the end of the war. Can the common features be explained from the same nomadic past (cf. Judg. 11: 24)?

The Moabites had settled east of the Dead Sea under similar circumstances to the Israelites, but at an earlier date.

(c) Finally this thesis is supported from an apparently remote parallel. In the ancient Near East the Assyrians were notorious for the cruel wars of conquest with which they subordinated to their god Ashur both neighbouring and more distant lands. W. von Soden has argued for the view that the real hardening of the Assyrian conduct of war took place precisely in the wars against the Aramaeans (*Iraq* 25 (1963), p. 137). This connection too suggests that this particular manner of fighting was not a general oriental one (so M. Weippert, ' "Heiliger Krieg" '), but was a heritage of former nomadic peoples. The struggle for life is more merciless on the edge of the wilderness (cf. the saying of Cain, 'whoever finds me will slay me' (Gen. 4: 14, 23f.))

If the name Israel means 'god fights or battles' (cf. Gen. 32: 28 [Heb. 32: 29]; Hos. 12: 3 [Heb. 12: 4]) – although other translations such as 'God reigns' are also possible – this is another indication that the war tradition goes back to an early period.

2   Israel first experienced the fact that 'Yahweh is a man of war' (Exod. 15: 3; cf. Isa. 42: 13) in Palestine. The 'wars of Yahweh' (Num. 21: 14f.; 1 Sam. 18: 17; 25: 28; cf. Exod. 17: 16) were essentially carried out in the period between the entry and the rise of the monarchy. Then the ancient form of fighting gradually fell into disuse, because the professional army of mercenaries appeared in place of the levy of the whole nation, and the permanent institution of the ruler replaced the *ad hoc* call of the leader of the army. The most trustworthy attestation of it from the period of the judges is the Song of Deborah (Judg. 5), which tells of a battle against a coalition of Canaanite city-states. It praises the tribes which were prepared to go to war, and reproaches those who stayed at home, who could have taken part. Just as here only ten tribes are mentioned in all (without the southern tribes of Judah and Simeon), so in other wars of Yahweh only particular tribes appear, not all Israel. In response to the attacks of hostile neighbours the directly affected and neighbouring tribes joined together on each occasion under the direction of a spirit-endowed leader. So Gideon marched against the plundering Midianites (Judg. 6f.), or Jephthah against the Ammonites (Judg. 11). These 'major judges' accordingly had only a limited sphere of activity both in space and in time; they only led particular tribes in a single military action (1 Sam. 11).

It remains dubious how far the basic elements of the institution of the holy war can be reconstructed from the scattered individual accounts of a later period. The only historically trustworthy facts seem to be that at a time of oppression by enemies Yahweh raises up a deliverer by the gift of the spirit, who calls the surrounding tribes to the levy (Judg. 6: 34f.; cf. 1 Sam. 11: 6f.) and perhaps in confidence of victory proclaims as the decision of God that 'Yahweh has given the enemy into your hands' (Judg. 3: 27f.; 4: 7, 14; 7: 9, 15 et al.). Finally the booty is at the end made over to Yahweh – by the ban, that is, killing (1 Sam. 15: 3ff.). Apparently it is the words and the demand of the charismatic leader that characterize the impending war as a 'war of Yahweh'. So it is a religious, but not in the strict sense a cultic occasion, if regular performance, a specific place and a specifically appointed priesthood constitute a cult; for these three indicators are here lacking.

3   The tradition of the deliverance from oppression by enemies in the period of the judges had various after-effects upon the Old Testament, which also change the understanding of this war itself. At first it is regarded as a collaboration of God and man: Israel can 'come to the help of Yahweh' (Judg. 5: 23) or exploit the terror imposed by Yahweh upon the enemies (4: 15f.). But the war comes to be seen more and more as exclusively an act of Yahweh, in which Israel only looks on (cf. above, §4b). So on the one hand the distance between God and man increases (they no longer appear alongside or with one another), on the other hand men put their trust more and more completely in God's power alone. The recognition of the transcendence of God means at the same time the acknowledgement of God's power or sole activity, and so the admission of man's own powerlessness: the power of man cannot help. So the work of God and of man can be contrasted:

A king is not saved by his great army;
    a warrior is not delivered by his great strength.
The war horse is a vain hope for victory,
    and by its great might it cannot save.
Behold, the eye of Yahweh is upon who fear him,
    on those who hope in his steadfast love.
                                        (Ps. 33: 16–18; cf. Isa. 7: 4ff.; 30: 15)

Here the fear of God is identified with trust in God's power, which saves the individual.

The prophets too make room for the tradition of the war of Yahweh in their future hopes (Isa. 9: 3), and in doing so alter it in two ways. First the recollection of a salvific intervention of Yahweh can change into an announcement of disaster. The war of defence which Yahweh conducted on behalf of Israel against the nations becomes a war of attack against Israel (Amos 2: 13–16; Isa. 28: 21; 29: 1ff.; Jer. 21: 4ff. et al.; cf. Lam. 2: 4ff.) On the other hand the tradition, in the form of a declaration of salvation for Israel (Isa. 42: 13; 49: 25 et al.) is given universal reference. Because the pictures of war fill out the detail of expectations of the 'day of Yahweh' they are extended to form a judgement on all nations (Joel 2; Zech. 12; 14; cf. Ps. 46: 8ff. [Heb. 46: 9ff.]).

EXCURSUS 3:   THE 'SPIRIT' OF GOD

In the descriptions of theophanies Israel pictures how God's presence can alter nature; in the 'wars of Yahweh' it experiences how God intervenes in the world of history and of politics. It is clear precisely from these 'archetypal' occasions that Israel understands God as a power that is active upon earth.

This power can be manifested in the gift of the spirit. Its occurrence is unpredictable. It does not come to rest permanently upon its bearer, but it 'comes upon' the one called (Judg. 3: 10; 6: 34; 11: 29; 1 Sam. 11: 6 et al,), drives him to actions, and is withdrawn again. It makes a hitherto unknown man into a leader and victor. So the essential nature of the spirit is predominantly not one of lasting presence but of becoming active; it is power because it becomes powerful. It is a movement that puts its recipient in movement.

Did Israel come to know this appearance of the spirit only under Canaanite influence in the cultivated land, or was this phenomenon already familiar to the nomads? It is predominantly restricted to the premonarchical period, but is seen also in one other area. The spirit takes hold of the (early) prophets as well as of the judges, makes groups of them fall into frenzy and ecstasy (1 Sam. 10: 6ff.; 19: 20ff.; cf. 1 Kgs. 18: 12; 2 Kgs. 2: 9ff.; below §14a, 2), or makes them speak (Num. 24: 2f.; later Ezek. 3: 12ff.; 8: 3; 11: 1, 24; Joel 3; Zech. 13). It achieves both the heroic deeds of political history, and also ecstasy and inspiration, it creates both good and evil (1 Sam. 16: 13f.; 1 Kgs. 22: 21f.). The spirit is what makes the hero a hero and the prophet a prophet; the spirit equips a man for action by changing him: 'you will be turned into another man' (1 Sam. 10: 6). The spirit does not create here a mystical unity of God and man, but is experienced by man as different in that it 'comes upon' him and equips him for action. Perhaps in some sayings echoes are still heard of nature-based concepts of an impersonal power of the spirit, but fundamentally the gift of the spirit is a way in which God becomes active in man in the world, though no longer directly but through an intermediary. Because God's power on earth becomes present through it, spirit can be used occasionally in contrast to 'flesh' to express the distinction between God and man as one of power and weakness (Isa. 31: 3).

The basic meaning of the word (ru^ah) however indicates how little 'spirit' is thought of in terms of a contrast to body or nature, and how little it is either a higher principle or a form of self-awareness. It means (perhaps originally onomatopoeically) breathing or blowing. From this the transition on the one hand to breath, wind, storm, and on the other to mind or intellect can be understood. This complexity of meaning starts from an activity or movement, and can therefore bind together the physical and the mental. Just as here the internal and the external, the essential nature and the activity, are thought of as a unity, so in the event of the spirit God's being is understood as action. The spirit can bring about both the unusual, the miraculous, and also 'natural' life in its daily manifestations. The essential nature of the spirit is then its continuity, not the special once-for-all event, but permanent activity (Ps. 51: 10–12 [Heb. 12– 14]). This group of ideas is based on a completely different concept, which does not originally go together with the experience of the spirit which singles out particular men rather than others. Ancient Near Eastern parallels speak of the breath of life; similarly the spirit of the Old Testament is the power which gives and renews life. Its removal means death:

When thou hidest thy face, they are dismayed;
   when thou takest away their breath, they die
   and return to their dust.
When thou sendest forth thy spirit, they are created.

(Ps. 104: 29f.; cf. 33: 6)

The spirit of God has made me,
   and the breath of the Almighty gives me life.

(Job 33: 4; cf. 34: 14f.; Ezek. 37: 9ff.)

Man is not in control of the spirit as the power of life; this makes him experience his dependence. Man does not 'have' what makes his life possible. In what really constitutes his life he is outside his own control.

Finally in the hope of the prophets the once-for-all gift of the spirit becomes a lasting possession. It is given to particular individuals, the Messiah (Isa. 11), the servant of God (Isa. 42), or all men (Ezek. 36: 26f.; Isa. 44: 3; Joel 2: 28–32 [Heb. 3]). However the spirit is understood, as occasional or permanent, as special or general, in each case it gives the capacity to do something, and is what makes achievement of it possible.

§8 The Tribal Confederacy

1 In the early period God, people and land seem to form a unity. Yahweh is the 'God of Israel' (Judg. 5: 3, 5 et al.) as conversely Israel is called 'the people of God' (5: 11, 13 et al.). Israel's enemies are 'the enemies of Yahweh' (5: 31; Num. 10: 35); an attack on the nation and the land affects Yahweh himself (so still Joel 3: 2f. [Heb. 4: 2f.]). He conducts Israel's wars and so takes the part of one side, just as the god Chemosh cares for his worshippers, 'the people of Chemosh' (Num. 21: 29), that is the Moabites, and drives away their enemies (Judg. 11: 23f.).

A national religion seems to be the mark of a particular cultural stage, in which faith is not the decision of an individual, but God is a God of the people. But this is not itself a matter of course: 'the concept of the people, which is central for the thinking of the Israelites, is not a concept known in Babylonia. Men were distinguished primarily by the lands from which they came or by social groups' (W. von Soden). The worship of god or gods takes place within the borders of the people or land, though frequently with a more extensive claim. The inhabitants of the land may be simply called 'the men', and the actual sanctuary is regarded as the centre of the earth. So Delphi claims to be the 'navel of the earth', just as the Greeks called all foreigners barbarians. Examples of this are attested in the ancient Near East.

Occasionally the concept of the navel of the earth is attested in the Old Testament too (Judg. 9: 37 of Gerizim; Ezek. 38: 12 of the land of Judah or of Jerusalem). Zion in particular in the late period attracted the myth of the centre of the world (cf. below, §13:, 4). But the idea that only Israel is essentially and properly entitled to the name 'man' is unknown to the Old Testament. It made its own distinction between itself and others (Num. 23: 9 et al.).

An ancient seeming, or at least unusual tradition is preserved by the so-called 'song of Moses', the dating of which is much disputed:

When Elyon (the Most High) gave to the nations their inheritance,
    when he separated the sons of men,
he fixed the bounds of the peoples
    according to the number of the sons of 'El' (God).
For Yahweh's portion is his people,
    Jacob his allotted heritage. (Deut. 32: 8f.)

Taken literally these verses tell us in a highly mythological form that El Elyon (who is known from Gen. 14: 18ff. as the city god of Jerusalem) divides up mankind into nations, fixes their frontiers and assigns the individual peoples to the 'sons of El'. The scene implies a form of universalism. The ruler of the whole world divides up his realm. Each deity of the pantheon has a nation assigned to him, which worships him. In this primeval act Yahweh receives Israel as his portion. Does the text preserve the memory of a time in which the God of Israel is still subordinate to the deity (El) Elyon? But the Old Testament equates Yahweh and Elyon here as it does elsewhere, understanding Elyon only as an epithet 'the highest', and reduces the sons of El to heavenly beings whose status is that of loyal servants. In this way the passage acquires a new sense: while Yahweh as the highest God assigns the nations to the 'sons of gods', he reserves Israel for himself as his property. So the saying becomes an instance of a universalism in the Yahwistic faith. The area of dominion of the gods is attributed to an act of Yahweh, and they and their nations are ultimately subordinate to him (Ps. 82: 8). This indirect world dominion of Yahweh is matched by a direct election of Israel. The mythological scene in heaven explains the difference between Israel and the other nations. Israel's election (below Excursus 5) indicates the privilege of directly belonging to Yahweh, but does not suggest a disparagement of the nations. Particularism and universalism are not exclusive contrasts in the Old Testament, but are thought of together (Gen. 12: 3; Amos 3: 2 et al.) But the form of the relationship is being thought out constantly anew in the history of Israel. The tendency towards universalism grows with time (below, IV, 2; §17, 5), but never triumphs completely. A measure of particularism is inevitably given through the first and second commandments. They form the basis for the choice of Israel (cf. Deut. 6: 4), exclude rites and customs of foreign religions (Deut. 10: 12ff.; 14; Lev. 11: 43ff.; 19; Ezek. 20: 5 et al.) and make election without obligation unthinkable. So God remains at the same time a God of the nation.

2   Even in the early period the covenant with God which sets out the relation of fidelity between Yahweh and Israel, and the covenant which unites the tribes together, are not simply identical. In fact the term 'covenant' is not even used for the tribal confederacy, and the Old Testament does not have another term for it either. In external oppression the threatened tribe or the leader of the levy calls on the tribes living near for help (Judg. 6: 35 et al.). 'This cry for help to the neighbour . . . and the results achieved by it are the most unquestionable, the most essential, and the most vital manifestation of Israelite unity which is known to us from that time' (R. Smend, *Yahweh War and Tribal Confederation*, Nashville, Tenn., 1970, p. 21). But beyond these individual actions was there anything which permanently united all the tribes which worshipped Yahweh, in times of peace too? If Israel was not yet a political unity, perhaps there was another comprehensive organization in which the community of faith was expressed. But there is no direct attestation of any permanent institution which formed the basis for the linking of the Israelite tribes together and preserved it; the Book of Judges portrays the early history of Israel as a situation of unregulated complexity.

The existence of an early tribal organization has been deduced from the combination of different and independent themes. The starting point was the striking persistence of the number twelve for the tribes, which persists although the individual constituents change (Gen. 29: 31ff.; 49; Deut. 33 et al.). Within the twelve sons of Jacob–Israel, the personification of the tribes (sons of Leah, Reuben, Simeon, Levi, Judah, Issachar, Zebulun; sons of Rachel, Joseph and Benjamin; sons of Rachel's handmaid Bilhah, Dan and Naphtali; sons of Leah's handmaid Zilpah, Gad and Asher) it is especially Levi that is missing in later forms of the lists (e.g. Num. 1: 26). The number twelve is then maintained by dividing up Joseph into Ephraim and Manasseh, who are regarded as grandchildren of Jacob–Israel. How far is the number twelve just a symbol (of the completeness of the whole), how far does some reality underlie it? The number twelve cannot be derived from the period of the monarchy, when the tribal structure came to lose its importance (cf. the division into districts in 1 Kgs. 4: 7ff.).

On the evidence of the Old Testament the number twelve is attested not only in Israel, but also among its neighbours: among the Aramaeans (Gen. 22: 20–4), Edomites (36: 10–14) and Ishmaelites (25: 13–16), and it is found also in completely separate areas, as in Greece and among the Etruscans in Italy. There the tribes met for the common worship of a god around a central sanctuary, for instance, that of Apollo at Delphi. Was Yahweh in a similar way a covenant God of such a sacral community, of an 'amphictyony' (M. Noth, *Das System der zwölf Stamme Israels*, 1930)? In that case people and state of Israel would be secondary phenomena by comparison with this cultic federation. The existence of such an amphictyony is still however a disputed question, since it is not attested directly; and in the early period Israel did not have a central sanctuary common to all the tribes (below §9a). It is also disputed how closely the southern tribes, especially Judah, were linked in the pre-Davidic period with Israel, which had its centre in central Palestine (Gen. 33: 20 et al.). No historical connection with the sacral confederacies of Greece can be traced. Or are there connections by way of Asia Minor, where the Kashkeans formed a twelve-tribe group?

Until recently the period from the entry until the formation of the state was portrayed as a history of the sacral institutions. But various doubts have been cast upon this picture. The 'amphictyony' cannot any longer be simply understood as the transmitter of the various traditions from the early period. A return has therefore been made fundamentally to an older less unified picture, and the questions which the hypothesis of the amphictyony sought to answer are open again: 'What does Israel originally mean? How can the number twelve for the tribes, which goes back to the early period, be better explained?' Some consciousness of belonging together, which finally led to the inauguration of the monarchy, must have appeared already at an earlier date.

An offence was called 'folly in Israel' (Gen. 34: 7; Judg. 20: 6; cf. 2 Sam. 13: 12 et al.). It is possible that the 'judges in Israel' (cf. the lists in Judg. 10: 1–5; 12: 7–15; also 4: 4f.; 1 Sam. 7: 16f.) held an office in pre-monarchical Israel.

It remains uncertain however whether there was an enduring unity, going beyond the solidarity that appeared at times of crisis, and consisting of all and not only particular tribes, and what form the reality of this association took.

Israel came to be the group name for the twelve tribes. But at an older period there seems to have been another smaller Israel already. The stele of Pharaoh Merenptah or Merneptah (c.1220 BC) tells of a destruction of Israel, which cannot refer to the twelve-tribe confederacy: '(the people of) Israel lies fallow and has no seedcorn' (*ANET*, p. 378; *DOTT*, p. 139).

The division of the twelve tribes or sons among the mothers too is not just a colourful narrative trait, but reflects old connections. In particular the connection of Reuben, Simeon, and probably also Levi, which by contrast to their later significance stand at the head of the twelve tribe group, seems to reflect a common history in central Palestine (cf. Gen. 34; 49: 5–7; also Josh. 15: 6 et al.). Possibly before the immigration of the Rachel tribes, among whom the tradition of the stay in Egypt seems originally to have been at home (above §4) there was a six-tribe confederacy of tribes of Leah, which did not worship the God Yahweh, but as the name Israel suggests, the God El (cf. the name of the altar at Shechem 'El the God of Israel', Gen. 33: 20).

3   According to the account of Josh. 24 Israel as a whole seems not yet to have worshipped Yahweh, or not in the right way, as was presupposed by the tradition of Exodus and of the Sinai revelation. It has been conjectured that the 'assembly at Shechem' was the event at which the tribes bound themselves to one another in the worship of Yahweh. Joshua calls 'all the tribes of Israel' to Shechem 'before God', and demands of them a decision, to choose Yahweh, or foreign gods. Who are these 'other gods', the gods of the land or of the foreign empires (above §3, 1)? After the agreement of the people Joshua makes the covenant (cf. 2 Kgs. 23: 3 et al.), stipulates the statutes and law, and erects a stone as a witness. The whole chapter is strongly theological, and constructed under the influence of the later understanding of faith, in order to set out the obligation of the nation to obedience. The question is whether we have here an account of a historical event at all.

The attempt has often been made to separate a later redaction from an old tradition. But this cannot be done convincingly without destroying the whole. The basic sequence of events (esp. vv. 1, 25–7) seems to be older than the speeches (vv. 2–24). But the events, which also are related only in the later (Deuteronomistic) style, presuppose the speech section, and it is in this that the heart of the narrative lies: 'I and my house wish to serve Yahweh' (vv. 14f.). There are no compelling reasons to separate these central sentences as the oldest material from the whole context; for they seem late in style as well as in content. Certain indications, like the strange detail about the worship of foreign gods, and perhaps too the proclamation of the law in Shechem, do suggest an older tradition. It is peculiar however that this place plays a significant part in demonstrably later passages (Deut. 11: 29f.; 27; Josh. 8: 30ff.). The historical basis of Josh. 24 cannot therefore be clearly determined. It is therefore better for the sake of caution to give no great significance to this passage in the reconstruction of the early history of Israel. (To this extent the situation is similar to that in the account of the covenant making in Exod. 34, above, §5c).

4   The structure of Josh. 24 and of other Old Testament passages which picture the covenant between God and nation seems however to have striking parallels in the structure of ancient Near Eastern international treaties. In particular the

treaties which the Hittite king made with his vassals suggest that the two forms should be compared. After the introduction of the great king ('thus says' with name and descent) there follow in a not completely fixed pattern an account of the earlier history of the relationships between the Hittite empire and its allies, the basic and particular terms of the mutual relationship of fidelity, sometimes a clause about the preservation of the treaty and its reading aloud, an appeal to the gods as witnesses, and curse and blessing. However the structure of the Old Testament passages is only similar, never completely identical; important elements are always missing. Josh. 24 shows particularly close connections, but does not contain blessing or curse, while the treaties on their side do not tell of the actual making of the treaty itself. The significant sequence of historical account and lawgiving follows from the situation itself; for a legal ordinance needs an explanation which only history can give.

There are historical objections too to a dependence of the Old Testament 'covenant formulary' upon Hittite treaties. The Hittites live only on the margin of the ancient Near East, in the centuries before Israel's entry into the land. After the fall of the empire the small states of north Syria, which had lain previously in its area of influence, maintained the Hittite culture. But it is the treaties that are preserved from just this area, which joins together Asia Minor and Palestine, those of Sefire, that do not have the same strict form. It was generally customary in the ancient Near East to place treaties under divine protection, so that the deity punished transgressions of them in accordance with the curse uttered in them. Finally the treaties do in fact regulate the relationship between kings and states, and in consequence have a different content, while 'a treaty between a god and his people is hitherto unattested from outside the Old Testament' (F. Nötscher, 'Bundesformular und "Amtsschimmel" ', *BZ* 9 (1965), p. 191).

This fact is important in another respect too. According to Judg. 8: 33; 9: 4 a Ba'al Berith, 'lord of the covenant' (as protective god or guarantor of an alliance?) was worshipped in Shechem. While the text says that Israel fell away from Yahweh to this deity, the contrary case has been conjectured, that Israel took over from the population of Shechem the custom of making a covenant – perhaps even in the form of state treaties. First, however, the tradition is not uniform about the name of this God: he is also called El Berith (Judg. 9: 46), although El and Ba'al are different deities (below, §10). Secondly the linking of God and man by a covenant does not fit well with what is otherwise known of ancient Near Eastern, especially Canaanite, religion, while the word 'covenant' is not attested in this connection in the west Semitic lands. It remains very dubious whether Israel borrowed the idea that God makes a covenant with men from the Canaanites, or more generally from the ancient Near East.

In any case the earliest Old Testament tradition of the Sinai event cannot be explained from the form of the national treaties. The characteristic structure arises through the subsequent conjunction of originally independent sections (both in the Sinai pericope Exod. 19–24 and in Deuteronomy), or from secondary redaction (Josh. 24). Influence of the treaty style upon the Old Testament covenant forms therefore occurred only at a later period, if at all. Possibly Israel concluded similar national treaties during the period of dependence upon the Assyrian empire. At this period the relationship with God could have been interpreted from the concept of treaty, and so in a certain measure been given a legal understanding. At least the contacts we know, especially in the curses (Deut. 28 et al.), could be explained this way. Apparently the end of the monarchical period, coupled with Deuteronomy, brought about a radical change in the theological thought of Israel.

EXCURSUS 4: 'COVENANT'

1   The word covenant does not completely render the corresponding Old Testament term (*berīth*). It signifies usually not an agreement of equal partners, who grant each other mutually determined rights and duties, nor a testament as the statement of one's last will, but a fixed formal assurance, a promise or a commitment (A. Jepsen, 'Berith', in A. Kuschke (ed.), *Verbannung und Heimkehr*, Tübingen, 1961; E. Kutsch, *Verheissung und Gesetz*, Berlin, 1972). So the covenant is comparable with an oath (Ps. 89: 3 [Heb. 89: 4]; 105: 9; Josh. 9: 15; cf. Gen. 21: 27, 31f.; 26: 28; Ezek. 17: 18f. et al.). In an archaic rite also attested in the ancient Near East, when a covenant is concluded animals may be divided up, and it is perhaps for this reason that the Old Testament speaks of cutting a covenant rather than concluding one. (The basic meaning is however sharply disputed; according to Kutsch it is to 'establish an obligation'). The one who guarantees the covenant goes between the two halves of the animal and so takes a curse upon himself: if he does not act in accordance with his word, he is to experience the same fate as the animals (Gen. 15: 9f.; Jer. 34: 18).

2   In schematic form we can distinguish three types of relationship between the partners.

A covenant is primarily an assurance which the stronger makes to the weaker, the higher to the subordinate (this is a self-obligation). Joshua gives the Gibeonites, who humiliate themselves and become servants, a guarantee to leave them alive, and so makes peace with them (Josh. 9: 6–15; cf. on the other hand 1 Sam. 11: 1f.). The covenant is ratified by a meal (Josh. 9: 14; cf. Gen. 31: 46, 54; 26: 30) and has after-effects for centuries (2 Sam. 21: 1ff.). The agreement to release the slaves is an obligation which king and nation undertake, but break (Jer. 34: 8ff.; cf. Hos. 10: 4). Finally David, after he had become king over Judah, (2 Sam. 2: 4) is made king of Israel too by a covenant 'before Yahweh' (cf. 2 Kgs. 23: 3); that is, he gave perhaps a promise to the elders of Israel to care for prosperity and peace, and was thereupon anointed as king (2 Sam. 5: 3). David's offer is justified by the already existing fellowship or relationship (cf. 5: 1 with Gen. 2: 23).

There is also the possibility of the more powerful participant laying an obligation upon the subordinate (this is the obligation of another). The king of Jerusalem as vassal has to take an oath of allegiance to the Babylonian king Nebuchadnezzar (Ezek. 17: 12ff.; cf. 1 Kgs. 20: 34 et al.).

Finally a covenant can be concluded as a bilateral treaty between equal partners (a reciprocal obligation) as, for example, between king Hiram of Tyre and Solomon (1 Kgs. 5: 26; cf. 15: 19; Gen. 21: 27, 32; 26: 28, 31; 31: 44 et al.).

Hos. 2: 18 (Heb 2: 20) appears to know of yet another form of covenant making, of mediation through a third party: God compels the animals to peaceful behaviour towards Israel.

3   In the relationship between God and man the third understanding is excluded; the covenant is not a treaty, i.e. not an agreement between equals. God's covenant with Israel is rather a promise which God gives (cf. Gen. 15: 9ff. et al.) and/or an obligation, which God imposes upon man, or which they take upon themselves, being in fellowship with him, and therefore under his protection, (cf. Exod. 19: 5; 24: 7; Josh. 24: 25; 2 Kgs. 23: 3 et al.). In both cases God himself concludes the covenant and so gives the basis to the relationship (cf. Gen. 17: 2, 10, 13f.; Exod. 34: 10, 27 et al.; exceptions include 2 Chr. 29: 10; 2 Kgs. 11: 17; cf. 23: 3 et al.).

It is hotly disputed whether the term 'covenant' was current in Israel at an early date (cf. Gen. 15: 18; Exod. 19: 5; 24: 7f.; 34: 10, 27; Hos. 6: 7; 8: 1) or has only been in use from a later period. Probably it only represents the subsequent reinterpretation of a relationship between God and nation which existed already. The substance of it is therefore substantially older than the actual term. Apart from the Abraham tradition, the Sinai pericope and the promise to David it is found primarily in Deuteronomy and the Deuteronomistic history, and in P. For example Deut. 5.2f. presents the Decalogue as the terms of a covenant which God has concluded with the generation now living, not with the past generation; this interpretation is not known to the Sinai pericope itself. The Sinai story links the Decalogue (Exod. 20) and the covenant (Exod. 19; 24; 34) only very indirectly. It is therefore probable that the concept of covenant has only secondarily been brought into the older tradition, and so is only one possible term among others for the relationship to God. Only this supposition makes it possible to understand why prophets like Amos, Isaiah or Micah (less certainly Hosea) do not refer back to the covenant.

Köhler (*ThR* 7 (1935), pp. 272f.) was already arguing against Eichrodt, who built his *Theology of the Old Testament* upon the concept of the covenant, that 'the concept of the covenant does not have fundamental significance in the prophets. Amos does not know the word at all (1: 9 speaks of the relationship between Tyrians and Edomites); Hosea uses it in two passages (6: 7; 8: 1), but makes nothing significant of it; Isaiah knows nothing of a covenant between God and Israel; Micah does not have the word at all. If however these prophets had read Eichrodt's theology, it would have constantly been heard and alluded to. . . . How can he constantly speak of Yahweh as a god of the covenant, when not one single name given to Yahweh recalls the covenant, but all the usual divine names, and still more all those in frequent use, derive their content from outside the concept of the covenant?'

4   The two basic possibilities of covenant, promise and obligation, do not need to be mutually exclusive. Mal. 2: 5 expressly describes the call of Levi as both gift and task:

My covenant with him was a covenant of life and peace, and I gave them to him, that he might fear; and he feared me.

In various traditions the character of covenant as demand seems even to come out more strongly with time:
The covenant with Abraham (Gen. 15: 9–18; 17P; cf. Exod. 2: 24; 6: 4f.; Lev. 26: 42; Deut. 4: 31; Ps. 105: 9 et al.), the promise of descendants and of land, is primarily an assurance by God, but has a commitment on the part of man as a consequence (Gen. 17: 9ff.).
God promises through the prophets that the dynasty of David will endure for ever (2 Sam. 7, esp. vv. 11f., 16). This relationship between God and David is later interpreted by means of the concept of covenant (2 Sam. 23: 5; Ps. 89: 3f., 28f. [Heb. 89: 4f., 29f.]; cf. Isa. 55: 3; Jer. 33: 21; 2 Chr. 13: 5; 21: 7) and made dependent upon a commitment of the king (Ps. 132: 12; 89: 30–33 [Heb. 89: 31–34]; 1 Kgs. 2: 4; 8: 25, et al.; Isa. 7: 9).
The fellowship granted by God upon Sinai (Exod. 24: 9–11) appears increasingly strongly as a commitment which man takes on (24: 3–8; 34: 10ff.; and the growth of the collections of laws).
So covenant can assume the sense of instruction (cf. 2 Kgs. 22: 8, 11 with 23: 2f.; 17: 15; Ps. 78: 10 et al.), and man is given the task of keeping the covenant, i.e. the commandments (Exod. 19: 5; Deut. 4: 13; Jer. 11: 3f. et al.).

5   Deuteronomy and its school connect covenant closely with the Decalogue (Deut. 4: 13; 5: 2f.); the tables of the law are called tables of the covenant (9: 9) and the place where they are kept, the Ark, is called the Ark of the covenant (10: 8; 31: 25f.; Josh. 3: 3, 6 et al.). The covenant is particularly interpreted by means of the primary commandment of the Decalogue, the demand for exclusiveness, so that the transgression of the first (and second) commandment is regarded as constituting the real breach of the covenant (Deut. 4: 23; 31: 16, 20; Josh. 23: 16; Judg. 2: 19f.; 2 Kgs. 17: 15, 35, 37f. et al.).
Wellhausen introduced the name 'Book of the four covenants' (Q = *liber quattuor foederum*) for the Priestly writing. In fact the course of history is divided by P into four periods (each with a cultic act); creation (Gen. 1: 1–2: 4a; God's rest on the seventh day), Noah (Gen. 9: prohibition of consuming blood and of manslaughter), Abraham (Gen. 17: circumcision) and Sinai (Exod. 16: keeping of the sabbath; Exod. 25ff., cultic laws). But creation and (perhaps in criticism of the tradition (Exod. 24: 3–8; 34: 10ff.)) the revelation at Sinai (24: 15ff.; 40: 33f.) are not represented as covenant; P reserves this term for the promises of God to Noah (Gen. 9 against 8: 21f.J) and Abraham. Certainly the covenant with Abraham is primarily God's declaration, the promise of multiplication and of the gift of the

land, with the goal 'I will be their God' (17: 2–8), but it is not a pure covenant of grace (W. Zimmerli, *Sinaibund und Abrahambund: Gottes Offenbarung*, n.d., p. 205ff.) for the promise begins with 'I am El Shaddai. Walk before me and be blameless' (17: 1; cf. 6: 9; Deut. 18: 13; Ps. 15: 2). This association of first-person address on the part of God and demand is reminiscent of the Decalogue, and in the exhortation to walk aright before God the first Commandment is to be found in another form. Accordingly P, although it does not contain a Decalogue, assigns this a preeminent place. God reveals himself to Abraham as El Shaddai, not as Yahweh (Exod. 6: 2), but the relationship to God is already characterized by exclusiveness.

The prophets, who contest the continuation of the relationship of God and people (Hos. 1: 9 et al.), and so, to put it more strongly, the everlasting character of the covenant (Gen. 17: 7, 13 P; cf. Lev. 26: 40ff.) expect a new covenant, which will itself be everlasting (Jer. 31: 31–34; cf. 32: 40; Ezek. 34: 25; 37: 26; Isa. 55: 3; 61: 8; also 42: 6 et al.).

EXCURSUS 5: ELECTION

Like covenant, election represents only one possible way of thinking of the relationship between God and people – though a possibility which emphasizes that God's action precedes all human action (cf. Jer. 1: 5; Isa. 49: 1, Ps. 139: 16). Election in the Old Testament does not however refer to a decision made before all time, but to a historical action, and therefore does not imply an unalterable condition of 'being chosen'; God reserves the freedom to withdraw the election (of Israel 2 Kgs. 21: 14; of Zion 23: 27 et al.). So man cannot gain election, but can lose it.

In ordinary language 'to elect' (*bāḥar*) means to seek out for oneself, to prefer, or even to desire (Gen. 6: 2). A child learns 'to refuse the evil (that which threatens life) and to choose the good (what is useful)' (Isa. 7: 15). Man can certainly 'choose' God's way (Ps. 25: 12) or life (Deut. 30: 19), but can also choose foreign cults (Isa. 1: 29; 65: 12; 66: 3f.) or gods (Judg. 10: 14); however only once does the term refer to a decision for God: 'choose this day whom you will serve' (Josh. 24: 15, 22).

From the earliest times Israel was conscious of having been delivered and called by its God, before it understood this relationship as God's election. In the older version of the traditions of the patriarchs (cf. Neh. 9: 5), of Exodus and Sinai, the verb is not yet used, and is first found frequently in the Deuteronomic and Deuteronomistic literature, in Deutero-Isaiah and in the Psalter. So the substance is older than the word.

In agreement with ancient Near Eastern ideas the earliest instances in the Old Testament speak of God's 'election' of the king (1 Sam. 10: 24; 16: 8ff.; 2 Sam. 6: 21; 16: 18; cf. Ps 89: 3ff. [Heb. 89: 4ff.]), and this usage is maintained over a long period of time (Deut. 17: 15; Hag. 2: 23; 1 Chr. 28: 4f.).

Just as here selection and commissioning are one, in later texts the installation of priests (Num. 16: 5, 7; 1 Sam. 2: 28) or Levites (Deut. 18: 5 et al.) in office too is regarded as election. However the call of the prophet is never termed 'election' (except that of the servant of God in Isa. 42: 1) Did they not hold an office in the strict sense, or does their call take place unpredictably?

Deuteronomy finds a new basis for and a fresh interpretation of the cult from the viewpoint of election. While Israel celebrated its feasts in older times at the different local sanctuaries, Deuteronomy elevates the one 'place which Yahweh chooses' (12: 5, 11ff.; 14: 23ff.; 16: 2, 6ff. et al.) to be the only place of cultic life in Israel.

Through the reform of King Josiah (621 BC) Jerusalem becomes the one 'chosen' place (1 Kgs. 8: 16, 44, 48 et saep.). It is no doubt on the basis of this profoundly significant historical event, that is, in consequence of Deuteronomy, that Ps. 78: 68ff. and 132: 10ff. (1 Kgs. 8: 16) speak of the election of the king and of Zion, and thus understand monarchy and temple on the basis of the same theological principle.

It is especially the relationship of God to Israel that is rethought by means of the word 'choose'. Again Deuteronomy contains the *locus classicus* of election theology (T. C. Vriezen, *Die Erwählung Israels nach dem Alten Testament*, Zurich, 1953), in giving no sort of discoverable or demonstrable explanation for the preference of Israel over against the nations, and letting it rest on God's love alone:

For you are a people holy to Yahweh your God; Yahweh your God has chosen you to be a people for his own possession, out of all the peoples that are on the face of the earth.

This assurance (cf. Ps. 33: 12; 135: 4) is explained, with a transition now from the second person singular to the plural:

It was not because you were more in number than any other people that Yahweh set his love upon you and chose you, for you were the fewest of all peoples, but it is because Yahweh loves you. . . . (Deut. 7: 6–8)

This expresses really pointedly the relationship between Israel and the others: election does not allow any appeal to a righteousness of one's own (9: 4f.), but because of the exclusiveness of the relationship, includes obligation (14: 1f. et al.).

Israel as 'the fewest of all peoples' (7: 7) has nothing to claim on behalf of itself, and is in itself unworthy. This theme has parallels in narratives of the election of the lowly, be it Gideon (Judg. 6: 15), Saul (1 Sam. 9: 21; 15: 17) or David (16: 1–13); cf. also Mic. 5: 1; Isa. 60: 22.

Probably prophetic preaching already has an influence on the theology of Deuteronomy, having had to take up a critical attitude to the popular belief in the special position of Israel (Amos 3: 2; 9: 7; Mic. 3: 5, 11; Jer. 5: 12; cf. Isa. 63: 16).

Jeremiah threatens Israel with the end of election: 'Refuse silver they are called, for Yahweh has rejected them' (6: 30; 7: 29; 12: 7f.; 14: 19ff.; cf. Deut. 8: 19f.; Lam. 3: 45 et al.). In the time close to the exile election and rejection appear as to have been seen as two equally possible actions of God. While the freedom of God compared with his people is expressed here, the Old Testament soon holds fast again to the superior power of God's love when set over against all the man's questionable actions. God is asked not to reject his people (Deut. 9: 25ff.; 1 Kgs. 8: 57; cf. Lam. 5: 22), and the (ultimate) rejection of Israel is actually denied (Lev. 26: 44; 1 Sam. 12: 22; Jer. 31: 37; Ps. 94: 14 et al.).

In particular the exilic prophet Deutero-Isaiah consoles the exiles, who believe themselves to have been abandoned by God (Isa. 49: 14), with the idea of election (41: 8f.; 44: 1f. et al.) and declares that in spite of the recent execution of judgement the election of Israel continues into the future. As a basis for hope, it is at the same time a commitment: Israel is to appear before the nations as a 'witness' of the uniqueness of God (43: 10, 12; 44: 8; 55: 5).

§9 Sanctuaries and Feasts

a SANCTUARIES

Israel in its early period gathered around various different sanctuaries. Perhaps some groups or tribes at first practised a cult of their own in one place or another, until a common worship of Yahweh was practised everywhere, and drove out all foreign traditions. In any case the unity of all Israel in faith does not seem to have been expressed predominantly, still less exclusively, at one particular place. Just as only the neighbouring tribes joined in the holy war, so the sanctuaries did not take in the tribes as a whole, but only these who lived in the immediate or more distant neighbourhood. Different places had very varying degrees of importance, and the position must have been different in each case. Neither the tent, nor the Ark, nor the local sanctuaries, assured all Israel of the presence of God.

1 The 'tent of meeting' was, as the name itself indicates, a place of worship for tent-dwellers. In fact it is only clearly attested in the wilderness period, and nomadic tribes elsewhere had similar tent sanctuaries. According to the older tradition it was to be found outside the camp, divided from the general living area as a holy place (Exod. 33: 7–11; Num. 11: 16f., 24ff.; 12: 4f., 10; Deut. 31: 14f.); as it was conceived of in late traditions it was the centre around which the camp was arranged. The tent seems to have disappeared at a very early date; the later accounts of its stay in Shiloh (Josh. 18: 1; 1 Sam. 2: 22 et al.) or Gibeon (1 Chr. 16: 39 et al.) are less reliable. Is the tent which David caused to be newly erected in Jerusalem with an altar for the Ark (2 Sam. 6: 17; 7: 2; 1 Kgs. 1: 39, 2: 28ff.; cf. 8: 4) still the old site at which God 'met' men?

Everyone, not only the priest, could question God at this moving sanctuary (Exod. 33: 7); it was therefore apparently an oracle centre and a place of appearances as the same time. This encounter with God was understood in the form of an event: he does not 'dwell' constantly in the tent as he does in the sanctuaries of the settled lands, but comes there when he is sought. Since it is never mentioned together with the Ark in early passages, the two must originally have existed independently of one another (cf. however 2 Sam. 7: 2). It is the later Priestly writing with the tabernacle that makes the tent the shelter for the Ark, in large measure transferring the situation in Jerusalem back into the wilderness period; the temple with the Holy of Holies becomes a combined building, consisting both of tent and of wood, which can be dismantled (Exod. 25ff.). So traditions of tent, of Ark and of temple, that is of nomadic and of cultivated land materials, are fused together: God wishes to 'dwell' in a sanctuary (Exod. 25: 8, as he does in the temple 1 Kgs. 8: 12) and to 'appear' there (Num. 14: 10); he meets men (as in the tent) 'over' the Ark (Exod. 25: 22; 29: 42ff.).

2   The origin, antiquity and significance of the Ark are still strongly disputed. It has even been conjectured that there were different arks; but the Old Testament sources are insufficient to establish this hypothesis. Either the Ark goes back into the wilderness period, and forms the sanctuary of another not yet sedentary group, or the original home of the Ark is to be looked for in the lands of civilization. Both assumptions can be supported by parallels. On the one hand beduin sanctuaries for the conduct of war and the reception of oracles are known from much later times, which are however carried not by men but by camels, or borne upon carts; nor is their form and significance identical with that of the Ark. On the other hand in the lands of cultivation there are similar thrones of God or procession sanctuaries. But they too do not give us a close comparison in every respect. So it is difficult to decide clearly whether the ark was a moving sanctuary or whether, as seems less probable, it was taken over from the Canaanites. It has features from both backgrounds, and this is an argument for suggesting that an originally nomadic understanding has been overlaid by concepts from the lands of cultivation.

In just one attestation in the Pentateuch (Num. 10: 33ff.) the ark appears to be a nomadic war palladium. God is present 'sitting' upon it, and intervenes in battle. The 'ark sayings' address God:

Arise, Yahweh, and let thy enemies be scattered;
(and let them that hate thee flee before thee).
Return (or, come down), Yahweh,
to the ten thousand thousands of Israel.

However these sayings do not mention the Ark itself, so that it may be doubted whether the two belonged together from the beginning: and they do not fit smoothly into the present narrative framework. The introduction does not speak of a departure to fight against enemies, but only of setting out in a change of camp. Originally too the Ark cannot, like, for example, the pillars of cloud and fire, have been understood as a protective leader, which guided the wandering band on its way, and indicated the camp-sites, because it must itself be carried by men or animals, if it is to indicate the way (cf. however 1 Sam. 6: 7ff.).

After the entry the Ark is attested in several localities, but the historical value of our information varies. Only late texts, which harmonize the old traditions, speak of the Ark in Shechem (Josh. 8: 30) and Bethel (Judg. 20: 27f.). In Jericho the Ark was present only briefly during the time Israel passed through (Josh. 3ff.). In these circumstances the assumption of a regular movement of the Ark from one fixed site to another is a hypothesis with no secure historical support. Possibly the Ark was used in Jerusalem as a processional shrine (Ps. 24: 7ff.; 48: 12f. [Heb. 48: 13f.]; 132; below §11a, 6; 13: 3).

The account of the stay in the Ark in the temple at Shiloh is really reliable (in the eleventh century; 1 Sam. 3: 3ff.). So strictly speaking the history of the Ark can only be followed for a short stretch from there to Jerusalem. Since Shiloh was situated in the area of Ephraim, the Ark was perhaps a special sanctuary of this tribe, or more generally of the tribes of Rachel, that is, of the house of Joseph, or also of Benjamin. The so-called Narrative of the Ark (1 Sam. 4–6; 2 Sam. 6) tells explicitly of the loss of the 'Ark of God' to the Philistines and of its return. David brought it (strictly having no legal right to do so) solemnly to Jerusalem (2 Sam. 6: Ps. 132) after the hole-and corner existence which it had had after the loss of the war (1 Sam. 7: 1f.), and so created a continuity between the old days and the new capital. It linked traditions from Shiloh in the north with Jerusalem, and so justified and legitimated this city as a cultic centre. Was it through this action that the ark became the symbol of the presence of God for all Israel? Solomon finally had the Ark brought into the Holy of Holies of the temple, and so withdrew it from public view (1 Kgs. 6: 23–28; 8, below, §13, 3). It was perhaps burnt there in the destruction of the temple by the Babylonians in 587 BC, and was in any case lost then.

In the course of this varied history the Ark came to have some quite different meanings. In the struggle against the Philistines it was brought out as a symbol of the presence of God as a last resort, but its power could not prevent a second defeat. It was also occasionally carried out in war (cf. Num. 14: 44; Josh. 3f.; 6; 1 Sam. 4; 2 Sam. 11: 11; 15: 24ff.), in times of crisis if not regularly; for it is usually not mentioned in connection with the wars of Yahweh. But how is the presence of God conceived? According to the title 'he that sits upon the cherubim', which the God of the Ark bears, the Ark seems to have been regarded as the throne of the invisible God (cf. Ps. 24: 7–10; Jer. 3: 16f.), perhaps as the footstool of the throne (Ps. 99: 5; 132: 7; 1 Chr. 28: 2; Lam. 2: 1; Ezek. 43: 7; Isa. 66: 1) or alternatively as the stand for the throne (M. Metzger *Königsthron und Gottesthron*, forthcoming). This picture of an empty throne of God belongs not to the wilderness but to the cultivated lands.

The title 'he that sits upon the cherubim' very probably only came to be connected with the Ark in the course of history; for it is only according to very late accounts (Exod. 25: 18ff. P) that the Ark bears two cherubim upon its lid. The instances of this divine name come mostly from the Jerusalem cult terminology (Ps. 99: 1; 2 Kgs. 19: 15 et al.). It is natural to connect it with the enormous pair of cherubim which stood with outstretched wings in the Holy of Holies of the temple in Jerusalem and overshadowed the Ark (1 Kgs. 6: 23ff.; 8: 6f.). These mixed creatures, which seem to have been like an upright sphinx, with the head of a man, the body of an animal and wings, are therefore independent of the Ark and serve to protect it. The title 'he that sits upon the cherubim' presupposes a different understanding however, of cherubim as supporters of the throne of God or of God himself; perhaps there is an original connection with the kingship of God (below, §11a). This gives significance to the older occurrences of the title in the time of Shiloh (1 Sam. 4: 4; 2 Sam. 6: 2); they do not need to be a retrojection of the position in Jerusalem to an earlier period. We know in fact very little of the temple at Shiloh, which no doubt was under some Canaanite influence. Was it here that the attribute 'he that sits upon the cherubim' was transferred to the God of the Ark? Probably this is a Canaanite divine epithet, which Israel either took over directly or reinterpreted in dependence upon Canaanite models. In a similar way the formally comparable epithet of the weather God Ba'al 'who rides upon the clouds' (as his war-chariot) was ascribed to Yahweh (Ps. 68: 4, 33 [Heb. 68: 5, 34] et al.). On one occasion the two different concepts of the one who sits upon the cherubim and the traveller upon the clouds are combined in a description of a theophany strongly influenced by foreign religious ideas: 'and he (Yahweh) rode upon a cherub' (Ps. 18: 10 [Heb. 18: 11]).

The position is similar with the much more frequent title 'Yahweh Sabaoth'. It is not found until the book of Judges, and appears for the first time in Shiloh (1 Sam. 1: 3, 11); here the Ark is twice explicitly and emphatically called 'the Ark of Yahweh Sabaoth, who sits upon the cherubim' (1 Sam. 4: 4; 2 Sam. 6: 2). Since however the attribute 'Sabaoth' appears later in independence of the Ark (1 Sam. 15: 2 et al.), and is, especially in the prophetic literature, closely connected with Zion (Isa. 6: 5; Ps. 24: 9f.; 46; 48; 84) the question arises again whether it originated in Shiloh and was transferred from there to Jerusalem, or whether it was retrospectively attributed to Shiloh. Probably it is originally a title, which like 'he that sits upon the cherubim' is associated with the Ark, and which perhaps also is under Canaanite influence. However its foreign origin is less certain, and the decision depends upon the disputed meaning of the name Sabaoth. It undoubtedly contains a statement about the might of Yahweh, so that the Septuagint can with some justification translate the word by *pantokratōr*, all-powerful. Either the confession of the all-powerfulness of Yahweh is to be understood abstractly (Sabaoth = power) or the title is related to the hosts of heaven (so in late texts Ps. 103: 21; 148: 2) or to the levy of Israel (Josh. 5: 14; 1 Sam. 17: 45; I Kgs. 2: 5). In the latter case the term is connected with the holy war, in which the Ark too is from time to time employed. Probably we find traces in the course of time of several interpretations; the meaning changes and is therefore no longer firmly determined. The unusual spread of the term indicates a complicated history; it even appears to be avoided in certain parts of the the Old Testament, for reasons which cannot now be determined.

In the course of time therefore different divine names have been connected with the Ark, which in part at least still show signs of foreign origin; the concepts of a throne of God or of a footstool of the throne do not seem to be original. The old, general term 'Ark' or 'Ark of God' suggests rather a chest which served as a container (cf. Gen. 50: 26; 2 Kgs. 12: 10f.) But there is no mention in early texts of any content for it. It is only Deuteronomy (10: 1–5; 1 Kgs. 8: 9), at a time at which the Ark had long since lost its significance or even perhaps no longer existed, that makes of it a chest for the tables of the law from Sinai. P takes over this interpretation for its 'Ark of the testimony' (Exod. 25: 10ff.; 26: 33f.; 37: 1ff.), changes the bare chest into a gold-covered cult object with a lid, and cherubim, and puts it in the tent. Here the Ark is for the first time described, but according to the ideas of the later period, in which however old traditions still live on. It has been conjectured that the Ark originally contained an image of God, a collection of treasure, holy stones or some sort of documents; but all these hypotheses lack any basis in the text. Probably the Ark was in fact simply empty; this fits best a God of whom no images are permitted. Even if quite different concepts from the period in the wilderness and that in the cultivated lands meet and change in the course of time, the Ark in any case was understood in Israel as the place of revelation of the God who could not be portrayed. Even at the sanctuary his presence remained invisible.

3   Originally each settlement must have had its own sanctuary. In later polemic against the cult 'on every high hill and under every green tree' (Jer. 2: 20 et al.; cf. Hos. 4: 13) there are still traces of the fact that these local sanctuaries had been open to foreign customs, indeed in part had already been Canaanite cultic sites. At various places excavations have come across the foundations of temples, but most of the high places probably only had an altar under the open sky (1 Sam. 9: 12ff.; 2 Kgs. 17: 9f., 29; 23: 5, 8). Some of the many local cultic sites stood out as marked by particular events or circumstances. They served as the sanctuary of a whole tribe, or were even visited by surrounding neighbours, perhaps because they lay upon the border between individual areas. Indeed some holy sites were a goal of pilgrimage for tribes living far away. Here the three great feasts of the year were celebrated; for they were 'before Yahweh' (Judg. 20: 26; 21: 19ff.; 1 Sam. 1: 3ff.; cf. Exod. 23: 14ff.; below, §9b). Undoubtedly men also took their personal concerns there in prayer before God, and experienced his presence. But the significance of many sanctuaries went far beyond the cultic element; they were in another sense too meeting-places and centres. Markets were held here, the levy of the surrounding tribes gathered here before the war, and here the king was later chosen by the nation or its elders.

The most important sanctuaries of the time of the judges and the kings are not to any great extent the same as the places which are known from the time of the patriarchs (above, §3c). Apart from Shechem (Josh. 24; above, §8, 3), the later centre of the northern kingdom (1 Kgs. 12) and Shiloh, which housed the ark in a temple (1 Sam. 1ff.; cf. Judg. 21: 19ff.; Jer. 7: 12ff.) there are the following:

   The mountain peak of Tabor, rising up from the plain of Jezreel, seems to have been the place of worship for the neighbouring tribes of Issachar, Zebulun and Naphtali (Josh. 19: 22, 34; cf. Deut. 33: 19; Hos. 5: 1; Ps. 89: 12 [Heb. 89: 13], and also Ps. 68?). Here men met under Barak's leadership before the battle against the Canaanites (Judg. 4: 6, 12, 14). In pre-Israelite times Ba'al Tabor will have been worshipped upon the mountain; although the name of the deity is only attested at a later date.

   At Gilgal in the Jordan valley memories were preserved of the entry into the land (Josh. 3f.). Here the levies of the surrounding tribes later met (1 Sam. 10: 8; 13: 4ff.; 15: 12, 21 et al.) here Saul was called to be king and crowned (11: 14f.) and David reacknowledged (2 Sam. 19: 41ff.). After the division of the kingdom Gilgal was a much visited pilgrimage centre for the northern kingdom; this makes understandable the attacks of the prophets Amos (4: 4; 5: 5) and Hosea (4: 15; cf. 9: 15; 12: 12). Elisha too lived at Gilgal in the circle of his band of pupils (2 Kgs. 4: 38; 2: 1). It is however not certain that it is the same place that is in question on each occasion. When Jeroboam made Bethel the royal sanctuary of the northern kingdom as a counter-foundation to Jerusalem (1 Kgs. 12: 29ff.; Amos 7: 13) he could certainly link up with the old-established significance of the place (Gen. 12: 8; 28:

10ff.; 35: 1ff.; cf. Judg. 20: 26f.; 21: 1ff.; 1 Sam. 7: 16; 10: 3 et al.). Here Amos began his ministry (3: 14; 4: 4; 5: 5 et al.) and was driven out (7: 10ff.).

Mizpah (Judg. 20f.; 1 Sam. 7: 5ff., 16) after the destruction of Jerusalem by the Babylonians became the centre for those who had remained in the land (2 Kgs. 25: 23ff.; Jer. 40: 7ff.). It may be wondered whether this was the place of origin of the Deuteronomistic history (Deut.-2 Kgs.).

The tree-sanctuary of Mamre at Hebron was not only associated with the tradition of Abraham (Gen. 18); in this city of the tribe of Caleb David was also chosen as king over the southern tribes (2 Sam. 2: 1–4; cf. 5: 3; 15: 7).

Beersheba, still further south, in which stories were told of Isaac (Gen. 26: 23ff.; cf. 46: 1) seems also to have been a centre of pilgrimage for the northern kingdom in the time of the monarchy (Amos 5: 5, 8: 14).

To a large extent therefore it is only particular individual events that are recorded of particular places; what occurred regularly is not described. But the events recorded do allow conclusions about the significance of the cultic sites in the different periods and areas. However the sanctuaries did not follow one another in time, so that the role of one place was passed on to another; they remained in existence alongside one another, and struggled against one another for position. So Wellhausen's verdict is justified that 'any strict centralization is for that period inconceivable, alike in the religious as in every other sphere' (*Prolegomena to the History of Ancient Israel*, London, 1885, p. 19). The local sanctuaries were able, in spite of prophetic criticism (Amos 4: 4; 5: 5 et al.) to hold their own beside Jerusalem, which was only invested with unique significance for Yahwistic faith through Josiah's reform (621 BC; 2 Kgs. 22f.). Through this change, after all the earlier complexity, the worship of Yahweh attained a unity of place as well as of belief. The exclusiveness of the first commandment demanded the exclusiveness of the central sanctuary (Deut. 12), until in prophetic hope (Zeph. 2: 11) the God who may not be portrayed could give up even this last local connection, to be present everywhere in the same manner.

b FEASTS

The oldest tradition of regularly observed feasts in Israel is offered in closely similar form in the two calendars of feasts in the Book of the Covenant (Exod. 23: 14–17) and in the Ritual Decalogue (Exod. 34: 18, 22f.). (The differences between them have been given varied explanations). These details do not go back to the nomadic past, but to a relatively early time after the settlement. Exod. 23: 14–17 runs:

> Three times in the year you shall keep a (pilgrimage) feast to me: You shall keep the feast of unleavened bread; as I commanded you, you shall eat unleavened bread for seven days at the appointed time in the month of Abib, for in it you came out of Egypt. None shall appear before me

empty-handed. You shall keep the feast of harvest, of the first fruits of your labour, of what you sow in the field.

You shall keep the feast of ingathering at the end of the year, when you gather in from the field the fruit of your labour.

Three times in the year shall all your males see the face of the Lord Yahweh (later corrected to 'appear before Yahweh', cf. Exod. 34: 23; Deut. 16: 16).

The later cultic calendar of Deut. 16 with its radical demand for cultic centralization offers a still more advanced step in the development, but it too only makes three feasts in the year (v. 16) obligatory. The more detailed arrangements of feasts in the Code of Holiness of Lev. 23 and the sacrificial calendar in Num. 28f., go beyond this, including the sabbath (Lev. 23:3; Num. 28: 8f.), which was originally not a cultic occasion, in any case not a feast (above, Excursus 2), New Year's Day and the Day of Atonement (Lev. 23: 23–32; Num. 29: 1–11). These later Priestly passages point however to a more extensive reform; while Deuteronomy united the feasts in one place, Lev. 23 and Num. 28f. fix the time of the feasts, replacing the older more generally expressed indications of time so far as possible by exact dates. The course of historical development is successively reflected in such changes and expansions.

The three great pilgrimage feasts mentioned in the older cultic calendars (Exod. 23; 34; Deut 16) are agriculturally based, and ordered by the seasons of the year. They form a cycle (perhaps from the beginning, and in any case for the account we have of them in Exod. 23: 14ff. et al.), which covers the whole harvest season:

the Feast of Unleavened Bread (later united with the Passover), at the beginning of the harvest in the spring;
the Feast of Harvest or of Weeks after the conclusion of the grain harvest,
the Feast of Ingathering or of Tabernacles in the autumn at the end of the year.

All three are agricultural feasts, and so no doubt of ancient local custom. The nomads as they became sedentary apparently took them over from their Canaanite neighbours, no doubt at the different holy places in the land (cf. above, §9a, 3); for pilgrimage feasts were celebrated at the local cultic places at particular times, perhaps by several villages or groups of tribes together (cf. Judg. 9: 27 on the feast of ingathering in the temple at Shechem; also Judg. 21: 19ff.; 1 Sam. 1: 3 tells of an annual pilgrimage to Shiloh). Deuteronomy (16: 2, 6f., 11, 16 et al.) first makes the demand to journey to a place chosen by God.

Since all three feasts attested in the pre-exilic period reflect the cycle of nature, foreign influence on the Israelite cult can be clearly traced. Is there anything distinctive of Israel that can be found in the feasts of Yahweh? This problem was one of the reasons for proposing to reconstruct a feast of definitely Israelite character, but not directly attested in the Old Testament, like the Covenant

Festival. But the distinctiveness of Israel is more clearly to be seen in the reinterpretation of what they took over than in the introduction of new feasts. The foreign material is taken into Israel's own faith; the feasts are to be kept 'to me, Yahweh' (Exod. 23: 14), they are feasts 'for Yahweh' (Lev. 23: 6, 28, 34, 40; cf. 23: 25ff. of sacrifices; Exod. 20: 10 of the sabbath etc.). What is the essential meaning of this reinterpretation? Was Israel able to introduce the experiences of its past into the structure of the feasts, or even to open them up to what was historically new and unforeseeable? In fact Israel sought to incorporate the events of nature as they are portrayed in the feasts into history, and so to give the feasts a new character over and beyond thanksgiving for harvest: that of remembering decisive events from Israel's early history (Exod. 23: 15; Lev. 23: 42f.; cf. Deut. 26 et al.). The priority given to the once-for-all and historical aspect over the annual and cyclical aspect was certainly a gradual process; it can be understood as 'a rigorous demythologizing process' (G. von Rad, *Old Testament Theology*, vol. 1. Edinburgh, 1962, p. 27). This historicization, the subsequent insertion of phenomena which were originally not understood historically into historical thought, is distinctly unusual in the ancient Near East, and betrays a different understanding both of God and of man. So F. Heiler (*Erscheinungsformen und Wesen der Religion*, Stuttgart, 1961, p. 155) takes the view, 'Here one of the biggest revolutions in the history of religions took place.' It is however not known in detail what subsequent effects this new understanding had on the actual course of the feast; for we know relatively little for certain about the worship of Israel, and much is only hypothetical. This reinterpretation (and with it the historical change at the same time) comes out most clearly in the Feast of Passover and of Unleavened Bread.

1   The Feast of Passover and Unleavened Bread

The Feast of Passover or of Unleavened Bread, the main Jewish feast in the New Testament period (Mark 14: 1, 12, 14 et al.) unites two originally completely different rites, which like the two forms of sacrifice mentioned in Gen. 4: 3f., can be derived from two ways of life, the nomadic and the sedentary.

The Passover (Hebrew *pesaḥ*) goes back to a nomadic origin. As a rite of shepherds it was not tied to a holy place, and was not performed by priests at an altar but by the elders of the clan. The feast, with the slaughter of the animals, sprinkling with blood, and common meal, at which the meat was consumed in roasted form, took place by night, probably in the night of the full moon after the spring equinox. The blood with which the entrances were smeared (Exod. 12: 22f. J; 12: 7, 13P) most probably had an apotropaic significance: it warded off disaster, and gave protection to man and animals against a demon of the wilderness, the 'destroyer' (Exod. 12: 23J; cf. Heb. 11: 28). Accordingly the Passover was not a sacrifice, not even a sacrifice of the firstborn (cf. Exod. 13: 2, 11ff.; 34: 19f.); Passover was intended neither to create fellowship with the deity nor to atone for sin (cf. however Ezek. 45: 21 ff.). On an attractive conjecture of Rost the nomads performed the blood ritual regularly before setting out from the winter pastures of the steppe to the summer pastures of the cultivated lands; for on the migration they were exposed to great dangers, and therefore had need of special protection ('Weidewechsel und altisraelitische Festkalender' [1943], in *Das kleine Credo und andere Studien zum Alten Testament*, Heidelberg, 1965). If this particular explanation is not accepted, it must more generally be assumed that the action served for the protection of those involved.

The Feast of Unleavened Bread (Exod. 23: 15; 34: 18; 12: 15ff.P; 13: 3ff. et al.) was originally a Canaanite agricultural pilgrimage feast, which was performed at the beginning of the grain harvest: after the first cutting of the barley (cf. Deut. 16: 9) they ate the first bread of the year unleavened. The custom was perhaps filled out into a seven-day feast only in Israel.

These two rites, so completely different in their intention, were linked together by the Passover being slain on the eve of the seven-day Feast of Unleavened Bread; however it is Deuteronomy that first attests this development (16: 3f. in secondary combination; cf. Lev. 23: 5f.; Mark 14: 12 et al.). It was possible to combine both ceremonies because they occurred in temporal proximity (in March–April); it was after the barley harvest that the stubble fields of the cultivated land were available to the shepherds. It has been wondered whether cakes of unleavened bread (and bitter herbs) had from the beginning been consumed at Passover. However the evidence is very uncertain (cf. Exod. 12: 8 P with vv. 15ff.; 12: 34, 39J; Deut. 16: 3a).

Since the Feast of Unleavened Bread was very early on connected with the Exodus from Egypt, fixed in a particular month (Abib) and celebrated for a full week, alongside the view sketched out it has also been held that Israel itself developed the Feast of Unleavened Bread in the land from the Passover (J. Halbe, 'Passa-Massot im deuteronomischen Festkalender', *ZAW* 87 (1975), pp. 147–168). But then it is difficult to explain why the arrangements for celebration of Passover and Unleavened Bread stand separate but side by side and why the older cultic calendars mention the feast of Unleavened Bread in place of Passover.

As a result of the no doubt subsequent combination of the two cultic acts Passover was changed into a pilgrimage feast, which was performed at the sanctuary; thus on the analogy of the Feast of Unleavened Bread (Exod. 23: 15; 34: 18 et al.) it was possible to speak too of the Feast of Passover (34: 25; 12: 14). The character of the feast was however increasingly determined by the Passover customs, and by history, not by the harvest, so that Passover could finally serve as the common name for the two (Luke 22: 1).

It is Deuteronomy that explicitly transfers the Passover (16: 2, 5f) from the realm of the family (cf. Exod. 12: 21J) in the various localities to the one central sanctuary. (It remains however unknown for lack of evidence whether it was Deuteronomy that first reinterpreted the Passover to be a common feast of pilgrimage, or whether this development took place earlier (in two stages) through a postulated pre-Deuteronomic connection of Passover and Unleavened Bread, and the demand for centralization only transferred the different local pilgrimage feasts to the central sanctuary.) The development of the Passover into a sacrifice seems to have occurred with the change in the cultic action (cf. the verb 'to slay' in Exod. 12: 21J, 6P with 'sacrifice' in Deut. 16: 2, 4, 6 and 'present' in Num. 9: 7, 13P; also Ezek. 45: 21ff.; 1 Cor. 5: 7).

According to 2 Kgs. 23: 21f. King Josiah in the course of the Deuteronomic reform celebrated such a common Passover in Jerusalem (the historicity of this is disputed, as is still more the account of the first celebration of Passover in the land, Josh. 5: 10f.; cf. Num. 9: 5). This arrangement was preserved, although the rules governing it continued to be refined (cf. 2 Chr. 30; 35; Ezra. 6: 19ff.).

Since P in the context of the story of Passover and Exodus in Exod. 12: 3ff. has to infringe its own theological pattern of allowing cultic laws only after the erection of the sanctuary upon Sinai (Exod. 25ff.), and perhaps too wants to create regulations for the time after the destruction of the temple, it goes back to the older arrangement and makes the feasts take place not in the temple but in the individual families. Less in this respect, but more with regard to the individual details in which P revived the pre-Deuteronomic position it has come to win the day: only a young male selected from the sheep or goats is permitted (Exod. 12: 3ff.), not from cattle (which Deut. 16: 2 permitted in the course of the change of Passover into a sacrifice; cf. Ezek. 45: 21ff.). Again the meat may not be boiled (against Deut. 16: 7; cf. of sacrifice 1 Sam. 2: 13f.; Ezek. 46: 24 et al.), but only roasted (Exod. 12: 9P; cf 2 Chr. 35: 7f., 13).

Judaism of the New Testament period observed the Passover both in the temple, where the killing took place, and in the houses in which the meat was consumed.

If the feast of Passover and Unleavened Bread in its origins reflects a syncretism of nomadic ritual and of Canaanite agricultural feast, neither of the two feasts is in origin Israelite or Yahwistic. Both are connected with the rhythm of nature, the recurrence of the seasons. Nevertheless the rite became a 'Passover for Yahweh' (Exod. 12: 11, 14: 27), that is, exclusive to Yahweh. What does this mean in real terms?

1   Already in the older cultic calendars, which mention the Feast of Unleavened Bread but not yet in connection with the Passover, it takes place in the month of the Exodus from Egypt (Exod. 23: 15; 34: 18, both probably with secondary expansions and explanations; cf. Exod. 13: 3ff.; Deut. 16). The Passover too is already integrated into the events of the Exodus in its earliest literary occurrence (Exod. 12: 21–23J; cf. vv. 11f.P; Deut. 16: 1). Older forms can in both cases only be recovered by deduction (and analogy). The usage of Passover, as a protection against the last plague, is together with the Feast of Unleavened Bread already fully incorporated into the story of the Exodus (Exodus (Exod. 12: 1–20P). Probably a reciprocal relationship underlies this: while the rite is interpreted from the Exodus event, it has in turn influenced the narrative. In any case it was through the combination of Passover and Exodus tradition that the mixture of legal ordinance and historical narrative which is now characteristic of Exod. 12 originated.

The historical retrospect is itself documented externally in the rite: the participants in the Passover meal are always to maintain the situation of its beginning, by preserving the memory of readiness to set out hastily with clothes for travel – with loins girded, sandals and staff, (the weapon of the shepherd against wild beasts, cf. 2 Kgs. 4: 29; 1 Sam. 17: 40, 43) and in anxious haste. This mood of departure, although only attested late (Exod. 12: 11P; cf. 12: 39; Deut. 16: 3) seems to be a constant between the original nomadic ritual and the Israelite feast; only now it symbolizes the Exodus from the land of servitude.

2 The name of the feast (the original meaning of *pesaḥ* remains uncertain) has been explained as 'to pass by, to spare' (*pāsaḥ*, Exod. 12: 23J, 13P, 27 Dtr. cf. Isa. 31: 5): the divine judgement passed over Israel.

The wilderness demon which attacks man and beast then becomes a sort of angelic being which at Yahweh's command carries out his sentence (cf. Exod. 12: 23J with v. 29J). Since the 'destroyer' only carries out the divine will to slay (cf. 2 Sam. 24: 17; 2 Kgs. 19: 35), Yahweh exploits both the old belief in demons and the ritual. P finally gives up completely the personal nature of the Angel of Death: the 'blow of the destroyer' (Exod. 12: 23) turns into a blow of destruction (v. 13).

3 As a result of the subordination of the Angel of Death to Yahweh, who 'leads them out of Egypt', the threat caused by the demon changes its former character from a regularly recurrent event, into a once-for-all event in the night of the Exodus. The Passover is explicitly understood as a day of remembrance reminding men of the Exodus (Exod. 12: 14P; Deut. 16: 3, 12; cf. Ps. 111: 4; Lev. 23: 24). The danger that history is cultically 'repeated' at an annual feast through its relationship to the Passover custom is averted, even if the salvation experienced in it is preserved for 'today' (Exod. 13: 3f.).

4 Finally the date of the feast is yet more sharply separated from the course of the agricultural year, since after the transfer of the new year into the spring a fixed date was set (the fourteenth to the twenty-first of the first month, later called Nisan) (Exod. 12: 21ff.P; cf. Ezek. 45: 21; Ezra 6: 19; 2 Chr. 35: 1).

Thus the Passover lost its original meaning, for it no longer conveys protection through its own power. The rite as such does not achieve anything, no longer gives any magical guarantee. The blood on the doorposts is only a sign (Exod. 12: 13P) of God's passing by, as the rainbow and circumcision are signs of the covenant (Gen. 9: 13; 17: 11P).

Unlike the original rite of protection the historicized Passover custom does not have independent significance of its own. [The history of the past is not made present in a cultic dramatic representation, but] is brought near to the participant in the cult through an act of proclamation, and interpreted for its significance for the present. . . . It may be wondered whether the dramatic themes of the Passover Feast, which are intended to evoke thought, are not to be understood in P only in the sense of a symbolic action, which effects an understanding of the actuality of the events which are interpreted in signs. (W. Schottroff, '*Gedenken' im Alten Orient und im Alten Testament*, 2nd edn., Neukirchen-Vluyn, 1967, pp. 315 ff.)

The once-for-all character of the event is held on to firmly in recognition of the temporal distance of the event but with the relationship to the present in mind. The past has significance for later generations, which can be drawn into the past by 'remembering'. Therefore the Passover, like circumcision (Gen. 17: 13P) can be commanded as an ever valid ordinance, as an 'ordinance forever' to all generations (Exod. 12: 14P).

How does the 'remembering' take place in specific terms? The Passover with its note of departure should lead the children to ask their fathers about the meaning of the action: 'What do you mean by this service?' (Exod. 12: 26f.). The cult is therefore simply an occasion for proclamation. What it leads to is the narrative; the annually recurrent ritual has the task of building up to it (Exod. 12: 24–27a; 13: 8, 14ff. Dtr). This pedagogical orientation fits a tendency of the Deuteronomist, who constantly calls men to the instruction of their sons (4: 9f.; 7ff.; 20ff. et al.) and so turns an older custom into a law, by which it is not the priest but the father of the family who gives instruction in the matters of the faith. The generations who grow up with other experiences are also to experience this history and grasp it as their own (Exod. 12: 27: 'he spared *our* houses'; cf. 13: 8), and so are called to trust and thankfulness.

The Passover thus gives an instructive example of the force with which the faith of the Old Testament stamps its own character upon an (alien) custom. According to a general principle in the history of religions the practice is preserved while the interpretation changes. Since the meaning of a rite does not lie in itself, the ritual action as such is open to several interpretations; it is given a single sense only through language (e.g. Job 1: 20f.). It needs the spoken word, therefore, especially in a faith which depends upon history.

2   *The Feast of Harvest or of Weeks*

The Feast of Harvest marked the end of the grain harvest in summer (Exod. 34: 22). 'the first-fruits of your labour, of what you sow in the fields', sheaves, and bread (now leavened, not as in the Feast of Unleavened Bread) (Exod. 23: 16; Lev. 23: 17) were brought to the sanctuary, so that this one-day feast is also called 'the day of the first-fruits' (Num. 28: 26).

It remains uncertain however whether the delivery of the first-fruits (Exod. 23: 19; 34: 26: Deut. 26: 1ff. et al.) took place exclusively at this feast or also at other times.

The probably later name 'Feast of Weeks' (Exod. 34: 22 et al.) was coined upon the basis of the date: it took place seven weeks after the sickle was put to the standing grain (Deut. 16: 9f.). The exact period of fifty days (hence the Greek term *pentēkostē* 'pentecost') was apparently later adapted to the Israelites' sabbath numeration (7 × 7 + 1) (Lev. 23: 15f.).

Both the calculation of the date of the feast in weeks and also the name Feast of Weeks are surely not of Canaanite origin, since they presuppose the rhythm of the seven-day period and the sabbath, which has hitherto not been found for certain among Israel's neighbours (above, Excursus 2). Ezekiel's reconstruction programme does not mention the Feast of Weeks (this is perhaps a Jerusalem peculiarity), but rather mentions only the Feast of Passover and the autumn feast in the first and seventh months (Ezek. 45; 21–25). It is doubtful whether the calendar of feasts of the Code of Holiness (Lev. 23) which mentions only these two feasts (M. Noth, *Leviticus*, London, 1965, 2nd edn., 1977 pp.165ff.) goes back to an older form.

The Feast of Weeks apparently acquired an historical connection only at a late date; Deut. 16: 12 in an exhortation to allow slaves too to take part in the joy of the feast, calls to mind Israel's vassalage in Egypt. It is possible that this less important feast held out longer against historicization, and remained simply a feast of thankfulness for harvest. In the post-exilic period however it became for Judaism the feast of the giving of the covenant and law (cf. 2 Chr. 15: 10 and Jubilees), that is, it provides a remembrance of the revelation upon Sinai. Perhaps P already has this historical link, since it puts the revelation at Sinai, according to Exod. 19: 1, in the third month, and so at the time of the Feast of Weeks, if the later character of the feast did not simply develop upon the basis of Exod. 19: 1.

3 The Feast of Ingathering or of Tabernacles

The Feast of Ingathering (Exod. 23: 16; 34: 22) was celebrated in the autumn, when the fruit of threshing-floor and winepress, with fruit, olives and grapes (cf. Jer. 8: 13), was brought in (Deut. 16: 13; Lev. 23: 39ff.). Originally the dance in the vineyards and the banquet were part of the feast (Judg. 21: 19ff.; 9: 27).

From the custom of living in booths (Lev. 23: 42, 40: Neh. 8: 14ff.) the feast acquired the name of Tabernacles or Booths (Deut. 16: 13ff.; Zech. 14: 16ff. et al.). Like the Feast of Unleavened Bread it lasted, at least at the later period (first attested in Deut. 16: 13), for seven days, and after the exile, when the attempt was made to have the feasts independent of the time of the end of the harvest and to give them exact dates, took place from the fifteenth day of the seventh month on (Lev. 23: 34ff.; Num. 29: 12ff.; Ezek. 45: 25; Neh. 8: 18; 2 Chr. 7: 8f.). The last of the three great annual feasts was also the most important; for this reason it was also called 'the feast of Yahweh' (Judg. 21: 19; Hos. 9: 5; Lev. 23: 39) or simply 'the feast' (1 Kgs. 8: 2, 65; 12: 32 et al.).

Like the Feast of Passover and Unleavened Bread, the Feast of Tabernacles too was connected with the stay in Egypt. However such a historicization is not attested until P. According to Lev. 23: 42f. the tabernacles were to remind the Israelites of their manner of dwelling when they set out from Egypt, and therefore to remind them graphically of the beginning of its existence. This interpretation contains an anachronism at least to this extent that the dwellers in the wilderness certainly lived in tents made of cloths and skins, and not in huts made of branches. In the stay in booths an old custom lived on of 'erecting temporary dwellings during the harvest, as still happens today, in the vineyards and olive gardens, a custom which is simply transferred (now as a holy custom) to the area of the temple and to Jerusalem' (K. Elliger, *Leviticus*, 1966, p. 323). Thus a custom of the settled lands is given a basis in the nomadic life. Here we have a clear example of how both traditions meet in Israel, and how the nomadic has the priority not in the real life style but in the interpretation given of it.

As 'the feast (of Yahweh)' without qualification the autumn festival was not tied to history only by thanksgiving for harvest and by remembrance of their history. According to 1 Kgs. 8: 2 it was on this occasion that the temple of Solomon was dedicated. Deut. 31: 10f. makes the demand that on the Feast of Tabernacles every seventh year the law is to be read; whether the requirement goes back to an already existing custom and how far it was carried out at all remains uncertain. According to Neh. 8 Ezra read to the community at the beginning of the seventh month each day at Tabernacles from the law. Finally Zech. 14: 16 expects that the remnant of the nations that is left from the battle of the nations will go on pilgrimage annually at Tabernacles to Jerusalem, to worship Yahweh as king (cf. Jer. 41: 5). Is it possible in spite of these few brief indications that the Old Testament itself contains of this most significant feast of the pre-exilic period to conjecture that it had a quite different character? After the discovery of the significance of the cult the attempt was made (following P. Volz and S. Mowinckel) to fill out the gap by transferring all sorts of reconstructed festal items to this autumnal feast: the enthronement feast of Yahweh (below, §11a, 6), the feast of the (renewal of the) covenant (cf. Ps. 50; 81), the enthronement of the king (Ps. 2; 110), the royal feast of Zion (cf. Ps. 132), etc. The cultic action has also been filled out with different actions: theophany, battle with the sea and with the nations, creation, but also the death and resurrection of the God, the sacred marriage, etc.; these various rites are supposed to have served primarily for the preservation of the world and of society. While it is in any case questionable how far they are common to the ancient Near East, the Old Testament instances themselves are insufficiently strong to carry the weight that is put upon them. A cultic background can indeed be conjectured for particular themes; but hardly once is it possible to reach a firm conclusion, especially about the manner of cultic representation.

Roughly since the exile two further feasts were observed in the seventh month, in which the harvest festival was celebrated. Apparently these days were separated off from the autumn festival and located before it in time, so that they came to have a significance of their own. The Code of Holiness in Lev. 23 attests this development; but it is not yet found in Deut. 16. New Year's Day on the first day of the seventh month (the year begins in the older system in the autumn, by the later dating in the spring) is really distinguished only by 'trumpet blasts' and (like all feast days since the Code of Holiness) by rest and sacrifice (Lev. 23: 24f.; Num. 29: 1ff.; cf. Neh. 8: 2).

The Day of Atonement on the tenth day of the seventh month, on which the command to rest applies particularly strongly, serves first for the purification of the temple, and secondly for the purification of the community, which 'afflicts itself' (Lev. 23: 26–32; 25: 9; Num. 29: 7–11; cf. Ezek. 45: 18–20). The rite described in Lev. 16 (esp. vv. 7–10, 21f.), but no doubt older, was transferred to this day: a lot chooses between two he-goats; one is offered to Yahweh as a sin offering, the other has the guilt of Israel 'laid upon it' by the imposition of hands upon the head and confession of sins, and then is driven into the wilderness – to Azazel, probably a demon.

4 Other feasts

The Feast of Purim arose in the Jewish diaspora of the Persian period; the book of Esther forms its (no doubt secondary) festival legend (9: 16ff.). The feast is distinguished by its strikingly profane character, its joyful atmosphere, and the mutual giving of presents; in remembrance of preservation from persecution the Jews are to 'keep days of feasting and of gladness, send gifts to one another and give presents to the poor' (9: 22, 19). Both the name (*pūr* means 'lot', 3: 7; 9: 24ff.) and also the place of origin suggest an originally foreign (spring) feast, perhaps a Persian or Babylonian New Year festival. Like the great Israelite feasts this feast would then have achieved a subsequent historical basis, which however does not go back directly to historical events.

G. Gerleman (*BK* XXI, pp. 26f.) interprets the plural *pūrīm* as 'parts, portions', and understands 'the mutual giving of presents as a typical expression of the diaspora situation, and a manifestation of the special solidarity which the Jews had in the diaspora'. Since the book of Esther seems to allude to the events of the Exodus, it has perhaps the purpose of 'putting Purim in place of the old Passover as the central cultic observance of the Persian diaspora'.

The remembrance of the rededication of the temple during the wars of the Maccabees in 164 BC was celebrated in the feast of the dedication of the temple (Hanukka) (1 Macc. 4: 36ff.; 2 Macc. 1f.; 10; John 10: 22; cf. already after the rebuilding Ezra 6: 16f.).

Obviously there were also feasts which took place irregularly according to the occasion: family feasts like weddings (Gen. 29: 21ff.; Judg. 14: 10ff.; Song of Songs esp. 3: 11; of the king, Ps. 45) or burials (Gen. 50: 10f.; 2 Sam. 3: 31ff. et al.), perhaps also the accession of a new king (1 Kgs. 1: 33ff.; 2 Kgs. 11: 4ff.; cf. Ps. 2; 110).

In an emergency, such as defeat in war, epidemic or famine (1 Kgs. 8: 33ff.; 2 Chr. 20) the call went out for a public lamentation by the people, the so-called fast (1 Kgs. 21: 9, 12; Jer. 36: 9; Jonah 3: 5; Joel 1: 5ff.; 2. 15 et al.). Someone, perhaps a cultic prophet, uttered intercession for relief from distress (Jer. 14; 1 Sam. 7: 5ff.; Ps. 74: 9 et al.). Since such services of intercession were not characterized by sacrifices and therefore were independent of the temple, they could be retained in exile. It is even possible that the gradual evolution of a form of worship characterized by words and with no sacrifice, which signifies a profound alteration in the expressions of the faith, developed from this or of cultic life. In any case because of the continuing distress after the fall of the southern kingdom solemn occasions of communal lament became a regular practice, in which the events surrounding the fall of Jerusalem and of the temple (2 Kgs. 25) were recalled (Zech. 7: 3, 5; 8: 19; cf. the psalms of lament, Ps. 44; 74; 79f. et al.).

EXCURSUS 6: SACRIFICE

1 As the sacrificial laws (Lev. 1–7) and the sacrificial calendar (Num. 28f.; also Josh. 22: 23ff.; 2 Kgs. 16: 12ff. et al.) indicated, Israel had various different forms of sacrifice. They had both in themselves and in their relationship to one another a history of extensive changes, which cannot be given here.

The burnt offering ('ōlā) is, with the exception of the skin, which is given to the priests, killed and consumed as a whole, burnt upon the altar (Gen. 8: 20; Judg. 6: 26; 13: 15ff.; 1 Kgs. 18: 23, 32f.; Lev. 1; 6: 2–6). For this reason it is also called 'whole offering' (kālīl: 1 Sam. 7: 9 et al.). It is especially offered at public festal occasions (9: 25; 18 et al.) and is regarded in the later period as the most important form of sacrifice. In Gen. 22 the ritual, slaughtering before burning, is altered for the sake of the sparing of Isaac. The principal objects of sacrifice are cattle, sheep, goats and doves.

The communion sacrifice (zebaḥ) on the other hand is a sacrifice of fellowship, which was originally held within the family or in a larger invited circle (Gen. 31: 54; 46: 1; 1 Sam. 1: 21; 2: 13ff.; 9: 12f.; 16: 2ff. et al.) as a meal, and only later came to involve the participation of a priest, who then also received a share (cf. Lev. 7: 34). The fat pieces, as belonging to God (cf. Gen. 4: 4; Lev. 3: 16; Deut. 32: 37f.; Isa. 43: 24) are burnt upon the altar, the blood is poured out, and the flesh consumed among the participants. It is after this sacrifice and the verb that goes with it 'to slay, sacrifice' (zābaḥ) that the altar is called 'place of slaying' (mizbēaḥ). Perhaps originally all slaughterings of animals were sacrifices (cf. 1 Sam. 2: 13; 9: 13; but Gen. 18: 7f.) In any case Deuteronomy, in order to carry out its demand (12: 15f.; 20ff.) that sacrifice should only take place at the one central sanctuary, explicitly allows for secular slaughter.

The sacrifices of completion, of prosperity or of peace (peace-offerings: the translation of shᵉlāmīm is disputed), of which sprinkling with blood is characteristic, are originally offered after the burnt offerings (Exod. 20: 24; Deut. 27: 6f.; Josh. 8: 31; Judg. 20: 26; 21: 4; 2 Sam. 6: 17f.; 24: 25; 2 Chr. 31: 2 et al.), and are apparently only secondarily joined with the communion sacrifices to form a unity (Lev. 3; 7: 11 ff. et al.).

The word for food offering (minḥā) denotes at first generally the (bloody or unbloody) gifts (Gen. 4: 3ff.; Judg. 6: 18; 1 Sam. 2: 17, 29 et al.) and only comes to have in the course of time the significance of a vegetable offering of groats, meal, oil, salt or cakes (Lev. 2; 5: 11ff.; 23: 16f.; 1 Kgs. 18: 29, 36; 2 Kgs. 3: 20; 16: 15 et al.) This sacrifice loses its independence completely, and serves as an accompaniment to animal sacrifices (Lev. 9: 3f., 16f.; Num. 15: 3f.).

In the post-exilic period particular sin offerings (ḥaṭṭā, Lev. 4f; 6: 17ff.; 8: 14ff.; 12: 6ff.; 16) and guilt offerings ('āšām, Lev. 5: 14ff.; 7; 14: 12ff. et al.)

become steadily more important (e.g. Ezek. 40: 39; 42: 13; 43: 18ff.). In particular the blood, 'the soul of the flesh', has atoning power and belongs to Yahweh (Lev. 17: 11, 14).

We find also drink offerings (*nesek*, Gen. 35: 14; 1 Sam. 7: 6; 2 Sam. 23: 16; Num. 15: 5ff.) and incense offerings (Lev. 10: 1, Exod 30; Num. 16; Ps. 66: 15; cf. Jer. 6: 20) and on particular occasions thank offerings (Lev. 7: 12ff.; Ps. 107: 22; 116: 17; cf. Jon. 1: 16), free-will gifts (Deut. 12: 6, 17; Amos 4: 5) or votive offerings (Lev. 7: 16; 22: 18ff. et al.).

2   The stay in the wilderness appears to Hosea as a time of uninterrupted fellowship with God (2: 2ff. [Heb. 2: 4ff.]; 9: 10; cf. Jer. 2: 2), and in two additions to the books of the prophets we find the fundamental question, 'Did you bring to me sacrifices and offerings the forty years in the wilderness, O house of Israel?' (Amos 5: 25), or even the assertion 'For in the day that I brought them out of the land of Egypt, I did not speak to your fathers or command them concerning burnt offerings and sacrifices' (Jer. 7: 22). Nevertheless Israel's ancestors in the nomadic period were undoubtedly familiar with sacrifices. The peace offering or communion offering is most likely to come from this period (Gen. 31: 54; 46: 1; Exod. 5: 3; 22: 20 [Heb. 22: 19]; 34: 25 et al.; cf. above, §9b, 1 on the Passover), while the burnt offering could have been taken over from the Canaanites in the cultivated land (cf. the addition in Exod. 18: 12; Gen. 22 is no doubt originally the cultic legend of a local sanctuary). The burning of sacrifices was customary in the ancient Near East only in the west Semitic, Canaanite and Greek lands, not in Mesopotamia or Egypt (Rost, 'Erwägungen zum israelitischen Brandopfer', in J. Hempel and L. Rost (ed.), *Von Ugarit nach Qumran*, Festschrift O. Eissfeldt, Berlin, 1958, also in *Das kleine Credo und andere Studien zum alten Testament*, Heidelberg, 1965). Further it is burnt offerings that are of significance in the struggle with the religion of Ba'al (Judg. 6: 25ff.; 1 Kgs. 18), and it can hardly be an accident that burnt offerings are also employed in connection with the offering of human sacrifices (Gen. 22; Judg. 11: 31; 2 Kgs. 3: 27; cf. 16: 3 et al.). The Old Testament does still state God's right to the (human) first-born (Exod. 22: 29f. [Heb. 22: 28f.]; 13: 2, 12f.; 34: 19f.; Num. 18: 15; 3: 1 ff.; Deut. 15: 19); but human sacrifices are replaced even at a very early date by animal sacrifices, and, even if they reappeared at the end of the period of the monarchy, are regarded as forbidden (cf. further Lev. 18: 21; 20: 2ff.; Deut. 12: 31; 18: 10; Jer. 7: 31; Ezek. 20: 25f. et al.). While the present version of the narrative of the sacrifice of Isaac (Gen. 22) is intended to represent how Abraham in his fear of God resisted a temptation (vv. 1, 12), the subject of the original core of the tradition was no doubt the replacement of human sacrifice by animal sacrifice.

3   While the right to offer sacrifice was later restricted to the priests (Lev. 1ff.; Ezek. 43: 18ff.), in the nomadic period the patriarchs acted as priests as well as prophets (above §3b). In the period of the judges fathers of families could still offer sacrifices themselves (Judg. 6: 19, 25; 13: 19ff.; 1 Sam. 1: 3; 2: 13; 9: 12f.).

The priests were originally called to their office by their 'hands being filled' (Judg. 17: 5, 12; Exod. 28: 41); they lived off portions of sacrifices (1 Sam. 2: 12ff.; 21: 5ff.; Num. 18), but could also possess lands (1 Kgs. 2: 26; Amos 7: 17). The duties of the priests included putting questions to God (1 Sam. 14: 18f., 36f.; 23: 9ff.; 30: 7f.), instruction (*torah*) over holy and profane, pure and impure things (Hag. 2: 10ff.; Lev. 10: 10f.; 13: 8ff. Ezek. 44: 23), decisions about the right form of sacrifice (Lev. 1: 3f.; 7: 18; 19: 5ff.; Mal. 1: 10), giving an assurance that prayers of lamentation are heard (1 Sam. 1: 17; cf. Ps. 107: 19f.), and the blessing of the community (Num. 6: 22ff.). Apparently the priests also guarded the legal traditions (Ezek. 44: 24; Deut. 17: 8ff.; cf. Num. 5: 12ff.; Ps. 15).

While it is difficult to see clearly the history of the priesthood, the early statements about Levi are still more disparate.

On the one hand Levi, which in the (older form of the) list of the twelve tribes comes in the Leah group, appears as a tribe which tried to settle in central Palestine, but was scattered (Gen. 34; 49: 5–7). Did the descendants of the scattered tribe take over priestly tasks, or is there only an accidental similarity of name with the later Levites?

On the other hand Levi is the name for a group which in its zeal for Yahweh loosed its ties of kinship (Exod. 32: 29; Deut. 33: 9) and gave up the possession of land (10: 9: Num. 18: 20f.; Ps. 16: 5f.) so that they lived as protected citizens in a status with lower social rights in Israel. According to Deut. 33: 8ff. the Levites had to operate the lot oracle and to teach the *torah*. They are not automatically priests, but can become priests and, because they have dedicated their lives to Yahweh, are given preference in appointments to the office of priest (Judg. 17: 7ff.; cf. 19: 17ff.).

Although Deuteronomy speaks of 'levitical priests' (18; 1ff. et al.), and so can identify priests and Levites, the two are strictly distinguished in the post-exilic period (Ezek. 44; P; Chr.). The priests are regarded as descendants of Aaron; the Levites, who perform humbler services, are subordinate to them. At the head is the anointed High Priest (Lev. 21: 10; 4: 3ff.), who also wears royal insignia (Exod. 28f.; Lev. 8: 4ff.).

4 It is only rarely that the Old Testament indicates what meaning was given to the particular sacrifices. Certainly different motives come together here: gift (Exod. 23: 15; 34: 20), homage, thankfulness, communion with God and of the participants with one another, atonement, expiation, deliverance from impurity, etc. The understanding of sacrifice as feeding God is still to be heard in some expressions (Lev. 3: 11, 16; 21: 6, 8, 17, 21; Num. 28: 2; Ezek. 44: 7; cf. Gen. 8: 21; 1 Sam. 26: 19; Isa. 43: 24; Judg. 6: 18ff.; 13: 15ff. et al.), but had long been given up as a conscious intention. This is clearly expressed by a word of God which was perhaps uttered by a prophet:

For every beast of the forest is mine,
    the cattle on a thousand hills.
I know all the birds of the air,
    and all that moves in the field is mine.

If I were hungry, I would not tell you;
for the world and all that is in it is mine.
Do I eat the flesh of bulls,
or drink the blood of goats? (Ps. 50: 10–13)

5   Thus the Old Testament itself enters into dispute with the sacrificial cult. The prophets in particular, going on from their threat of disaster to God's people as a whole (Amos 8: 2; Hos. 1: 9 et al., below, §14b, 2) and the sanctuaries in particular (Amos 5: 4f.; 9: 1; Mic. 3: 12; Jer. 7; 26 et al.) proceed to a radical criticism of sacrifices. The prophets take up priestly expressions (like 'to hear, to accept with good pleasure'), and turn them into their opposites; the institutions of worship are regarded only as human occasions, no longer as the ordinance of God ('Your sacrifices'; Amos 4: 5, 'So you love it') and reject not only particular sacrifices but all sacrifices (Amos 5: 21ff. et al.). The generalized character of the prophetic announcement of judgement explains the general character of the attack on sacrifices, and both are uttered as the word of God. The prophets do not intend to utter a general and timelessly valid instruction, but to address the men of their own time; but the present, in view of the sort of future that has been announced, comes to have fundamental significance.

The harshest criticism of sacrifice is to be found not perhaps in the older prophets Amos (4: 4f.; 5: 21ff.; 8: 10), Hosea (2: 11 [Heb. 2: 13]; 6: 6; 8: 13), Isaiah (1: 10ff.) or even Jeremiah (6: 19ff.; 7: 21ff.; 14: 11f.) but in Deutero-Isaiah, who in a retrospect to the pre-exilic period gives the general verdict:

You have not brought to me your sheep for burnt offerings,
or honoured me with your sacrifices,
I have not burdened you with offerings,
or wearied you with frankincense.
You have not bought me sweet cane with money,
or satisfied me with the fat of your sacrifices,
But you have burdened me with your sins,
you have wearied me with your iniquities. (Isa. 43: 23f.; cf. 66: 3)

6   Nevertheless criticism of sacrifices is much older than written prophecy. According to 1 Sam. 15: 22 Samuel argues to Saul that obedience is better than sacrifices. A similar tendency is also found in wisdom (cf. the various criticisms of the cult in Prov. 15: 8, 29; 17: 1; 20: 25; 28: 9 et al.). Like Egyptian wisdom before it, Israelite proverbial wisdom (even in the earliest collection, Prov. 10–22: 16) shows a certain distance from cultic matters. Ethical and cultic behaviour can be distinguished, and compared with one another; right action is more pleasing to God than sacrifice:

To do righteousness and justice
is more acceptable to Yahweh than sacrifice. (Prov. 21: 3)

A saying in the same collection, while it does not value social behaviour to one's fellow man more highly than performing worship, makes the qualification that it is only the worship of the righteous that is valid before God:

The sacrifice of the wicked is an abomination to Yahweh,
   but the prayer of the upright is his delight. (15: 8; cf. 21: 27; Sir. 35: 8ff.)

In fact the saying goes beyond this contrast, since it not only contrasts the behaviour of the righteous with that of the evildoer, but also contrasts prayer to sacrifice, and thus indirectly devalues the latter. Another saying is probably only fully understandable if it is regarded as an indirect criticism of the priestly view that atonement can be made through expiatory sacrifices:

By loyalty and faithfulness iniquity is atoned for,
   and by the fear of Yahweh a man avoids evil. (16: 6)

The two together, the fear of God and evidence of fellowship with him, bring about good. Later Jesus son of Sirach (Sir. 35: 1–5; cf. Heb. 13: 16) equates the fulfilment of the commandments and sacrifice:

He who keeps the law makes many offerings;
   he who heeds the commandments sacrifices a peace offering.
He who returns a kindness offers fine flour,
   and he who gives alms sacrifices a thank offering.
To keep from wickedness is pleasing to the lord,
   and to forsake unrighteousness is atonement.

If wisdom can value the upright life as true worship, it becomes understandable that prophets like Amos or Isaiah can achieve such insights.

The sceptical Preacher comes to a quite different view, both developing and going beyond prophetic wisdom thought (Eccles. 9: 2). Since ethical behaviour cannot alter the fate of death for man, any more than can his attitude to sacrifice, both threaten to become indifferent:

One fate comes to all, to the righteous and the wicked, to the good and the evil, to the clean and the unclean, to him who sacrifices and him who does not sacrifice.

7   As well as direct criticism of sacrifice (Ps. 50: 9ff.; cf. 40: 6; 51: 16; 69: 30f. [Heb. 40: 7; 51: 18; 69: 31f.) the psalms also contain indirect criticism, or at least a replacement of sacrifice by the word, when they speak before the community in a transferred sense of sacrifice as praise and thanksgiving:

Offer to God a sacrifice of thanksgiving, and pay your vows to the Most
  High . . .
He who brings thanksgiving as his sacrifice honours me. (Ps. 50: 14, 23)

O Lord, open thou my lips,
  and my mouth shall show forth thy praise.
For thou hast no delight in sacrifice;
  were I to give a burnt offering, thou wouldest not be pleased.
My sacrifice, O God, is a broken spirit;
  a broken and contrite heart, O God, thou wilt not despise.

(Ps. 51: 15–17 [Heb. 51: 17–19]; cf. 22: 25f.
[Heb. 22: 26f.]; 27: 6; 54: 6 [Heb. 54: 8];
95: 2; 107: 22; 116: 17; 119: 108; 141: 2 et al., against 66: 13ff.)

While praise was originally uttered at the offering of sacrifice, it was later
separated from it and made independent. In this way the word comes to take the
place of sacrifice, and so itself become an act of sacrifice. How far this 'spirituali-
zation' (cf. H.J. Hermisson, *Sprache und Ritus im altisraelitischen Kult*, Neukirchen,
1965) is an event within the cult, and how far a certain distancing from the cult is
expressed in it, is difficult to decide; probably both tendencies are at work in the
complex statements of the psalter. In any case in the identification of word and
sacrifice an original insight emerges: sacrifice is self-offering. In the offering of
sacrifice this intention comes to expression in the rite of the laying on of hands,
which is variously interpreted as transference of ownership, as identification, and
especially according to the Old Testament evidence as transfer of sin: the
sacrificer lays his hand upon the head of the animal (Lev. 1: 4, 3: 2, 8, 13; 4: 4, 15,
24; 16: 21 et al.). According to these statements in the psalms man is no longer
represented by sacrifice, but appears on his own behalf (Ps. 51: 17 [Heb. 51: 19];
cf. Rom. 12: 1).

III THE PERIOD OF THE MONARCHY

1   As individual tribes had united for common battle in the face of the danger from the Canaanites (Judg. 5), under the continual threat from the Philistines (cf. 1 Sam. 9: 16) a state came to be formed. The situation made common action of all the tribes under permanent leadership desirable. So Israel was welded together to form a state by the necessity of war; but it remained a single political entity only for a brief period.

The origin of the monarchy is connected with the name of Saul (*c.*1000 BC). After his brief and ultimately unsuccessful reign the house of Judah and its smaller neighbours made David king (2 Sam. 2: 1–4), but the ten northern tribes made Saul's son Ishbaal king. The independence of north and south was thus clearly revealed; both parts had in some measure had a separate existence from the beginning. After the death of Ishbaal David became king over Israel too by a treaty agreement (2 Sam. 5: 1–3). He ruled at first in the remote city of Hebron, but soon created for himself a new capital in Jerusalem, which lay on neutral ground (in the middle between the two kingdoms) and was independent of the tribes. Further David conquered it not by the levy of Israel but by his own mercenaries. The special connection of Jerusalem with the person of the king is indicated by the name 'city of David' (5: 6–9); the Davidic monarchy and the city are closely connected right down to the time of the later messianic expectations. In the course of time not only did David incorporate the Canaanite city-states into Israel, but his empire extended over the neighbouring peoples (esp. 2 Sam. 8). From the nation-state of Saul David built up an empire such as had hitherto not been known in Syria-Palestine.

Although David seems to have treated Jerusalem politically as his own personal possession, he made it into the cultic centre of Yahwistic faith by transferring the Ark there (2 Sam. 6), and this was confirmed by Solomon's subsequent building of the temple (1 Kgs. 5–8). The city became for the first time the main cultic centre of all Israel (below, §13). So Israel acquired a unity in the person of the king and in the central cultic place. A prophetic word from God confirmed the election of Zion and of the Davidic dynasty (2 Sam. 7; 23: 5; Ps. 89: 3 [Heb. 89: 4]; 132: 11ff.). As in the old tradition of Sinai, Yahweh is again connected with a place, and at the same time with a ruler who becomes the 'son of God' (Ps. 2: 7; 89: 26f. [Heb. 89: 27f.]). By contrast with the charismatic call of the leader of the tribal levies, the dynasty which was to rule 'for ever' on the throne in Jerusalem was something essentially new. The question is whether it is possible for the

Yahwistic faith, coming from the nomadic period, to take over the completely alien institution of monarchy without breaking up.

While Saul and David were directly designated king by God, Solomon begins a dynastic succession. After his death not only did the empire break up into small states, but the newly won political unity of Judah and Israel fell apart (926 BC). But the Yahwistic faith remained the state cult, which David had made it, in the two divided kingdoms. Jeroboam I appointed two old cultic centres, Bethel and Dan, as royal sanctuaries (Amos 7: 13), at which also Yahweh was worshipped (1 Kgs. 12: 28f.; cf. Exod. 32: 4; Hos. 8: 4ff.; 10: 5). Historically this counter-foundation had more justification than the choice of Jerusalem as the central sanctuary, for both places, especially Bethel, were connected with the Yahwistic faith by a long tradition (Gen. 28: 10ff.; Judg. 17f.). In fact political and national motives were the decisive factor: the sanctuaries of the northern kingdom were meant to prevent pilgrimages to Jerusalem, so that pilgrims to Zion should not acknowledge the Davidic dynasty. The final capital of the northern kingdom (in which unlike the south there was a succession of dynasties) was Samaria; and the history of the north was in external relations strongly dominated by the need to repel the Aramaeans, with their capital at Damascus.

In spite of their shared faith the north and south remained separated for centuries, until the fall of Israel to the Assyrians (722 BC) and Judah to the Babylonians (587 BC), both predicted by the prophets. In fact the rivalry between these two parts of the country continued beyond this breach into the contrast between Jews and Samaritans.

2 A state which united Israelites and Canaanites was bound to tolerate the religion of the Canaanites or even (as was done later by Omri and Ahab (c. 880–850 BC) in the north) to seek for political reasons to introduce an official syncretism.

At the time of Israelite dependence upon the great empires the borrowing of foreign state cults was actually necessary. The subjection to Assyrian power meant at the same time the recognition of the God Ashur, who had to be represented by an altar in the temple of Jerusalem (2 Kgs. 16: 7ff). In this situation, whether officially or through popular piety, the worship of sun and star deities (Amos 5: 26; Zeph. 1: 5; 2 Kgs. 17: 29ff.; 21: 3, 5; 23: 4f., 11ff.) and of the Queen of Heaven, probably Ishtar, the goddess of the planet Venus, (Jer. 7: 18; 44: 15ff.), was accepted.

Nevertheless not only did prophetic polemic oppose this multifarious syncretism (Jer.; cf. Mic. 5: 13 [Heb. 5: 12ff.] et al.), official reforms too may have tried to eliminate it (1 Kgs. 15: 12f.; 2 Kgs. 18: 4). In particular the Deuteronomic reform under Josiah (621 BC), which made the central cultic place at Jerusalem the only one (2 Kgs. 23), was concerned to bring into force the first command-ment against the worship of Canaanite and foreign deities. But even this did not succeed in eliminating syncretism for ever (Ezek. 8; 23; Jer. 44; Isa. 57: 3ff.; 65: 2ff.; Mal. 2: 10ff. et al.).

But what happened at the beginning of the monarchy is of more significance than the events at the end of it, since this had considerable consequences for the Yahwistic faith itself. It could no longer shake off these influences, since they became too deeply embedded. David after the conquest of Jerusalem probably already allowed much that he found there to remain (below §13). Since he made himself the king of the city, Jerusalem concepts of monarchy were certainly transferred to the Davidic dynasty. Just as Israel in the early period took over Canaanite sanctuaries, so particular forms which were already known in the surrounding world were taken over in the arrangement chosen for the temple in Jerusalem. The temple in which God dwells is characteristic of the lands of civilization. The bull image in Bethel (and in Dan) in particular combined the native faith of Israel with conceptions drawn from foreign religions.

The new relationship of Yahweh to dynastic monarchy on the one hand and to Zion on the other profoundly altered and enriched Israel's beliefs about God; but Canaanite conceptions of God also had a profound influence. The Yahwistic faith, quite apart from the borrowing of cultic usages, made borrowings directly or with alterations from the neighbouring religion, which must now be discussed. In this way it developed and in the course of the relationship evolved something new.

§10 The Significance of the Canaanite Gods in the Old Testament

Palestine as a land of transit was exposed to varied cultural influences from north and south, especially from Mesopotamia and Egypt (above, §1, 1). It is therefore a harsh oversimplification to speak only of Canaanite religion and to seize either exclusively or predominantly on its relationship to the Old Testament. Nevertheless the influences of the ancient Near Eastern empires were rarely transmitted directly, but were predominantly mediated through Canaan.

1 Until a few years ago what little was known of Canaanite religion was derived from polemical utterances of the Old Testament, passing statements of neighbouring nations, and accounts in some Greek writers (Philo of Byblos' Phoenician History in the *Praeparatio Evangelica* of Eusebius of Caesarea; the *De Dea Syria* of Lucian of Samosata; Plutarch on Isis and Osiris). In consequence excavations of cities in Syria-Palestine, and especially the discovery of the texts of Ras Shamra or Ugarit (on the northern Syrian Mediterranean coast, destroyed *c.* 1200 BC, that is, about the time of the settlement of Israel) were able extensively to correct the ideas which had been formed earlier of Canaanite religion. Certain conclusions are also possible from numerous inscriptions from Asia Minor and northern Syria on the basis of divine and personal names occurring in them, but only in Ugarit are there preserved as well as rituals, lists, and the like, extensive myths of gods and epics of kings, in which the inhabitants themselves speak of their religion. In this international harbour city, which linked together the Mediterranean and Babylonia, Asia Minor and Egypt, a mixture of languages and of nations was no doubt to be found, but particularly in religion the Canaanite basis seems to have been essentially preserved. Even though there was no historical connection between this remote city-state and Israel, and there were substantial differences in Syria-Palestine between north and south, coast and interior, the verbal agreements of Old Testament and Ugaritic texts are so extensive that this position can only be explained by the assumption that the religious literature of Ugarit is entirely typical of Canaanite religion.

2 The content of the Ugaritic myths is all the more striking. On the basis of the allusions in the Old Testament we would expect evidence of a worship of nature (cf. Jer. 2: 20ff.; Isa. 1: 29f.; 57: 5 et al.). Hosea accuses Israel that following Canaanite practice it seeks oracles from 'wood and staff' (4: 12). Jeremiah rebukes even more clearly those who 'say to a tree, "You are my father", and to a

stone, "You gave me birth" ' (2: 27; cf. 3: 9; Hab. 2: 19). The reference here is clearly to tree and stone worship. Ezekiel states this directly when he forbids Israel to think, 'let us be like the nations, like the tribes of the (other) countries, and worship wood and stone' (20: 32; cf. however also Deut. 4: 28; 2 Kgs. 19: 18 et al.).

The texts of the Canaanites themselves hardly speak at all however of holy stones, trees or springs, in which the deity appears (above §3e). The understanding of Canaanite religion as a simple fertility cult, which only serves to satisfy the needs of agriculture, is much too one-sided. Sacral prostitution (cf. Hos. 4: 13f.), which portrays and symbolizes the relationship of god and goddess, is not mentioned directly at all. (However among the groups of professions there appears alongside the priest the *qadesh*, 'the dedicated one'; cf. Deut. 23: 18; 1 Kgs. 14: 24.) Finally, surprisingly little significance is ascribed to the sun and moon gods. Instead a large structured pantheon like that of the Greeks is found. The gods are arranged in a family as husband and wife, brother and sister, or linked, with a change of generation, as 'sons of gods'. Similar yet more extended systems of gods are known from Egypt and Mesopotamia. But the Canaanite pantheon as it appears in Ugarit and elsewhere in west Semitic inscriptions, is independent of these. Such a family of gods only emerges in a long historical development; originally independent deities are connected on the basis of a political amalgamation. So earthly power relationships are reflected in the world of the gods. The city state which has won precedence places its city god at the head of the pantheon. But the universal deities do not simply grow out of individual unimportant local deities which have extended their dominions.

In the pantheon of Ugarit El and Ba'al, who are also mentioned frequently in the Old Testament, are dominant; beside these leading deities the others are of less importance. But the religions of different populations have already been assimilated to one another in the peaceful coexistence of the two deities. 'El' is a common Semitic deity perhaps already known to the nomads, but the west Semitic weather god Ba'al is a typical phenomenon of cultivated lands. Neither is associated with a place in the myths, in the way that the Old Testament speaks of an El of Bethel (Gen. 31: 13) or of Ba'al Hermon (Judg. 3: 3). There is no sign in the myths of a city god of Ugarit, who might struggle for predominance with another city god. El and Ba'al appear without any qualifying epithets as universal deities. Cosmic rather than political contrasts are found: Ba'al's opponents are the sea god Yam, the god of death, Mot, or the evening star Ashtar, never local deities. Similarly later west Semitic inscriptions mention such all-embracing deities as Ba'al Shamaim, the 'lord of heaven'.

Certainly a uniform religion must not be assumed for Syria-Palestine; we must draw careful distinctions between the different local cults, and between their deities. However is spite of the political divisions of the land, which did not naturally come to form a single large state, but fell apart into a multiplicity of warring city-states, there was a relative degree of unity in religion, which in the course of time remained surprisingly constant for millennia, so far as we can judge in retrospect. It is only the Yahwistic faith which in this area does not fit into the usual pattern: the religion of the old covenant represents a complete break with the traditional, and a distinctive innovation. Nvertheless there were certain points of contact, which altered the Yahwistic faith. Yahweh made certain borrowings from both deities, El and Ba'al, so that the character of each needs to be briefly described.

3   First however a possible misunderstanding must be excluded. If one comes from reading the Genesis narratives about the 'god of the fathers', it is very striking that the Canaanite deities are in most cases, if not all, connected in some way with nature. Some are even drawn in, through their dying and coming back to life, into the cycle of nature, its growth and passing away. But the gods are not identical with the course of nature; they cause it. Even if they are in origin personifications of natural events, they are explicitly distinguished as persons from the events, and stories are told of them which go far beyond natural events. The gods are not themselves the vegetation, but are the power which bestows life. So Ba'al is not the earth, but, as his title indicates, the 'prince' or 'lord of the earth'.

There are no nature deities in the strict sense. Even if the gods appear in nature and its manifold phenomena, they are always concerned for man. Even sun, sky and weather deities are not foreign to man. They protect the royal house, watch over justice, grant life and blessing, answer prayer (cf. e.g. 2 Kgs. 1: 2). Nature deities are therefore not essentially neutral impersonal powers, which can be basically detached from any 'I-thou' relationship. The contrast of natural and personal gives a one-sided treatment to individual features much too strongly to be useful for the distinguishing of religions. The contrast of universal nature religion and particular religion of history, a contrast governed by the opposition of nature and personal freedom, is also inadequate.

a   THE GOD EL

El appears in the Old Testament throughout not as a particular deity but as a title for Yahweh. At most echoes are heard now and then of El as a proper name (Isa. 14: 13; Ezek. 28: 2). So the name Israel is compounded not with Yahweh but with El (above §6, 2). But as a rule El is simply a general term for god. In Deutero-Isaiah Yahweh makes the claim to be El alone, that is, a god, and there is no other (Isa. 45: 22; 43: 12 et al.). Here however the element of proper name in El has completely receded; an identification is no longer implied, because the prophet knows only one true God: 'To whom will you liken El (God)?' (40: 18). For this reason there is no evidence either or any subordination of Yahweh to El (cf. Ps. 82; Deut. 32: 8f.; above, §8, 1).

1   So throughout the history of Israel Yahweh may be called El. The gods of the fathers are already identified with El (above, §3c, e); later Jerusalem is apparently

the decisive location for the taking over of conceptions of this god (see above, §3. According to Gen. 14: 18–20, which has been inserted into its context as an isolated section, Melchizedek, King of Salem (i.e. Jerusalem; Ps. 76: 3) and 'priest of El Elyon' blesses Abraham; he pays him as a return gift the 'tenth of all', and thus gives legitimation to the claim of the Jerusalem priesthood to a tenth. This El Elyon, the 'highest god', was probably the city god of Jerusalem, as an El Olam, god of eternity, is known from Beer-sheba (Gen. 21: 33). There is however a possibility that Elyon, unlike the other epithets of El (above, §3c) was himself originally an independent deity. In the oldest instance outside the Old Testament, in the inscriptions of Sefire, there is found in a list of deities the pair El and Elyon. At a late period Philo of Byblos knows of an Elyon, who is called the most high, and distinguishes him from El-Kronos. The two passages can also be explained on the assumption that Elyon was originally an epithet of El and became hypostatized and independent, but it cannot in the last resort be decided with certainty whether it is the unity or the separation of the two deities that is original. In any case El and Elyon go readily together. In the Old Testament too the two names several times go together; they are also found in alternate parallelism, and so are equated (Num. 24: 16; Ps. 73: 11; 77: 9f. [Heb. 77: 10f.]; 82: 1, 6; Isa. 14: 13f. et al.).

The conjecture that the city god of Jerusalem, the tradition of whom lives on in the psalms of Zion (Ps. 46: 4; 47: 2; 48: 1f. [Heb. Ps. 46: 5; 47: 3; 48: 2f.]), was only called Elyon is opposed by the fact that David gave names compounded with El to his sons who were born in Jerusalem (2 Sam. 5: 14ff.); while personal names compounded with Elyon are not attested.

So El and Elyon appear to have been closely connected already in pre-Israelite Jerusalem.

2   While El Elyon according to the Old Testament (Gen. 14: 19, 22) was worshipped as 'creator of heaven and earth', only the title 'El, creator of earth', is attested in the various inscriptions (from Karatepe, Leptis Magna, Palmyra and perhaps Boghazköi). There is no non-biblical attestation in which the creation of the world is ascribed to the god El; indeed no myth of the creation of the world at all is so far known from Canaanite territory. It has therefore often been conjectured that in the Old Testament title 'creator of heaven and earth' the titles of two quite different gods have been conjoined. But so far no parallel to 'El, creator of earth', such as 'Elyon creator of heaven' has been found. Ba'al is connected with heaven, but he is not called creator; as Ba'al Shamaim he is 'lord of heaven' in which he dwells. On the other hand in the Ugaritic myths the creation of gods and men is ascribed to El in attributes such as 'father of the gods', 'father of mankind' or 'creator of the creation'; in the west Semitic inscriptions mentioned the creation of earth too is ascribed to him, and finally in the Old Testament the creation of heaven and earth. On this evidence El can be regarded as the creator

god, even if no cosmogony is preserved. In the world around Israel a strong distinction was apparently made between the creator god and the vegetation god (below, §11f) who dies and rises again, and thus preserves nature or makes it live again. This distinction is found elsewhere too in the history of religions.

3 El, as the 'king' who is regarded as holy and wise, stands at the head of the pantheon in the Ugaritic myths. But El is not the 'highest' god in the cult. The chief temple in Ugarit was dedicated to Ba'al; a temple to El has not yet been discovered. Because Ba'al as the giver of life was more important to his worshippers, he played a larger part too in the cult. Ba'al is the 'near' god, El the 'far' god, who in the terminology of the phenomenology of religion seems to occupy more and more the place of the *deus otiosus*. This is supported not only by his property of being the creator, his kindly and generous nature, his antiquity, but also in the spatial picture of him by his dwelling place, which is far away in the mythical world. He is placed 'at the source of the two rivers, among the floodbeds of the two abysses', that is, where the waters of the world above and of the underworld meet. El is not directly affected by the battles which shake the world of the gods, but he is not driven out of his lordship either. He has not yet become a so-called high god, who has no longer any task in the life of the community and therefore does not enjoy worship either. El still receives sacrifices in myth, or appears as the protector of the dynasty, reveals himself to the king in a dream, to promise him descendants (in this being like the gods of the fathers).

Nevertheless in later west Semitic inscriptions the importance of El is yet more reduced. Ba'al comes to occupy first place, El is driven into second place. Finally in Palmyra at a late date and elsewhere Ba'al becomes the leading deity. The god El too has a history.

b   THE GOD BA'AL

While the Old Testament contains no polemic against the god El, it certainly does have one against Ba'al. Israel had probably come into collision with him in the period of the judges, and in any case did so intensively in the period of the monarchy. The opposition gradually intensified, so that the struggle between Yahweh and Ba'al became religio-historically the most significant event. We already find Gideon, whose real name was Jerub-ba'al, 'Ba'al fights', tearing down an altar of Ba'al with the Ashera (Judg. 6: 25ff.; cf. the cultic fellowship with Ba'al Peor in Num. 25; Hos. 9: 10). Elsewhere too the Old Testament tells of an altar or even a temple being dedicated to Ba'al and of sacrifice being made to him (1 Kgs. 16: 31f.; 18: 25f.; Hos. 11: 2; Jer. 11: 13, 17 et al.) Men kiss the bull image which represents Ba'al (1 Kgs. 19: 18, Hos. 13: 2). Priests and prophets serve him; he is able to answer prayers (1 Kgs. 18: 19ff.; 2 Kgs. 10: 19ff. et al.) and to heal (2 Kgs. 1).

1   On the evidence of Elijah and Hosea, apostasy to Ba'al seems to have taken place earlier and more strongly in the northern kingdom. In the south it is Jeremiah at the end of the seventh century who first attacks the Baalization of the Yahwistic religion (not the earlier Isaiah or Micah, nor Amos in the north). Was the struggle of Ba'al and El not known before? Further only brief mentions are preserved of a temple of Ba'al in Jerusalem (2 Kgs. 11: 18; 21: 3; 23: 4; Jer. 2: 28; Zeph. 1: 4 et al.). Personal names on the inscriptions of Lachish and Arad also establish by contrast with the ostraca of Samaria that in the south the worship of Ba'al was much less widespread.

We have detailed accounts from Israel. It was roughly in the middle of the ninth century that the struggle between the two religions broke out. The wife of king Ahab, the Phoenician princess Jezebel, brought with her from her home the worship of Ba'al. In the capital Samaria a temple of Ba'al was built, which Jehu destroyed (1 Kgs. 16: 31f.; 2 Kgs. 10: 18ff.). This cult was not a complete innovation; it had taken place from the beginnings in local sanctuaries scattered round the land. Now it became the official state worship which was practised and protected by the royal court itself. The frequent personal names compounded with Ba'al at this period show clearly the danger to the Yahwistic faith. It remains unknown however in which of his manifestations Jezebel introduced Ba'al: was Melkart, the city god of Tyre, or the 'Ba'al of heaven', now worshipped in Israel? In the contest upon Mount Carmel (1 Kgs. 18: 16ff.) the deity is nowhere more exactly named, for instance as Ba'al Carmel. If the individual narratives have not been secondarily generalized, the struggle was not with the god of a locality in his specific form, but with Ba'al himself, who can appear under different names. Similarly the god in the Ugaritic myths does not appear in a special local form, but as the universal Ba'al. Only King Ahaziah, in the scene which leads to the confrontation with Elisha (2 Kgs. 1), puts an inquiry to the particular deity 'Ba'al Zebub, the God of Ekron'; but this title 'god of the flies' is probably a distortion of the general title Ba'al Zebul, 'prince Ba'al'.

In the course of time the picture which the Old Testament gives of the Canaanite god comes to lose clarity; it becomes more and more general and colourless. The prophets Hosea (2: 15, 19) and Jeremiah (2: 23; 9: 13), to a large extent the Deuteronomistic history (Judg. 2: 11; 3: 7 et al.) and the Chronicler entirely, speak of Ba'al in the plural. While originally perhaps the local manifestations were treated polemically and contemptuously as different local deities, 'the Ba'als' finally becomes a term for 'foreign gods' as a whole (1 Sam. 7: 4; cf. Hos. 3: 1). The first commandment is therefore substantially directed against the Ba'als and Asheras (Judg. 2: 11ff.; 10: 6ff.; 1 Sam. 12: 10 et al.). How far this view is justified, how far it was developed in retrospect after the centralization of the cult, it is hard to decide. If the holy places were exposed to the danger of Baalization or even succumbed to it, it was Yahweh that was still meant under these other names. The difference between false worship of Yahweh and true worship of Baal had become blurred. There must have been in Israel some identification of Yahweh and Baal, even if only within marked limits of space and time (cf. the personal name Bealiah 'Baal is Yahweh', 1 Chr. 12: 6); only so can we understand the prophetic criticism, which is directed both against the worship of idols and against the distortion of true worship of God. In any case a history of opposition between Yahweh and Ba'al can be traced from the time of the judges, through Elijah, Hosea, Jeremiah, down to the Deuteronomic history and the work of the Chronicler, with development, high point, and decline into merely typical and general mentions, until on account of the promise of Hos. 2: 17 [Heb. 2: 19], the word Ba'al in personal names is distorted into Bosheth, 'shame' (2 Sam. 2: 8ff. against 1 Chr. 8: 33ff.).

2   In spite of the lively struggle of the Old Testament with Canaanite religion the real character of Ba'al does not come out clearly. Perhaps Ba'al, 'lord, owner', is only a title of the god, and his real name is Hadad (cf Zech. 12: 11); the two are identified at an early date, because they do at least have the same area of activity. Another god of similar character is Dagan (cf. 1 Sam. 5: 2ff.). Ba'al is the god of the weather, who rules over wind, clouds and rain, and appears in thunder and lightning (hence his title 'rider upon the clouds', above, §9, 2). At the same time he is a god of vegetation, who gives the earth its fertility. His presence decides the life or death of man; for nature dies away if Ba'al goes down into the underworld, and breaks out again into life if he returns to earth (below, §11c, 2). So Ba'al appears in the polemic of Hosea (2: 5, 8ff. [Heb. 2: 7, 10f.]) as the giver of corn and oil, of wool and of flax. In the Ugaritic myths he is called 'the strong, the mighty' (aliyan), 'the prince' (zebul) or 'judge, ruler' (shophet); images and representations of him in statues show him in battle attitude, for example with a club in his right hand, and wielding the lightning, like a lance, in his left hand. The young victorious god both claims, and has, power. The extensive cycle of myths from Ugarit which tells of the fortunes of the god, describes the battle of the gods among themselves for dominion, which includes at the same time dominion over man. Ba'al in the fight with the sea-god Yam obtains the kingdom, and wins recognition of his victory by building a temple or palace. If the opposition of land and sea is reflected here, the struggle for dominion with the god of death, Mot, reflects rather the annual succession of summer and winter, of dry and rainy season, although the myth does not mention a regular annual recurrence of the events, but represents the course of nature only indirectly and partially.

3   The youthful god occurs usually with a goddess. Often this is the 'virgin Anat', sister and wife, goddess of fertility and of war at the same time. She is mentioned in the Old Testament only in place names and in personal names (Judg. 1: 33; 5: 6 et al.). On the other hand Ba'al is often mentioned with Astarte (Judg. 2: 13; 10: 6; 1 Sam. 7: 3f. et al.: the Babylonian Ishtar) or with Ashera (Judg. 3: 7; 1 Kgs. 18: 19), who is represented in a wooden cultic image, a tree or post (1 Kgs. 15: 13 et saep.; cf. Deut. 16: 21; Isa. 17: 8).

Anat and Astarte are probably united in Atargatis, the Dea Syria, the Syrian goddess of the Hellenistic and Roman period.

In Canaanite religion the female goddess appears to have been worshipped less as the 'great mother', but rather as a virgin goddess of love. This marriage of god and goddess is repeated on earth by imitation in the fertility cult; it symbolizes what happens in heaven. In any case the Old Testament often suggests that sexual orgies were connected with the cult of Ba'al (Jer. 2: 20ff.; Hos. 4: 13f. et al.; Exod. 32: 6, 25 in connection with the golden calf) and sees here a danger which threatens from the Canaanite side (Gen. 9: 21ff.; 19; 34 et al.). In the myth too the procreative power of the deity can be represented by a bull, although the deity is basically thought of as having the form of a man. It is attested by Greek writers that the wife before marriage underwent a once-for-all sexual rite. Both ancient Near Eastern and Old Testament passages speak of male and female 'devoted ones' (qᵉdēšîm) living in the temple, who were devoted to prostitution (Deut. 23: 18; 1 Kgs. 14: 23f.; 2 Kgs. 23: 7 et al.). Later the foreign cult is referred to in stereotyped form by the expression 'to whore after the gods' (Exod. 34: 15f. et saep.).

The prophets (Hosea; Jer. 3; Ezek. 16; 23) took up this cultic myth of the marriage of the god, and reinterpreted it in terms of the relationship of god and nation; at the same time they destroyed it through the announcement of the end of the marriage. Thus the first commandment changed the form of the myth. Israel could not acknowledge at least in principle the concept of a partnership of god and goddess, but it had to and could take from Ba'al the blessing of fertility. Now it was Yahweh that gave the rain (so already Gen. 2: 5; 7: 4; 8: 22J; 1 Kgs. 17f; Jer. 5: 24; Zech. 10: 1f.) and with it the fruit of the land (Hos. 2; Deut. 11: 13ff.; 28: 2ff.; 33: 13ff. et al.). The responsibility of Ba'al was transferred to Yahweh, for it was he who had led Israel into the cultivated land. Thus nature was understood from the point of view of history. Because the first commandment had to apply in the new setting of life as well, the nomadic god of the Exodus and the leader in the holy wars became also the bestower of fertility.

§11   The New Beliefs about God

a   THE KINGDOM OF GOD

The New Testament expectation of the reign of God, for which the Lord's Prayer also prays, 'thy kingdom come', followed on from Old Testament hopes. But was the belief in a kingdom of God, which seems to describe the power and activity of God in a basic and comprehensive way, originally shaped by Israel's understanding of God?

1   Just a look at the dictionary shows that the concept of 'kingdom' in the Old Testament did not have a correspondingly great significance. The instances, which as a whole are relatively few in number, are very unequally spread, and are only frequent in the hymnic parts of the psalter. This position of itself argues against the assumption that the concept of the kingship of God was an archetypal element in Israel's faith. Buber wished to demonstrate 'the religious idea of a fold-kingship of God as an actual historical one for the early period of Israel' (*Kingship of God*, London, 1967, p. 14), and described the covenant at Sinai as a royal covenant. Others too have been ready to distinguish between the two concepts of Yahweh as the king of the nation and as the king of the world. In the concept of Yahweh's kingship over Israel a nomadic and old Israelite tradition was found, which was later expanded into a proclamation of the world dominion of Yahweh. The few relevant texts in the Pentateuch which speak of the kingship of Yahweh (Exod. 15: 17f.; Num. 23: 21; Deut. 33: 5, 26) all come however from the time after the entry, or are even not to be dated before the beginnings of the monarchy. Finally personal names which are compounded with *melek*, king, only become frequent during the exile. A kingship of God is therefore unknown to the early traditions of Israel; neither the God of the patriarchs, nor the God of Sinai, nor the God of the Exodus was worshipped as 'king'.

2   After the entry into Canaan however the Israelite tribes encountered the belief in an extensive family of gods, with a royal ruler at their head. In order to deprive the foreign gods of their dominance in the land, Yahweh drew to himself basic features of these gods, and Israel proclaimed 'Yahweh (and not El or Ba'al) is king'. In the oldest definitely datable passage which speaks of the kingship of Yahweh, there are still echoes of the argument with the religion of the Canaanites. The vision of the call of the prophet Isaiah (6: 1–5) offers a typical picture in the scene in heaven:

Isaiah sees the Lord sitting upon a high exalted throne. Six-winged seraphim stand before him and call to one another:

Holy, holy, holy is Yahweh Sabaoth;
the whole earth is full of his glory.

Then Isaiah breaks into a lament: 'Woe is me! I must be silent . . .; for my eyes have seen the king, Yahweh of Sabaoth.'

The same association of ideas, the divine king who is regarded as holy, and is given glory by the heavenly court, is found several times. The so-called thunderstorm psalm (Ps. 29: 1f., 9), for which a Canaanite origin has long been conjectured, calls upon the sons of God to give glory to the heavenly king. Ps. 97, a hymn to Yahweh as king, even exhorts the gods to bow down before Yahweh (v. 7; similarly Ps. 96: 7ff. et al.; cf. below, §11b, 2). Yahweh appears each time as the head of a group of beings obedient to himself.

The whole tradition complex was borrowed by Israel; it is found attested in quite similar form in the Ugaritic myths. As the Old Testament calls to gods and sons of gods to bow down before their king, so the gods there offer glory to the king El in homage. El is called by the title king precisely as the head of the congregation of the gods. When Yahweh is enthroned amid a band of divine beings obedient to him, it looks very much as if Israel has transferred to Yahweh the mythical ideas which centred around the Canaanite king and god.

But Yahweh has also assumed features of the kingship of Ba'al. In the same myths Zaphon is regarded as the holy and beautiful mountain on which the weather god sits enthroned after his victory over his enemies. The Old Testament attaches to Yahweh's dwelling place upon Zion these concepts of a royal mountain of the gods in the north:

His holy mountain, beautiful in elevation,
    is the joy of all the earth,
Mount Zion, in the far north,
    is the city of the great king. (Ps. 48: 1f., Heb. 48: 2f.; cf. also Isa. 14: 13f.)

The confession 'Yahweh reigns as king for ever' (Ps 146: 10; Exod. 15: 18; Ps. 29: 10 et al.) may also go back to Canaanite ideas. In the myth Ba'al is promised a royal dominion for an unlimited future:

You shall take your eternal kingdom,
    your dominion for ever and ever.

A later psalm (Ps. 145: 13) offers an almost word for word parallel to this promise; such formulaic language could have persisted over a long time in the cult:

Thy kingdom is an everlasting kingdom,
and thy dominion endures throughout all generations.

Finally, is an echo of the kingship of Baʿal to be found in the statements about Yahweh's judging in power the gods and the earth (Ps. 82; 96: 13; 98: 9)?

3   When it is recognized that a divine kingship over Israel is not securely attested before the entry, but that it is common in Canaanite and generally in ancient Near Eastern religion, and that there are a number of connections between the Ugaritic and the Old Testament texts, the conclusion cannot be escaped that Yahweh's kingship is an inheritance of Canaan. Israel's God has united in himself the kingship of both gods, El and Baʿal.

Both characteristics point to Jerusalem. Here we find not only the concept of the court (Isa. 6) but also of the mountain of God (Ps. 48: 2 [Heb. 48: 3]) at home; the king is enthroned in the temple (cf. later Jer. 8: 19; 17: 12; Ezek. 43: 7; Zech. 14: 16f. et al.). Perhaps the pre-Israelite city god of Jerusalem was already worshipped as king; for the name of the priest-king is in fact Melchi-zedek, '(my) king is (the god) Zedek'. But the transference of the concept of kingship need by no means have taken place only in Jerusalem; for the various local El deities may also have been king-gods. However these various points of contact throughout the land are not accessible to us through the facts given in the Old Testament. The concept of the throne, which is attested in connection with the ark (1 Sam. 4: 4; 2 Sam. 6: 2: 'who sits upon the cherubim') but also independently of it (1 Kgs. 22: 18ff.) outside Jerusalem, could give support to the conjecture that Yahweh was already proclaimed as king in the temple at Shiloh. We do not have however a clear instance of Yahweh's kingship from the premonarchical period.

4.   Clearly the title 'king' originally designates in a mythological way the one god as ruler over the other gods. This is true not only for the Ugaritic myths, but similarly for the whole of the ancient Near East. In Egypt for instance Amun is regarded as king of the gods, and similarly Marduk in Babylon. The kingship of God is not therefore primarily a statement about the relationship of God to his worshippers. God is superior to men just as God, while the title 'king' indicates one who is exalted among his like. However the area of dominion of the God-king includes both earth and men.

Israel transferred this mythological conception to Yahweh:

For Yahweh is a great god,
a king above all gods. (Ps. 95: 3; cf. 96: 4; 97: 7, 9)

But faith was not content with Yahweh's priority over the other gods, but deprived them of their power completely. The king of the gods became a ruler over heavenly beings subordinate to him who are put under his power, and are at his service (Ps. 103: 19ff.; Job 1f.). So the pantheon, venerated among Israel's neighbours, but now deprived of its power in the Old Testament, forms Yahweh's court, until Yahweh's claim to exclusivity leads to the denial of the existence of the gods at all (cf. Ps. 96: 5).

The change which the concept of the divine king undergoes in Israel goes yet deeper. Is it only accidental that we do not find in the Ugaritic myths analogies for Yahweh's frequent title 'king of Israel', or 'our, your, my king'? No doubt in Canaan as elsewhere in the ancient Near East the address 'my king' must have been possible in prayer. But only the myth gives the grounds for the kingship of god by telling how the god obtained his supremacy. This myth was lacking in Israel. This meant that basically at least those concepts in which the heavenly kingdom was thought of on the analogy of the earthly social structure, with the king at the head of the state (cf. above, §6b, 4) were abandoned. As the marriage of god and goddess in the myth are reinterpreted in prophetic simile of the relationship of God and nation, the king of the gods becomes king over Israel: 'Yahweh is our king; he will save us' (Isa. 33: 22).

5 Yahweh's royal dominion was therefore not originally restricted to Israel, and only then spread across the world. The course of its history was rather the opposite: the 'king upon earth' (this title is attested in the myth) became king of the nation. A sentence like 'Yahweh is king over all the earth' (Ps. 47: 7 [Heb. 47: 8]) still falls in principle within the realm of Canaanite concepts of God; for the extension of his dominion over the earth and over men comes together with the conceptual pattern grouped around divine kingship (cf. further Isa. 6: 3 or the perhaps traditional title 'lord of the whole earth', Josh. 3: 11, 13; Ps. 97: 5 et al.). To this extent universalism is a characteristic of Canaanite religion. Israel had already encountered it in Palestine and therefore did not need to develop it itself in the late period. But the earlier view of a religio-historical development is to this extent justified, that the cosmic and universal approach was in many ways expanded and developed in the Old Testament.

Even the passages which proclaim Yahweh's kingship over the nations (Ps. 47: 8 [Heb. 47: 9]); Jer. 10: 7; Zech. 14: 13ff. et saep.) do not go directly back to pre-Israelite traditions; for the statement that a god who is king rules over the nations is apparently not attested elsewhere. Perhaps in Israel mythological concepts of the battle of the gods have been reinterpreted to give the battle of the nations (cf. below, §13, 5); in any case a worldwide dominion of God is proclaimed in such language. The spatial delimitation of his dominion in Ps. 103: 19, which develops the Canaanite conception of the king of heaven in the midst of his court, is unsurpassable:

Yahweh has established his throne in the heavens,
    and his kingdom rules over all.

The spatial extension made by the Old Testament of the divine kingship is matched by an extension to 'all times' (Ps. 145: 13; Dan. 3: 33; 4: 34 [Heb. 4:

31]). But this pressure towards the cosmic does not ignore the individual. The individual cries out in full trust to the God whose kingdom is without end in space or time, 'My king and my God' (Ps. 5: 2 [Heb. 5: 3]; 84: 3 [Heb. 84: 4]; 145: 1 et al.) Just because God rules everywhere and at all times he is the god of the individual; universalism and individualism belong together (cf. Ps. 103: 1f., 19). This coud be summarized a little exaggeratedly, by saying that Yahweh from being king over the earth became king over the whole world and over all time, but from being king over the gods became king over Israel and the individual.

6   In the late period the kingship of Yahweh becomes more and more the promise of a reality that will come to pass only in the future. Deutero-Isaiah proclaims for the immediate future a new Exodus of the people in exile in connection with an accession of God which is of worldwide importance:

> How beautiful upon the mountains
>   are the feet of him who brings good tidings,
> who publishes peace, who brings good tidings of good,
>   who publishes salvation,
>   who says to Zion, 'Your God reigns'.
> Hark, your watchmen lift up their voice,
>   together they sing for joy;
> for eye to eye they see
>   the return of Yahweh to Zion.
> Break forth together into singing,
>   you waste places of Jerusalem,
> for Yahweh has comforted his people,
>   he had redeemed Jerusalem. (Isa. 52: 7–9)

While Deutero-Isaiah in his preaching can anticipate the occurrence of a coming event, calling men in the present to offer praise already for the future action of God (Isa. 42: 10–13), similarly he goes far beyond the exilic situation in seeing the messengers of victory already hastening to Jerusalem. Dramatically he describes how the feet carry the herald from mountain to mountain into the city, to bring it the message of peace: 'your God has become king'. This is not an enthronement cry with which the new ruler is installed in his office on his accession, but a proclamation which announces the event, which has already taken place, to the land (cf. Ps. 96: 10: 'Say among the nations, Yahweh has become king', and 2 Sam. 15: 10). This message is not completely new to the listeners (Ps. 47: 5 [Heb. 47: 6]; 93: 1 et al.); the cry is also familiar to Israel's neighbours.

According to the Babylonian creation epic *enuma elish*, which was read at the New Year festival, the gods acknowledge 'Marduk is king'; at a procession to the temple of the god Ashur a priest cried out 'Ashur is king', and in the Ugaritic myth it is proclaimed '(the sea god) Yam is dead, Ba'al is king'.

A similar cry is attested in the Old Testament at the enthronement of an earthly king: '... has become king' (2 Sam. 15: 10; 2 Kgs. 9: 13; cf. 1 Kgs. 1: 18).

On the basis of this and of the Babylonian parallel Mowinckel deduced (in 1922; a similar theory had already been put forward by Volz in 1912) a Feast of the Enthronement of Yahweh, which was observed at the autumn or New Year festival (cf. §9b, 3). The main pieces of evidence are the enthronement psalms 47; 93; 96–99, also called 'songs of Yahweh as king'. The cry 'Yahweh has become king', or, as it can also be translated, 'Yahweh rules as king', is common to them. It remains highly disputed whether Israel really celebrated such a feast; there may at least have been a cultic action associated with this cry, for instance in a procession of the Ark (cf. Ps. 24: 7ff.).

The enthronement psalms are strongly hymnic in character, but lack formal unity and come from different periods. Ps. 47 and 93 are the most likely to be pre-exilic, while the other psalms have incorporated later concepts. The tradition then is old and was available to Deutero-Isaiah, and must have continued to have influence in the late post-exilic period (Zech. 14: 16ff.).

Deutero-Isaiah understands the reality of this word as still in the future, and announces it as imminent. Further he changes the traditional formula 'Yahweh has become king' into an assurance 'your God', just as he speaks not of 'the word of Yahweh' but of 'the word of our God' (40: 8), to bring out more clearly within the framework of his message of consolation the love of God for his people. Although it is Deutero-Isaiah who promises a revelation of God to 'all the ends of the earth', he never makes use of the royal title in the absolute, but declares to the listeners that God is 'your king' (43: 15), the 'king of Israel' (44: 6; 41: 21, in contrast with foreign gods). The specific situation of the exile is traceable finally in the recasting of the picture itself. Although God enters his city as victor, it lies in ruins; for the Babylonians have destroyed Jerusalem. The watchers see not only the messengers, but God himself 'eye to eye' as he returns home to Zion. Because the prophet makes use of the dramatic medium of the 'view from the wall' he does not need to describe the coming of God but only the accompanying circumstances. God himself does not become an image, only his coming is described. It is however so significant that it completely drives out the real occasion of the proclamation, the return of the exiles.

It is not certain whether Deutero-Isaiah was the first to look for a reign of God. A saying in Ezekiel could be only a little older or of the same age; there too the kingdom is regarded as a future historical event; God will exercise dominion.

With a mighty hand and an outstretched arm, and with wrath poured out, I will be king over you. I will bring you out from the peoples and gather you out of the countries where you are scattered, with a mighty hand and an outstretched arm, and with wrath poured out; and I will bring you into the wilderness of the peoples, and there I will enter into judgement with you face to face. (Ezek. 20: 33–35)

The new Exodus, unlike the first, will not only bring a particular people out of just one land (Egypt), but will bring back those widely scattered among the nations. However the saying has a twofold character: by this act of liberation God displays his royal power, but at the same time sets up his royal judgement. Return and leading back through the wilderness are not only acts of salvation, but bring in the judgement, which in direct encounter 'face to face' (cf. 1 Cor. 13: 12) distinguishes between the faithful and the unfaithful. The criterion is again the first commandment: anyone who has taken part in the worship of idols will not experience the new entry into the land.

In Deutero-Isaiah's message of the end of vassalage, the expectation of a return of the nation has saving character only. But both prophets agree in uniting two traditions which did not originally belong together: the Israelite tradition of Exodus, and the concept of the king (cf. also Lam. 5: 17ff.). In this they have successors. Although Deutero-Isaiah's imminent expectation of the coming of the kingdom of God in the return to Jerusalem was not fulfilled, his hope was carried on, and the belief in a future which changes the present remains. In particular a series of additions to the different books of the prophets link the proclamation of the kingdom of God with the announcement that the scattered will be brought home. Israel in the late period needed assurance in the situation in which it found itself, and so it adds its hopes onto the words of the prophets who had threatened present distress in their messages of disaster.

> I will surely gather all of you, O Jacob,
>   I will gather the remnant of Israel . . .
> He who opens the breach will go up before them . . .
> Their king will pass on before them,
> Yahweh at their head.

In this insertion into Micah (2: 12f.) the threat of judgement has fallen away once for all. God as the one who 'opens the breach' leads the united nation, northern and southern kingdom, on the way to freedom. God's power carries out the act, and so the gathering and reuniting of Israel is followed by the final reign of God. It will be of unlimited duration, and will also make of the diaspora the remnant, the basic element of a new people:

> And the lame I will make the remnant;
>   and those who were cast off, a strong nation;
> and Yahweh will reign over them in Mount Zion
>   from this time forth and for evermore.   (Mic. 4: 7)

The recovery of the lost may be accompanied by the renewal of old rights of ownership, so that ancient injustice is put right; but, in spite of all the restoration of things lost, Yahweh, not Israel, has the dominion (Obad. 19–21). When political and national expectations such as freedom and unity of the nation in their own land are associated with the concept of the kingdom of God, the hope remains specific. The king is apparently understood as leader of the returning band. So through the superimposition of the Exodus tradition the civilized land concept of the kingdom of God is nomadized, or made mobile.

Later writers, whose concepts are already preparing the way for apocalyptic, reach out further in their expectation. Zech. 14 threatens on 'that day' judgement upon Jerusalem and upon other nations, but only as a preliminary to salvation. The division which (upon the analogy of the selection of a remnant in Israel which takes place in the war of Yahweh) is made among the nations, is only the preliminary condition for the participation of the nations in the worship of Yahweh. 'Yahweh himself has brought the nations on to the stage in order to defeat them in battle, and so bring them to a recognition of his kingship' (H.-M. Lutz, *Jahwe, Jerusalem und die Völker*, 1968, p. 53). Those who do not take part in the war or who emerge from it saved will go on pilgrimage every year to Jerusalem in order to worship Yahweh as king:

> Then everyone that survives of all the nations that have come against Jerusalem shall go up year after year to worship the King, Yahweh Sabaoth, and to keep the feast of booths. (v. 16)

While the hope goes beyond Israel to include the other nations, it holds fast to the essential criterion of Yahwistic faith, its exclusivity. So the ancient Near Eastern mythological concept of divine kingship is radically reinterpreted in accordance with the mind of Israel's faith, stamped by the first commandment, and redirected towards the future:

> And Yahweh will become king over all the earth; on that day Yahweh will be one and his name will be one. (v. 9)

The so-called apocalypse of Isaiah (chs. 24–27) expands yet more strongly the area of dominion of the king 'upon mount Zion': Yahweh will assert himself not only against earthly powers but also against heavenly powers until he reigns unrestrained (Isa. 24: 21–23). Finally the conclusion of Ps. 22 (vv. 28–32) seems to go beyond 'all the ends of the earth' and the afterworld to include even the dead in the kingship of God.

However the kingdom of God is never solely expected for the future, but is always also believed in as present (cf. §16b, 5); it is hope and confession, prayer ('thy kingdom come') and confidence that the will of God is already being done, 'thine is the kingdom'.

Conceptually the expectations of the kingship of God and of the reign of the Messiah remain separate one from another and exist alongside one another unharmonized. The Old Testament only very rarely contrasts divine and earthly kingship (1 Sam. 8: 7; 12: 12; cf. Judg. 8: 22f.) or connects the two into a unity (1 Chr. 17: 14; 28: 5; 29: 11f., 23 et al.; cf. Ps. 110: 1). It is not that the distinction developed only later; the two declarations come from different traditions (even the ancient Near Eastern 'royal ideology' (below, §12a, 1) is hardly connected directly with the concept of a king of the gods) and keep their independence by and large into the New Testament period (cf. 1 Cor. 15: 28 et al.). The apocalyptic of the post-Old Testament period did sometimes make the two reigns follow one another: the rule of God follows that of the Messiah. But this chronological arrangement leaves unanswered the problem of their relationship.

In summary the title of king has undergone a threefold change since it was taken over into the Old Testament: the reign of God was focused upon man, spatially and temporally extended to infinity, and finally expected in the future.

b THE 'HOLY' GOD

In his well-known book *The Idea of the Holy*, Rudolph Otto begins with the statement that 'there is no religion in which [the holy] does not live as the real innermost core, and without it no religion would be worthy of the name' (Oxford, 1923, p. 6) and S. Mowinckel takes up this insight from the phenomenology of religion: 'religious practice has always known that it stood over against something that was "holy" (*Religion und Kultus*, Göttingen, 1953, p. 31). In the same way holiness has been regarded as 'the essential character of the God revealed in Israel'. Both 'Yahweh's nature, his character' and 'the essence of Old Testament religion' were found in it, so that it could be portrayed as a 'religion of holiness' (J. Hänel, *Die Religion der Heiligkeit*, Gütersloh, 1931). It was argued that the understanding of the holiness of God was what distinguished the Mosaic faith from the religions of the surrounding countries. This evaluation was until recently supported by our religio-historical knowledge as well. Graf Baudissin summarized his studies as follows: 'in the non-Old Testament area a formation from the root *qdš* (= holy) with application to the deity cannot be demonstrated with certainty for early times' (*Kyrios* III, Giessen, 1929, p. 208 n. 1).

1 But is the belief in the holiness of Yahweh really fundamental from the beginning for the faith of Israel?

> God came from Teman,
> and the Holy One from Mount Paran. (Hab. 3: 3)

Certainly this description of a theophany from Sinai is not intended strictly historically. Can it nevertheless in one point be taken literally? Is 'the Holy One' an epithet of the God of Sinai? Older passages (Deut. 33: 2; Judg. 5: 5) which similarly describe God coming from the mountain, do not contain the epithet. In fact it is only very late that statements are found in the Old Testament about the inherent quality of holiness of God.

Before the Ark, which had brought them disaster, the Philistines cry in horror, 'who is able to stand before Yahweh, the holy God?' (1 Sam. 6: 20). This question however presupposes an acknowledgement of Yahweh, and has been at least as far as the wording goes put into the mouth of the foreigners. The concept of holy occurs only rarely in connection with the Ark, and not in old and significant passages. If the psalms, which are difficult to date, are ignored, sayings from the prophets Amos, Isaiah and Hosea, from the eighth century, are the oldest instances. The Old Testament only makes a different impression because the late Priestly writing uses the concept of holiness in such varied ways in the Pentateuch. The instance in Amos is uncharacteristic: 'The Lord Yahweh has sworn by his holiness' is only an introductory formula to an address by God (Amos 4: 2; 'so that my holy name is profaned' is an addition in priestly language in Amos 2: 7). The saying of Hosea 'for I am God and not man, the Hole One in your midst' (11: 9) which declares God's freedom to forgive, cannot be firmly placed traditio-historically (the parallels in Isa. 31: 3; Ezek. 28: 2 lack the expression in question). The occurrence of the expression in Isaiah indicates its origin all the more clearly.

The call scene, in which the choir of seraphim begin singing 'Holy, holy, holy is Yahweh of Sabaoth' (Isa. 6: 3) gives the impression that the prophet experienced the holiness of God here authentically for the first time. But with the concept of the throne we encounter the inherited tradition complex of the heavenly court (cf. esp. Ps. 29: 1f., 9f.; above, §11a, 2). The 'sons of gods' are already regarded as holy in the Old Testament:

> Who is like thee, Yahweh, among the gods?
> Who is like thee, majestic in holiness? (Exod. 15: 11)
> Let the heavens praise thy wonders, O Yahweh,
> thy faithfulness in the assembly of the holy ones!
> For who in the skies can be compared to Yahweh?
> Who among the heavenly beings is like Yahweh,
> a god feared in the council of the holy ones,
> great and terrible above all that are round about him? (Ps. 89: 6–8)

Both times a question is asked about the incomparability of him who rules over the holy gods or 'sons of gods', and information from the surrounding world confirms that Israel inherited these expressions. In west Semitic inscriptions (Yehimilk, Eshmunazar) there is mention of the 'holy gods', and a magic text from Arslan Tash calls the gods 'all the holy ones'. The Old Testament seems to have reduced the heavenly beings again to spirits that do service (Job, 4: 18; 5: 1; 15: 15; Zech. 14: 5; Dan. 4: 10; 8: 13 et al.). But in the Ugaritic myths the god El probably also bears the title 'the kindly and the holy', while the gods, who are usually called 'sons of El', are perhaps called 'sons of the holy one'. Finally one ancient Near Eastern goddess is directly called 'the holy one' as her name. 'Holy' is therefore an old term for god, familiar from the world around Israel. Even leading gods are given this epithet. On this evidence the Canaanite understanding of holiness is not at all impersonal or material; nor can anything specifically Israelite be seen in the fact that 'the Old Testament first and foremost calls God himself holy'.

Rather this term is common to Israel and to the Canaanite world. Indeed to all appearances Israel first learnt from the Canaanites to call Yahweh holy. Several connections suggest this conclusion. The nomadic traditions were not familiar with this title, any more than they were with that of king. Neither the gods of the fathers nor the God of Sinai are called holy in really old tradition; before the entry into the cultivated land and the encounter with Canaanite religion Israel does not appear to have worshipped Yahweh as holy; at least the term is lacking. But this is something peculiar in the history of religions. Commonly the unusual power which religions experience in things, persons and the deity himself is understood as holy, while Israel originally did not make this equation of power and holiness. The distinction of God and man, like the activity of God, was expressed in other ways.

It can perhaps be recognized, as with the title of king, where particularly Israel took over the concept of holiness; again Zion plays a decisive part. Ps. 48: 1 (Heb. 48: 2) transfers to it the mythological concept of Ba'al's 'holy mountain' in the north (cf. Ps. 2: 6 et saep.). Ps. 46: 4 (Heb. 46: 5) speaks of 'holy habitations of Elyon' which are now regarded as the dwelling place of Yahweh (cf. 68: 5 [Heb. 68: 6]; 47: 8 [Heb. 47: 9]). So the Jerusalem city god (El) Elyon seems to have been worshipped as holy, and Yahweh has succeeded him in this. In this way the strong connection of the concept of holiness with Jerusalem, 'the holy city' (Isa. 52: 1; Joel 3: 17 [Heb. 4: 17] et al.) can be explained.

2 If the Old Testament connects God's holiness with his 'honour', 'glory' (*kābōd*), this may be following an inherited association. The sons of gods according to the Ugaritic myths as well as according to the Old Testament offer 'glory' to the holy king of the gods; the cry not only rings out however in the realms of the heavens (Ps. 29: 1f., 9; 19: 1 [Heb. 19: 2]), but extends right down to earth (Isa. 6: 3) and is here taken up (Ps 96: 7; 24: 7ff.; cf. 97: 6; 57: 5, 11 [Heb. 57: 6, 12]). It is not therefore going too far to assume that the concept of the glory of God, which was again local to Jerusalem, especially to the temple (Ps. 26: 8), comes from Canaanite religion. The Old Testament itself perhaps still offers evidence of the fact that the ascription of glory was originally made to the god El; Ps. 19, the first part of which has for long been considered to derive from Canaanite thought-forms, begins:

The heavens are telling the glory of El.

The Old Testament increasingly developed and altered this tradition; 'glory' becomes more and more an epithet or even the manner of revelation of Yahweh. In P the glory of God is God's light-filled appearance from heaven and his presence upon earth, which forms the basis for the cult upon Sinai (Exod. 24: 15ff.; 40: 34f.; Lev. 9: 23f.) and acts to save as well as to guide the wanderers in the wilderness (Exod. 16; Num. 14; 20; cf. 16f.). According to Ezekiel (1: 28; 10: 18f.; 11: 22f.) the 'glory' of Yahweh leaves Jerusalem once it is doomed, to return only in the future new temple (43: 2ff.). The connection of holiness and glory is at home in both P and Ezekiel: when God glorifies himself, he 'shows himself holy' (Exod. 29: 43; Ezek. 28: 22ff.; 36: 20ff. et al.). Finally Deutero-Isaiah proclaims the impending appearance of God's glory, of his victorious might (Isa. 40: 5), to all nations (cf. 60: 1ff.; 62: 2; 66: 18f.; 11: 10; Ps. 97: 6).

Glory is therefore not something which Yahweh has in himself or is, but which is active in the world. Correspondingly Israel too understands the holiness of Yahweh as an event. Even in the call of Isaiah it is not confined to the heavenly stage; because of his impurity man cannot take part in the song of the choir of seraphim (Isa. 6: 5); but the purification is his call to prophetic speech. The opposition of holy and impure is not simply a fixed one, but can be reduced or even removed by touching (cf. Exod. 29: 37; Lev. 6: 11, 20). God's holiness is expressed in men; characteristic changes must therefore be recognized here too, which have taken place since Israel adopted the concept. In particular this is shown by the divine name, which has already become a set expression 'the holy one of Israel'. This term, which seems to be modelled on the title 'God of Israel', and which was already in the tradition for Isaiah to take over (cf. Ps. 89: 18 [Heb. 89: 19]; 71: 22; 78: 41) appears in his work usually in accusations and warnings (Isa. 1: 4; 5: 19, 24). Its meaning appears most clearly in a secondary passage (5: 16; cf. 2: 8f.): The 'holy' God shows himself holy in judgement of his people and so maintains his holiness. As Yahweh's holiness can be defined as jealousy (Josh. 24: 19f.), here it is interpreted in accordance with the first commandment: God alone has power (cf. Ezek. 28: 22; Deut. 32: 51). Deutero-Isaiah maintains this concern, but using the same expression, 'the holy one of Israel', announces God's salvation and the coming deliverance of the people (Isa. 41: 14, 16; 43: 14f. et al.).

3   Just because holiness is understood from the viewpoint of God's relationship to man, it is in the course of time concentrated ever more strongly upon God. The laws of P also speak of material holiness: cultic objects are 'holy' (in future expectation, Zech. 14: 20f.), and can transmit this quality by touch. 'Holy' is distinguished from 'very holy' and both again from mere purity, and so it is laid down how men are to deal with material things. But only the late period uses the title 'the holy one' absolutely for Yahweh (Hab. 3: 3; Prov. 9: 10 et al.). When Deutero-Isaiah inquires like a teacher of wisdom (40: 25),

> To whom then will you compare me,
>   that I should be like him?
>   says the Holy One

there may still be an echo of the old idea of God who sits enthroned among the holy company of heaven (Exod. 15: 11). But the contrast is more acute here: the one stands over against all others (again in the sense of the first commandment) as the only one:

There is none holy like Yahweh
– there is none beside thee –,
there is no rock like our God. (1 Sam. 2: 2; cf. Deut. 32: 51 et al.)

When the distinction between God and man is defined by holiness, this holy one nevertheless remains near to men: 'holy is Yahweh, our God' (Ps. 99: 9, 3, 5; cf. 22: 3 [Heb. 22: 4]); Hos. 11: 9).

For thus says the high and lofty one
who inhabits eternity, whose name is Holy;
I dwell in the high and holy place,
and also with him who is of a contrite and humble spirit,
to revive the spirit of the humble,
and to revive the heart of the humble contrite. (Isa. 57: 15)

The Code of Holiness finally (Lev. 17–26) sees the holiness of man as grounded in the holiness of God, when it commands men to imitate God: 'You shall be holy; for I Yahweh your God am holy' (19: 2; 11: 44f.; 20: 26; cf. Exod. 22: 30 et al.). Perhaps this statement of principle, which summarizes all the individual ordinances beforehand, is meant not only as a demand but also as a statement: 'you are holy, for I am holy', just as Deuteronomy (14: 1) heads its laws with 'You are sons to Yahweh your God'. But if we are meant to pick up both possibilities of interpretation, the meaning of the sentence would be that man should behave as he actually is already by God's creation.

c   THE 'LIVING' GOD: CONCEPTS OF THE DYING AND RISING GOD

Under the term 'the living God' the Old Testament seems to sum up in one expression an attitude that is central to it: God is not an abstract idea but is encountered as concrete and personal; he does not remain remote from human events, but intervenes in history, and on each occasion gives a new definition to the present. So this concept expresses better than any other how man is affected by God.

But the actual occurrence of the combination does not of itself give support to this understanding: if the oath-formula 'as Yahweh lives' is excluded, the expression 'the living God' in its various forms is confined in all to just ten occurrences; in fact the Old Testament only rarely makes statements about the essential character of God. This shows that the epithet 'living' is not a theological concept of basic significance from the earliest period on. In fact at first it does not express anything specifically Old Testament. We have again a foreign term for God which Israel took over: the 'living God' is not originally the God of history, who constantly does new things, but the God of myth. However Israel has so reinterpreted the concept that it was able to express through it its own experiences of God.

1   The concept of God's 'life' is found most frequently in the oath, which had to be undertaken for instance at a sanctuary, with hand raised: 'as truly as Yahweh lives' (Judg. 8: 19 *et saep.*). A similar oath formula is also applied to other gods. A problematic saying from Amos (8: 14 – usually Amos does not attack alien cults but social corruption) announces judgement on this:

> Those who swear by the guilt [but instead a divine name, Ashima or Ashera, should perhaps be read] of Samaria, and say 'as thy god lives, O Dan', and 'As the way [pilgrimage?] of Beersheba lives', they shall fall, and never rise again.

Whether the threat is directed against a real cult of foreign deities or only against the worship of Yahweh under alien form (bull images?), the confession is hardly one of Yahweh alone. The oath formula 'as truly as God lives' can apply equally to Yahweh and to foreign gods; other nations turn to their own god (cf. Jer. 12: 16; Zeph. 1: 5; also Gen. 31: 53). The oath is not made generally by the life of God, but calls upon the name of a particular god; so swearing by other gods can be prohibited (Josh. 23: 7 et al.). Since one's own God is named solemnly as witness and judge, the oath acquires at the same time the character of a confession of faith. Because however the expression 'as Yahweh lives' is lacking in the early Pentateuchal passages, Israel seems to have coined it only in the land of cultivation in dependence upon foreign customs. For the immediate Canaanite neighbourhood however an expression like 'Ba'al lives' is not attested as an oath formula. But corresponding expressions are attested from Egypt at the beginning of an oath 'as Amon lives', etc.).

2   The oath formula is similar in wording to the praise with which the intercessor with general applicability summarizes his thanksgiving to God for deliverance from distress:

> Yahweh lives, and blessed be my rock.
>   and exalted be the God of my salvation. (Ps. 18: 47)

The God who is able to bring about salvation is praised as 'living'. Perhaps we have here however a transferred sense of the word. It is not really the one who gives life that is living, but he who has life. What is the original context of the usage which contrasts dead and living? There is an equivalent of the cry 'Yahweh lives' in the cry in the Ugaritic myth which breaks out in the world of the gods when nature reveals the return of Ba'al to life:

> Aliyan [= strong] Ba'al lives,
> the prince, lord of the earth exists!

This cry has a strict parallel in a lament which is heard upon the death of Ba'al:

Dead is Aliyan Ba'al,
dead is the prince, the lord of the earth.

Here we have the home of the contrast of the life and death of the god. As late as the Hellenistic period Lucian (*De Dea Syria* §6ff.) tells us that the god Adonis comes back to life. Both instances come from the myth of the dying and rising god, which is told in the ancient Near East in various versions: a young god is slain, the gods mourn, a goddess looks for the dead god until she finds him. While the god is in the underworld, nature dies upon earth, but it springs up again when the now living god returns to earth. Canaan tells this myth of Ba'al Hadad and Anat, Egypt of Osiris and Isis, Asia Minor later of Attis and Cybele, and finally Phoenicia and the Greeks of Adonis and Aphrodite. (Mention could also be made of Melkart of Tyre or of the god of health Eshmun, and in a broader sense among the Germanic peoples, of Baldur.) The fate of the god seems in each case to have been portrayed in cultic representations. The later mystery ceremonies identify the initiated mystic with the deity; because he shares the experience of his fate, man obtains redemption. In the ancient Near Eastern period however the performance of the myth, with the exception of the Egyptian Osiris ritual, does not yet give man any share in the resurrection of the deity.

The Old Testament itself mentions such resurrection gods in passing. The lament for the death of the Sumerian and Babylonian god Tammuz, who does not seem in the strict sense to belong to the dying and rising gods, is mentioned in the vision of the prophet Ezekiel: he sees in the gate of the temple 'women weeping for Tammuz' (8:14). Small flowerbeds – vessels or sherds filled with earth – were supposed to portray the fate of the god Adonis with their quick flowering and wilting (Isa. 17:10f.; 1:29); for the dying and rising god is also a vegetation god. The lament for the god Hadad Rimmon is mentioned in Zech. 12:11; the 'one beloved of women' in Dan. 11:37 (cf. also Jer. 22:18; 34:5). In the story of Jephthah's daughter too (Judg. 11:34ff.) traces of a corresponding occasion of lamentation have been found. In any case Israel knew this myth; indeed it took over various of its motifs in an altered form.

3   It is especially in the message of the prophet Hosea, who attacks the Baalization of the Yahwistic faith in all sorts of different expressions, that allusions can be found to such concepts. The announcement of judgement, that Yahweh is withdrawing from his people, forms the occasion for a song of penitence which the people sing, or which the prophet puts in their mouths:

Come, let us return to Yahweh;
for he has torn, that he may heal us;
   he has stricken, and he will bind us up.
After two days he will revive us;
   on the third day he will raise us up,
      that we may live before him.

Let us know, let us press on to know Yahweh;
   his going forth is sure as the dawn,
he will come to us (as surely) as the showers,
   as the spring rains that water the earth. (Hos. 6: 1–3)

In distress the people seem to find their way back to their God: he will help them again out of the disaster which he brought upon them; he who punished can also heal (cf. 2 Kgs. 5: 7). So the lament changes quickly into trusting certainty: soon God will give new life – as certainly as the new morning comes. The whole passage could have been formed from features of the myth of the dying and rising god: 'rising again' after a short break of two to three days (attested similarly for Osiris and elsewhere; cf. Jonah 2: 1), 'healing' (the rising god is at least at a later period also a god of healing, cf. 2 Kgs. 1: 2), perhaps 'pressing on' (following the god into the underworld) and the comparison with the rain (the gift of the vegetation god) all remind us of this connection. The Greek translation contains in addition the motif of finding (the search for the dead god); and when Hosea in the immediately preceding word of judgement announces that Yahweh is 'returning again to his place' (5: 15) he may be alluding to it too. The accumulation of so many varied motifs is surely not accidental. But the song associates these features no longer with God, but with the nation; and it paints a picture of one wounded, who will be healed by the treatment he receives, and not of the resurrection of one that is dead. This distinction between what the text says and the tradition it draws on should be noticed also in the other allusions to the myth. Hosea possibly picks up the theme of seeking and finding (5: 6; cf. 2: 7 [Heb. 2: 9]) or of mourning (10: 5; cf. 7: 14) to give them a new significance which alters their sense in an entirely different context: the lament is no longer for the recurrent mythical event, but for a once-for-all historical event, the coming judgement.

   The proverbial expression of joy in harvest, which follows upon tears in the sowing, may also be occasioned by an ancient Near Eastern rite, which imitated the fate of the vegetation god:

Those who sow in tears
   will reap with shouts of joy.
He that goes forth weeping,
   bearing the seed for sowing,
shall come home with shouts of joy,
   bringing his sheaves with him.   (Ps. 126: 5f.)

Is the weeping just a pictorial expression for hard wearisome work and the pain which will give way to future joy? Possibly religious customs in agriculture live on in the image. Sowing, with the breaking up of the ground and the sowing of the seed in the earth, was like the burial of the dead god, and was therefore a time for sorrow. Greater significance was given especially in the ritual of Osiris to the so-called 'hoeing of the earth' as the 'killing and sinking of Osiris in the lap of the earth'; 'for in the sowing Osiris, who is himself the corn, is sunk into the earth, indeed trodden into the earth' (H. Bonnet, *Reallexikon der ägyptischen Religions-geschichte*, Berlin, 1952, p. 168). On the other hand the springing up of the seed is a sign of the rebirth of the deity, who does not remain in the earth, and therefore was greeted with joy. The Old Testament itself mentions the performance of the ritual in the case of the so-called gardens of Adonis (Isa. 17: 10f.; 1: 29).

Since the death of the god can also be called 'sleep' and his return from the underworld 'waking up' (cf. Hab. 2: 19), it is from this circle of ideas that we can understand the words in which Elijah pours out his mockery upon the prophets of Ba'al, whose sacrifice and prayers are not heard:

> Cry aloud, for he is a god; either he is musing, or he has gone aside, or he is on a journey, or perhaps he is asleep and must be awakened. (1 Kgs. 18: 27)

The Old Testament employs the same originally mythical expression many times for its own beliefs about God. After Ps. 78 has narrated the events in the early history of the nation down to the destruction of Shiloh, it describes the historical turning point with the words: 'Then the Lord arose as from sleep'. It is hardly accidental that in this context (vv. 64–6) we hear of the weeping of the people, and metaphorically even of God's frenzy and of his victory over enemies. It is the laments that call upon God to 'wake up, to rouse himself' as a prayer to intervene on behalf of the oppressed (Ps. 7: 6 [Heb. 7: 7]; 35: 23; 59: 4f. [Heb 59: 5f.]; esp. 44: 23f. [Heb. 44: 24ff.]).

> Rouse thyself! Why sleepest thou, O Lord?
> Awake! Do not cast us off for ever!
> Why dost thou hide thy face?
> Why dost thou forget our affliction and oppression?

Such expressions just allude to the mythical sleep of God; the new meaning of the borrowed expression is clear in the context. The story of the fate of the god has changed into a prayer for deliverance from distress by man. Sleep in these psalms is just 'an image for the behaviour of the *deus absconditus*, the god who is silent and does not intervene, who does not, or not yet, display his life and his power to the suffering' (H.-J. Kraus, 'Der lebendige Gott', *EvTh* 27 (1967)). The Old Testament has so little preserved the original content of the idea, which thought of an interruption of the activity of the god for a time of sleep, that in quite the opposite sense the words become an expression of God's continuing care and protection:

> Behold, he who keeps Israel
> will neither slumber nor sleep. (Ps. 121: 4)

Perhaps Deutero-Isaiah goes back to the same tradition when he proclaims in similar language that God 'does not faint or grow weary' and interprets this expression as 'he gives power to the faint' (Isa. 40: 28f.). The words of the psalms and of the prophets may however not necessarily be of mythical origin, but could have been transferred, without an underlying model, from human circumstances to God, in order to deny them in his case. If however the language is of mythological origin, once again the concept has been turned into a statement about God's actions towards men.

4   Expressions about God's 'living' seem to come for the most part, but not exclusively, from this mythological area of dying and rising again. The life of God was probably understood in a more comprehensive sense from the beginning. Already in the Egyptian Old Kingdom there are personal names in which the gods are called 'possessors, givers and preservers of life'. In Mesopotamia expressions like 'god lives' or 'is the living one', which were well known in Egyptian religion, were not customary; however the gods bear the title 'lord of life'. In Ugaritic texts the term 'life' is also connected with the god El, who is not one of the gods of vegetation. The oath formula 'as the god lives' is not associated only with dying and rising gods. The ancient Near East is not bound therefore to have conceived the 'life' of a deity only in contrast to his death, that is, in the framework of natural growth and decay. Or do we have here a somewhat extended linguistic usage, because the gods are involved in mortality? They belong 'to the realm of what is created', and are therefore, over and above the dying and rising gods, 'subject to the fate of death' (S. Morenz, *Egyptian Religion*, London, 1973, p. 24).

This is not how the Old Testament understands God; it guards against the transfer of death and resurrection to Yahweh.

> Art thou not from everlasting,
> O Yahweh my god, my Holy One, who does not die? (Hab. 1: 12).

The disagreement with the myth, which appears elsewhere only indirectly, comes out explicitly here as an exception: God does not die, but is from everlasting. In saying this 'Israelite thought does not mean the eternity of pure being, but the eternity of activity'; for all times and so for the present too it is God's 'being at work' that is believed in (K. Elliger). This is the meaning too of the confession 'Yahweh lives' (Ps. 18: 46 [Heb. 18: 47]; cf. Josh. 3: 10). As the laments can take up the idea of God's awakening out of sleep in order to move him to intervene in distress, so this song of thanksgiving (Ps. 18) can indicate the deliverance that has taken place with the formula which among neighbouring religions announced the return of the god of vegetation to life. The mythological language is preserved, but with a quite different sense, to express God's willingness to help. To borrow a summary formulation of W. Graf Baudissin, the concept of the life of God is borrowed, but the Old Testament 'has eliminated the overcoming of death, but preserved the concept itself'; the expression 'living God' characterizes Yahweh 'as the god who shows himself active in operation' (*Adonis und Esmun*, Leipzig, 1911, pp 507, 466).

5   When the Old Testament itself uses the distinction of living and dead in relation to God, the contrast takes on another meaning. In David's fight against Goliath (1 Sam. 17: 26, 36) and in the distress of Hezekiah in the siege of Jerusalem (2 Kgs. 19: 4, 16) the living god is invoked: let Yahweh not let himself be mocked by the enemies as powerless, but (unlike the mortal gods of the already defeated nations (19: 18)) prove himself living, and intervene to save. In accordance with the thought of early Israelite tradition (above §7), the 'living God' is the leader in war. Probably here already, as frequently at a later period, the foreign, dead idols are contrasted to the living, that is, the true God: 'Yahweh is the true God. He is the living God and the everlasting King' (Jer. 10: 10). This meaning undoubtedly does not fit the original understanding, since it effectively determines the meaning of the 'life' of God from the first commandment.

The individual too in his lamentation seeks the God who is able to change distress into deliverance, and to preserve life (Ps. 42: 2, 8 [Heb. 42: 3, 9]; 84: 2 [Heb. 84: 3]):

> As a hart longs for flowing streams,
>   so longs my soul (i.e. I) for thee, O God.
> My soul thirsts for God, for the living God.

Certainly God is never in the Old Testament called 'the life'. As the 'living one' he is not originally the creator (and for this reason the term is lacking in both creation narratives in Gen. 1 and 2) and this may be significant both for the antiquity of the title and for its religio-historical origin: in Canaan the creator god is not the dying and living god of vegetation. But the Old Testament can call Yahweh the 'fountain of life' (Ps. 36: 9 [Heb. 36: 10]; Jer. 2: 13; 17: 13; cf. 38: 16); the God of history, who has appropriated the title 'the living one', reaches out into the realm of creation.

Because the living God is able to give life, the psalmist sets his hope upon him. It is thus that the promise in Hosea (1: 10 [Heb. 2: 1]) can be understood, under which God can create life beyond any humanly calculable scale:

> Yet the number of the people of Israel shall be like the sand of the sea, which can neither be measured nor numbered; and in the place where it was said to them, 'You are not my people', it shall be said to them, 'Sons of the living God'.

The unusual expression 'sons of the living God', which unites two expressions originally foreign to Israel, and which come from the world around, 'sons of God' (below, §12b) and 'living God', points to the God 'who because he himself is life and has life can give beyond human understanding' (W. Rudolph). Thus the Old Testament has associated the concept of the life of God with the relationship of God and man (cf. 1 Sam. 2: 6; 2 Kgs. 5: 7 et al).

Already in the myth the epithet 'living' is given to the god who effects the preservation of the world: the resurrection of the dead god means also the springing up of the vegetation. Even if Israel did not originally describe the activity of Yahweh as life, it did from the beginning know the activity of its God. Even the name Yahweh can be interpreted as 'he shows himself'. Perhaps then the activity of God is the common theme which allows the borrowing of the term. This in any case is what is important to the Old Testament.

d THEOPHANY

1   In some very varied passages in the psalter and in the prophetic literature the Old Testament describes what terrible consequences an appearance of God has for nature. These strange accounts often sound peculiar in their present contexts, but are strikingly similar to one another. The heading later prefixed to the book of Amos is a good example of this in its brevity: it is meant to announce the judgement of God of Jerusalem upon the northern kingdom:

> Yahweh roars from Zion,
>   and utters his voice (of thunder) from Jerusalem;
> the pastures of the shepherds mourn,
>   and the top of Carmel withers.   (Amos 1: 2)

This single verse is clearly constructed on a two-part pattern: the first half describes a theophany, the second its effects. Certain prophetic announcements of judgement have a similar structure:

> For behold, Yahweh is coming forth out of his place
>   to punish the inhabitants of the earth for their iniquity,
> and the earth will disclose the blood shed upon her,
>   and will no more cover her slain.   (Isa. 26: 21; cf. 30: 27ff.; 66: 15f. et al.)

In the strict sense God does not 'appear' at all; it is only the consequences that are visible, and only they are described in detail. In contrast to the patriarchal narratives of Genesis, the story of the call of Moses or the visions and auditions of the prophets, God does not actually reveal who he is or what he wants. In fact (with the single exception of Ps. 50) in such appearances God does not speak at all. Mostly too he comes not to intervene with salvation and deliverance upon behalf of one oppressed (cf. Deut. 33: 2ff.), but to bring confusion and destruction. What is fixed starts to shift, the hills are shaken, heaven and earth are in turmoil. Nature is certainly not here felt to be beautiful or even protective; what happens in it is terrible. Many descriptions of theophanies set the scene by incorporating ever more extensive further motifs (cf. Ps. 18: 7–15 [Heb. 18: 8–16]; 77: 16–19 [Heb. 77: 17–20]; 97; Nah. 1; Hab. 3); but all the presentations are so distinctive and are so closely connected in form and manner of expression that they can undoubtedly be treated as a unity.

2   Although nature theophanies are certainly less specifically Israelite, they are found in the Old Testament more frequently than are similar appearances of God in history. Natural phenomena as powerful accompaniments of the revelation of God are indeed (somewhat in contrast to the person-related faith of the patriarchs) an indication of the religion of the cultivated lands. In fact the Old Testament passages can be related to similar ancient Near Eastern descriptions, and then it is seen that these pictures of the terrible appearance of God were common to Israel and its neighbours, and indeed that Israel borrowed them and transferred them to Yahweh. In particular the gods of fertility and weather, the Sumerian Ishkur, 'who rides upon a storm wind', the Hittite Teshub or the Babylonian and Syro-Canaanite Ba'al-Hadad (like the Germanic Thor) appear in nature, in storm, clouds, lightning, thunder, rain, fire and earthquake. Representations depict the weather god with the lightning as a spear in his hand, and the Ugaritic myth says of Ba'al;

> He raises his (thunderous) voice in the clouds,
>   hurls the lightnings to earth.

The introduction to Amos quoted above compares the voice of Yahweh with the roar of the lion and the thunder of the storm god, who does not now bring rain and fertility, but destroys the vegetation (cf. Ps. 29). Similarly the lightning can become Yahweh's weapon (Ps. 18: 14 [Heb. 18: 15]; 77: 17f. [Heb. 77: 18f.]) and the clouds can be his chariot. As ancient Near Eastern gods spread an aura of terror around themselves, so Yahweh can have a radiance. He draws near in that he shines out:

> Out of Zion, the perfection of beauty,
>   God shines forth.
> Our God comes, he does not keep silence,
>   before him is a devouring fire,
>   round about him a mighty tempest.
>   (Ps. 50: 2f.; cf. 18: 12 [Heb. 18: 13]; Deut. 33: 2f.; Hab. 3: 4)

3   It is rare that the appearance of God goes out from Zion (cf. Amos 1: 2) as in this example; usually Yahweh appears from heaven, and in the oldest texts Sinai is the starting point:

Yahweh, when thou didst go forth from Seir,
  when thou didst march from the region of Edom,
the earth trembled,
  and the heaven dropped,
    yea, the cloud dropped water.
          (Judg. 5: 4f.; Deut. 33: 2; Ps. 68: 8 [Heb. 68: 9] et al.)

It may be argued therefore that it is sufficient to seek the origin of the descriptions of the theophany in the Sinai revelation, and that we need not look to foreign ideas. Both sets of texts have the connection of thunder and lightning and volcanic phenomena, and describe Yahweh's appearance as 'coming down' (Exod. 19: 18; 34: 5 and Mic. 1: 3; Ps. 18: 9 [Heb. 18: 10]). Certainly the tradition of the revelation at Sinai has had an effect upon the descriptions of theophanies; but it cannot simply have been the model for them (J. Jeremias, *Theophanie,* Neukirchen-Vluyn, 1965). On the one hand the two concepts, of Yahweh's theophany at Sinai and his coming from Sinai, must be distinguished (above, §5d). On the other hand the disturbance of nature is unknown to the Sinai account; thunder and lightning are regarded only as accompaniments of the appearance of God, not as God's weapons. These features can only be explained from the representations of foreign storm gods. It was possible for Yahweh to draw to himself some of their properties because the old Israelite tradition told of similar things.

4   While the Sinai narrative in the Pentateuch tells of a revelation of Yahweh in the past, the theophany passages in the psalter speak of a coming of God in the present. When however the prophets take up this idea they use it to announce the appearance of God in the future. As they reshape the nature theophany as a revelation of history in the future, the mythological concept turns into expectation:

For behold, Yahweh is coming forth out of his place,
  and will come down and tread upon the high places of the earth,
and the mountains will melt under him
  and the valleys will be cleft . . .
All this is for the transgression of Jacob
  and for the sins of the house of Israel . . .
Therefore I will make Samaria a heap in the open country,
  a place for planting vineyards. (Mic. 1: 3ff.)

Such descriptions of theophanies can be directed against Israel itself or against foreign nations (Isa. 30: 27ff.; 19: 1) in the prophetic message of judgement, and can either paint the threatening 'day of Yahweh' (Joel 2: 10ff.) or turn into promise (Isa. 31: 4; 40: 10; 42: 13). The nature theophanies only speak of fearful consequences; they do not yet know this double possibility, because salvation or disaster can only be worked out in history for man.

5   Both the hymns of the psalter and the sayings of the prophets are intended to proclaim God's power, which neither nature nor history can resist. This conception is not conceived in general terms, but is related to particular events; God comes ready for action. Even the oldest witness to such a theophany sings of Yahweh's victorious intervention in battle (Judg. 5: 4ff.). Israel was able to take over the descriptions of theophanies from the religions of the surrounding countries because they speak of an act of God. While the act of God is perhaps repeated regularly in the vegetation myth of the dying and rising god, it is here understood as being a specific event. The descriptions of theophany do not depend on a feeling for a universal presence of God in nature.

If the deity was originally known and experienced in destructive storm and in earthquakes, by the time of Israel's appearance the ancient Near East had long ceased to equate the gods with events in nature (above, §10, 3). The different phenomena only accompany his appearance. Only in this sense could the Old Testament understand the natural phenomena as consequences of the presence of God. Probably this language in Israel no longer implied its original context, since it was taken over from the surrounding world, where indeed it was very widely distributed. At least the prophets who take over such descriptions only hint at what happens when God comes. The world cannot stay as it is. The high is made low, as they put it in other words (Isa. 40: 4; 1 Sam. 2: 6ff. et al.). The descriptions of theophany with their two basic elements – God's appearance and its consequences – seek to express both the relation of God to the world and the distinction between God and world; they speak of God because they describe the effects of his presence.

e   THE FIGHT WITH THE CHAOS MONSTER

1   In the descriptions of theophanies there are frequent allusions to a fight of Yahweh with a monster, or rather with the sea. Both mythological ideas are intended to glorify God's power by their terribleness, since they portray how he wins victory against his enemies in nature.

> When the waters saw thee, O God,
>   when the waters saw thee they were afraid,
>   yea, the deep trembled.
> The clouds poured out water;
>   the skies gave forth thunder;
>   thy arrows flashed on every side.
> The crash of thy thunder was in the whirlwind;
>   the lightnings lighted up the world;
>   the earth trembled and shook.
>   (Ps. 77: 16–18 [Heb. 77: 17–19]; 29: 3; 93: 4; 114: 3; 18: 15
>   [Heb. 18: 16]; Nah. 1; 4 et al.)

If God's appearance can cause an earthquake and the uproar of the sea, it is a natural conjecture the theophany and sea battle are not two originally separate traditions, but only two different features of a single myth complex. The representation of a God who in the one case walks upon the clouds in storm and thunder, and hold the lightning as a weapon, and in the other victoriously conquers the sea, can easily be explained as the borrowing of characteristics of Ba'al: the weather god also won the battle with the sea.

In the very frequent echoes of a fight of Yahweh with the sea in the Old Testament, especially in hymns and laments in the psalter, but also in the prophetic books, influences of the Babylonian myth of creation were found at first after the decipherment of cuneiform. In this the god Marduk catches the sea goddess Tiamat and her brood of serpents with net and storm, divides the monster, forms the heaven out of the upper half, while he creates the earth, with hills and rivers, from the other parts of the body. In the Old Testament influences from Babylonian mythology are found here and there (e.g. in the Flood story), probably mediated by the Canaanites. But the Ugaritic texts have shown us that the mythological conceptions of the Canaanites are by no means necessarily identical with those of the Babylonians; even the names of the warring participants are different. The Egyptians had other conceptions again, and their cosmogonies vary from city to city. So we must not attempt to make a unity out of the ancient Near Eastern traditions.

While the fight between Marduk, the city god of Babylon, and the sea goddess Tiamat is a fight with chaos, which ends with the creation of the world, the fight between Ba'al and the sea god Yam, told in the Ugaritic myths, presupposes that the world already existed. Apparently Ba'al with his victory gains dominion over the gods for the first time; Marduk had already been proclaimed king. In particular Ba'al does not need to create the earth; as dying and rising vegetation god he is only the preserver of the world, who by his rain gives fertility. For this reason the fight with the sea is not a repetition of creation. If the concept of chaos is to retain its specific meaning, it is best thought of as restricted to the situation of the world before creation (cf. Gen. 1: 2 et al.). In that case the earthquakes and movements of the sea which are evoked by a theophany are not a situation of chaos, because they do not make a re-creation of the world necessary (cf. e.g. Ps. 46: 2 [Heb. 46: 3]).

2   This distinction which we have made in non-Israelite texts, between act of creation and fight with the sea, is found also in the Old Testament, although this only displays fragments of the myth. The two traditions are expressed in completely different language. Deutero-Isaiah portrays the miracle at the Red Sea in the Exodus from Egypt in terms of the concept of the fight with the sea monster (similarly Ps. 77: 15ff. [Heb. 77: 16ff.]; 74: 14 [Heb. 74: 15]). Here the mythological event has lost its independence; it only serves to make a historical event more vivid:

Awake, awake, put on strength,
O arm of Yahweh;
awake, as in days of old,
the generations of long ago.
Was it not thou that didst cut Rahab in pieces,
that didst pierce the dragon?
Was it not thou that didst dry up the sea,
the waters of the great deep? (Isa. 51: 9f.; cf. 43: 16f.)

The prophet answers this cry for help with an assurance of salvation, which is no longer based upon the deliverance at the Red Sea (the beginning of the history of Israel), but on creation (the beginning of the world):

I, I am he that comforts you; . . .
your maker, who stretched out the heavens
and laid the foundations of the earth. (Isa. 51: 12f.)

As the language shows, the distinction between the two traditions has persisted over a long period. Similarly the Old Testament in a number of other passages (Ps. 77: 16–19 [Heb. 77: 17–20]; 93; Isa. 27: 1; Nah. 1: 3f.; Hab. 3: 8) alludes only to the fight with the sea. If one wanted to understand these too as representations of the fight with chaos, it would be left completely unexplained why the climax of the course of events in the myth, the creation of the world, is missing. However the Old Testament also contains passages which cannot be derived so clearly, because different ideas run together in them (Ps. 74: 12ff.; 89: 9ff. [Heb. 89: 10ff.]). The individual variants cannot be composed into a uniform picture; for the origin of the mythical motifs is not confined to one cultural area. Israel came also under Mesopotamian and Egyptian influence (cf. Ps. 104). Furthermore in the course of time its contacts with the world around altered.

3   Nevertheless the contacts with Canaanite myths, which have become known through the discoveries of Ras Shamra (Ugarit) are particularly close, even down to details. The Old Testament when it praises God's victory over the hostile sea, tells also of the conquest of particular sea monsters. In the same way the Ugaritic myths tell of the struggle both with the sea god and also with individual sea monsters, which have the same or very similar names: Tannin, 'the wounded snake, the tyrant with seven heads' or Lotan/Leviathan (cf. Ps. 74: 13f. et al.; Rahab is found only in the Old Testament). In both Israel and Canaan it remains ultimately unclear whether these monsters are different or are one single mythical being, which is identical with the sea (so Job 7: 12).

A later text shows yet more clearly the borrowing and transformation of the mythological concept of the primeval snake. In the Ugaritic myth of god Ba'al is thus addressed:

> When you (also) slew Leviathan,
>> the slippery snake,
>> made an end to the wounded snake,
> the tyrant with seven heads.

In the Old Testament this scene is inserted into an apocalypse to describe the end of time. The antiquity of a description and its fixing in writing can therefore diverge considerably; mythical motifs appear in the Old Testament both early and late. Although there is roughly a thousand years between the two occurrences, even the very wording has in part been preserved:

> In that day Yahweh with his hard and great and strong sword will punish Leviathan the fleeing serpent, Leviathan the twisting serpent, and he will slay the dragon that is in the sea. (Isa. 27: 1)

With this degree of verbal agreement the divergences of substance are all the more striking. The sea dragon in the Old Testament no longer constitutes the sea, but an animal that 'lives in the sea'. The story of creation (Gen. 1: 21) understands the monsters of the sea, which were once seen as older than the gods, as created beings. 'The primeval chaos monsters have been turned into a strange sort of fish, which figure among the other created beings' (H. Gunkel, *Schöpfung und Chaos in Urzeit und Endzeit,* Göttingen, 1895, p. 120). Finally the hymn Ps. 104: 26 ironically completes the process of deprivation of power, by reducing the sea monsters to a divine plaything.

Further the change in the concept in the Old Testament again brings with it a projection into the future; even the fight with the dragon was altered in Isa. 27 into an expectation. This meant that it had to give up its hold on reality; the stage properties of the myth appear now only as a symbol for particular historical kingdoms (cf. Isa. 24: 21).

4   Similarly the Old Testament connects the battle with the dragon elsewhere with the passing through the sea. Because the myth tells of an action of God, it can be used to portray vividly the activity of God. Then however the historical events run into the danger of being transferred into an unhistorical primeval time: 'the deeds of Yahweh' become 'wonders of old' (Ps. 77: 11 [Heb. 77: 12]; cf. 74: 12; Isa. 51: 9f.). The historicization of the myth threatens to become a mythicization of history. However myth and history do not stand on an equal footing in the Old Testament. Where the two modes of thought are mixed up it is the historical reality that is the purpose of the statement: Yahweh 'works salvation in the midst of the earth' (Ps. 74: 12). The recollection of God's actions in the past, which is given mythological form, is at the same time a confession of trust and a prayer, 'may God show his power now as in the past!' The myth can therefore be inserted even into man's personal life. The individual can pray for a theophany which will

save him from the waters of the primeval flood, or gives thanks for his deliverance (Ps. 18; 144: 5–7; cf. 32: 6; 42: 7 [Heb. 42: 8]; Job 7: 12 et al.). In this context the cosmic dimension of the myth which becomes decisive again for apocalyptic (below § 16b, 1) seems to be entirely lost, so that it becomes a mere image.

f CREATION

1   Although cosmogonies had a fundamental significance for the religions of the developed lands of the ancient Near East, Israel apppears originally not to have had an independent creation story of its own. At least there is no mention of a belief in creation, or rather, a creator, in the oldest traditions from the nomadic period (the promise to the patriarchs, Exodus, Sinai).

This fact would be very surprising if the name 'Yahweh' had the basic meaning 'he makes to be, calls into being'; but this is not very probable (cf. Exod. 3: 14f.; above, §6a, 2).

Perhaps the belief in a creator is the main inheritance Christianity has received from Israel; nevertheless statements about creation are not typical of the whole Old Testament. Outside the primeval history (Gen. 1–2) they are significant only in three areas, in the psalter (especially in the psalms of creation, 8; 19A; 104; cf. 33; 136; 148 et al.; also in later hymnic elements in the books of the prophets, such as Amos 4: 13; Jer. 10); in the wisdom literature (Proverbs and Job) and in Deutero-Isaiah. Concepts of creation are relatively rare in the pre-exilic period, are first found in the early monarchical period (in the saying at the dedication of the temple, 1 Kgs. 8: 12; Gen 2J; 14: 19ff.; perhaps Ps. 19; 24: 2; Prov. 14: 31 et al.) and become frequent from the time of the exile on. While one or another tradition, in particular the earliest oral form of the Yahwistic narrative of Gen. 2, may go back to the early Israelite period, clearly no importance attached to the belief in a creator in the older period.

Israel did make confession from early times of Yahweh's power over nature (Exod. 14–17; 19: 16ff.), but also over foreign nations and their land (Gen. 12: 10ff.; 20 et al.), but Yahweh appears originally not to have been worshipped as creator. Israel experienced its God primarily as a deliverer in distress. When it learnt to understand nature and world together as the work of Yahweh, and mankind as his creation, it was certain from the start that the creator was the deliverer and redeemer.

Israel did not need therefore to base its faith upon the creation, and to work back from it to God, or from nature to salvation. The Old Testament looks back from history to creation, which joins up with history as an event in time, and indeed inaugurates it as its beginning (Gen. 1; cf. Ps. 136). In God's word of blessing (Gen. 1: 28) through which the transmission of life onwards is conveyed, the future is explicitly in mind, and the stories of creation lead on to the genealogies (4: 1f.; 17ff.J; 5: 1ff.P).

The situation after the entry made an extension of their understanding of God necessary. It was probably only in Palestine, perhaps only after the early monarchical period, but certainly before the exile, that Israel took over concepts of creation from the surrounding religions and in debate with them spoke of Yahweh as creator. The borrowing of Canaanite ideas is clearly seen in Gen. 14: 19ff. (above, §10a, 2).

2 Israel shares its mythical concepts of the beginning of the world with the ✓ ancient Near East, and has indeed borrowed them from here. Gen. 1 in the sequence of the individual works of creation (sea and its division; stars; announcement of the creation of man and its achievement; divine rest) shows certain agreements with the Babylonian epic of creation *enuma elish* ('when from above . . .'), which was recited each year at the New Year festival in Babylon. However, the biblical creation narrative is not directly dependent upon this cosmogonic myth (the differences are too great for this); but both texts share the same traditio-historical context.

The Babylonian narrative of the creation of the world itself depends upon foreign tradition. The two leading ideas are already attested in the Sumerian version of the myth: in the beginning there was only water; and the world came into being through a division. In the Babylonian epic the sea is called progenitor or mother of the gods, and the victorious god Marduk after the battle with the sea goddess Tiamat forms the heaven out of her upper parts, and the earth from the lower parts.

> Then the lord rested and contemplated her corpse,
> intent on dividing the form and doing skilful works,
>   he split it like a dried fish,
> set up half and made it the firmament. (*NERT*, p. 83; cf. *ANET*, p. 67)

After the creation of the stars there follows as the last and crowning work the creation of man out of the blood of the gods; he is given the task of serving the gods:

> Blood I will mass and cause bones to be,
> I will establish a savage, 'man' shall be his name.
> Verily, savage-man I will create.
> He shall be charged with the service of the gods
>   That they might be at ease!
> They bound him (the god Kingu), holding him before Ea.
> They imposed upon him his guilt and severed his blood (vessels).
> Out of his blood he (Ea) fashioned mankind,
> He imposed the service and let free the gods. (*ANET*, p. 68)

The creation of the world and of man, which perhaps originally belonged to different conceptual worlds (cf. R. Albertz, *Weltschöpfung und Menschenschöpfung*, Stuttgart, 1974) were therefore already found together in the Babylonian creation epic, so that Israel inherited this combination. As in Gen. 1 the creation of man is declared by a divine word. But the Old Testament does not see man's destiny in 'the service of God', but promises man dominion over the earth with his being made in the image of God. No blood of the gods is needed for the creation of man (but according to Gen. 2: 7 only the breath of God), just as the whole act of creation is no longer thought of as a battle.

While Mesopotamia went on expanding traditional ideas of creation (*enuma elish*) and connected them with other material to form a primeval history down to the flood (the Atrahasis epic), the Egyptian cosmogonies are much more varied, since they differ from place to place. But here too we find the two basic concepts of the primeval sea as the beginning of the world, and of the division of heaven and earth.

The great systems of Hermopolis, Heliopolis and Memphis have each a quite different form. The Shabaka Stone, sometimes called 'the memorial of the theology of Memphis', describes the creation of the world through the thought and word of the god Ptah: 'each word of God arose through what was thought out by the heart and commanded by the tongue.' In the cosmogony of Hermopolis important elements known from Gen. 1: 2 appear as four primeval pairs of gods: the primeval waters (Nun and Naunet), boundlessness (Huh and Hauhet), darkness (Kuk and Kauket) and the gentle breeze (Amun and Amaunet). These eight primeval gods (in Heliopolis nine) personify the world before creation. Water (Nun) is the basic material, and the other deities are properties (boundlessness, darkness) of the primeval situation.

In Greece too echoes can be found of ancient Near Eastern traditions, when for instance Homer calls Okeanos the 'father of the gods', or when according to Thales water is the origin of matter.

From Canaanite territory we have isolated expressions (above, §10a, 2) but no comprehensive narrative of creation. Viewed comprehensively the ancient Near Eastern cosmogonies, in spite of similar basic concepts, take on very different forms.

3   The multiplicity of Old Testament concepts of creation shows that Israel could take over and reshape very varied traditions. They do not form any sort of unity, and the individual variants of the myth of the battle with the sea cannot be drawn together to make a single course of events.

According to the Priestly writer's story of creation (Gen. 1) after the formation of light and its division from the darkness, there come from the primeval sea, which is there from the start, through continued division, the heavenly and earthly ocean, and then the land, upon which the plants are able to spring up and the animals can live. When men are made, the world is ready for them. Several originally independent cosmogonic conceptions have been brought together in a unity in this narrative: the world is formed from the primeval water, which (on the analogy of the widespread myth of the division of heaven and earth) is divided into an upper and lower half, while the dry land appears out of the water. The expressions 'God made' and 'God spoke' alternate; and these must in turn be distinguished from 'God called'.

While in the countries around Israel the powers of chaos are fully deities with creative power, Gen. 1 excluded any independent activity of the primeval material (v. 2: 'the earth was without form and void' is simply a description of the situation). The pieces of primeval material which originated through the great cosmic acts of separation, are transformed in their basic essence by God's naming of them, and only so are they incorporated into the formed world (v. 5: the darkness as night; cf. vv. 8, 10). The primal material no longer appears in the world when it is created. So the earth is not like a little island in a chaotic sea which constantly threatens to destroy all life. The world no longer has a frontier, it is not threatened by a return to formlessness; it is now open to future history. The understanding of the world is thus basically altered; in place of an uncertainty very conscious of the threat to life, comes a universal confidence: 'and behold, it was very good'.

The introduction prefixed to the story, 'in the beginning God created heaven and earth (i.e. everything)' summarizes the meaning of the Old Testament creation narrative, and at the same time indicates the way in which it should be read. It is expressly indicated by a special verb 'create' (*bārā'*) that God did not have need of any already existing material. Since this word is reserved for God alone in the Old Testament, creation is deprived of any similarity to human action, and so of concreteness. A conception of the activity of God is only possible when there is some analogy to human action. The word in question does not (even now) imply creation *ex nihilo* (cf. 2 Macc. 7: 28; Rom. 4: 17), but says nothing more about the manner of the origin of the world; it leaves open the question 'how it happened', and preserves God's unrestricted freedom.

This is also the task of the concept of the creation of the world by the word, which was probably prefixed to the older tradition of God's 'making', so that God's action becomes merely the confirmation of the word of God. The formula 'he spoke . . . and it was so' does not attempt to portray the event; for one can represent a craftsman at his work, but not a word that calls material objects into existence through being uttered (cf. Ps. 33: 6, 9; 148: 5 et al.). Certainly there is not only one valid representation among the various ways in which the Old Testament speaks of creation; for they are all intended to contrast creator and creation. But some particular expressions do more justice to this distinction, and so are more appropriate to faith. So the Old Testament chooses from within the possibilities available to it; mythological conceptions of the craftsmanlike activity of God, and still more those of battle and birth, recede in importance. Finally Israel, which originally had no independent language of creation, creates its own language by means of the concept of 'create' (*bārā'*).

In accordance with this understanding Gen. 1 only tells that God created man; how he came into existence and where he comes from are not even hinted at. How much more has for instance the Babylonian creation myth to tell us! This means that mythological 'knowledge' about the origin of man and of the world was more and more restricted in the Old Testament. The story of creation certainly depends upon the scientific knowledge of its date. But the unity of declaration of faith and explanation of the world begins to be dissolved, because conceptions relating to the origin both of the world and of man are reduced in significance or even removed.

With the same critical purpose the creation narrative understands mythical beings as God's creatures. The sea dragons, originally embodiments of the primeval water, are now only harmless animals in the sea without any power of their own (Gen. 1: 21; cf. above, §6b, 8).

The names sun and moon, which in the lands around Israel connoted deities (cf. Ezek. 8: 16) are avoided (vv. 14–18); Gen. 1 does not concede a single word to this alien faith. The stars are bodies of light created by God, which no longer 'govern' human fate, but only day and night, that is, distinguish the times. Because the mythological personification has been given up, the stars can be treated purely materially as objects to be found in the world. So faith leads to a way of thinking that is concerned with what is accessible to observation, with the phenomena themselves.

Gen. 1 as priestly instruction is intensively concerned with the correct language for creation, and as such has been influential. Because of its cosmic breadth and its basic importance this creation narrative rightly begins the Old Testament. Compared with it the older Yahwistic picture in Gen. 2: 4bff. in spite of its fresh beginning seems like a development and an illustration of it. But it is insufficient to characterize this story as an account of the origin of man; for Gen. 2 tells of far more than the creation of man. The world does not come into existence in seven days, but God builds up by means of fields, plants and animals the restricted world of the farmer around man, who originally is on his own. Here the primeval sea is not already there; God's act of creation takes the form of, a watering of a wilderness. The sea with its fishes, which is far from the life of the countryside, is not within the author's field of vision at all; nor are the stars mentioned. While according to Gen. 1 God seems to create man at once as a whole, the second narrative speaks only of a human pair, who are 'formed' or 'made' one after another.

According to Gen. 1: 26ff.P God transfers to man the dominion over the other created beings, but according to 2: 19f.J he brings the animals to man, so that he may give them their names. Thus man wins a share in God's power, and from the start is by no means only dependent, but is himself to try out in freedom what suits him, and to this extent share a little in God's creation.

Certainly the animals can give help in man's work, for instance in farming (2: 5, 15; 3: 23); but man finds his true opposite number, the helper that matches him (2: 18) in woman. With his cry of joy and consent, 'This at last is bone of my bones and flesh of my flesh' (2: 23) he declares that God's promise 'I will make him a helper fit for him' becomes reality. The two form a community, a unity ('*one* flesh'). The subordination of the woman to the man seems not to be part of the will of the creator, but appears only as a consequence of the curse which befalls disobedience (3: 16). Similarly work (2: 15) becomes toil and sorrow (3: 17ff.).

Through the fact that the creation narrative goes on to the story of the garden of Eden and of the disobedience of man, the Yahwist indicates his purpose of understanding existence in its duality. Man is created (Gen. 2), but is troubled and heavy-laden (Gen. 3). Good and evil are placed side by side; but evil, with the guilt of man and the difficulties of existence, is not regarded, or not without qualifications, as God's creation. The world as it is now does not correspond to the will of the creator. (However the story sees in death only the end of toil, not yet, as in Rom. 5: 12; 6: 23, the consequence of sin.)

A similar difference between what is in accordance with creation and what is actually found recurs in P; for God's full approval is only given to the world in which there is still no pouring of blood (Gen. 1: 29ff.). When violence comes upon earth, God takes the opposite view (6: 12f.P corrects 1: 31). The toleration of the killing of animals does allow a situation of fear and terror to arise, but man himself is protected as the image of God (9: 2f., 6P; cf. below, §12c, 6).

4   Since the first commandment forms a criterion for the borrowing and adaptation of inherited traditions, certain motifs which are irreconcilable with it are excluded. But occasionally ideas are found which do not even contain the general idea that creation is an act of God. The basis for the confession 'Yahweh, thou hast searched me out and known me" is given as

> My frame was not hidden from thee,
>   when I was being made in secret,
>   intricately wrought in the depths of the earth.
> Thy eyes beheld my unformed substance. (Ps. 139: 15f.)

As it is pictured here (though v. 13 has a different picture) God only looks on, as man is 'wrought' in the bosom of the earth. The home of man is according to a widespread myth 'mother earth', which brings everything living out of itself (cf. Gen. 1: 11f., 24; Ps. 90: 2f.; Job 1: 21; 38: 8, 28; Isa. 55: 10). So concepts of creation proper, according to which God forms man or the world through his work, could be distinguished from cosmogonic conceptions, according to which man independently proceeds from an original material out of the earth or the world. But the Old Testament suppresses such motifs, and they are only preserved in a few places.

According to other passages God can stretch out the heaven like a tent, and stamp down the earth like a plate (Isa. 42: 5; 44: 24), found the earth (48: 13; 51: 13, 16; Prov. 3: 19), that is, perhaps, build upon foundations in the water (Ps. 24: 2; cf. 104: 5; Job 38: 4ff.), form the earth, the mountains, and man and the animals like a potter (Isa. 45: 18; Amos 4: 13; Gen. 2: 7, 19; cf. Jer. 18: 3f.), etc. It is easily possible therefore to list a number of completely different concepts of creation. As concepts they cannot simply be equated and harmonized, may indeed contradict one another; there is not originally a single agreed narrative of creation, probably not even a uniform picture of the world. Since the picture which the individual passages give is so variable, the purpose of the concepts cannot lie in the ideas themselves. The varied juxtaposition is only really to be explained by the assumption that the actual terms for the manner of creation were already not of decisive importance for the Old Testament itself. It is able to mix up all sorts of motifs together, and have fundamentally different ones (like Gen. 1 and 2) follow directly one upon another. A certain measure of freedom is perhaps expressed thereby.

5   The confession of faith in a creator is rather the consequence than the presupposition of the faith in salvation. But in this context a certain change enters

in from the exile on. After the destruction of the temple, the end of the Davidic monarchy and the expulsion from their homeland have destroyed some basic promises, Deutero-Isaiah can base his preaching upon creation (Isa. 40: 12ff.; 43: 1; 45: 7f.; 54: 4f. et al.). As past history lost its importance the belief in a creator became important. Perhaps the dispute with foreign gods also played a part here (cf. Isa. 40: 25f. against astral religion). In any case the increase in statements about creation at this period arises not only from the effect of Babylonian religion, but out of a basic need in Israel itself.

While this change is understandable for historical reasons, it is still an innovation. It is the newly uttered promise of salvation after the accomplishment of judgement in exile that is grounded for the first time not upon an historical event, like leading or election, but upon creation. This change is also hinted at in Gen. 1, when the origin of the world leads on to God's rest, which anticipates Israel's hallowing of the sabbath in an exemplary way. In particular many of those who pray the psalms place their trust in the power of the creator:

> I lift up my eyes to the hills.
>   From whence does my help come?
> My help comes from Yahweh,
>   who made heaven and earth. (Ps. 121: 1 f.; cf. Ps. 33 et al.)

He who supports the individual and the group, and can help in distress, is creator; thus the return to the beginnings of the past can help in the understanding of the present (cf. Jonah. 1, esp. vv. 9, 16).

The theology of creation has a similar function in the wisdom literature. A man's relation to the oppressed is in good as well as evil circumstances his relationship to the creator:

> He who oppresses a poor man insults his Maker,
>   but he who is kind to the needy honours him. (Prov. 14: 31; cf. 17: 5)

Egyptian wisdom already bases ethical behaviour upon a reference to the creator god:

> Do not mock a man who is in the hand of God . . .
>   Man is clay and straw
>   and God is his builder. (Amenemope, ch. 25; NERT p. 61; ANET, p. 424)

In Job creation is a witness to God's power and righteousness against the weakness and injustice of man (4: 17; 7: 17f.; 9: 1ff.; 10: 3ff.; 26: 6ff. et al.), but also to the equality of men together: 'Did not one fashion us in the womb?' (31: 14ff.; cf. 33: 4ff.; Mal. 2: 10). Creation joins together rich and poor, levels off differences among men, is a ground common to all (Prov. 22: 2; 29: 13).

Koheleth, the Preacher, for all his doubts holds fast to belief in God's creative power; God's work remains complete, but is unrecognizable for men:

He has made everything beautiful in its time; also he has put eternity into man's mind, yet so that he cannot find out what God has done from the beginning to the end. (Eccles. 3: 11)

Thus a note of qualification enters into the theology of creation, such as was not known to the creation narratives of Gen. 1f.

Such a confession as Ps. 121 makes clear to what extent Israel's faith could take concepts of creation into itself. The declaration 'who has made heaven and earth' becomes a characteristic epithet of Yahweh (Ps. 115: 15; 124: 8; cf. Exod. 20: 11; Neh. 9: 6 et al.). In fact such an opposition between creation and history cannot be maintained. Deutero-Isaiah even equates the two. Redemption, like election, is a creative action of Yahweh (Isa. 43: 1, 20f.; 44: 1f., 20f., 24; 45: 7 et al.). Creation is not an independent area, and does not take place only at the beginning, but also now in the present. God 'forms' the individual (Jer. 1: 5; Isa. 49: 5; cf. Ps. 139: 16) and the nation (Isa. 44: 2; 27: 11 et al.), and as creator achieves new history: 'Behold, I am doing a new thing' (43: 19; 48: 7; Jer. 31: 22 et al.).

Thus not only what is never changing, but also what is new and event-filled is drawn into the belief in a creator. Creation becomes eschatology, because eschatology is God's creation; creation is not only the remembered past, but also the expected future (esp. Isa. 65: 17; 66: 22 et al.). Just as in apocalyptic before the coming reign of God human history becomes a unity, so by contrast to the creator the world becomes a unity. The Old Testament expresses this conceptually by the double expression 'heaven and earth' or occasionally by the single world 'all' (Isa. 44: 24 et al.). So the worship of Yahweh as creator implies a confession of the God of the world.

g   RESULTS: BORROWING AND APPROPRIATION –
THE 'INCOMPARABILITY' OF YAHWEH

It appears that Israel has borrowed a number of terms used of God from its environment. This is true probably for the attributes 'holy' and 'living', the title king, the proclamation of honour and glory, and the descriptions of theophany and of the fight with the chaos monster. The confession of Yahweh as creator probably represents the greatest expansion of his dominion. In other declarations about God too foreign influence is probable. In particular the Zion theology, as it is contained in the psalms of Zion and the words of the prophets, attracted a mass of mythological motifs. When for instance Jerusalem is called 'the righteous city' (Isa. 1: 21 et al.) pre-Davidic traditions can probably be traced here (below, §13, 2). But the praise of Yahweh's righteous deeds (Judg. 5: 11) is closer to early Israelite thought, so that when the Old Testament speaks of righteousness native and foreign traditions meet.

The transition to Canaan meant therefore a decisive change for Israel's beliefs about God as a whole. It would not do justice to this change if the view were summarily expressed that Israel 'made use of' alien expressions and forms of speech. Such an approach does not really take into consideration the whole phenomenon. The contrast of content and form, or the image of core and husk, are also inadequate; they are still more inadequate if a timeless centre is separated from a time-conditioned outer edge, which alone is affected by the course of history (cf. above, §1, 2). Indeed in many respects the attempt to express in words Israel's understanding of God apart from the influence of Canaan proves difficult. For example it cannot simply be said that although Yahweh was not invoked as king in the early period, he was from the beginning as lord, for the title lord ('ādōn) probably also represents an originally Canaanite epithet for God. Nor however would it do justice to the whole development to call it syncretism, and say that because Israel has in large measure taken over material from another religion, Old Testament religion is a syncretistic religion. Just as the general expressions monotheism or monolatry (above, §6b, 3) do not reveal what is specific and historical, the term syncretism does not simply identify a phenomenon but also obscures it.

The distinctive character of Yahwistic faith cannot be described if we only have regard to its connections with its environment; for its specific character cannot be adequately explained as a composition from given ancient Near Eastern elements. If however syncretism as a combination of different religious elements presupposes an 'integrating principle prior to the different elements' (W. Pannenberg, Basic Questions in Theology, vol. 2, London, 1971, p. 88 n. 37), this driving force must be looked for in the demand for exclusiveness, although the second commandment, the historically linked character of the faith and probably also the understanding of revelation by the word should also not be forgotten as further determining characteristics (see below).

Certainly Israel in Canaan did not only develop what was contained in embryo in its nomadic traditions. The external influences brought in something genuinely new, and were really important for the faith of Israel, as is shown by the example of institution of kingship. But Israel did not leave unaltered what it took over from its environment and claimed 'for Yahweh' (cf. above, Excursus 2, 2; §9), but reached a new understanding of it. This reinterpretation apparently took place in two directions in particular. The king of the gods is worshipped as the king of the nation. The 'holy' God becomes the 'holy one of Israel', who shows himself holy in judgement (Isaiah) or in deliverance (Deutero-Isaiah). The living God is called upon in laments as the giver of life (Ps. 42). So on the one hand properties of God become actions which are done to man. Words with mythological content become terms for relationships, which characterize the relationship between God and man.

On the other hand almost all the expressions are reinterpreted eschato-logically. As the reign of God in the Old Testament becomes a hope, so from the institution of the earthly kingdom emerges the promise of a future Messiah.

God's glory is yet to appear, his holiness will yet become universal. The theophany is still expected, and the new creation is still in the future. Thus the already universal coverage of the traditions (above, §11a, 5) is extended yet further; the kingdom of Yahweh is both spatially and temporally unlimited, his glory will be visible to all (Isa. 40: 5), and his power as creator embraces the world as a whole. Conversely however the traditions can also be related to the individual: he can call upon Yahweh as king (Ps. 5: 2 [Heb. 5: 3]), or living God (Ps. 42) or pray for a theophany (144: 5ff.).

Generally Israel has reinterpreted the originally foreign material especially in the direction of the relationship of God to man, and in the direction of the future. This profound change prevents us however from speaking of syncretism. The process of interpretation permits us in a limited sense to say that even when foreign material enters into Israel, the Old Testament makes the decision what the borrowed concepts mean: what, for instance, is the meaning of the kingdom of God?

Similar remarks could be made not only about concepts but also about actual passages. The literary type of 'lamentations' (e.g. Ps. 13; 51) shows a surprising kinship in structure (invocation of God – lament – prayer – vow) and motifs with Babylonian psalms of lamentation. Possibly Israel has taken over whole psalms; Pss. 29 and 82 in particular show strong Canaanite influence. Apparently however there is no passage in the Old Testament which Israel has taken over unaltered. It has at least imposed its own character upon them by additions (cf. e.g. Ps. 29: 11; 93: 5).

The borrowing of foreign material did not therefore take place wholesale, but was an extremely critical action, which is therefore evidence for Israel's dispute with neighbouring religions. When Israel transferred a mythological action to Yahweh, it removed from a foreign deity the right to base his own claim to dominion upon this demonstration of power. It claims the meaning of the myth for its own faith; the incomparability which is asserted of particular gods in the pantheon now describes Yahweh's exclusivity:

What god is great like our God?
  Thou art the God who workest wonders,
  who hast manifested thy might among the peoples.
(Ps. 77: 13f. [Heb. 77: 14f.])

For who in the skies can be compared to Yahweh?
  Who among the heavenly beings is like Yahweh?
(Ps. 89: 6 [Heb. 89: 7]; cf. Exod. 15: 11; Deut. 3: 24 et al.)

The superiority of one God to other gods thus turns into a statement that there is no analogy: 'greater than' changes into 'other than'.

There is none like thee
and there is no God beside thee
(2 Sam. 7: 22; cf. 1 Sam. 2: 2; Ps. 18: 31 [Heb. 18: 32] et al.)

The Old Testament is not content with the superiority which a comparison makes possible. The highest God (Ps. 47: 2 [Heb. 47: 3]; 97: 9 et al.; cf. §10a, 1) becomes the only one:

Let (the nations) know that thou alone,
whose name is Yahweh,
art the Most High over all the earth. (Ps. 83: 18 [Heb. 83: 19]).

The word 'alone', known already from the legal clause (Exod. 22: 20 [Heb. 22: 19]; cf. Deut. 32: 12) recurs in quite different contexts: God alone performs miracles (Is. 72: 18; 136: 4; cf. Isa. 44: 24; 63: 3; Job 9: 8), alone knows the hearts of all men (1 Kgs. 8: 39; cf. Ps. 51: 4 [Heb. 51: 6]), and his name is exalted alone (Ps. 148: 13). When the confession is made 'thou alone art God' (86: 10; 2 Kgs. 19: 15; Neh. 9: 6), a future is expected in which this will be generally acknowledged (Isa. 2: 11, 17; Ps. 83: 18 [Heb. 83: 19]; 2: Kgs. 19: 19).

To deprive other gods of their supremacy, Yahweh drew essential characteristics of these gods to himself, while Israel rejected what could not be combined with its own faith. Yahweh was not simply identified with one God (El), while he opposed the other (Ba'al) in irreconcilable hostility. The double process of recognition and rejection cuts across the foreign gods themselves, since he encounters and chooses their properties and their activities one by one. It could not indeed have been otherwise, since no area of divine activity could have been omitted from Yahweh's power. So Yahweh had for instance to dethrone Ba'al as giver of fertility and life, and also as victor in the battle with the sea, but on the other hand to hold at a distance the character of a nature god: Yahweh could not in the last resort be represented as a bull, nor could he die and rise again.

It remains unsatisfactory however simply to state this polarity of contact and rejection. After the religio-historical comparison has been made, the question (for which there is historical justification too) is bound to arise: what made possible for Israel this history in which it deprived Yahweh's opponents of their power? What was the criterion which allowed rejection on the one hand, borrowing and change on the other? This is a difficult problem, and one to which the same answer cannot be given in every case. But Yahweh's demand for exclusivity and the prohibition of images are bound to be cited as the decisive criterion.

The first commandment (in however many ways it was broken in the history of Israel) excluded in principle polytheism. This made permanently impossible all ideas and mythological narratives which presuppose several deities, such as the conjunction of god and goddess. Creation cannot ultimately be represented as a battle of the gods; the pantheon survived at most as a heavenly court subject to Yahweh. The 'holy' God is in accordance with the mind of the first commandment understood as jealous (Josh. 24: 19), and the living God is defined by contrast to the dead idols (Jer. 10: 10).

The law of exclusivity and the prohibition of images are however ruled out as reasons for the fact that Israel kept concepts of dying and rising separate from Yahweh, although it was able to take over and alter the concepts contained in this myth. Here the rejection may have been because the cyclical recurrence of death and resurrection exclude the once-for-all character of history. The relationship of history to faith (above, §2, 1; §6d) represents one further criterion for Israel's relationship with other religions.

§12   The Monarchy

In the ancient Near East the king is assigned a role of decisive significance in religion: he is the mediator between God and man; he represents divinity on earth and his subjects before the powers of heaven. The pharaoh for instance is the head priest, who actually creates the contact with the divine world, even if subordinate priests carry out the cultic ritual in his name. The double character of kingship is illustrated by the example of the pharaoh. In his own person he embodies the unity of God and man; he upholds the order of life in nature and in society, and guarantees the continued existence of the world. However the king does not have the same position everywhere and at all times in the broad area of the ancient Near East. Kingship does always function by virtue of a divine ordering, but the relationship between God and king is different in every instance; and even in one and the same area it can alter in the course of history.

1   In Egypt the king is already in the earliest period regarded as Horus, the hawk god of heaven; probably this relationship is even then not thought of as one of identity. As the worship of the sun god Re increases, the king appears from the fourth dynasty on as son of Re. Does a sharper distinction between God and king here appear, although his divine character is maintained? 'According to a generally held principle which was especially strong in the ancient Orient, a son is responsible to a more powerful father' (S. Morenz, *Egyptian Religion*, London, 1973, p. 35). The new title expresses both the relationship of trust (the king is entrusted with dominion as God's representative on earth) and also subordination: the pharaoh carries out what God commands. The title son does not drive out the older Horus title; both terms are found unharmonized alongside one another. Since later on the relationship of the pharaoh to other gods like Atum and Amun was also thought of as a father-and-son relationship, the greater emphasis may have been on the new title. The distinction beween the human and divine nature of the king seems from early on to have been connected with a distinction between person and office. It is said of the earthly person 'that the pharaoh in the Old Kingdom was in no way regarded as a god, but was primarily a man. . . . It is not the king who is divine, but the office exercised by him, of which he is the holder, (H. Goedicke, *Die Stellung des Königs im Alten Reich*, Wiesbaden, 1960, pp. 89f.). Although appointed as ruler from birth on as son of God (below,

§12b, 1), the king acquires divinity only through the ritual at his accession. But it is only the dead king who is regarded entirely as god; the living king embodies both divine and human nature. So the person of the king does not receive worship in his lifetime; but his statue may enjoy divine honours in the temple, and the dead king is worshipped at his tomb, having through the performance of specified rites become one with the dying and rising god Osiris (thus since the fifth dynasty).

In Mesopotamia there appears not to have been generally so far-reaching a unity of god and kingship. If a basic concept is sought in the varied history of the area, in which several peoples with different concepts of kingship succeeded one another, it is to be found in the view that kingship is instituted by the deity. The king is not god incarnate, but appointed, elected and blessed by God.

For the narrower environs of Israel, which was in the sphere of influence and of conflict of these two cultures, no clear decision can be made, since we do not have such extensive evidence from this area. King Zakir of Hamath says of himself on a stele: 'the Ba'al of heaven made me king' (*KAI* No. 202; *NERT*, p. 231; *ANET*, p. 655). Probably the kings of the two very different political patterns, the Canaanite city-states and the Transjordanian tribes related to Israel, were not worshipped as gods.

2 In the Old Testament a large part of these ancient Near Eastern concepts recur; pre-Israelite ideas, including some of Egyptian origin, seem to have remained significant, especially at the court in Jerusalem. The king is regarded as in the area around as 'chosen' (1 Sam. 10: 24; 16: 8ff. et al.):

> I have made a covenant with my chosen one,
> I have sworn to David my servant:
> I will establish your descendants for ever,
> and build your throne for all generations. (Ps. 89: 3f. [Heb. 89: 4f.])

In addition he can bear other (already given) titles, which describe his close relationship to God or his meaning for the people: 'son' (Ps. 2: 7; 2 Sam. 7: 14 et al.), 'servant' (7: 5, 8; Ps. 132: 10 et al.), and 'light of Israel' (2 Sam. 21: 17; cf. Lam. 4: 20). 'Glory and majesty' are ascribed to God (Ps. 96: 6 et al.) as well as to the king (21: 5 [Heb. 21: 6]; 45: 3 [Heb. 45: 4]); both are called 'shepherds' (Isa. 40: 11 with 2 Sam. 5: 2; Jer. 23: 1ff. et al.). If the name of God is usually invoked in an oath (above, §11c, 1), one can also swear by the life of the king (1 Sam. 17: 55; cf. 12: 3, 5; Gen. 42: 15f.). Conversely a man is punished for 'cursing God and the king' (1 Kgs. 21: 10). At least occasionally the king takes on priestly tasks (2 Sam. 6: 13–18; 8: 18; 24: 25; 1 Kgs. 9: 25; cf. Ps. 110: 4 et al.). The king can exceptionally even be addressed as 'god'; but this single instance does not allow the conclusion that the king was regarded as equivalent to God, or at least belonged to the divine sphere:

Your throne, O God, endures for ever and ever.
Your royal sceptre is a sceptre of equity;
you love righteousness and hate wickedness.
(Ps. 45: 6f. [Heb. 45: 7f.]; cf. 2 Sam. 14: 17, 20; Zech. 12: 8)

Here the continuance of the throne is associated with right behaviour. In the same way legal protection and prosperity were always expected from the king (Ps. 72; 45: 4, 7 [Heb. 45; 5, 8]; Prov. 16: 12ff.; 20: 28; 29: 14; 1 Sam. 8: 20; 2 Sam. 8: 15; 1 Kgs. 3; Jer. 22: 15f.; Isa. 9: 7 [Heb. 9: 6] et al.). It is a good ancient Near Eastern tradition that the ruler issues the law and defends the needy (e.g. the Code of Hammurabi); justice and with it the well-being of the nation, and even the fertility of nature (cf. Ps. 72: 3ff.) may be dependent upon the king. It is for this reason that he is wished a long life (21: 4 [Heb. 21: 5]; cf. 1 Kgs. 1: 25ff. et al.) and worldwide dominion. So universal hopes are associated with kingship, no doubt as a result of the establishment of David's empire, which provided the occasion for the taking over of ancient Near Eastern traditions (Ps. 2; 18: 43ff. [Heb. 18: 44ff.]; 72: 8ff.; 110).

These few references to the dominating position of the king, which could be greatly expanded, come for the most part from the psalter, especially from the royal psalms. This is not accidental. Israel took over numerous ancient Near Eastern concepts in its cultic and court language. On the other hand the historical accounts in the books of Samuel and Kings are stamped to a far lesser degree by pre-Israelite and non-Israelite concepts, so that we can expect more expressions here which are typical of Israel. The picture formed of kingship in Israel differs therefore according as it is formed more from the historical material or from the psalms, which cannot be arranged in historical order, and accordingly appear almost timeless, or even taken from the messianic expectations such as Isa. 11, in order to draw conclusions about reality from the prophetic hopes.

Perhaps when a contrast is made it can be said in general terms that the ancient Near Eastern king was understood in a more strongly mythological way, while the king in Israel conversely was more a historical figure, to whom certain mythological features were ascribed. The declaration of the Babylonian king-list 'when kingship came down from heaven' (*NERT*, p. 88; *ANET*, p. 265) was impossible for Israel; for it did not forget the origin of its kingship in history, but rather described it (cf. §6d). Furthermore the institution of the monarchy was treated much more strongly as a human development: the nation itself made Saul or David king (1 Sam. 11: 15; 2 Sam. 2: 4; 5: 3; also Judg. 8: 22 et al.). Possibly critical voices were soon heard (cf. the fable of Jotham, Judg. 9: 7ff.; the 'ways of the king' (1 Sam. 8: 11ff.; also 10: 27). In any case there could not be said of the Israelite king what was said of the pharaoh: 'His life from birth or even from his mother's conception of him, through his coronation and the royal feasts down to his death and his transfiguration, is a mythical event, his way of life and his actions are divine revelation. . . . As the appearance of the king represents a repetition of the creation and ordering of the world, so the historical event of the foundation of the monarchy recurs in his coronation' (E. Otto, 'Die Religion der alten Ägypter', in *Religionsgeschichte des Alten Orients,* Leiden, 1964, pp. 26f.). While the pharaoh is in certain respects nearer to God than to men, the distance between Yahweh and the Israelite king is certainly greater than that between king and nation.

3   Israel was conscious that with the introduction of monarchy it was behaving 'like all the nations' (1 Sam. 8: 5, 20; Deut. 17: 14). Israel accordingly asks itself how it can incorporate the alien institution into its own faith. The king is regarded as 'chosen' by God, but obedience to God's commands and faithful submissiveness to him are insistently stipulated. Already 2 Sam. 23: 3f. declares:

> When one rules justly over men,
>   ruling in the fear of God,
> he dawns on them like the morning light.

The law of the king in Deuteronomy (17: 14–20; probably only the negative regulations are original) provides at least theoretically for specific restrictions of the power of the king; it is still more astonishing that there does exist a law that binds not the ruled but the ruler, and subordinates him to God and his law:

> The lawgivers were also conscious of this and intended it: they give the king a law as they do even to the smallest farmer and demand of him obedience on pain of losing the blessing of God. (H. Schmidt)

The Deuteronomistic history evaluates the individual kings in accordance with their attitude to the law of Yahweh – passing from assent (2 Kgs. 18: 3ff.; 22: 2: 23: 25), through certain qualifications (1 Kgs. 15: 11, 14; 2 Kgs. 17: 2) on to complete rejection (1 Kgs. 16: 30, 33; 21: 25f. et al.). The promise of the everlasting continuance of the dynasty of David (2 Sam. 7: 11ff.; later interpreted as a 'covenant': 23: 5; Ps. 89: 3, 28 [Heb. 89: 4, 29]; cf. Excursus 4) seems to have been made at first without conditions, but is then made increasingly dependent upon the king's keeping of the commands of God (Ps. 132: 12; 1 Kgs. 2: 4; 8: 25; 9: 4f.; Zech. 3: 7; cf. 1 Sam. 12: 14f., 24f. et al.). Divine and kingly rule, which in Ps. 2 appear indissolubly linked, are more and more distinguished (Ps. 110: 1; 20: 6ff. [Heb. 20: 7ff.]) until finally they can be contrasted to one another (Judg. 8: 22f.; 1 Sam. 8: 6f.; 12: 12):

> A king is not saved by his great army;
>   a warrior is not delivered by his great strength.
> The war horse is a vain hope for victory,
>   and by its great might it cannot save.

Behold, the eye of Yahweh is on those who fear him,
on those who hope in his steadfast love.
(Ps. 33: 16–18; cf. 144: 3f., 147: 10f.)

4   Because kingship is treated with a measure of reserve, it finds an opponent
from its very origin in the prophetic movement, which exhorts, reprimands or
rejects the ruler in office because of his behaviour (1 Sam. 15; 2 Sam. 12: 24; 2
Kgs. 1; below, §14a, 2 and 5). This attitude of critical dissociation comes to a
climax in the preaching of Hosea. While Amos has shortly before (7: 9, 11)
announced death to the 'house of Jeroboam', according to Hosea (1: 4; cf. 3: 4),
Yahweh makes an end not only of the existing dynasty, but of 'the kingdom of the
house of Israel' as a whole. The prophet sees in kingship as a whole emphatically
only a human institution without God:

They made kings, but not through me.
They set up princes, but without my knowledge. (8: 4)

When he nevertheless derives the monarchy from God, he does not recognize it
as a proof of God's grace, but from beginning to end as a gift of his wrath:

I have given you kings in my anger,
and I have taken them away in my wrath. (13: 11)

This complete rejection, exceeding individual prophecies of doom, applies only to kingship
in Israel; for Hosea appears in the northern kingdom, from which he comes. But are his
words intended to except the southern kingdom with the dynasty of David in Jerusalem, or
are they to be understood basically as a criticism of the institution as such? The answer to
this question depends primarily on the authenticity or inauthenticity of the disputed
prophecy of salvation in Hos. 1: 10–2: 1 [Heb. 2: 1–3], which expects the reunification of
both kingdoms under one 'head'. But even in this saying the coming ruler is not called
'king', which again indicates a certain reserve; he only bears the title of a charismatic leader
of the pre-monarchical period (Num. 14: 4; Judg. 11: 8; 1 Sam. 15: 17). Nor is it said that
the single common head is a Davidite; the dynasty of David is never contrasted favourably
in Hosea with the Israelite ruling house. Just as the Judahite Amos did not argue in Israel in
favour of the sanctuary of Jerusalem and the Davidic monarchy, the northern prophet
Hosea is not likely to have spoken against his home country in favour of the south. Later
Isaiah specifically utters criticism of the ruling member of the line of David, but holds fast
to the institution in his future expectation (Isa. 7: 9ff.; 11: 1).

The historical development of the monarchy had a different course in the two
kingdoms. In the north there were changes of dynasty (especially 2 Kgs. 9f.). By
contrast in Judah and Jerusalem there was an established dynasty, which in spite
of violent changes in the incumbency of the monarchy (2 Kgs. 11 et al.) remained in
power for almost five hundred years until the time of the Babylonian exile. So this
form of monarchy, to which the promise of Nathan had given an assurance of

everlasting continuance (2 Sam. 7), came to have much greater significance for faith. But even in the southern kingdom the attitude to the ruling house was far from unanimous; there were, as in Israel, differences between court and nation, the men of Jerusalem and the country Judahites (cf. 2 Kgs. 11: 14; 14: 21; 21: 24; 23: 30; and also Mic. 5: 2 [Heb. 5: 1]). In all these differences in the understanding of kingship, both between northern and southern kingdoms, and within the groups in the nation, it becomes clear that ideas from varied traditions overlap in the Israelite conceptions of kingship. Inheritances from Israel's nomadic past, influences from the lands of civilization, no doubt especially from the Canaanite city-states, but also from elsewhere, and finally the example of the ancient Near Eastern empires, are all found together.

As in the pattern of the civil service (1 Kgs. 4: 2ff. et al.) it seems to be primarily some particular Egyptian forms that live on in the coronation ritual of Judah (1: 32ff.; 2 Kgs. 11: 12; Ps. 2; 110 et al.). Because however the ritual is never described as a whole in the Old Testament, its reconstruction is difficult and disputed.

From these varied traditions it will be clear that the Old Testament takes up all sorts of attitude towards kingship, from approval celebrating it in hymns, through critical reservation, to total rejection.

It is precisely in Jerusalem, where the institution of kingship seems to have become firmly established through the dynasty that ruled 'for ever', that the question is again reopened. When the Old Testament transferred traditional beliefs about God into the future, the formal statements about the king were transformed into expectation, and so finally incorporated into its faith. The real ruler is not the present king but the one to come: this is promised by the messianic predictions (below, §12d). The exilic prophet Deutero-Isaiah, who reserves the title 'king' for Yahweh (Isa. 52: 7), and transfers the title 'anointed' to the Persian king Cyrus (44: 28ff.) goes yet further in his reinterpretation of the Davidic tradition, when he announces to the exiles as the word of God:

> I will make with you an everlasting covenant,
>   my steadfast, sure love for David. (Isa. 55: 3)

This saying is reminiscent of the prophecy of Nathan (2 Sam. 7 et al.), but in contrast to that is not now uttered to the Judahite royal house. The promise to David is broadened out to the nation, and so loses its distinctive character, that of the election of a dynasty from within the nation as a whole. What God granted to David alone he now gives to all. Israel becomes 'a leader (not king) and commander for the peoples' not through war, but as a 'witness' for Yahweh (55: 4f.; 43: 10 et al.).

b SON OF GOD

1 'Son of God' in the ancient Near East refers primarily to the king. The pharaoh held the title from the Old Kingdom on; later it was given mythical elaboration. The folktale in the Westcar papyrus tells how the sun god Re has intercourse with a priest's wife, and she bears triplets, the three coming rulers. Here it is not a once-for-all miracle of the distant past that is being described. It was customary from the eighteenth dynasty on to represent the conception and birth of the king in murals (e.g. in Der-el-Bahri, the temple of the dead of Queen Hatshepsut, or in Luxor, Philae or Edfu): the most high god goes in the form of the pharaoh to the wife of the ruler. The ruler of the day is accordingly regarded as the son of the god and of the queen in person (H. Brunner, *Die Geburt des Gottkönigs*, Wiesbaden, 1964).

The title 'son of God' for the king is not unknown in Mesopotamia. The Babylonian rulers call themselves 'son of Marduk (city god of Babylon)', 'Son of (the moon goddess) Sin', and similar titles. Here too the title can be expanded to a more comprehensive representation of sonship. So Gudea of Lagash in his hymn for the building of the temple addresses the local goddess:

I have no mother – you are my mother,
I have no father – you are my father,
my seed you have received,
have born me in the sanctuary.
(*Sumerische und akkadische Hymnen und Gebete*, ed. A. Falkenstein
and W. von Soden, 1953, p. 140)

Or the goddess Ishtar reminds the Assyrian king Esarhaddon of his youth, to attest her gracious attitude: 'When you were small, I took you in my arms' (*ANET*, p. 450). In Syria too the royal title 'son of God' is current. In the Ugaritic myths King Keret is called 'son of El', and the son of the king is suckled by the goddesses Ashera and Anat. Similarly Egyptian illustrations show the king sitting in the lap of the goddess, who offers her breast to him; in this way divine strength is supplied to the coming ruler. In the Hellenistic world the oriental title 'son of God' still lives as a term for rulers (Alexander the Great) and heroes (Heracles); even at this late period the divine generation can still be represented materially.

2 The same myth of the union of God and man is also alluded to just once in the primeval history with the narrative of the marriage of the sons of God (Gen. 6: 1–4). The 'sons of god' – the gods and divine beings are called sons of God too in the ancient Near East, since they are brought into genealogical connection with a high God (above, §11a, 2) – take themselves daughters of men as wives; the mixing of the heavenly and earthly is according to the tradition the origin of the giants. But the text of the Old Testament no longer regards the giants as the

offspring of this union of the divine and the human; the heroes now simply appear at the same time as the marriages of the gods. If the myth was originally intended to tell of a power-filled event, the story in its present form declares the sin of man and the judgement of God; it turns something exalted into something reprehensible. As the myth of divine birth is distorted in content in this way, so also Israel takes up the ancient Near Eastern idea of the king as the son of God only in an altered form.

At a later period the Old Testament expresses the mutual relationship between Yahweh and Israel through the covenant formula, 'I will be their God, and they shall be my people' (Jer. 31: 33 et al.). Similarly 2 Sam. 7: 14 determines the mutual relationship between God and king by the promise and warning, 'I will be his father, and he shall be my son'. Ps. 89: 28f. [Heb. 89: 27f.] also juxtaposes demand and promise:

> He shall cry to me, 'Thou art my Father,
>   my God, and the Rock of my salvation.'
> And I will make him the first-born,
>   the highest of the kings of the earth.

On the other hand the perhaps older version of Ps. 2: 7 speaks one-sidedly of the promise of God alone, without mentioning a commitment on the king's side: 'You are my son, today I have begotten you.' But even in this saying, with which a prophet may well have addressed the future ruler, the sonship does not exist from birth on, but is declared. The first part of the sentence agrees formally with the adoption formula current in the ancient Near East. (According to the Code of Hammurabi §170f. the father acknowledges the children of the slavewoman as having equal rights with the words 'you are my children'; cf. Isa. 49: 3, 'You are my servant', as a call formula; also Jer. 2: 27; Hos. 2: 23 [Heb. 2: 25]; Esther 2: 7; Exod. 2: 10 et al.) In the second clause 'today I have begotten you' something of the idea of physical birth from the gods is still heard, but with the temporal indication 'today' the saying points forward to the accession, no longer to the conception. It must be left undecided whether this gives us an antithesis with the world around; for even in the Egyptian concept the pharaoh obtains his divine character only at his enthronement. In any case the king is no longer physically of heavenly origin, nor is he a god incarnate; a man is designated heir by appointment. In this way the difference between god and man is at least more strongly expressed. It is not the ruling king, but the expected future ruler who is called 'Everlasting Father'.

3   The really big change achieved with the taking over of the title 'son of god' in Israel, lies in the extension of this relationship to the nation as a whole. Just as the Old Testament reinterprets old mythical ideas of the relationship between God and nation, it extends expressions which were originally reserved for the king and emphasized his special position in relation to his subjects, to all men (cf. above,

§12a, 4 on Isa. 55: 3). This 'democratization', which is already beginning in the ancient Near East, comes to have such fundamental significance in the Old Testament that the father-son relationship much more often characterizes the relationship of God and nation than that of God and king.

But when the date of the texts is noticed, it becomes clear that the word 'son' is used very rarely of Israel in the early period. Although it would be particularly well suited to express Yahweh's affection for Israel, it first occurs substantially in the prophets, and is therefore found mostly in words of God. Later ages use it freely; at first the father-son relationship appears to have been transferred only with some reserve to Yahweh, because concepts abhorrent to Israel's own faith were too easily linked with it. For this reason it does not show signs of the nomadic and patriarchal way of life of the early period either. But the image of 'son' is so readily suggested by the idea of bringing up (Isa. 1: 2; Prov. 13: 24 et al.) that borrowing from the surrounding world cannot (unlike the use of the term 'son' about the king) be demonstrated with the same certainty. In the language of the court it comes out more clearly that Israel borrows foreign concepts.

Some personal names, like Ab-ram 'the (divine) father is exalted', Eli-ab 'my God is father' or Ahiezer 'my (divine) brother is help' are still echoes of a religion which interpreted the relationship between the divinity and his worshippers as one of kinship. These traces point to the 'gods of the fathers' of the patriarchal period. But even this clan or tribal god was not simply regarded as related by blood to his worshippers; or at least this relationship is not sufficient to characterize it adequately (above, §3b). Furthermore it is hard to decide how far a metaphorical significance is already found in these names in the early period, as it is later.

In another area the father-son relationship can be traced back to the nature cult. If the prophet Jeremiah is not deliberately heightening his polemic against those 'who say to a tree, "You are my father," and to a stone, "You gave me birth" ' (2: 27), his saying presupposes that in the individual local cults the worshippers could derive their existence from holy trees and stones (cf. above, §10, 2, 3). Just possibly in Hosea's savage description 'children of harlotry' (2: 4 [Heb. 2: 6]; 1: 2) for Israelites who have succumbed to the Ba'al cult an antithesis can be found to a mythological father-son relationship. Yahweh himself is not represented in the Old Testament as ancestor or progenitor of mankind – apart from the image which applies the activity of both father and mother to God: you forgot 'the Rock that begot you, the God who gave you birth' (Deut. 32: 18). Again in the Song of Moses it is no doubt foreign ideas that are at work when this says to the people:

Is not he your father, who created you,
who made you and established you? (Deut. 32: 6)

Certainly the idea of procreation is replaced by that of creation, but the interpretation of the father as creator (also in Isa. 64: 7; 43: 6f.; 45: 9ff.; Mal. 2:

10) is not in origin a specifically Old Testament correction of a physically understood relation. It is already in existence, and only taken further by the Old Testament. In the Ugaritic myths the god El is in relation to Ba'al called 'his father, who has established him', which agrees almost verbally with Deut. 32: 6. El is at the same time worshipped as 'father of mankind', and his consort, the goddess Ashera, as 'creatress of the gods'. So all the instances both in and outside the Old Testament do not support the conjecture that in the world around Israel the relationship of God and of the individual man was as a rule thought of in a physical way. What was said here and there of the king, that he was begotten by the deity, was not true, or only exceptionally so, of everyone. For this reason it should not be thought that Israel assumed its descent from Yahweh in the early period, and later changed this idea to one of adoption by free choice.

4   Strictly, a distinction needs to be made between the transfer of the concept of father to Yahweh and the description of man as 'son' of God. Both titles can occur together (2 Sam. 7: 14; Jer. 3: 19 et al.), but they do not necessarily belong together originally. The address 'son' appears to occur only rarely in the ancient Near East for the individual, apart from personal names, while the invocation of God as 'father' is well known, but in Egypt is generally reserved to the king.

Hosea already goes further than the application of the title 'son' to Israel, in filling out the image of sonship from the reality of life. The ancient Near Eastern concept of the king as son of God can be filled out similarly: the deity takes the child on his lap and brings it up. The relationship to God is therefore not only found in the title, but (as in the marriage metaphor, Hos. 2) interpreted as solicitous guidance and upbringing.

> When Israel was a child, I loved him,
>   and out of Egypt I called my son.
> The more I called them,
>   the more they went from me;
> they kept sacrificing to the Ba'als,
>   and burning incense to idols.
> Yet it was I who taught Ephraim to walk,
>   I took them up in my arms;
>   but they did not know that I healed them. (Hos. 11: 1–3)

The prophet looks back to the origin of the people: Yahweh chose his son in Egypt. This representation of childhood excludes any sort of physical relation. It is specifically a matter of call, not of descent. In this way the relationship of adoption is anchored in time: sonship has a beginning. The metaphor is given the task of representing Israel's historical self-understanding.

This understanding of sonship, based on the love of God, is taken over by the later prophets: God must answer with compassion the lament of the 'dear son' Ephraim (Jer. 31: 20; cf. 31: 1ff.), so that God's grace can be entreated with the petition 'our father' (Isa. 63: 15f.; 64: 7f.; cf. Jer. 3: 4, 19; Mal. 3: 17) or we can be assured of his goodness:

> As a father pities his children,
>> so the Lord pities those who fear him. (Ps. 103: 13; cf. Prov. 3: 12 et al.)

But the son does not respond to the 'call' of the loving father. Hosea's whole picture, carefully done down to the details, of a father's dealings with his adopted son is intended only to demonstrate the sin of the nation, which turns away in disobedience to the first and second commandments from its guardian to the Ba'als. The later prophets take up this message too:

> Sons have I reared and brought up,
>> but they have rebelled against me. (Isa. 1: 2)

Wisdom concepts in particular come into the picture here: the obedient son heeds the exhortations of the father (Prov. 6: 20ff.; 23: 24ff.) Similarly Isaiah, with specific terms like 'corrupt' (1: 4), 'rebellious' (30: 1) or 'lying sons' (30: 9), and also Jeremiah (3: 14, 19, 22; 4: 22) emphasize the corruption of sonship.

By the image of the son, then, Hosea and his followers express at the same time the love of the father and the disobedience of the son. So the father-son relationship comes to have a particular sense in the prophetic message. The idea that the father can legally claim the authority of the paterfamilias, to whom respectful obedience is owed (Mal. 1: 6) fades in importance; the relationship is described in personal or affectionate terms rather than in legal ones. The actual authority of the father forms the background for the imagery, but it is constantly the affection of the father, which endures in spite of all the disobedience of the son, that is emphasized. Sonship nowhere appears as a task to be fulfilled, or as a destiny which has to be realized. It has to prove itself in history, but this is not demanded beforehand in laws, like 'You shall be sons!' Sonship is simply stated, whether it is negatively portrayed in failure and then in accusation as partaking of sin, or whether it is granted positively in address. So the word of Yahweh according to Exod. 4: 22f. (probably a later addition to the Yahwist) says, 'Israel is my first-born son.' As in Hos. 11: 1ff. the call from Egypt and the title of son go together; but unlike that passage we are here given no explanation; only a conclusion is drawn (release from vassalage to foreigners and punishment of the sin upon the 'first-born son' of pharaoh in accordance with the law of talion). Similarly in Deut. 14: 1 sonship is promised to the nation without reasons being given: 'You are the sons of the Lord your God.' This form of address is reminiscent of the adoption of the king, 'You are my son' in Ps. 2: 7; again sonship is not claimed to be natural and obvious, but goes back to a word of Yahweh. It is prefixed to the law as a general principle, from which the prohibition of particular ritual actions is then deduced, because they are incompatible with worship of Yahweh. While the relationship of son to God may be so assured, or, as in the prophets, denied or promised, in no instance it is really something that one has to obtain.

5   Sonship is not reserved for the nation as a whole (as in Exod. 4: 22 et al.), but is often applied (to a noticeable extent within the Old Testament) to each individual (as in Deut. 14: 1; 32: 5 et al.). The general address in prayer 'my father' is not yet current. It is not found among the various titles for God in the psalter; Ps. 89: 26 [Heb. 89: 27] relates only to the king: 'He shall cry to me, "Thou art my Father." ' Only the nation as a whole says 'my father' (Jer. 3: 4, 19; said critically 2: 27) or 'our father' (Isa. 63: 16; 64: 7). Similarly God is only rarely addressed as 'my king' (Ps. 5: 2 [Heb. 5: 3]). On the other hand the absence of the address 'father' does not mean in turn that the relationship of God to the individual is not thought of as a relationship to a son.

In a saying of the prophet Hosea (2: 2 [Heb. 2: 4]) Yahweh demands of the sons that they should take a stand against their apostate mother; he therefore calls upon the individual Israelites against Israel as a whole: 'Plead with your mother, plead – for she is not my wife, and I am not her husband!' Here the father-son relationship is expanded into a family image with the help of the image of marriage; the father seeks to get the children upon his side and to separate them from their mother. However precisely this distinction between the individual and the whole, that is, the nation or the country, is meant, it is in any case true that 'the collective idea . . . noticeably breaks down' (H. W. Wolff, *Hosea*, Philadelphia, 1974, p. 33). It matches this circumstance that Hosea not only calls Israel 'son' (11: 1), but also speaks reproachfully of 'sons' (2: 4 [Heb. 2: 6]; 5: 7). Isaiah and Jeremiah follow him, and Deutero-Isaiah promises the exiles in the style of a divine oracle of salvation:

Fear not, for I am with you;
    I will bring your offspring from the east,
and from the west I will gather you;
I will say to the north, Give up,
    and to the south, do not withhold;
bring my sons from afar
    and my daughters from the end of the earth,
everyone who is called by my name,
    whom I created for my glory,
    whom I formed and made.   (Isa. 43: 5–7)

Not only those addressed are to obtain freedom; all the members of the people of God are to experience homecoming from the four corners of the earth. After the collective address 'Fear not', the saying speaks quite unexpectedly in the plural of 'sons' and 'daughters' (cf. 49: 22; 45: 11). God sees the individual and calls him into fellowship, just as Deutero-Isaiah in another passage (44: 5; cf. 55: 7) expects a decision of the individual for God. When finally Hosea (1: 10 [Heb. 2:

1]) promises that the nation will bear the name 'sons of the living God' (above, §11c, 5), the Old Testament has again let an assurance for the present become a hope for the future. But then it really becomes clear that sonship is not something that man can make a reality for himself.

c   THE IMAGE OF GOD

1   The description of man as the 'image of God' had so far-reaching consequences outside the Old Testament itself that it is difficult to establish the original meaning of the concept. After a distinction came to be made frequently in the history of the Church, following on from Irenaeus, between natural and supernatural likeness to the image of God, exegesis was concerned for a long period to get beyond this distinction, which has no basis in the Old Testament. But even then quite different views of it were to be found. While many commentators found the similarity with God in the intellectual character of man, other opposed this understanding: 'the first man is similar to God in form and appearance . . . accordingly this "image of God" is related primarily to the body of man' (H. Gunkel). Reference was made particularly, following ancient concepts, to man's upright stance as an indicator which thoroughly distinguishes man from animals (L. Köhler 'Die Grundstelle der Imago-Dei-Lehre, Genesis 1. 26', *ThZ* 4 (1948)). The Hebrew concept of 'image' does not however argue clearly for this understanding; it can, but does not have to, refer to a representation in sculpture. Furthermore the Old Testament does not make a distinction between body and mind or soul: 'spirit' is not contrasted to body, but is thought of as the power of life (above Excursus 3). So some commentators looked for a compromise, emphasizing that spiritual and corporal are to be seen together, while others avoided this terminology altogether, and defined man's being made in the image of God as the lordship of man over the animal world. It was remembered that the great kings of the ancient Near East set up images of themselves in distant lands of their kingdom, in order to be present there too, and correspondingly man was interpreted as God's governor or representative. But is not this dominion rather a consequence of man's being made in the image of God? Finally Karl Barth's teaching brought a new approach (*Church Dogmatics*, vol. III, pt. I, Edinburgh, 1958, pp. 184ff.): being made in the image of God is 'not a quality of man'. 'It does not consist in anything that man is or does. It consists as man himself consists as the creature of God. . . . He is the image of God in the fact that he is man'. Certainly Barth, following here Bonhoeffer, then recognizes the image of God in the 'confrontation and reciprocity of man and man', more exactly in 'that of man and woman', which repeats the contrast of I and Thou in God. Where however the Old Testament alludes to the image of God outside Gen. 1: 26f., the relationship of man and woman is not mentioned. For this reason those commentators who take over Barth's thesis have modified it, speaking generally of the personality of man, of the partnerlike relationship between God and man, and the responsible relationship of cooperation and mutual care. However

justified this statement is (cf. Gen. 2: 18), does it really render what is meant by 'God created man in his own image'?

2   The difficulty the expression 'the image of God' makes for understanding, consists in the fact that the Old Testament contains only three or four instances of it at all (exclusively in the Priestly writer, Gen. 1: 26f.; 5: 1ff.; 9: 6; cf. Ps. 8: 4ff. [Heb. 8: 5ff.]) and never explains more fully these brief allusions. This suggests that it was a concept which Israel borrowed. Further, the language is strikingly fixed. Even if God is the subject of the sentence, the attribute can be 'after the image of God' instead of 'after his image'. So 'image of God' seems to be a fixed technical term. Where does it come from?

Ps. 8, the only parallel which the Old Testament itself offers (and then one of substance, not of language) determines the nature of man dialectically: he is on the one hand too little before God (v. 4, [Heb. 5]), on the other almost equal to God (vv. 5–8 [Heb. 6–9]), littleness and greatness in one. The psalm describes the sovereignty of man in describing him as king. The language is rooted in that of the court even down to the details (cf. e.g. Ps. 21: 5 [Heb. 21: 6]; 110: 1f.). In the creation narrative too likeness to the image of God is connected with man's dominion (Gen. 1: 26ff.; 9: 6f.). The king is indeed never called in the Old Testament 'image of God'; but may the ancient Near East, in which the king had a position equal or similar to that of God, have been familiar with the term?

3   Especially in the New Kingdom of Egypt (approximately the period from the seventeenth century BC) the pharaoh is regarded as the image of the creator and sun god. The title is preserved down to the Hellenistic period. The terminology as a whole is very varied. Expressions like 'image of Re, Amun, Atum' are very common, often filled out as 'holy image' or 'living image on earth'. It is interesting that as in the Old Testament the image of God and creation can be connected. Amenophis III is once addressed by the deity Amon Re as 'my living image, the creation of my limbs', and another time: 'you are my beloved son, coming from my limbs, my image which I have put upon earth. I have let you govern the earth in peace.' Like the older term 'son of god' the expression 'image of god' describes the close relationship between god and king, although it perhaps also emphasized more strongly the distance between the two. In any case the pharaoh as image of god is a visible sign to men that god is near them.

In Mesopotamia the title is much less common. But the king, with a word corresponding to the Hebrew (Heb. ṣelem, Akk. ṣalmu), can be called 'image of Marduk' or 'image of Shamash', and we read in a letter directed to him:

The father of the king, my lord,
    was the image of Bel,
and the king, my lord,
    is the image of Bel.

In both cultures the title is composed as a rule of a (varying) expression for 'image' and the proper name of a particular deity. The expression 'image of God' is found on the other hand only rarely in Egypt. Similarly the Old Testament does not think just of an equality of man with divine or heavenly beings (cf. Gen. 3: 22 with 3: 5), but rather of a likeness of the creator god. 'Elohim' does have a far wider meaning than 'god', but the subordinate heavenly beings are called 'sons of God' (Gen. 6: 2, 4; Ps. 29; Job 1f.) rather than 'gods' (cf. Ps. 82). A qualification is at most recognizable in the fact that Ps. 8 compares man only with 'God' (v.5 [Heb. v. 6]) rather than with 'Yahweh' (v. 1 [Heb. v. 2]); for elsewhere too the Old Testament occasionally distinguishes between 'God' and 'Yahweh', avoids the proper name, and uses the generic term, perhaps in order in this way to safeguard the distinctiveness of Yahweh (cf. e.g. 1 Sam. 16: 14ff.). But this consideration does not hold for the creation narrative, which speaks throughout of 'God'. In Gen. 1 and the dependent passages there cannot really be established a qualification in any form, not even through the parallel expression 'likeness'. It is the Greek (and Aramaic) translation, which seeks to avoid anthropomorphisms, that reduces the concept of 'image of God' to 'image of angels' (cf. Heb. 2: 6f.), but at the same time gives the expression a more mythological form. However in the Old Testament too the nearness of man to God does not mean identity.

4　Ancient Near Eastern myth also has the concept of an image of god, though in other, not so explicit, terms. The Gilgamesh epic describes the birth of the hero Enkidu; Araru created Enkidu 'in his heart after the image of Anu', and the story of Ishtar's journey to the underworld tells us that: 'Ea created in his heart an image, created Asushunamir.' The imagery is again derived from creation, but it also comes out much more strongly that the deity is the model upon which the human creature is modelled. On the other hand the royal titulature is already much more formulaic. What is decisive is not that the ruler truly represents the deity in appearance (cf. above, §6c), but that he embodies him on earth. It is for this reason that the pharaoh can be regarded at the same time as image of a female and of a male deity, as in Philae: 'image of Isis, likeness of Onophris'. It is the Old Testament that places no emphasis on the fact that God is the heavenly model (cf. Exod. 25: 9, 40) and man his image. Israel does appear to have conceived of God completely as in human form, but in P, especially in the creation narrative, such ideas recede in importance (cf. above, §11f. 3). At least an external identity or similarity between God and man is not emphasized. To raise the question how far God is the model for man is to alter completely the tone of the statements in the text. 'Man's being made in the image of God is not intended to state something about God, about his form, his appearance, his nature and character; the relationship is the exact opposite, that the distinctive character of man ... is to be stated' (Horst, *Gottes Recht*, 1961, p. 277f.). Since the term 'image of God' is taken over by the Old Testament, it need not have reflected upon the outward form of God, whatever the original meaning of the expression may have demanded. In any case the Old Testament does not tell how man's likeness to the image of God originated, but only states that man was created 'as the image of God' – this translation is more apt than the usual 'in the image of God'. The 'image of God' is no longer conceived in the Old Testament as strongly mythological, but is only a title which does not imply any event.

The relationship of God and man expressed thus cannot be interpreted as one of kinship. In the Egyptian terminology it must be left open whether the parallel expression 'son' whom the deity has 'begotten' still means a physical relationship and does not rather refer to creation and coronation (cf. above, §12a, 1). The Mesopotamian instances do not allude at all to sonship or kinship. In the Old Testament too the 'image of God' is not explained by terms which might be misleading in this context such as 'son of God'. Man is not therefore the 'image of God' because he is the 'son' that has come from God, and he does not through his special position gain any 'share' in God.

5   It is of the essence of an image that it allows something to be seen. Just as the ancient Near Eastern king as the 'image of God' represents the deity upon earth, man as the image of God is an attestation of God upon earth. While already in Egypt the royal privilege is occasionally extended to all men (best known is the saying from the teaching of Merikare: 'they are his (i.e. the creator god's) images, which have proceeded from his limbs'), what is called democratization is again basically complete in the Old Testament. The title is only used here of man, never of the king. The Old Testament has generalized, and assured everyone, not only the members of a nation, but all humankind, man and woman alike (Gen. 1: 27f.), of what once was basically only assigned to the king, that they would exercise dominion as 'image of God'.

It remains however clear from the origin of the tradition that the image of God is not a part, or a feature, that is to be sought in, or on, man; it rather goes with man's being the creation of God, and independently of social rank, nationality or sex. The likeness to the image of God is not related therefore specially to the spiritual character of man, nor to his bodily posture, but as with the king, to his 'office', his position in the world. The image of God cannot be acquired by action any more than can sonship (above, §12b, 4f.); for man's position as image is given by God.

On an Egyptian inscription about the appointment of a vizier the pharaoh gives reasons for his desire that the son should follow his old father in his office: 'it is good to be replaced by one's like! Uncover your image. . . . Your representative he is to be.' Just as here the physical son as 'image' of his father is his 'representative', so Adam according to Gen. 5: 3 begets a son 'in his own likeness, after his image'. This does not only mean that the son looks like his father externally, but that the father reappears in his son. The son 'repeats' his father; for the father is intrinsically present in the son.

Accordingly the likeness to the image of God in man can be understood as deputizing for God on earth. Perhaps the concept of 'image of God' cannot be strictly defined at all, because in the tradition itself we catch the note of several themes: the appearance of God, his actualization, his representation by another, and also governorship on his behalf. The creation narrative does separate the commission as ruler from the theme of the image of God, and promises it to man in a separate blessing (Gen. 1: 28), but the two remain closely connected. How far can office and task, essential nature and consequence be separated from one another? The expression 'image of God' does describe the presence of God at a place – in the world; so that it includes simultaneously situation and function. As representative of God man is God's governor upon earth; he exercises his position as 'image of God' in creation.

6   It is astonishing that the Old Testament does not set limits in any way to this freedom of man in the world. The image of God is not lost through sin (cf. Gen. 5: 1; 9: 6; the Priestly work does not have a 'fall' story); it is not even made dependent upon responsible behaviour distinguishing between good and evil. Dominion is assured to man by God, but it is given unconditionally. While Ps. 8 speaks expressly only of the superiority of man over the animal world, and proclaims an expansion of his area of power at most in the declaration 'thou hast put all things under his feet', the creation narrative expressly demands of man, in particularly harsh words, that he should subdue the earth – ruthlessly, not considerately. The Old Testament does not envisage that the dominion of man could be detached from God who gives the authority for it and become un-scrupulous and destructive. Certainly it does not see man as 'the measure of all things', but as a creature in God's creation, though certainly one preferred by God, and addressed by him. Further the commission to dominion includes as yet, according to Gen. 1: 28ff., no shedding of blood (cf. above, §11f., 3), and even after the killing of animals was permitted, the Old Testament exempts man himself from man's dominion. The 'image of God' as a reality between God and world has a special position, from which a legal statement draws the conclusion:

Whoever sheds the blood of man,
by man shall his blood be shed;
for God made in his own image. (Gen. 9: 6)

d   THE MESSIAH

Among the successors of prophecy the hopes of the late period (4 Ezra; John 4: 25) are directed towards the Messiah, the 'anointed'. On the other hand the Old Testament does not have this title for the future ruler. 'The anointed of Yahweh' is for centuries (from 1 Sam. 24: 7 down to Lam. 4: 20; Zech. 4: 14) a title of the king, and even the Persian king Cyrus can exceptionally be so entitled as Yahweh's representative (Isa. 45: 1).

1   That anointing should form an important part of the coronation ritual (e.g. 1 Kgs. 1: 39; 2 Kgs. 11: 12; cf. 2 Sam. 19: 11) is by no means a matter of course in the ancient Near

East. It occurred occasionally at the installation of high Egyptian officials, and Pharaoh Thutmosis III made a Syrian vassal prince (according to one of the Amarna letters) king by 'putting oil upon his head', but we do not have clear evidence of the anointing of the king himself either from Egypt or from Mesopotamia. So it seems to have been unknown in both areas. However the Hittite king was often anointed by the people or nobility, in a way like that often mentioned in the Old Testament. So it is a likely conjecture that 'the rite in Israel and Judah goes back to a Hittite custom', Canaan perhaps serving as the 'mediating link'; the legal position of the queen mother, the 'dowager' (1 Kgs. 15: 13; 2 Kgs. 10: 13 et al.) may also go back to a Hittite precedent (Kutsch, *Salbung und Rechtsakt im Alten Testament und im Alten Orient*, Berlin, 1963, p. 56).

In any case the anointing of the king comes to have paramount significance in Israel. It can be performed either by the people, or by a prophet in the name of Yahweh (so in the case of David in 2 Sam. 2: 4; 5: 3 and 1 Sam. 16: 13). It is uncertain how far the corresponding prophetic narratives (1 Sam. 9: 1–10: 16; 16: 1–13) really portray the historical reality, and are not written subsequently to illustrate the divine authority of the king; the account of the anointing of Jehu by a prophetic follower of Elisha (2 Kgs. 9) has more claim to historicity. Otherwise however the anointing of the king is better attested in the southern kingdom than in the northern.

So while it cannot be reliably proved, it is very likely that every king of Judah (and perhaps also of Israel) was anointed on his accession. In whatever form and by whoever this act was carried out, it was the specific occasion for and origin of the royal title 'anointed of Yahweh' (Ps. 2: 2; 20: 6 [Heb. 20: 7]; 132: 10, 17; 1 Sam. 12: 3 et al.). With this action Yahweh put the future king under his protection, so that he was sacrosanct (24: 7, 11; 2 Sam. 1: 14ff.; Ps. 89: 20ff. [Heb. 89: 21ff.]), and at the same time commissioned him (1 Sam. 9: 16). When the gift of the spirit, with which God called the leaders of the Judges period directly to a task, was regarded as a consequence of anointing (1 Sam. 10: 1, 6; 16: 13f.; 2 Sam. 23: 1f.), an institution of the lands of civilization was linked with an inheritance of the nomadic period. Finally the prophetic gift of the spirit was also connected with anointing (Isa. 61: 1; 1 Kgs. 19: 15f.; cf. Ps. 105: 15 said of the patriarchs), although the prophets were certainly never anointed. Already in the Old Testament therefore the loss of the rite is followed by an expansion of its traditional significance; the anointed is the authorized representative.

2   Since the title 'Messiah' is not used of the future king, but is only echoed in the image of the two 'sons of oil' (Zech. 4: 11ff.) the term 'messianic prophecy' is not unambiguous. It could cover a very broad area, for the Old Testament has some very different eschatological expectations, which are not dominated by a messianic figure in the narrower sense: the hope of the achievement of the reign of God or of the coming of the Son of Man (after Dan. 7: 13f. especially in the Similitudes of Enoch 37–71, and 4 Ezra 13). Even on a stricter interpretation of the expression 'messianic prophecy' it is not easy to delimit the relevant passages.

Do the obscure saying from the Blessing of Jacob in Gen. 49: 10f., about the 'coming' of a ruler (?) and the saying of Balaam in Num. 24: 17f., which promises the rise of a star in Jacob, refer to a future ruler figure at all? We have rather what are called *vaticinia ex eventu*, which are made to look forward to David from a contemporary or even later situation. The ambiguous Immanuel prophecy in Isa. 7: 14ff. must be left aside too.

Messianic prophecies which are directed to the future, and to this extent are 'genuine', are first found in the major prophets. But what is the occasion and the reason for the origin of the messianic hope? The assumption that there is a constantly repeated disappointment over the reigning king of the time (because he does not fulfil the ideas which one has of a true ruler) is certainly not a sufficient explanation; for in the Old Testament quite other areas, like Exodus or creation, become eschatological too. Further we lack sufficient clear ancient Near Eastern precedents which could have given the impetus to Israel's messianic expectation (cf. later Virgil's Fourth Eclogue). Is its origin then to be sought in the prophecy of Nathan in 2 Sam. 7? The Messianic hope does seem to have originated in the south, in which the house of David reigned for centuries. However the prophecy of Nathan promises the 'everlasting' continuation of the dynasty of David, not of one single new ruler, who furthermore can appear in contrast to the royal house. Further the messianic passages look forward to a definitive final position ('peace without end' Isa. 9: 6), not a succession of events (unlike Jer. 33: 17f.). Would they not have had to quote the prophecy of Nathan at least occasionally, if it had had such fundamental significance?

The two sayings of Amos and Hosea, which announce a reestablishment of the rule of David (Amos 9: 11f.; Hos. 3: 5), are generally and rightly regarded as secondary. In that case Isa. 9 opens the sequence of messianic prophecies. Is the 'messianic concept' born here? Certainly the authenticity of almost all the promises is disputed. Objective criteria like vocabulary studies do not give a clear decision. For this reason the problem of when the sayings are to be dated and whether they have been rightly placed in the individual prophetic books will be left out of consideration as far as possible. Prophecies of salvation leave their original historical situation so difficult to discern because they are not explained in terms of human behaviour, can deliberately speak in non-concrete and general terms ('The people who walked in darkness have seen a great light', Isa. 9: 2 [Heb. 9: 1]) and go beyond what is possible in history (especially 11: 6–8). So it can only be said with qualification that the Messiah was originally a historical figure; for experience is transcended in hope.

3   The promise of a 'great light', which brings joy to those who dwell in darkness and in the dominion of death, is based in Isa. 9 primarily upon liberation from political oppression and the destruction of military booty, while there is added as the third and last ground (vv. 6f. [Heb. vv. 5f.]):

For to us a child is born,
   to us a son is given.
and the government will be upon his shoulder,
   and his name will be called

Wonderful Counsellor, Mighty God,
   Everlasting Father, Prince of Peace.
Of the increase of his government and of peace
   there will be no end,
upon the throne of David, and over his kingdom,
   to establish it, and to uphold it
with justice and with righteousness
   from this time forth and for evermore.

The appearance of the king's son forms the chief occasion for joy, and is therefore also described in the most detail, from his birth, through the gift of dominion and bestowal of his name, on to the manner of his rule. He is introduced emphatically as ruler, but as a 'peaceful ruler'. This title is given him not only because the elimination of the state of war is final, and so the peace is unsurpassable, 'eschatological'. The Messiah himself (this term will be used of the figure in question) carries out no more acts of war. The war, which removes the political pressure, and therefore must precede the kingdom of peace, is conducted by God himself. All the activity rests with him alone: God brings or is the light, he creates the joy and breaks the yoke (vv. 2–5 [Heb. vv. 1–4]), so that the final sentence can say in summary (v. 7 [Heb. v. 6]). 'The zeal of Yahweh Sabaoth will do this.' In this way the Messiah is driven into a strange passivity: he exercises his just dominion only after victory is already won. Traditio-historically this strange position is to be explained by the fact that the royal tradition, and the Messianic expectation that is built upon it, have incorporated the older Israelite tradition of the holy war which God alone conducts (above, §7, 3). This strict distinction between the reign of God and the reign of the king can already be noticed in the royal psalms (Ps. 110: 1, 5f.; cf. above, §12a, 3). In any case such a demand as God makes of the king according to Ps. 2, 'Ask of me the nations to destroy them', has become impossible in the case of the Messiah. Even in the war that precedes the reign of peace this 'humanization' takes effect. While the older tradition can report that in the war of Yahweh all the booty including all the prisoners was put to destruction (1 Sam. 15), Isa. 9: 5 [Heb. 9: 4] speaks only of the burning of the weapons of war. There is no longer mention of the killing of man or beast. No nation is now subjected; the war as such seems to have been done away with. It may in fact be asked whether the title of king would not be inappropriate for such a future ruler, and whether therefore it is quite deliberately omitted in the promise.

Even if the rule of God and of Messiah are sharply distinguished in Isa. 9, the Messiah still stands close to God himself. The Old Testament probably nowhere else (apart perhaps from Ps. 45: 6 [Heb. 45: 7]) puts the present or future king into so close a relationship with Yahweh. Following the pattern of the usual throne names of the pharaoh, the prophet gives the Messiah honorific titles. The two first names 'who plans wonderful things' and 'divine hero' are no doubt honorific epithets for God (cf. Isa. 28: 29 and Ps. 24: 8), and 'father' too is easily understood as a divine name (cf. above, §12b, 3). The Messiah is almost equal to God; he is capable of doing what God can do. Such exalted utterances were not regularly applied by Israel to the earthly ruler; at least there is some heightening of the normal for the Messiah here. 'Religio-historically speaking the contents of the ideology of divine kingship have only been fully realized in Israel in the course of eschatological reinterpretation' (H. Wildberger, 'Die Thronnamen des Messias', *ThZ* 16 (1960), p. 331). Except with great reservations Israel could only incorporate the ancient Near Eastern kingship ideology into its hope. For this reason the frequent attempts to reconstruct from Isa. 9: 6f. [Heb. 9: 5f.] the course of the coronation ritual in Jerusalem (e.g. adoption? – transfer of authority – giving of name – proclamation of reign) must be viewed with scepticism. A prophetic saying so changes the underlying reality that this is only reflected in it in very changed form.

4   The Messianic expectation, which in Isa. 9 is only a part of the future hope, has expanded in Isa. 11: 1–5 and become independent; Isa. 11 seems to take Isa. 9 further. The arrival of the ruler, his gifts of the spirit, his tasks, and in addition also the paradisiacal consequences (vv. 6–8) are described:

> There shall come forth a shoot from the stump of Jesse,
>   and a branch shall grow out of his roots.
> And the Spirit of Yahweh shall rest upon him,
>   the spirit of wisdom and understanding,
>   the spirit of counsel and might,
>   the spirit of knowledge and the fear of Yahweh. . . .
> He shall not judge by what his eyes see,
>   or decide by what his ears hear;
> but with righteousness shall be judge the poor,
>   and decide with equity for the meek of the earth;
> and he shall smite the earth with the rod of his mouth,
>   and with the breath of his lips he shall slay the wicked.
> Righteousness shall be the girdle of his waist,
>   and faithfulness the girdle of his loins.

Just as the 'prince of peace' reigns from the throne of David (Isa. 9: 7 [Heb. 9: 6]) the promised ruler in Isa. 11 is similarly in origin a Davidide. He does not come however from the existing royal family; rather the branch comes out of the root. This return to origins (Jesse was David's father, 1 Sam. 17: 12ff.; 2 Sam. 23: 1) is a criticism of the existing royal house; in fact the whole history of Israel since David is set aside, or erased completely (cf. Isa. 7: 9ff.) The existing situation cannot be continued. The future dominion can only be hoped for to the accompaniment of criticism of the past and present one; so messianic prophecy comes to have a strongly contentious character. The Messiah receives as gifts of the spirit wisdom and insight, for which Solomon prayed (1 Kgs. 3: 12), counsel and might, which already characterize the 'prince of peace' (so wonderful counsellor, divine hero), knowledge and the fear of God – this too an ancient hope for the ruler (2 Sam. 23: 3). As a whole these characteristics do not go beyond what tradition has to offer. They do not place the Messiah as near to God as do the titles of Isa. 9: 6 [Heb. 9: 5]; but these virtues of a ruler too are realized by God and appear here, in contrast to the tradition, collected together and united. The traditional image of the king is expanded and intensified in the expectation. So the spirit will 'rest' for ever upon the future ruler (cf. Num. 11: 25; 2 Kgs. 2: 15), and will not be taken from him (in contrast to the heroes of the period of the judges, or the first king, Saul). It equips him primarily for the practice of justice. What it means for righteousness to be the support of the throne (Isa. 9: 6) is here made clear: justice is total, because the judge does not need to judge after appearances or what he hears; he sees how things actually are (cf. 1 Sam. 16: 7). He looks after the poor and needy. But he smites the man who does violence and injustice, although not with the royal sceptre (cf. Ps. 2: 9 et al.) but with the 'rod of his mouth'. His sceptre is – unusually – his word, but this word retains the sceptre's power.

This future 'king' (again the title is deliberately avoided) is a 'prince of peace'. We hear no more of war and victory, which in Isa. 9 are the presuppositions of 'peace without end'. The external peace is almost self-evident. The political and national sphere is omitted in the activity of the Messiah; his activity as ruler is restricted to the administration of justice. He proceeds against evil-doers, not against foreign nations in rebellion. An addition (vv. 6ff.; cf. Ezek. 34: 25ff.) expands the reign of peace further to the co-existence of man and beast, and of beasts among themselves. Even the first promise, which is directed exclusively to the future ruler, is not accounted for by the claim that 'still among the great writing prophets the figure of the Messiah .`. . has predominantly political features.' The text compels us rather to the view that the prophets have 're-arranged and destroyed the old picture' (H. Gressmann, *Der Messias*, Göttingen, 1929, p. 273).

5   As later additions expanded the message of Isa. 11 in a universal sense, so the prophecy of Mic. 5: 2–6 [Heb. 5: 1–5] seems to be marked by similar expansions, which however have affected the text itself. The promise of a Messiah, which describes again the origin and the task of the ruler (vv. 2, 4a, 5a, 6b [Heb. vv. 1, 3a, 4a, 5b]) has been expanded by the insertion of words directed to a group, which have been attracted to the singular stratum (vv. 1, 2b, 3b–4a [Heb. vv. 2, 3b, 4b–5a]). In them the power of the future king 'to the ends of the earth' is proclaimed (cf. Isa. 11: 10), so that the scattered elements of the nation can return home. The original text was something like:

> But you, O Beth(lehem) Ephrata,
>   who are littlest among the thousands of Judah,

from you will come (to me)
one who will be ruler of Israel.
His origin is in the distant past,
in ancient days.
He stands fast and feeds them in the strength of Yahweh,
in the exalted name of Yahweh his God.

The final verses are perhaps an addition:

And this shall be peace.
He shall save (us) from Assyria,
when he comes into our land,
and treads within our border.

Micah breaks yet more sharply with the ruling dynasty than does Isaiah; for the
Messiah is not even to come from the Jerusalem dynasty. Disaster threatens the
capital (Mic. 1: 6, 16; 3: 12), only Davidic rule persists, but this like David himself
will come out of the little place Bethlehem. So the distant past recurs in the
future; the mythological expression 'ancient days' is intended to remind us of that
early history (cf. Amos 9: 11; while the obscure reference to a secret birth in v. 2a
is an allusion to Isa. 7: 14). As Yahweh's representative the Messiah rules with
power and majesty, but is (in the disputed final verses) unlike the future ruler of
Isaiah politically active. He seems not only to bring peace, but to be called
'salvation, peace'; but he himself effects the deliverance from the impending
Assyrian threat. Micah's saying here is a profound alteration of the prophecies of
Isaiah, but in turn it prepares the way for future promises (Ezek. 34: 23) when it
assigns the Messiah the task of 'feeding his flock', following widespread ancient
Near Eastern concepts of the king or of God as 'shepherd'.

6   In the prophecy in Jeremiah (23: 5f.) the future king is again exclusively a
peaceful ruler. Here the hopes are given a traditional form, no doubt fixed by
Isaiah, and there is little distinctively Jeremianic. Justice and wisdom are the
attributes of the Messiah, not political power, so that not even the promised
security of the land is ascribed to his activity.

Ezekiel's message points in the same direction:

And I will set over them one shepherd, my servant David, and he shall feed
them. He shall be their shepherd. And I, Yahweh, will be their God, and my
servant David shall be prince among them; I, Yahweh, have spoken it. (34:
23f.; cf. 37: 22ff.; 17: 22ff.).

As in Jeremiah the prophecy grows out of a shepherd saying, and again God
'sets up' the Messiah. His power to rule is now so narrowly circumscribed that the
'servant' only receives the general commission to 'feed' his flock. 'It is striking

here too (as in 17: 22–4) that the activity of this shepherd is not portrayed in any more detail' (W. Zimmerli). When instead of 'king' he is given the venerable title of 'prince' (cf. Exod. 22: 27) it is tempting to explain this choice from the attempt to keep away from the Messiah anything political or military. The shepherd oracle, which surrounds the individual saying, incorporates the activity of the Messiah entirely within God's action. What once was the duty of the king is now at last transferred to God himself.

In the prophecy of salvation in Hosea (2: 2) the future ruler (again not a 'king', but only a 'head' (above, §12a, 4), comparable to the title prince) again has no task. He represents the unity of the previouly separated kingdoms, but is basically a person without a function.

When Haggai (2: 22f.) expects the shattering of the world in the near future, and calls Zerubbabel to be Messiah, all the action rests again in God alone, so that Zerubbabel, who will only be installed in his office after the end of the war, has no real responsibilities as ruler. He appears as an official in the kingdom of God, without a real area of competence of his own. The position is similar in Zechariah, although he speaks of '*two* sons of oil' (4: 1ff.; 6: 3ff.), the political and cultic leaders of the community. But the task of the 'political' Messiah is the building of the temple.

7   In the last Messianic prediction, Zech 9: 9f., the reinterpretation which the Old Testament undertook of the traditional image of the king reaches its climax. The future ruler is indeed called 'king' again (although he is no longer a Davidide), but he is stripped of all royal characteristics. All that remains to him is to proclaim peace (cf. Isa. 42: 1, 4). The 'righteous' man rides upon an ass, since the horse is regarded as an animal of war (cf. Mic. 5: 11 [Heb. 5: 10]). While the king elsewhere has the duty of helping the poor (Ps. 72: 12f.; Isa. 11: 4), the Messiah himself is now the 'poor', who must be 'helped' (cf. Ps. 33: 16; 20: 6, 9 [Heb. 7, 10]; Num. 12: 3; Isa. 53: 4). Has the ethos of the 'poor of the land' or at least the self-understanding of the post-exilic and no longer politically active community influenced the messianic hope? In any case the expectation is directed towards a powerless Messiah; all power is with God. (The first-person saying 'I will cut off the chariot and the warhorse' is to be understood as the word of God, who as in Isa. 9: 3 eradicates only the weapons of war; the Greek translation assimilates the statement to the traditional concept of the king who himself carries out the act, by altering it into the third person.) So the field of activity of the Messiah is extended 'to the ends of the earth'. While the dominion of the Messiah in the prophecies of Isaiah and Jeremiah only extended indirectly beyond Israel, because no foreign power can any longer threaten the subjects of the kingdom of peace with war, here a universal kingdom is specifically mentioned (cf. Mic. 5: 4b [Heb. 5: 3b]; Ps. 72: 8 et al.). Accordingly in the course of the history of tradition the power of the Messiah declined, but the extent of his dominion increased.

Perhaps features of the Suffering Servant songs (Isa. 42: 1–4; 49: 1–6; 50: 4–9; 52: 13–53: 12) had an effect upon this strange messianic hope, if it is not the case that there are certain mutual relationships between them and the messianic prophecies; for the Suffering Servant songs too show the tendency increasingly to restrict the usual concept of the king (so clearly Isa. 53: 2).

According to Dan. 7 even the Son of Man only appears after God has conquered the hostile powers and held judgement. He also awards dominion to the Son of Man (7: 13f.) as he does to the Messiah (Isa. 11: 2 et al.). We can again perhaps deduce from the similar structure of the statement a traditio-historical connection which characterizes both forms of future expectation.

In any case the Old Testament made increasingly sharp distinctions between divine and messianic power, until only the powerlessness of God's representative upon earth could be asserted. It was not sufficient for the Old Testament to transfer the ancient Near Eastern ideology into the future; it so reshaped it that it lost some of its basic characteristics.

§13 Zion

In the premonarchical period and still far into the period of the monarchy Israel had many cultic sites, which could also be the scene of political events (above, §9a, 3). While the local sanctuaries at first held their ground alongside Jerusalem, Zion soon became the most important, and then the only, sanctuary. Jerusalem owes its special position not so much to its natural situation as to particular historical events (A.Alt, 'Jerusalems Aufstieg', *Kleine Schriften* III, Munich, 1959); outstanding among these are the events of the period of David and Solomon, which provided the basis for the city's standing.

1   Some at least of the many and various local sanctuaries which Israel possessed in the earlier period were already centres of pilgrimage for the Canaanites. Jerusalem too was not originally an Israelite city. It is already mentioned almost a millennium before David in the Egyptian execration texts, and then in the Amarna letters of the fourteenth century BC, there are to be found letters of a city-prince of Jerusalem called Abdi-Khepa ('Servant of the god Khepa') to the pharaoh. According to Judg. 1: 21 Israel in the period after the entry did not succeed in conquering this Canaanite city-state, or at least not in settling it; the city of the Jebusites, as the inhabitants are called, remained a 'foreign city' (cf. 19: 10–12; Josh. 10; 15: 63, 8; 18: 16; not so in Judg. 1: 8; on which see K. D. Schunck 'Juda und Jerusalem in vor- und frühisraelitischer Zeit', in K. H. Bernhardt (ed.), *Schalom*, Berlin, 1971). It was in any case David who first won lasting success here. After he had become king of Judah and Israel, he removed the Canaanite barrier which separated the two kingdoms from each other, and apparently gave the conquered city a special position in law vis-à-vis Israel and Judah (Alt, 'Jerusalems Aufstieg'; cf. above, III, 1). This special position leaves its mark in the Old Testament when, for example, Jerusalem is mentioned separately over against the 'two houses of Israel' (Isa. 8: 14) or 'Jerusalem and Judah' are mentioned together as the two political units of the southern kingdom (3: 1, 8 et al.). David not only made the former Jebusite city the capital of the two kingdoms, but at the same time made it the cultic centre of the nation by having the Ark, the place of the invisible presence of God, brought to Jerusalem.

In the cultic measure of the transfer of the Ark, which David as king was strictly not entitled to carry out, there is seen at least in retrospect the will of God (so indirectly 2 Sam. 6: 9, 21f.) and it is acknowledged that Yahweh has 'chosen' Zion and David (Ps. 78: 68, 70; 1 Kgs. 8: 16 LXX; 2 Chr. 6: 6).

Probably the traditions collected in 1 Sam. 4–6 and 2 Sam. 6 of the fate of the ark, which is brought from Shiloh past both Philistine and Israelite stopping places to Jerusalem, once formed an independent Ark narrative, which represented a *hieros logos* or cult-legend of the temple in Jerusalem.

The cultic significance of the city was increased yet more by Solomon's building of the temple, and the extension of the existing Zion conceptions increasingly reduced the status of the Ark (cf. Jer. 3: 16).

After the division of the kingdom, or in other words the collapse of the personal union of Israel and Judah into northern and southern kingdoms, Jerusalem remained *the* holy city for Judah, but seems to have possessed an attraction beyond these limits for the Israelites of the north too (1 Kgs. 12: 27f.; later Jer. 41: 5).

In 701 the Assyrian king Sennacherib conquered Judah, but withdrew from the siege of Jerusalem for reasons which are no longer entirely clear (2 Kgs. 18f. = Isa. 36f.); but the southern kingdom became tributary (2 Kgs. 18: 13–16). The deliverance of Jerusalem at the last moment perhaps strengthened the concept of the inviolability of the city, but was not the origin of it.

The reform of King Josiah in 621 BC (2 Kgs. 22f.), in the course of which Deuteronomy obtained the standing of state law, led not only like previous attempts at reform (1 Kgs. 15: 12f.; 2 Kgs. 18: 4) to a cleansing of the cult from foreign elements, but through the removal of all other sanctuaries in Judah and Israel made of Jerusalem the only site where Yahweh 'let his name dwell'. It is this exaltation of Jerusalem to the position of the only sanctuary of Yahweh that explains the high significance which the city had for the faith of the last period of the Old Testament, and for Judaism. In spite of the conquest of Judah and Jerusalem by the Babylonians and the destruction of the city and temple in 587 BC the high standing of the city remained (Jer. 41: 5). It became a place of remembrance and longing (Ps. 137), the place to which prayer was directed (Dan. 6: 11), and even the source of new expectations (below). So in the course of history from being the political centre, the capital of the kingdom, it became more and more a 'religious' centre.

After the return of the exiles and the reconstruction of the temple inaugurated by Haggai and Zechariah (520–515 BC) the provincial capital Jerusalem was the spiritual home of the post-exilic community, to which Ezra and Nehemiah gave external and internal order. The once Canaanite, foreign Jerusalem (cf. Ezek. 16: 3) became accordingly a more or less purely Judahite city, which later only gradually and often with reluctance and resistance opened itself to Hellenization.

2   From a religio-historical point of view what is most significant is that 'in Jerusalem Israelite and Canaanite religious concepts not only confronted one another as elsewhere for one or the other to drive out its rival, but were mingled together with an intensity otherwise unknown. Jerusalem actually became the

gateway through which genuinely Canaanite and other foreign religious influences upon the official faith of Yahwism entered in' (J. Jeremias, 'Lade und Zion', in
H. W. Wolff (ed.), *Probleme biblischer Theologie*, Munich, 1971, p. 195). However
the survival of foreign concepts at other places cannot be verified in the same
degree, since we lack comparable material of any extent.

Religious traditions from pre-Israelite Jerusalem have not been preserved directly, but
have to be reconstructed (with caution) from three sources: (a) the Psalms of Zion (Ps. 46;
48; 76; cf. 84; 87; 122; 132) and other psalms in which distinctively Jerusalem traditions
remain alive; (b) echoes in the prophets, especially Isaiah (1: 21ff.; 6; 8: 6, 18; 28: 14ff.;
29: 1ff. et al.) and Deutero-Isaiah (52: 1f., 7ff. et al.); (c) with particular caution, from
ancient Near Eastern material, in so far as it may have been similar to Jerusalem concepts.

At the conquest of Jerusalem David seems to have spared its inhabitants, and
generally as far as possible to have retained the institutions that he found,
especially in the cultic realm. How close the contact between the two groups in
the population was can perhaps be illustrated by one detail: the priest Zadok, who
appears suddenly in David's entourage, with no indication of his origin, supported Solomon in the struggle for the succession and finally replaced Abiathar
who was from the older Israelite priestly family (2 Sam. 8: 17; 1 Kgs. 1: 7f., 34; 2:
26f., 35), was perhaps already a priest (although probably not like Melchizedek
actually the priest-king) in pre-Davidic Jerusalem. If there was not in fact such a
continuity of person, there was at least a continuity of tradition. So Ps. 110: 4,
which promises the king eternal priesthood in an oath of Yahweh, appeals to the
order of Melchizedek, who according to Gen. 14: 18ff. was priest-king of Salem
(i.e. Jerusalem; cf. Ps. 76: 2, [Heb 76: 3]) in the premonarchical period.

This name Melchizedek (Hebrew: *Malki-ṣedeq*) is probably not to be translated '(the god) Melek is just' but '(my) king is (the god) Ṣedeq'. The same divine
name is found again in the name of the king of Jerusalem mentioned in Josh. 10:
1, 3 (cf. Judge. 1: 5ff.), Adonizedek, '(my) lord is (the god) Sedeq', and also forms
the name Zadok. If deductions can only be made about the religion of the
Canaanites of Jerusalem here on the basis of proper names, external reports,
down to Philo of Byblos, who speaks of a god Suduk, confirm that the ancient
Near East knew Zedek as a divine name. On the evidence of the royal names this
God seems to have been worshipped especially in Jerusalem, or (to put it more
cautiously) this title was given precisely to the city god of Jerusalem. This explains
why the root *sdq* 'righteous' remained firmly anchored for a long time in the Zion
tradition, so that Isaiah (1: 26, 21), for example, calls Jerusalem 'city of righteousness'. It can possibly be discerned through one or another of the Old Testament
statements about 'righteousness' (e.g. Ps. 85: 10f., 13 [Heb. 85: 11f., 14]; 89: 14
[Heb. 89: 15]) that Zedek once had divine attributes (H. H. Schmid, *Gerechtigkeit
als Weltordnung*, Tübingen, 1968, pp. 76f.).

The name Jeru-salem itself seems to mean 'foundation of (the god) Shalem'.
Shalem also is attested outside the Old Testament, in the texts of Ras Shamra

(Ugarit) as the name of a deity (probably the dusk). It occurs again in the name of David's son (who was born in Hebron) Absalom (2 Sam. 3: 3), and perhaps too in the name Solomon – although this is also given a completely different interpretation. Furthermore there may be traces of this tradition in the Old Testament when we hear of *shālōm*, 'salvation, peace' in connection with Zion (Ps. 122: 6f. [Heb. 122: 7f.]; Isa. 60: 17; Jer. 33: 6; Hag. 2: 9 et al.). It can however no longer be established with certainty what concepts of righteousness and salvation the pre-Israelite inhabitants of Jerusalem connected with these divine names (perhaps fertility in nature, preservation of justice and of society by the king, deliverance from enemies?).

A third divine name can be deduced with considerable certainty from other Old Testament passages, Elyon, 'the highest', which lives on precisely in the Psalms of Zion (Ps. 46: 4 [Heb. 46: 5]; 48: 1f. [Heb. 48: 2f.]; also 47: 2 [Heb. 47: 3] et al.) and appears already in Gen. 14: 18ff. in the form El Elyon. This name too is attested in non-biblical occurrences; it is however uncertain whether El and Elyon represent two originally different and only later united deities, or were always linked with one another (above, §10a, 1).

So three divine names can be deduced from the Old Testament, which were probably all established in pre-Israelite Jerusalem, Zedek, Shalem and (El) Elyon.

Attempts have also been made to deduce still further gods of a Jerusalem pantheon (F. Stolz, *Strukturen und Figuren im Kult von Jerusalem*, Berlin, 1970, pp. 218ff.); but the Old Testament does not provide sufficient basis for such attempts. The worship of the sun-god Shemesh (cf. the place-name Beth-Shemesh, 'house of Shemesh') is not demonstrable with certainty for pre-Israelite Jerusalem. It is first attested in the late monarchical period, in which allowance has to be made for Assyrian influence (above, III, 2) (2 Kgs. 23: 5, 11; Ezek. 8: 16; Jer. 8: 2; also Deut. 4: 19; 17: 3 et al.).

It remains unclear how these titles are related, whether they denote different gods, perhaps thought of as related, or are epithets of the one Jerusalem city god (probably El Elyon). Since the attributes and cults of the deities cannot be determined more exactly, it cannot be said which elements in the religion of Jerusalem the faith of Yahweh had to reject. Zedek and Shalom are not found again as divine names in the Old Testament; at most we hear echoes here and there of the former divine character of these titles. Only Elyon is retained directly as a divine name, because the Old Testament could understand the former proper name simply as an epithet 'the highest'. As in the borrowing of the title 'El' God or of other originally foreign divine epithets Israel was able to fulfil the first commandment by applying it exclusively to Yahweh and by neglecting, suppressing or simply forgetting its personal name character.

3   As the name Jerusalem shows, the foundation of the city was attributed to a god. Accordingly it was from ancient times regarded as the site of the divine presence, and there must certainly have been holy places too in its area.

Was for instance the temple of Yahweh, which was built not by David (2 Sam. 7) but by Solomon in connection with a considerable expansion of the city (1 Kgs. 5: 1ff. [Heb. 5: 15ff.]) erected on the site of the old Canaanite sanctuary, giving a continuity of site as well as of cultic staff and of traditions? Did the 'holy rock' already serve the Jebusites as a cultic site? However the story of the building of the first altar in Jerusalem (2 Sam. 24: 16ff.; cf. 2 Chr. 3: 1) speaks explicitly of a threshing-floor (hardly used for cultic purposes) as the site of the altar of Yahweh.

Both the royal palace and the temple (1 Kgs. 6f.) were built with the help of Phoenician builders (5: 6ff. [Heb. 5: 20ff.]; 7: 13ff.) on foreign models.

In the temple, which was oriented to the east, a court with an altar of burnt offerings was followed by an entrance hall with the two bronze pillars Jachin and Boaz (6: 3; 7: 15ff., 21), a long rectangular main room (6: 2) and the Holy of Holies, perhaps raised up, in which the Ark was set up (6: 16, 19f.; 8: 6). It is disputed how far this was separate from or incorporated into the temple, so whether the temple with entrance hall and main room was in fact only a two-part construction. (cf. among others T. A. Busink, *Der Tempel von Jerusalem*, vol. 1, Leiden, 1970).

The two buildings, palace and temple, were sited close to one another (cf. 2 Kgs. 11; in criticism Ezek. 43: 7f.). As the temple was the property of the ruler, 'king's sanctuary and temple of the kingdom' (Amos 7: 13, said of Bethel), the priest too was an official appointed by the king and capable of being deposed by him (2 Sam. 8: 17; 1 Kgs. 2: 27, 35; 4: 2 et al.).

Only the Ark (above, §9a, 2) and the traditions which may possibly have been connected with it formed a counterweight to all these tendencies and institutions which were originally strange to Israel and endangered its faith. After the Ark had been transferred in to the Holy of Holies however it seems quite quickly to have lost status (cf. Jeremias, 'Lade und Zion'). It is very unusual for it to be mentioned again (Jer. 3: 16f.; Ps. 132; 24: 7ff.?); even its fate (at the destruction of Jerusalem in 587 BC?) is not specifically narrated. It was in any case no longer (just) the Ark that was the site of the presence of God, but the temple, the mount or even the whole city. Was it possible for the Yahwistic faith to hold its own in or indeed against the temple cult with its own emphases, with all its institutions, objects and actions, and not least its Canaanite ideas and foreign customs? The Ark, even when it was housed in the temple as Shiloh, remained movable, and could change its location (1 Sam. 4–6; 2 Sam. 6). The presence of God was now however connected with a specific fixed spot. Was the nomadic element now finally lost in the lands of civilization, and the God of Sinai who led men upon their way changed into a God of state and temple? Certainly this note of restlessness can scarcely any longer be detected.

4   Both the psalms of Zion and also some prophetic passages attest the close, almost too close, connection of Yahweh and Jerusalem. Yahweh now 'dwells for ever' in his house (according to the declaration at the dedication of the temple, 1

Kgs. 8: 12f.). For this reason he is called 'Yahweh Sabaoth, who dwells on Mount Zion' (Isa. 8: 18; cf. Ps. 9: 11 [Heb. 9: 12]; 74: 2; 135: 21; also Joel 3: 17, 21 [Heb. 4: 17, 21] et al.). Yahweh sets out from Zion for his theophany (Ps. 50: 2; Amos 1: 2; cf. Ps. 14: 7; 128: 5; 134: 3). Conversely 'to Zion' can mean to God (Jer. 31: 6) and the man praying who is far from Zion, feels far from God (Ps. 42); for just there one can 'see' God (42: 2 [Heb. 42: 3]; 84: 2, 7 [Heb. 84: 3, 8]).

Accordingly designations are found like 'holy mountain' (Ps. 2: 6; 15: 1; 48: 1 [Heb. 48: 2]; 110: 3 et al.), 'city of God' (46: 4 [Heb. 46: 5]; 48: 1, 8 [Heb. 48: 2, 9]; 87: 3; 101: 8; cf. Isa. 60: 14; Jer. 31: 6, 38 et al.), and 'holy city' (Isa. 48: 2; 52: 1; Neh. 11: 1, 18). Jerusalem is 'your city, your holy mountain' (Dan. 9: 16; cf. 9: 19, 24), the throne of Yahweh (Jer. 3: 17; 14: 21; 17: 12), a place of beauty and of world-wide joy (Ps. 48: 2 [Heb. 48; 3]; 50: 2; Lam. 2: 15).

While Jerusalem according to its name was a 'foundation of the god Salem', it was now understood as a foundation of the God of Israel (Ps. 87: 1f., 5; Isa. 14: 32; cf. 28: 16; Ps. 48: 8 [Heb. 48: 9]; 78: 68f.; 132: 13f. et al.). But the name 'God of Jerusalem' is only found rarely, in 2 Chr. 32: 19 and in an inscription found at Lachish. Was it felt to be important that the connection with the city should not become too narrow?

As city of God Jerusalem attracted mythological ideas which reach far beyond the reality and transcend both geographical and historical facts.

So Jerusalem lies on a 'river whose streams make glad the city of God' (Ps. 46: 4 [Heb. 46: 5]; cf. 65: 9 [Heb. 65: 10]; 87: 7; Joel 4: 18; Ezek. 47; Zech. 14: 8; Isa. 33: 20f.), although the actual water-supply of Jerusalem – by one or two springs, Gihon (1 Kgs. 1: 33f.; 2 Chr. 32: 30) and Rogel (Josh. 15: 7; 18: 16; 2 Sam. 17: 17; 1 Kgs. 1: 9) and the canal and pools of Shiloah (Isa. 7: 3; 8: 6; 22: 9ff.; 36: 2; 2 Kgs. 20: 20 et al.) – makes mockery of such a description. The image could have been borrowed from a city that had a river running through it, like Babylon on the Euphrates, but it is more probable that it derives from mythological ideas, since the universal cosmic significance of the 'river of God' is more easily explained from this. So the dwelling place of the god El according to the Ugaritic myths seems to be set on a mountain, near which two rivers, the world above and the underworld, flow together (above, §10a, 3).

Even the name Zaphon, familiar from the texts of Ras Shamra (Ugarit) as that of the high mountain of the gods in the north, is transferred to Mount Zion (Ps. 48: 2 [Heb. 48: 3]) – again unexpectedly, for the surrounding hills, like the Mount of Olives, are higher. Since Zaphon in Ugarit is regarded as the throne of God, it may be concluded that 'Ba'al is dethroned, and Yahweh takes his place' (O. Eissfeldt, *Baal Zaphon, Zues Kasios und der Durchzug der Israeliten durchs Meer*, 1932, p. 20); cf. above, §11a).

Close to the concept of the mountain of God is the understanding of Zion as the world-mountain, at which heaven and earth touch. This view too does not generally underlie the Jerusalem traditions; it is found in forms too varied for this; for instance, according to the vision of Isaiah (6: 1) God himself towers above the temple beyond any conceivable scale, while according to Isa. 2: 2ff. (= Mic. 4) Zion will become the highest mountain 'at the end of the days' (cf. Ps. 48: 1f. [Heb. 48: 2f.]; 78: 69; 150: 1; Lam. 2: 1; Jer. 17: 12; Ezek. 17: 22; 40: 2; Zech. 14: 10 et al.; cf. M. Metzger, 'Himmlische und irdische Wohnstatt Jahwes', *UF* 2 (1970).

City of God, river of God and mountain of God are originally separate ideas, which come together as a unity here. They all picture the distinctiveness of Jerusalem, but they are inconsistent in their pictorial character. So a spring, not a river, rises on the mountain, and 'the city set on a hill' is a later combination. Further the individual motifs are still found independently (e.g. Gen. 2: 10ff.; Isa. 14: 13; cf. Ezek. 28).

There are in addition motifs of the weather god, who conquers the rebellious sea (Ps. 46: 3, 6 [Heb. 46: 4, 7]; cf. 76: 6, 8 [Heb. 76: 7, 9]; 65: 9 [Heb. 65: 8] et al.; above, §11e). Occasionally Jerusalem attracts the concept of the navel of the earth, the centre of the world (Ezek 38: 12; cf. 5: 5; Isa. 19: 24; Judg. 9: 37). According to Gen. 22: 2; 2 Chr. 3: 1 the site of Abraham's sacrifice also lay upon the later temple area. Finally Isa. 28: 16 speaks of a 'keystone', which perhaps is intended to restrain the primeval flood in its subterranean place and at the same time to form the foundation of the temple. To summarize, Zion is 'the perfection of beauty' (Ps. 50: 2).

The mythical motifs of the lands of civilization are united with specifically Israelite concepts, so that new comprehensive mythological concepts are formed. The distinction between the basic ideas that were taken over by Israel, and the developments achieved by Israel itself, is important in method, but in the light of the sources as they are it is difficult to carry out, and is therefore a subject of disagreement among scholars.

The comprehensive picture of the Jerusalem tradition, which is painted by Stolz in *Strukturen und Figuren im Kult von Jerusalem* (Berlin, 1970) depends on a sometimes insufficient differentiation of the statements in the Old Testament. Neither its literary nor its historical context, that is, neither its development in each individual context, nor its alteration in the course of history, is sufficiently taken into account; unitary 'structures' are developed out of very varied references. But how far can the combination of traditions be understoon as inner-Israelite development? The Israelite share in the Old Testament concepts would have to be removed before they can be attributed to pre-Israelite origins. The comprehensive collection of material carried out by Stolz still needs to be re-examined from a strictly traditio-historical approach.

Like the early form of the Zion tradition, the date of the psalms of Zion is hard to establish definitely. Even if they received their present form in the course of time, or are actually late in origin, the Zion tradition recorded in the psalms can hardly have developed only after the experience of the deliverance of Jerusalem in 701 or even after the exile, as has been argued. Is not the Zion tradition presupposed also in Mic. 3: 11; Isa. 28: 15ff. et al.? Similarly in the enthronement psalms, a distinction must be made between the underlying motifs and the (later) present written form. An attempt at reconstruction could best start with the (more easily datable) message of Isaiah, and then work back to ask what ideas it presupposes.

5   As well as the basic themes of city of God and mountain of God the Zion tradition also contains more complex mythological concepts, especially of the fight of the nations and the pilgrimage of the nations.

The origin of the idea of a war of the nations threatening the city of God (Ps. 46: 6, 9 [Heb. 46: 7, 10]; 48: 4 [Heb. 45: 5ff.]; 76: 3ff. [Heb. 76: 4ff.]; cf. Joel 2; Mic. 4: 11; Zech. 12; also Isa. 8: 9f.; 17: 12ff.) has been given various explanations; from a generalization of historical experiences of Israel (especially of the withdrawal of the Assyrians in 701 or the revolts at the time of the Davidic and Solomonic empire), from the recollection of the attack of the sea-peoples living on in saga form, from a historicization of the fight with the primeval sea monster and finally directly from the taking over of pre-Israelite (cf. 2 Sam. 5: 8) ideas, especially those belonging to the Elyon cult. In ancient Near Eastern attestations gods appear in battle against human enemies, but precise non-biblical instances have not yet been found for the statement that many or even all of the nations attack the mountain of God or the city of God. (Ps. 2; 110; Isa. 41: 1–4; 45: 1–3 are related to an earthly king.) So it is probable that historically the concept of the battle of the nations (unlike the battle of the sea, cf. above, §11c) received its present form only in Israel, and in content presupposes a degree of monotheism such as is found only in Israel in the ancient Near East. In that case the related idea of the inviolability of the city of God in its strong form may also have developed in Israel: the general onslaught fails, Zion remains invincible (Ps. 46: 5 [Heb. 46: 6]; cf. 125: 1f.; Isa. 29: 5ff.; 8: 9f.; 17: 12–14; Zech. 12; also Hos. 1: 7 et al.) The man who 'calls upon the name of the Lord' is saved in Jerusalem the inviolable (Joel 2: 32; 3: 16f. [Heb. 3: 5; 4: 16f.]).

A distinction must in any case be made between the (later merging) concepts of the vain onslaught of the nations against Jerusalem, the war of Yahweh against the nations (Mic. 4: 12f.; Joel 3 [Heb. 4]; Zech. 14: 3, 13f.; cf. Ezek. 38f.) or against Jerusalem (Isa. 79: 1ff.; Zech. 14: 1f.) and of the foe from the north (Jer. 4–6; cf. Joel 2 et al.) (see H.-M. Lutz, *Jahwe, Jerusalem und die Völker* Neukirchen, 1968). The old Israelite tradition of the War of Yahweh (above, §7), at least in its later developed form, may also have had an influence in the formation of motifs upon the development of the Zion tradition. For instance the strikingly general statement that God breaks weapons apart (Ps. 46: 9 [Heb. 46: 10]; 76: 3 [Heb. 76: 4]; cf. Hos. 1: 5; 2: 18 [Heb. 2: 20]; Mic. 5: 10ff. [Heb. 5: 9ff.]; Zech. 9: 10), perhaps has 'its traditio-historical roots in the prophetic recognition of the irreconcilable opposition between Yahweh and military equipment, which in its turn is prepared for in the narrative tradition of the wars of Yahweh' (R. Bach, 'Der Bogen zerbricht, Spiesse zerschlägt und Wagen mit Feuer verbrennt', in H. W. Wolff (ed.), *Probleme biblischer Theologie*, Munich, 1971, p. 22; cf. Hos. 10: 13; 14: 3 [Heb. 14: 4]; Isa. 30: 15f.; 31: 1 ff. et al.).

If these conjectures (put forward only with reservations) about the origin of the concepts of the war of the nations are correct, then we would have the unusual if not unique position that Israel has not as in other instances taken over mythological material from neighbouring religions and reinterpreted them, but formed them itself, although not without foreign influence. However we do not have (in spite of Zech. 12; 14) mythological narratives in the strict sense, but rather mythological concepts and motifs, the purpose of which is to represent the special position of Jerusalem, the universal significance of the city of God, and finally the uniqueness of the one God (Ps. 46: 8 [Heb. 46: 9]; 48: 9f. [Heb. 48: 10f.]; 76: 10 [Heb. 76: 11] et al.).

This purpose comes out particularly clearly in the picture that balances the war picture, the hope of a peaceful pilgrimage of the nations to Zion (Isa. 2: 2–4; 60; 66: 20; Hag. 2; Zech. 8: 22; 14: 16f.; cf. Ps. 68: 31 [Heb. 68: 32] et al.). Again there are several rival attempts at derivation: from a generalization of the participation of non-Israelites in the worship of Yahweh, or the return of the exilic community to Jerusalem, from a reversal of the theme of the battle of the nations, or directly from the adoption of foreign examples. But there is again in the comparative material from the ancient Near East no real parallel material (e.g. corresponding to Isa. 2: 2ff.), so that in this case too Israelite development of borrowed motifs is to be assumed. It is the late passage Zech. 14 that first unites the two concepts of the war of the nations and the pilgrimage of the nations in a temporal juxtaposition: those among the nations who escape destruction in the war before Jerusalem will journey to Zion to worship God as king (cf. above, §11a, 6).

O. H. Steck (*Friedensvorstellungen im alten Jerusalem*, Zürich, 1972) following Mowinckel, going beyond these individual concepts, has characterized the Jerusalem cultic tradition as 'a totality of a whole complex of ideas', which finds expression not only in the psalms of Zion (Ps. 46; 48; 76), but also in the psalms of creation (Ps. 8; 19; 104; cf. 24: 1f. et al.), psalms of Yahweh as king (Ps. 47; 93; 96–9) and royal psalms (Ps. 2; 110 et al.), and includes roughly the following themes: the mountain of God, the throne of God, the creation and preservation of the world, the defeat of the revolt of the nations, the kingship and world dominion of God through the Davidic king as his regent. The distinctive character of the Jerusalem tradition over against specifically Israelite tradition is brought out strongly. But it remains doubtful whether the concepts attested in texts which are so different in category as well as in date comprise such a unity. Ps. 2: 6 for instance does indeed mention the installation of the king 'on Zion, my holy hill', but it is hardly accidental that the earthly king in turn has no place in the psalms of Zion, of Yahweh as king or of creation.

The striking discrepancy between the geographical and historical reality of Jerusalem on the one hand and its portrayal in the psalms of Zion on the other has often led scholars to derive this portrayal from prophecy; Gunkel called the category 'eschatological songs of Zion'. The remarkable agreement in basic motifs in both areas could serve as support for this view. But these psalms lack any direct reference to the future, and on general grounds it is more probable that the individual prophets refer back to the cultic traditions than vice versa. A 'contemporary history' treatment, which connected the psalms with quite specific actual events, has not won wide agreement. Their utterances go beyond any particular situation: 'they tell of something like a mythical event, viewed in a timeless distance or proximity' (G. von Rad, *Old Testament Theology*, vol. 1, Edinburgh, 1962, p. 46).

The songs of Zion sing of trust in God, in that they praise the place where God dwells. Only God's presence makes Zion a fortress. 'Yahweh of Sabaoth is with us, the God of Jacob is our refuge', says the refrain in Ps. 46: 7, 11 [Heb. 46: 8, 12]), and in Ps. 125: 1f. the security of Jerusalem even becomes an image for the security of those that believe in God. But the praise of God and the praise of the city (Ps. 48: 1ff. [Heb. 48: 2ff.] et al.) become one to a dangerous degree. God's protection is restricted to a particular place, just as the royal psalms bind God very narrowly to a particular man, the ruler (cf. above, §12a). The earthly institution (be it sanctuary or city or kingdom) is thereby apparently removed from the vicissitudes of history, so that trust in God threatens to harden into a supra-historical or non-historical security (the inviolability of the city). Would not the unity of God and place then have to be broken up again, and the historical development be put into reverse, so that trust in God could be separated from trust in a place? But perhaps this non-agreement of word and reality, of mythical concept and geographical and historical reality, is the really decisive and effective element in the Zion tradition. When it is taken up by the prophets they can build on precisely this difference: that which is not real becomes now the no longer real or the not yet real; the mythological concept becomes a critique or a 'Utopia'.

6   Isaiah in one place contrasts the splendour of Jerusalem as the city of right-eousness with present unjustice:

How the faithful city
  has become a harlot,
  she that was full of justice!
Righteousness lodged in her ...
I will restore your judges as at the first,
  and your counsellors as at the beginning.
Afterward you shall be called the city of righteousness,
  the faithful city. (Isa. 1: 21, 26)

The prophet takes up terms which seem to come from pre-Israelite tradition, but with a characteristic change: what the psalms of Zion describe as present reality becomes for him a lost past or a promised future, in any case a contra-diction of that which actually is at the present. What is important to the prophet is the difference, not the identity, so that he can hold the Zion tradition against his contemporaries. Only when the present has passed through judgement can the future correspond to the past and Jerusalem become that of which the Zion tradition speaks.

When Isaiah seeks to realize the assurances of protection in the David or Zion tradition, he makes it dependent on a particular requirement, that of faith: 'If you will not believe, surely you shall not be established' (7: 9; cf. 28: 16). Since the condition is not fulfilled, however, the announcement of disaster already experienced by him in the call vision (6: 9ff.) remains in force. A separate threat, which is without exception associated with Jerusalem, expresses it:

> Therefore Sheol has enlarged its appetite
> and opened its mouth beyond measure,
> and her nobility and the multitude go down,
>   her throng and he who exults in her! (5: 14; cf. 3: 8; 5: 17).

At a late period in his ministry Isaiah explicitly restates the radical announcement of disaster for the city and its inhabitants:

> For the place will be forsaken,
>   the populous city deserted;
> the hill and the watchtower
>   will become dens for ever,
> a joy of wild asses,
>   a pasture of flocks.
>   (32: 14; cf. 3: 16ff.; 22: 1–14; 28: 14–22; 29: 1–4; 30: 8–17)

The threat comes on behalf of Yahweh from the world power of Assyria (Isa. 5: 25ff.; 7: 18ff.; 8: 6ff.; cf. 10: 5ff.; 14: 24ff.) and so from Yahweh himself (8: 14; 29: 2f.).

Isaiah's message about Zion is however strongly disputed in detail. Are the assurances of salvation which follow the messages of disaster (10: 33f.; 29: 5–8; 31: 4f.; 32: 15ff.; cf. 10: 7; 28: 5f.; also 8: 9f.; 17: 12ff. et al.) to be regarded as secondary additions or (on the analogy of 1: 21–6) to be interpreted as the deliverance of Zion in the law-court?

Elsewhere too the prophets do not exempt Jerusalem or Zion from declaration of sin and announcement of judgement (Mic. 5: 10 [Heb. 5: 9]; 3: 10; Zeph. 1: 4, 12f.; Mal. 2: 11 et al.). As Amos (3: 14; 5: 5; 9: 1 et al.) or Hosea (10: 2, 8; 12: 11 [Heb. 12: 12] et al.) threaten the sanctuaries of the northern kingdom with destruction, so the temple in Jerusalem is not spared:

> Therefore because of you
>   Zion shall be ploughed as a field;
> Jerusalem shall become a heap of ruins,
>   and the mountain of the house a wooded height.
>   (Mic. 3: 12; cf. in retrospect Lam. 5: 18).

Jeremiah is acquitted after appealing to this saying, when a full hundred years later he calls trust in the temple a lie: 'This house, which is called by my name, has become a den of robbers' and the fate of the temple of Shiloh is pronounced upon it (7: 11f.; 26: 6).

Who will have pity on you, O Jerusalem,
> or who will bemoan you?
Who will turn aside
> to ask about your welfare?
You have rejected me, says the Lord,
> you keep going backwards;
So I have stretched out my hand
> against you and destroyed you –
> I am weary of relenting. (Jer. 15: 5f.; cf. 4: 31; 5: 1; 6: 6f.)

Instead of referring to the 'city of God' (Ps. 46: 4 (Heb. 46: 5] et al.) Jeremiah (19: 11ff.; 21: 4ff.) and Ezekiel (11: 2ff.) speak contemptuously of 'this city'. Jerusalem is like a vine which is good for nothing but to be burnt (Ezek. 15). With this image Ezekiel outbids his predecessors in his laments upon the 'city that sheds blood' (22: 2f.; 24: 6; cf. 16: 3ff.). He too proclaims judgement to her in symbolic actions and visions (4f.; 8–11 et al.), in which the temple is not spared: 'Behold, I will profane my sanctuary, the pride of your heart' (24: 21, 25).

So the prophets can combat precisely what the songs of Zion praise, trust in the house of God and the impregnability of the city of God. Here the use of the Zion tradition (like that of the David tradition) in the prophetic message is so complex that the history of prophecy could in substantial measure be described as a history of this relationship.

Lamentations looks back at the judgement accomplished upon Jerusalem and the sanctuary by the Babylonians in 587 BC: 'How lonely sits the city that was full of people! How like a widow she has become, she that was great among the nations!' (Lam. 1: 1; cf. 1: 4, 10; 2: 1, 6f.; 5: 17f.; also Jer. 42: 18; 2 Kgs. 24: 13, 20; Dan. 9: 12; Ps. 137). The question is now, 'Is the Lord not in Zion? Is her King not in her?' (Jer. 8: 19). After the fall of the city a reversal in the prophetic message takes place, now (again in contradiction of the views of their contemporaries) the Zion tradition becomes a promise of salvation.

In Ezekiel's vivid assurance of God's presence among the exiles what happened in the early days of Israel is seen as repeated: as the mountain God of Sinai did not stay in his place, but moved around with his wandering people, so centuries later God moves from Jerusalem to the exiles. The fixed throne of God acquires wheels and becomes mobile. It is only now that the throne concept of the civilized lands is completely acclimatized in the faith of Israel; God's love for men is shown to be greater than his bond with a particular place. The God who dwells upon Zion does not need to remain upon Zion (Ezek. 1).

Ezekiel finds a theological interpretation for the relationship between God's presence and the destruction of the city of God: Yahweh's 'glory' has already left the city (Ezek. 10: 18f.; 11: 22f.) and only returns in the 'for ever' of the future (43: 2ff.; cf. §11b, 2). So God himself is not affected by the destruction of the city and of the temple; in fact the judgement is only possible because of his absence.

The exilic prophet Deutero-Isaiah connects the expectation of the return of Yahweh to Zion with the proclamation of an impending reign of God (Isa. 52: 7ff.), and this hope runs through post-exilic prophecy in varying forms (Mic. 2: 12f.; 4: 7 et al. above, §11a, 6). Zion, once a geographical term for the hill upon which Jerusalem stands, now becomes, like the name of the city itself, a (salvation-)title for the community (Isa. 40: 2; 49: 14; 51: 16f.; 52: 1f.; 7ff.; cf. Ps. 147: 12 et al.).

This hope in a new return of God to Zion is found in almost the whole of prophecy or in additions to the older prophetic books (Isa. 4: 3ff.; Zech. 1: 17; 2: 1ff. [Heb. 2: 5ff.]; Joel 2: 32; 3: 16f. [Heb. 3: 5; 4: 16f.]; Obad. 17 etc.) The traditional declaration that God 'dwells' in his sanctuary, becomes an expectation now: 'lo, I come and I will dwell in the midst of you!' (Zech. 2: 14; cf. 2: 9; Ezek. 43: 7; Hag. 1: 8; 2: 9).

The appeal made in Trito-Isaiah also expresses with full clarity the fact that the expectation linked to the Zion tradition is the same as the hope in God's revelation:

Arise, shine; for your light has come.
    and the glory of the Lord has risen upon you.
For behold, darkness shall cover the earth,
    and thick darkness the peoples;
but the Lord will arise upon you,
    and his glory will be seen upon you. (Isa. 60: 1f.)

Already for Isaiah (1: 26) Jerusalem would recover its lost title 'city of right-eousness'. Now the city receives new names in the expectation of the later prophets, which express its altered status (Isa. 62: 2, 4, 12; Jer. 3: 17; 33: 16; Ezek. 48: 35; Zech. 8: 3). The size and form of the coming city is imagined, and it is equipped with undreamt-of splendour (Isa. 54: 11ff.; 62; 66: 10ff.; Jer 31: 38ff.; Ezek. 40ff.; especially 48: 30ff.; Zech. 14: 10 et al.). Jerusalem becomes a place of hope for the gathering together of the scattered nation (Isa. 27: 13; 35: 10; 51: 11; 62: 11; Zech. 6: 15 et al.), the prolongation of life (Isa. 65: 19ff. et al.; cf. below, Excursus 8, 5), a new and enduring fellowship with God (Zech. 8: 8; Isa. 11: 9 et al.), even the participation of the gentiles in this community (2: 2ff.; 11: 10; 25: 6 et al.). Nevertheless the critical purpose of the pre-exilic prophets is not completely lost. Trito-Zechariah takes over the tradition of the inviolability of Zion with a characteristic alteration: If the nations attack the city on their own initiative, it will be preserved (Zech. 12); if however they attack on Yahweh's instructions, Jerusalem will be captured, and its inhabitants will again have to suffer judgement (14: 2; cf. 13: 8).

Like the psalms of Zion the prophetic images of hope too go far beyond the reality which develops after the return from exile; the rebuilt Jerusalem is far from matching the expectations. The hope of Zechariah (2: 8f.) that Yahweh himself, because of the increase in the people of God, will be the wall of Jerusalem, also remained unfulfilled; Nehemiah (Neh. 3; Ezra 4: 6ff.) later built the city walls within very narrow bounds. So the hope in a new future Jerusalem was gradually converted into the post-Old Testament apocalyptic expectation of a heavenly Jerusalem above (cf. in the New Testament Rev. 21; Gal. 4: 26; Heb. 12: 22; 13: 14). But even the idea of a presence of the elements of salvation in heaven, which come down prepared to earth, is a hope in the removal of what is now at hand, namely the unsatisfactory historical reality (cf. below, §16b, 2).

§14 Prophecy

While the historical books tell of the past, the prophets declare the future. They do not start from the past, in order to stride forward into the future, but rather anticipate that which is to come, at first as judgement, later as salvation. The move into the future, which even the early tradition of patriarchs and Exodus contained, becomes now so dominant, that any sort of continuity threatens to be lost. The prophets do not wish to found a new faith. They presuppose the bond between God and nation, and come forward in the name of Yahweh – but they stand at a moment of radical change, which allows something fundamentally new to appear. They proclaim their freedom over against the past, in that that they reinterpret the tradition or even alter it to suit their purpose. This phenomenon of prophecy does not appear all of a sudden with Amos (c.760 BC) in a developed form, but appears in varying form in different times and areas.

The prehistory of prophecy reaches far beyond Israel. However only individual moments in its history can be discerned; its course as a whole cannot be described. The Old Testament itself says that prophecy is not an exclusively Israelite movement (e.g. Jer. 27: 3, 9), but new discoveries have made us fully conscious of this. Again we find both comparable material and also unique and incomparable elements. This relationship can be explained historically. In Israel something unmistakeably distinctive was made of the material taken over.

a ITS PREHISTORY

1 *Outside Israel*

Prophetic phenomena, both with and without ecstasy, are familiar to the history of religions generally; the only difficulty is to demarcate the phenomenon clearly from the various forms of prediction – whether through such media as hepato-scopy (inspection of the liver), augury (observance of the flight of birds) and observance of the stars, or the lot (cf. Ezek. 21: 26; 1 Sam. 14: 40ff.; Prov. 16: 33), or personally, as through dreams. We frequently hear of the deity speaking through the mouth of a man, who therefore receives and passes on oracles, is conscious of being called by God and of acting under his compulsion. The parallel examples are fewer if spontaneity is also considered a criterion for inspiration: the word must come unsought, and be passed on unasked for.

Different phenomena are certainly found together in the prophetic movement, so that its origin will perhaps never be determined more exactly.

1 Ecstasy was found predominantly, although not only, in the area of Asia Minor and of Phoenicia and Syria. The Old Testament tells us of ecstatic bands of the God Ba'al (1 Kgs. 18: 19ff.; 2 Kgs. 10: 19). These Canaanite prophets support their prayer by dance, and even wound themselves with knives and weapons, 'until the blood gushed out upon them', in order to bring themselves into a state of ecstasy (1 Kgs. 18: 28f.).

Can we see in the 'howling' and 'dancing' dervishes of Islam who appear roughly two thousand years later descendants as it were of such religious ecstatic groups?

Ecstasy is found very early, but not only in groups, but also in individuals, so that in this respect no deductions can be made about development. In the story of the journey of the Egyptian Wen-Amon (c.1100 BC) which is famous in the history of prophecy, we are told of a Phoenician who at a sacrificial feast unintentionally falls into a state of ecstasy, receives a message from God, and tells the Prince of Byblos uninvited:

Now while he (the Prince) was making offering to his gods, the god seized one of his youths and made him possessed. And he said to him (to the Prince) . . . . (ANET, p.26)

And in fact because of the message the Prince alters his attitude to Wen-Amon.

Another instance of a prophetic message (although in this case one that was sought) is offered by the inscription of Zakir of Hamath (c.800 BC); it tells of an apparently non-ecstatic group. The king, in the extremity of a siege, turns to his tutelary deity Baalshamem, 'Lord of heaven', who hears him through the medium of seers, and assures him of divine assistance in war:

[Then spoke] Baalshamem to me [through] seers and through messengers. [And] Baalshamem said [to me]: 'Fear not, for I have [made you] king, [and I shall sta]nd by you and I shall save you from all [these kings, who] have set up a siege wall against you!' (KAI No. 202; ANET, pp. 655f; NERT, p. 231; cf. the similar oracles of salvation in Deut. 20: 11f.; Exod. 14: 13; and to the king, Ps. 110: 1ff. et al.).

The Old Testament does not attest substantial prophetic phenomena before the time of Samuel, at the beginning of the millennium (1 Sam. 10: 5ff.; 19: 20ff.). Did prophecy then appear only after Israel became sedentary? Did the Yahwistic faith in fact take over the ecstasy which was familiar to the Canaanite world, and in time convert it into the distinctive institution of written prophecy? This view undoubtedly contains an element of truth, but it is not sufficient to explain the origin of prophecy. How could the strict restriction to Yahweh of prophecy (Elijah; cf. 2 Kgs. 9) have originated in such a relatively short time?

2   A deity invades a man with his word without his consent, the man so addressed turns to the king in order to give a message uninvited: this is found in letters from Mari (on the middle Euphrates) from the eighteenth century BC. The messages, which are not induced by oracle or lot, are regarded as revelations of the vegetation and weather god Dagan or Hadad, or of other deities; the messengers are aware of being 'sent' by God. Here we have the closest parallel so far known to Old Testament prophecy. The older court prophets Gad or Nathan are comparable, as are also later figures like Hananiah (Jer. 28; cf. 1 Kgs. 22: 11) who announce salvation to their own people, and disaster to foreigners.

As in the account of Wen-Amun someone was gripped by the god at a sacrifice, so here for example a man called Malik-Dagan had a dream-vision 'before Dagan', that is, probably before the image of the god in the temple. After the man praying had answered a question of the god, the commission was given him: 'Now go, I send you to Zimrilim (the king of Mari); you are to say yourself as follows . . . .' So the commission is fulfilled, as often in the call of the Old Testament prophets, in a two-part word of God: 'Go – I am sending you' (Isa. 6: 8f.; Jer. 1: 6f. et al.). Should it be concluded from the place of the reception of the revelation and the title which some messengers of God bear that we are dealing with officially legitimated cultic officials? It cannot however be clearly stated whether they receive their position permanently or only for a period. The recipient can be just an unnamed 'man' or even a married woman. So this prophecy seems at least not to be exclusively tied to the cult, as it also only has ecstatic features in part. The prophecies which those involved have to pass on contain demands for the cult or the building of a city gate or announce victory over the enemies of the land; the prophets can even, in the case of disobedience, threaten the king and have a critical encounter with him.

Is there not only an analogy between prophecy in Mari and in Israel, but a distant historical connection, since the tribes that had settled in Mari belonged like the ancestors of Israel to the so-called (proto-)Aramaic migration, which pressed forward out of the Syrian and Arabian deserts in the course of the second millennium BC into the cultivated lands of Mesopotamia and of Syria-Palestine? (See M. Noth, 'History and the Word of God in the Old Testament' [1949], in *Laws in the Pentateuch and other Essays*, Edinburgh, 1966, pp. 179–93.)

3   Did the two streams of tradition, from the nomadic past and the period in the cultivated land, flow together into the prophetic movement?

Earlier scholarship had already made a distinction between the seers exemplified in the non-Israelite Balaam (Num. 22–4; esp. 24: 3f.), who is now also attested in an inscription from Tel Deir Alla from c. 700 BC, and the prophets, and assumed that the individual seers were originally at home in nomadic life, but the bands of ecstatic prophets in the Canaanite cultivated land. 'Prophetism so-called has nothing at all to do with the position of the seer, which was at home from earliest times among the Semitic desert tribes . . . Israel took over ecstatic prophecy from the Canaanites; in its origin it is probably from Asia Minor' (G. Hölscher, *Geschichte der israelitischen und jüdischen Religion,* Giessen, 1922, p. 83; cf. *Die Profeten,* Leipzig, 1914, pp. 118ff.). On another view the history of religion teaches us 'that ecstasy and ecstatic prophecy are not confined to particular areas and not restricted to particular nations and races'; it is 'impossible to say when this phenomenon appeared in Israel' (J. Lindblom, 'Zur Frage des kanaanäischen Ursprungs des altisraelitischen Prophetismus', in J. Hempel and L. Rost (ed.) *Von Ugarit nach Qumran,* Berlin, 1958, pp. 98, 101).

Certainly ecstasy and prophecy on the one hand, appearance in individuals and groups on the other, cannot be derived straightforwardly from different origins – the nomadic way of life and a sedentary civilisation. Nor is prophecy necessarily later than priesthood; probably both existed early on alongside one another. The parallels produced by the discoveries at Mari have also made the great 'writing' prophets of the Old Testament stand out more clearly in their distinctiveness, even uniqueness. That which appeared new with Amos, the unconditioned announcement of disaster, which would affect not only the king, but the whole nation itself, remains unparalleled. Guilt and punishment are understood much more radically. Prophecy in Israel changed from being a marginal phenomenon of little significance to become a phenomenon which finally understood world history as world judgement. But it was only in the course of history that prophecy attained its universal significance.

2 *In Israel*

From its first appearance on, prophecy in Israel is by no means a unity. The multiplicity of its forms however makes it more difficult to discover its real beginnings, especially since only particular events are remembered from the early period, and the date of origin of the relevant narratives is much disputed.

1   Both the phenomena known from the world around are found in Israel too: about the beginning of the new millennium, at the start of the monarchy, there appear in close succession both bands of prophets and also individual prophets like Gad, Nathan or Ahijah of Shiloh, who are not characterized by ecstatic features but by the reception and transmission of the word. Nothing more is reported of the bands of ecstatics than that they can fall into ecstasy and transmit their condition, so that the man affected can 'be turned into another man' (1 Sam. 10: 5ff.; 19: 18ff.; cf. Num. 11: 25ff.). Frenzy is not brought on, as with the Ba'al prophets (1 Kgs. 18: 28f.), by wounds or blows (cf. only 1 Kgs. 20: 35ff.; Zech. 13: 6), but is perhaps induced by music and dance (cf. 2 Kgs. 3: 15). Perhaps the 'spirit' overtakes the prophets at least sometimes unintended; it is in any case not, as with the heroes of the period of the judges, the authorization for activity, but only effects a loss of self-awareness. If prophecy is held to begin with such ecstatic groups the questions cannot be avoided how the spirit changes into the power which gives the word (1 Kgs. 22: 24), so that address to a particular person

and intelligibility are basic. Prophecy at Mari makes it impossible to construct an oversimple or simplistic development, in which there developed out of the bands of ecstatics proclaimers of the word, who were divided up into court prophets, cultic prophets and writing prophets.

2 Prophetic phenomena in all their complexity are described by the Old Testament with the same word *nābī*, 'prophet'. This term too comes from outside Israel. It is most probably to be derived from an Akkadian word 'call' (*nabū*), but does not mean in the active the 'caller' who passes on the divine message, but rather in the passive 'the man called', who is apponted for a task by a revelation (cf. the same form *māshīaḥ*, 'the man anointed'). This explanation does not really fit the ecstatic, who is only characterized by a spirit-induced frenzy; nor can it be demonstrated that the concept refers specifically to the cultic prophet, who has a legitimate position in the cult, and was only later generalized. It is in any case noticeable that the title is avoided by several of the early writing prophets. Amos did not apparently use it of himself, but let himself be called 'seer' (Amos 7: 12–15; for 2: 11 and 3: 7 are secondary). Isaiah, who also does not use the term 'prophet' (only 8: 3 of his wife) perhaps also understood himself as 'seer' (cf. 30: 10; also 1: 1; 2: 1 against 37: 2 et al.).

Is the title *ḥōzeh* 'seer' (2Sam. 24: 11; Amos 7: 12 et al.) one already found in Aramaic (cf. the inscription of Zakir of Hamath cited above), and is this the reason why the prophets in describing their visions prefer to use another verb *rā'ā* 'see' (Amos 7f.; 9: 1; Isa. 6: 1; cf. 1 Sam. 9: 9 et al.)?

From the time of Jeremiah on, who was called to be a 'prophet to the nations' (1: 5; cf. 28: 5ff. et al.) the term prophet is current as a self-designation (probably not by Jeremiah himself, but by the redaction of Jeremiah), and then finds its way into the older prophetic books. What is the reason for the earlier reserve? Apparently Amos or Isaiah do not belong to a 'class' of (salaried?) prophets, and do not wish to be regarded as one of them, although they 'prophesy', and so perform a similar activity. The change in the name (cf. 1 Sam. 9: 9) indicates that prophecy originated from different phenomena, which were only later comprehended under a single term.

In retrospect Abraham (Gen. 20: 7) and more especially Moses (Deut. 18: 15; 34: 10; Num. 11f.) are also seen as prophets. Perhaps it is the Yahwist (in the tenth century, in which we first hear of a prophetic movement in Israel) who first describes the call of Moses as the sending of a prophet. Moses receives God's message, and passes it on to the nation (Exod. 3: 16: 'Go . . . and say to them" in accordance with the double commission of the prophet); conversely the 'I' of God, who promises the leading out of Israel, is found in his word. In any case it is the Elohist (3: 10ff.) who first represents the call of Moses in the form of a pattern (more or less fixed, and attested also in Judg. 6; 1 Sam. 9f. and Jer. 1) with the commission ('Go, I send you'), objection ('who am I?') and rejection of the objection ('I will be with you').

A similar interpretation governs the final scene, which was probably added later. When Moses again refuses to accept the commission as messenger – 'Oh my Lord, send, I pray, some other person' (Exod. 4: 13–16; cf. 6: 30–7: 2) – God commissions Aaron as messenger. Moses takes the position of God in relation to him, and 'puts the words in his mouth' (cf. Jer. 1: 9; 15: 19): 'He shall be a mouth for you, and you shall be to him as God.' The prophets must therefore have made a deep and lasting impression early on, for Moses or Miriam (Exod. 15: 20) to be understood as one of them.

3 The contrast between group of prophets and individual runs through the history of prophecy from the very beginning. In the Elijah stories the one isolated prophet of Yahweh contends against a multitude of prophets of Ba'al (1 Kgs. 18f.) for the retention of the purity of his faith. Elijah appears at a time in which the worship of Yahweh in the northern kingdom threatened to be lost, through the religious syncretism, probably supported by the state, which assimilated Yahweh to the god Ba'al. Elijah bluntly opposes this intermingling of faith in Yahweh and Ba'al religion with the incompatibility of the two forms of faith (cf. 1 Kgs. 18: 21). But he is probably not the first to represent this sharp contrast. In his words (the original date of which is again disputed) we hear traces of a sense of fellowship with other prophets: he is the only one left of the prophets of Yahweh, who were killed in the persecution of Queen Jezebel (18: 22; 19: 10, 14). They had apparently been equally concerned for the preservation of the Yahwistic faith (cf. Judg. 6: 11ff.; 2 Kgs. 9). So the growing realization of the distinctiveness and exclusiveness of the Yahwistic faith depends at least in part upon the prophetic movement, which is personified by Elijah (R. Rendtorff, 'Reflections on the Early History of Prophecy in Israel', in W. Pannenberg et al., *History and Hermeneutic,* New York, 1967, pp. 14–34). The whole confrontation could be understood as an actualization of the first commandment; Elijah presupposes it according to tradition at least in substance, and applied it in an intensified form – taking it through to its consequences. So he fulfils the demand of the Book of the Covenant ('Whoever sacrifices to any god, save to the Lord only, shall be utterly destroyed' (Exod. 22: 19) by the destruction of the prophets of Ba'al (1 Kgs. 18: 40), and threatens the king with death because he looks for healing from Ba'al and seeks an oracle from him (cf. 2 Kgs. 1: 3f. with Exod. 23: 13).

4 With Elijah's successor Elisha the relationship between the prophetic individual and the group appears as one of teacher and pupil. The 'sons of the prophets' sit before Elisha (2 Kgs. 4: 38; 6: 1; cf. 2: 15ff.; 4; 9) whether to gather for ecstatic practices (H. C. Schmitt, *Elisa*, Gütersloh, 1972) or to receive particular teaching from the master. This band of pupils seems at times to live a common life: they meet in a modestly equipped place, have meals together and are perhaps recognizable by a sign on their heads (1 Kgs. 20: 38ff.; cf. 2 Kgs. 2: 32). The prophets wear distinctive costume, the prophetic 'mantle' (1 Kgs. 19: 13, 19; 2 Kgs. 1: 8; 2: 8, 13f.; Zech. 13: 4; cf. Mark 1: 6). The relationship is personal rather than institutional, and therefore not to be compared with the

Egyptian wisdom schools for the training of government officials, or with the Greek schools of philosophers. It is not explicitly said what traditions were cultivated in this circle. Did the collection of the Elijah and Elisha narratives take place in it?

In any case the transmission of the words of the great writing prophets should be thought of on this model; for their message will not have been preserved in the temple, as was usual in the ancient Near East, because they themselves had an awkward relationship to the cult (Amos 7: 10ff. et al.). We do indeed hear nothing of such a group in the case of Amos; but in Isaiah there is explicit attestation that the prophet passed on his message to his disciples (8: 16; 30: 8), and Jeremiah dictated his words to his friend Baruch (Jer. 36). In the prophetic books certain narratives in the third person (like Amos 7: 10ff.; Isa. 7; 20) and certain additions which imitate the style of the master, or at least betray his influence, must come from these groups of disciples. Perhaps links between the great prophets themselves too are to be explained through mediation by these groups. A chain of tradition runs from Hosea to Jeremiah, and partially on to Ezekiel, another one from Isaiah to Deutero-Isaiah (Isa. 40–55), whose message is taken up in turn by Trito-Isaiah (Isa. 56–66). It could be for the same reason that these additions to Isaiah were made anonymously: the later prophets regarded themselves as pupils of their predecessor. These remarks are no more than suggestions; but in general the messages of the great prophets from Amos on agree in important features.

5   Finally, the clash between prophecy of salvation and of disaster is also illustrated by the contrast between individual prophets and group. According to 1 Kgs. 22 'the king of Israel' (Ahab) sought to question Yahweh through prophets in order to ascertain the result of a war he planned against the Aramaeans. Fully four hundred prophets predict for him the defeat of the enemy in the formulaic language of the war of Yahweh: 'Go up; for the Lord will give it (the city) into the hand of the king.' Micaiah ben Imlah, who is well known as a prophet of disaster and is consulted, also at first predicts good fortune and victory. Only when he is adjured to speak nothing but the truth does he tell his two visions, of Israel scattered like sheep upon the mountains, and of the lying spirit from the heavenly court which seizes the prophets.

This story, even if it has undergone secondary expansion, points forward even in detail to the prophecy of the future. The vision of the throne is reminiscent in language of the call of Isaiah (Isa. 6). While in the earlier prophetic future sayings to the king the nation was only secondarily affected by the disaster that was predicted, now Israel as a whole (v. 17, 'I saw all Israel scattered') is explicitly included. Only an individual event in question here, but we see here an anticipation of the radical message of disaster to the nation as such which Amos Hosea, Isaiah and others utter later.

The difference between the message of disaster of Micaiah and the assurance of salvation of the prophetic band also shows us the distinction between freedom and dependence in relation to the king. In contrast to the circle of disciples of

Elisha, the relation to the king is so close that they are called 'his prophets' (1 Kgs. 22: 22f.). Individual figures of an early date have already appeared as court prophets, Gad 'the seer of David', or Nathan, both of whom could also appear before the king with accusations (2 Sam. 12; 24: 11ff.). A connection with the court does not therefore necessarily imply dependence (cf. Num. 22: 37f.; 24: 13), and the contrast of group and individual is not necessarily identical with the contrast of dependence and freedom.

Prophets like Elijah can announce death to the ruler (1 Kgs. 21; 2 Kgs. 1; cf. 1 Sam. 13: 13f.; 15: 28; 1 Kgs. 14: 10ff.). When they designate someone as the coming king (2 Kgs. 9; cf. 1 Kgs. 11: 29ff.), at the same time they indirectly condemn the present ruler, and indeed the present dynasty. So the prehistory of written prophecy could be in large measure understood as a conflict with the monarchy (cf. above, §12a, 4).

Lastly, the story of Micaiah ben Imlah is indicative of the future in that it anticipates the contrast between the writing prophets and the majority of prophets. Only rarely do the writing prophets make common cause with their precursors (especially Hosea: 6: 5; cf. Jer. 28: 8 et al.); the greater part of their utterances about prophecy are polemical. Isaiah attacks 'priest and prophet', who 'are confused with wine' (28: 7ff.; cf. 9: 13f.), and Micah complains:

Thus says the Lord concerning the prophets
     who lead my people astray,
who cry 'Peace'
     when they have something to eat,
but declare war against him
     who puts nothing into their mouths.
Therefore it shall be night to you, without vision,
     and darkness to you, without divination.
The sun shall go down upon the prophets,
     and the day shall be black over them. (3: 5f.; cf. Jer. 6: 13f.; 8: 10)

Micah predicts an end of their prophetic activity to those who make their message dependent upon payment. Jeremiah makes bitter attacks upon those who speak in the name of Yahweh, but only utter lies, dreams and their own wishes: Yahweh has not sent them (14: 13ff.; 23: 9ff.; 27: 9ff.; cf. Ezek. 13; Lam. 2: 14; 4: 13). His opponents seem in part at least to have official positions in the cult (29: 26f.; 26: 1ff.) so that at least at his time (this cannot be demonstrated with certainty for the early period) there was a prophetic profession in the cult alongside the priests.

Are these identical with the court prophets, since the Jerusalem temple was a 'royal sanctuary' (cf. Amos 7: 13)? Sayings of such cultic prophets may be seen in the first person utterances of God in the psalms (such as Ps. 2: 7ff.; 110: 1), and perhaps also in additions to the prophetic books. Were Nahum and Nabakkuk, who appeared shortly before the exile, or Obadiah, who was active after the catastrophe of 587, cultic prophets? In any case the opponents of the writing prophets preached not only salvation but also disaster (Mic. 3: 5), although not to the nation as a whole; this remained reserved for the writing prophets (cf. J. Jeremias, *Kultprophetie und Gerichtsverkündigung in der späten Königszeit Israels*, Neukirchen, 1970).

b   THE MESSAGE

1   We hear mainly or exclusively of the predecessors of the writing prophets, like Elijah, in individual stories, which have been gathered together later to form a 'saga cycle'. Actual sayings are transmitted too. Brief assurances of salvation awake a hope of a better future, in which there will be no more anxieties about mere life as such:

> For thus says Yahweh the God of Israel,
> 'The jar of meal shall not be spent,
> and the cruse of oil shall not fail ...' (1 Kgs. 17: 14; cf. 2 Kgs. 4: 43)

But the majority of the sayings of the prophets are declarations of disaster. After the judicial murder of Naboth by Ahab, Elijah is commissioned to meet the king at Naboth's vineyard and to say,

> Thus says Yahweh:
> 'Have you killed,
> and also taken possession?'
> Therefore thus says Yahweh:
> 'In the place where dogs licked up the blood of Naboth
> shall dogs lick your own blood.' (1 Kgs. 21: 19)

The saying is in two parts; it names the action, of which the exact spot is known, and then deduces from the offence the statement of punishment ('therefore'). It is explicitly authorized by the messenger formula, 'thus says Yahweh'; God's word is present in the mouth of the prophet.

The part of the prophetic saying which gives the reasons is called invective, accusation, situation analysis, etc.; the announcement of a future of disaster is called threat or verdict, announcement of disaster, etc. In the cry of woe (Isa. 5: 8ff.) both parts are united. Historical retrospects (9: 7ff.), exhortations (1: 16f.) and other forms are also found.

Here we see the form of the prophetic message characterized: it is not issued as a well-formed utterance with a continuous sequence of thought, indeed is not even in writing, but in short individual sayings, independent in form, content and sense. They are from the start clear to understand, and without exception have a rhythmic, poetical form. Although originally embedded in a story, from the time of Amos they are almost completely freed from a narrative context. From his time on it is primarily individual sayings that are collected; their linking together, apart from a few longer compositions (like Amos 1f.; 7: 1ff.; Isa. 9: 7ff.) is secondary.

The transition to written prophecy, from Elijah to Amos, is not accidental. The sayings of the prophets, primarily announcements of disaster, giving reasons, and occasionally promises of salvation (Hos. 2: 14ff. [Heb. 2: 16ff.] et al.), come to have a general significance, and no longer refer to an individual offence; they are therefore now only occasionally directed to individuals (Amos 7: 10ff.; Isa. 22: 15ff.) as earlier to the king (Isa. 7) or groups (3: 16ff.), but rather to the nation as a whole.

Ecstatic phenomena diminish sharply, and are not certainly necessary accompaniments of the reception of revelation. Is a saying like:

My heart is broken within me,
    all my bones shake;
I am like a drunken man,
    like a man overcome with wine,
because of Yahweh
    and because of his holy words
        (Jer. 23: 9; cf. Isa. 21: 3f.; Hab. 3: 16; later Dan. 8: 18; 10: 8, 16f.)

still founded upon ecstatic experiences, or are such expressions only used in a metaphorical, transferred sense to express personal involvement?

The prophets appeal as a rule to the word, not to the 'spirit' (which is probably an addition in Mic. 3: 8). Only the book of Ezekiel, following older prophetic traditions (1 Kgs. 18: 12, 46 et al.) tells of the spirit possession of the prophet (Ezek. 3: 12ff. et al.). Not even fasting (cf. Dan. 9: 3; 10: 2ff.), 'which otherwise is regarded through the whole world as a means of preparing oneself for revelation, occurs in Amos and his followers' (H. Gunkel, in H. Schmidt, *Die grossen Propheten*, 1923, p. xix).

Because the prophets experience God in a word which presses on them, they can defend their activity as having the force of compulsion (Amos 3: 8; cf. Jer. 20: 9; 1 Cor. 9: 16). Perhaps they tell the story of their call to provide their own legitimation, but the account of their most personal experiences is turned into an address to their listeners (cf. Amos 7: 14f.; Jer. 26: 12). The prophet is already aware of the commission to preach which he has received when he tells the story of his call (similarly Isa. 40: 1: 'Comfort, comfort my people, says *your* God'). So there is insufficient material of a psychological interpretation inquiring into the subjective experiences of the prophets, even if this would not run completely against the intention of the prophets themselves. Each of them has his distinctive characteristics, but is so exclusively intent on uttering his word and on its being heard, that his personality recedes into the background. When their message is given a narrative framework (Amos 7: 10ff.; Isa. 7) it is intended to describe the situation which enables us to understand the saying.

2   The actual intention of the prophets is not primarily to proclaim the law, and to portray openly the guilt of the individual and of the nation. They do not start with a criticism of the circumstances of the time, and are not primarily interpreters of their own historical situation, 'the living conscience of their nation'. Amos at a time of peace revokes the salvific fellowship between God and nation:

The end has come upon my people Israel. (8: 2; cf. Ezek. 7)

All the rest of his preaching only develops further this message (5: 2, 18ff.; 7: 16f.; 9: 1ff. et al.), which declares something hitherto unheard of in Israel, the announcement of disaster to the nation as a whole. According to the tradition (Josh. 7 et al.) Israel can again experience salvation after eradicating evil. Although the later prophets go beyond Amos to preach salvation too, they take over, each in his own way, his radical announcement of judgement. Hosea's symbolic action, in which his children appear as signs of divine judgement, has as its climax a judgement of God, which possibly contests the divine assurance of Exod. 3: 14, 'I am who I am': 'you are not (any longer) my people, and I am not (any longer) your God' (Hos. 1: 9; cf. 2: 4 [Heb. 2: 6]; 9: 16f.; 13: 14). The charge to harden the heart of the nation,

Go, and say to this people:
'Hear and hear, but do not understand;
    see and see, but do not perceive.'
                    (Isa. 6: 9ff.; cf. 29: 9f.; also 22: 14; 28: 18ff.)

communicates to Isaiah not so much the content as the effect of his preaching. Jeremiah says in objection to those who preach salvation, that the time of grace and of salvation is past (Jer. 16: 5; 6: 13f.; 8: 11, 14f.; 23: 16ff.). Ezekiel is told to eat a scroll, with 'written on it words of lamentation and mourning and woe' on both sides (Ezek. 2: 10; cf. 7; 15: 6 et al.). So it is understandable from the message of the prophets that they had to suffer (Amos 7: 10ff.; 2: 12; esp. Jer. 26ff.).

In their forms of utterance (announcement of disaster with causes given, cry of woe, funeral lament, etc.) as well as in the themes of their preaching (criticism of the cult and of social matters, 'the day of Yahweh', Israel as a faithless wife, et al.) the prophets have so much in common that they cannot have preached independently of one another. These connections are best explained by oral tradition (above, §14a, 2, 4).

In some early sayings (e.g. Amos 5: 1–3) we do not yet have the list of sins which make the declaration of disaster 'compelling of agreement' (H. W. Wolff, 'Die eigentliche Botschaft der Klassischen Propheten', in H. Donner et al., *Beiträge zur alttestamentlichen Theologie*, Göttingen, 1977). In other instances a distinction is still made between the saying of God which contains the declaration of the future, and the complaint of the prophet himself (2: 1f.; Isa. 5: 8f.; Mic. 2: 1ff. et al.; though this does not mean that we have a 'pure' word of God, which is freed from the linguistic peculiarities of the prophet). In fact a foreboding of threatening disaster can only become specific knowledge with time, so that the future takes on more sharply outlined forms for the prophet. The visions show Amos only *that* and not *how* 'the end comes'; in his preaching he makes the judgement concrete in different ways, such as an earthquake (2: 13; 9: 1), war and exile (2: 14ff.; 5: 3; 7: 17 et al.). Even then however he does not name Assyria directly, but only hints at an exile 'beyond Damascus' (5: 27). Similarly Jeremiah speaks at first only of a 'foe from the north', not of the Babylonians, and in his vision of a boiling pot, the steam of which blows in upon him, he only hears that

> Out of the north evil shall break forth
> upon all the inhabitants of the land. (1: 14)

Here too we lack both a motive for and a more precise statement of the threatening disaster. Knowledge of the future does not therefore come from deep insight into the present reality, through a premonition of the necessary outcome of events; on the contrary it leads to an urgent analysis of the present situation, in Amos or Micah more to social criticism, in Hosea to criticism of the cult. The prophets therefore have different emphases, but social and cultic criticism merge together (Amos 5: 21ff.; Hos. 8: 4; Isa. 1: 10ff.).

The critique of sacrifices (above, Excursus 6, 4) is part of a comprehensive critique of the cult. While Amos (3: 14; 5: 5; 7: 9; 9: 1) and Hosea (10: 2, 8; 12: 11 [Heb. 12: 12]) predict the fall of the sanctuaries of the northern kingdom, later prophets, such as Micah (3: 12) and Jeremiah (7; 26), transfer the announcement of disaster to Zion (above, §13, 6). Even intercession for his nation is forbidden to Jeremiah (14: 11; 15: 1; cf. Isa. 1: 15).

As for the Old Testament as a whole (Prov. 14: 31; Ps. 15; 24 et al.), for the prophets in particular justice and relationship to God belong together. In the eighth century, in which social distinctions are sharply increasing, they criticize such trends as the accumulation of property (Isa. 5: 8ff.; Mic. 2: 1f.), luxury as a sign of pride (Amos 4: 1f.; Isa. 3: 16ff.) and corrupt legal practices (Amos 5: 10; Mic. 3: 9ff.; Isa. 1: 17). The upper levels of society (Isa. 3: 1ff.) and even the monarchy (Hosea; above, §12a, 4) are also criticized. Isaiah includes in the sphere of the poor who need protection (Amos 2: 6ff.; 8: 4ff.) widows and orphans (Isa. 1: 17, 23). But social criticism is part of the whole message of the prophet, and accordingly more a declaration of sin (Mic. 3: 8) than a call to improvement or even to the development of a new ordering of society.

3   The prophetic view of the future cannot be derived from a deeper knowledge of the past. According to 1 Kgs. 22 Micaiah ben Imlah in his oracle appeals to the same tradition of the holy war as does the band of prophets which in humble devotion to the king prophesy victory for him as he sets out to battle (vv. 6, 17). The tradition itself therefore allows no possibility for the evaluation of the situation; a 'knowledge' of salvation or disaster for the present or the future

cannot be deduced from it. The 'truth' of the prophecy is not decided by the tradition in which the prophet stands; for it is not the bare fact of their taking it over, but the manner of it that is important. As Amos later reverses their intention, and says that Yahweh conducts war not for Israel, but against his own nation (2: 14f.; cf. above, §7, 3), so Micaiah here employs the tradition critically against his own time, and asserts that he has received his insight into the present directly from God. Here we have (as also in the encounter of Jeremiah and Hananiah, Jer. 28) a contrast of two different judgements, both professing to be words of God; the listeners are not exempted from the need to make a decision. Prophecy does stand in a tradition, but it is not sufficient as a criterion for judging a situation; the contingent character of history makes it impossible that the past should answer clearly the problems of the present. Continuity is present, but only in discontinuity.

In the attitude to the reign of Jehu it again becomes clear how prophetic judgements on the same event can turn out to be totally different. Elisha has Jehu anointed king over Israel by a prophet who is a disciple of his, and Jehu exterminates the reigning house of Ahab; in the Deuteronomistic book of Kings (2 Kgs. 9f.; esp. 10: 30) this successful work of exterminating the worshippers of Ba'al is regarded as well pleasing to God. But because of the same act of violence which Jehu performed on the instruction of a prophet, he is rejected in a saying attributed to God in Hosea (1: 4). Hosea pronounces a new and different word upon the same event: 'a monarchy in Israel that bases its power upon blood letting can expect only a "No" from Yahweh' (H. W. Wolff, 'Die eigentliche Botschaft'). The ambiguity of history, but also conversely the historically rooted character of prophecy, could hardly be brought out more clearly.

4   A prophetic word about the future ultimately does not become a reality in the present; its fulfilment is either a hope or a realization in retrospect. Because history confirmed the preaching of the prophets of disaster, their words were also collected according to this criterion. Since Amos threatened an earthquake (2: 13; 9: 1), the superscription of the book of Amos tells us that the prophet began his ministry 'two years before the earthquake' (1: 2). The actualization of his message is therefore acknowledged at the very beginning of the book.

It is only when the predicted disaster has come to pass that it can be 'established' whether the prophet foresaw the future and was right. The law in Deuteronomy (18: 21f.) applies this standard in retrospect to prophecy in order thereby basically to control the phenomenon of prophetic preaching:

> And if you say in your heart, 'How may we know the word which Yahweh has not spoken?' – when a prophet speaks in the name of Yahweh, if the word does not come to pass or come true, that is a word which Yahweh has not spoken; the prophet has spoken it presumptuously, you need not be afraid of him.'

According to Jer. 28 the same law, but in a modified form, served the prophet Jeremiah as a weapon against his opponents. In a sharp dispute about the truth of his message of disaster, he demands only of the prophet of salvation that he should prove himself through the fulfilment of his words:

> The prophets who preceded you and me from ancient times prophesied war, famine and pestilence against many countries and great kingdoms. As for the prophet who prophesies peace, when the word of that prophet comes to pass, then it will be known that Yahweh has truly sent the prophet. (28: 8f.)

Jeremiah sees himself as in line of succession of the great preachers of disaster, like Amos, Isaiah and Micah. This common ground is for him a sufficient criterion of truth, so that he does not once refer explicitly to the actual course of history, which vindicated the words of his precursors. Certainly the problem of the truth of the prophetic message is not decided; what does come out clearly is how little help the criterion of fulfilment in the concrete situation is, because it fails to meet the situation of the listener. It puts off the problem of legitimization so far that it no longer needs an answer, but has become superfluous.

The prophet may hope that God does as he says, because he 'watches' over his word (Jer. 1: 11ff.; cf. 1 Kgs. 22: 27f.; Ezek. 12: 25 et al.), but in the actual situation he can only confront his listeners with his word alone. When accused before a court Jeremiah can only appeal to the commission he has received, 'Yahweh has sent me', and defend himself against doubts about his legitimacy by making the judges themselves the objects of his message (Jer. 26: 12–15). Similarly Amos in his encounter with the high priest Amaziah, who forbids him to speak, can only tell him the story of his call, and proclaim death to the man who opposes his preaching (Amos 7: 10–17; cf. 1 Kgs. 22: 24f.). The commission to harden the heart (Isa. 6: 9ff.) is the first to escape the criterion of fulfilment. The prophets' threats of disaster are by and large confirmed by history; but some of the prophetic sayings were never 'fulfilled', but were nevertheless preserved. In particular this is true of Deutero-Isaiah's message of the impending salvation and nearness of God (Isa. 40: 9; 52: 7); but nevertheless it was preserved as an 'everlasting' (40: 8) and effective (55: 10f.) word, read, and taken up and taken further by later prophets (Trito-Isaiah) (cf. below, IV, 3).

5   Prophecy does not 'have the task of "prophesying" the events of a distant future, so that a naive faith can be edified by the perfect agreement of prophecy and fulfilment. Their later imitators did indeed hold this view and complied with it, but the older prophets themselves know nothing of it, although there are found in them quite specific predictions over a short period of time' (B. Duhm, *Israels Propheten*, 2nd edn., Tübingen, 1922, pp. 3f.). From the certainty of impending disaster they announce a future which touches the present directly and inevitably (cf. Amos 1: 3ff.; 'I will not revoke'; also 7: 8; 8: 2 et al.). Exhortations and warnings, which challenge the listeners to perform an action or to let something happen (like Amos 4: 4f.; Isa. 1: 16f.), are rare in the older prophets, and occur in the context of their declaration of the future (esp. Amos 5: 5). The opportunity of

following the right way in trust in God has been missed: 'And you would not' (Isa. 30: 15; cf. 7: 1–17; 9: 12; 28: 12; Jer. 6: 16 et al.). Correspondingly the retrospect into the past serves as a demonstration of sin (Isa. 1: 2f.; 9: 7ff.; Amos 4: 6ff.; Hos. 11f.). Israel as a whole is guilty (2: 4 [Heb. 2: 6]; 9: 17; Isa 6: 5 et al.). Jeremiah is simply drawing the consequences of this realization with his view than man cannot change himself:

> Can the Ethiopian change his skin
> or the leopard his spots?
> Then also you can do good
> who are accustomed to do evil.
>
> (Jer. 13: 23; cf. 2: 22; 6: 10, 27ff.; Isa. 1: 18; Hos. 5: 4, 6; 7: 2;
> Ezek. 15f.; 20; 23 et al.)

In the experience of judgement, that is, in the exile, the prophetic word about the future is understood as a call to repentance, which has been sinfully ignored (Jer. 18: 7ff. et al.). It is for this later interpretation, rather than for prophecy, that Martin Buber's verdict holds good:

> But the relationship of the prophet to the future is not one of prediction. To prophesy is to place the community to which the word is uttered either directly or indirectly before choice and decision. The future is not as it were already at hand and therefore knowable, but rather depends substantially upon true decision, i.e. on decision that man makes at this hour. (*Werke* II, 1964, p. 238)

Although Isaiah (6: 10) receives a commission to harden men's hearts in order to hinder repentance, the call to repentance is a thematic summary of the message of Jeremiah (36: 3, 7) as of all true prophets (25: 5; 35: 15; Zech. 1: 4; H. W. Wolff, 'Die eigentliche Botschaft'). Similarly the (Deuteronomistic) books of Kings represent the prophets as warners who predict the threatening historical event in order still to make repentance possible. They announce beforehand what will happen, but because of the continuing disobedience towards the command-ments of God he allows the predicted disaster to take place (2 Kgs. 17: 13ff.; 24: 2f.). On this understanding the prophet issues his warning because he knows exactly what will happen, 'for the Lord does nothing without revealing his secrets to his servants the prophets' (so the added passage Amos 3: 7). Thus the self-understanding of the prophets is only partially reflected in the later inter-pretation.

6   For prophecy itself too the exile marks a deep break. The older prophets already expected salvation in or after the judgement (Hos. 2: 16f.; Isa. 1: 21ff.; 11: 1; Jer. 31: 2ff. et al.). Now Deutero-Isaiah proclaims to his despairing contemporaries (Isa. 40: 27; 49: 14; Ezek. 37: 11) in foreign lands, that their vassalage is ended, their iniquity paid for (Isa. 40: 2), God's future is certain.

> As I swore that the waters of Noah
>   should no more go over the earth,
> so I have sworn that I will not be angry with you
>   and will not rebuke you. (54: 9)

The new salvation is not based upon human behaviour, but upon God's forgiveness (Jer. 31: 31ff.; Isa. 54: 6ff.); he gives a new spirit and a new heart, so that man can change himself (Hos. 14: 5; Isa. 44: 3; Ezek. 36: 26; Joel 2: 28–32 [Heb. Joel 3]). With this expectation there is also room for the call to repentance (Jer. 3: 12; Isa. 44: 21f.; 55: 6; cf. Hos. 14: 2; Ezek. 18). Conversion and joy anticipate the promised future:

> Sing and rejoice, O daughter of Zion;
>   for lo, I come and I will dwell in the midst of you.
> (Zech. 2: 10 [Heb. 2: 14]; cf. 2: 13 [Heb. 2; 17]; 9: 9f.; Isa. 42: 10ff.; 52:
>   9 et al.; cf. above, §13, 6; below IV, 3)

EXCURSUS 7: THE 'WORD' OF GOD

1   The prophets occasionally speak directly of the process of reception and transmission of the word, which as a rule is apparently taken for granted; or they may reflect it, in the few cases in which they emphasize the activity of the word of God. The oldest writing prophet, Amos (c. 760 BC) refers already in his defence to the compulsion which rests upon him:

> The lion has roared – who will not fear?
> The Lord Yahweh has spoken; who can but prophesy?   (3: 8; cf. Jer. 20: 7ff.)

But man can also have the experience of receiving no word; if he seeks in vain for a word of God which he needs for the direction of his life, he has deep grounds for concern (1 Sam. 28: 15f.).

God's silence not only effects but already is a situation of inescapable judgement, as a threat for the future dramatically portrays in the book of Amos (probably a later addition):

> 'Behold, the days are coming', says the Lord Yahweh,
>   'when I will send a famine on the land;
> not a famine of bread, nor a thirst for water,
>   but of hearing the words of Yahweh.
> They shall wander from sea to sea,
>   and from north to east;

they shall run to and fro, to seek the word of Yahweh,
   but they shall not find it.'
                   (Amos 8: 11f.; cf. Hos. 5: 6; of prophets Mic. 3: 4, 6f.; Ezek. 7: 26)

2   In Isaiah the word becomes the subject of the sentence, and so the subject of
the action of the story:

   The Lord has sent a word against Jacob,
      and it fell upon Israel. (9: 7)

Like a superscription or a summarizing motto put at the head, the verse introduces a historical retrospect, which describes divine punishments which befell
the northern kingdom, without stirring up the necessary repentance. Do not the
character of the word as address and its content here recede too far behind its
powerful and destructive effect? 'It is not a word as transmitter of a message that
one ought to listen to, but as transmitter of an event, that one has to trace.' But
such a contrast tears apart what lies together in the text. The word 'sent' by God
is certainly that spoken by the prophet, which is regarded as the cause of the
catastrophe (cf. Hos. 6: 5).

3   Jeremiah later expressly attests that the word of God means the prophetic
message, which however participates in God's power, and seems not only to
announce but also actually to bring in the judgement:

   Behold, I am making my words in your mouth a fire, and this people wood,
   and the fire shall devour them. (Jer. 5: 14; cf. 1: 9, 11f.)

It is no accident that such generalized basic statements are found in Jeremiah,
who reflects on the position of the word in a contemporary debate with his
prophetic opponents. In this he is driven to make a distinction between well-
known forms of revelation, in that he criticizes the dream from the viewpoint of
the word, and comes 'perhaps for the first time to a definition of the word of
Yahweh' (J. Jeremias, *Kultprophetie,* p. 319):

   Let the prophet who has a dream
      tell the dream,
   but let him who has my word
      speak my word faithfully.
   What has straw in common with wheat . . .?
   Is not my word like fire, says Yahweh,
      and like a hammer which breaks the rock in pieces?'
                                          (Jer. 23: 28f.; cf. 23: 18ff.).

Certainly there is no 'definition' here seeking to determine the essential nature and character of the word, but a metaphorical comparison, which both asserts and also illustrates the power and effectiveness of the word (cf. 15: 16; 20: 7ff.).

4   Can we speak of a 'theology of the word' already in Jeremiah, or only in Deutero-Isaiah, the unnamed prophet of the exile? In any case there are found in his work two declarations of the power of the word of God which are striking just because of their location, and have the effect of programmatic utterances (Isa. 40: 8; 55: 10f.); they form a framework around the book of this prophet. The realization 'all flesh is grass' – that is, human power, even the force of the Babylonian oppressor, is transient (40: 6ff.; 51: 12) is met by the assurance,

The word of our God stands for ever.

Since the word possesses strength and duration in the context of what is earthly and transient, it can assert itself in a reality which has a different form and so gains trust even against appearances. Although it is formulated in surprisingly general terms, its declaration is not intended to be understood timelessly, but from its actual situation. The lastingly valid word is the promise of the end of the exile and of the revelation of divine glory before all the world (40: 1f., 5).

In Ezekiel's vision of the revival of the nation, which in the exile had no hope, the prophet receives the commission to address dead bones with the lifegiving word of the creator (Ezek. 37: 4ff.). The authority of the prophet is never more clearly expressed than in this promise.

The final sentences of Deutero-Isaiah, which reaffirm in summary the message of the prophet, point to release and return from exile: 'You shall go out in joy!' (Isa. 55: 12f.). Even the often cited contrasted pair 'my thoughts ... your thoughts, my ways ... your ways' (55: 9) does not express God's remoteness and freedom, and so the incomprehensibility of man's fate, as it is usually understood, but is intended to declare God's saving nearness. This contrast grows perhaps out of a disagreement with the self-understanding of the prophet's contemporaries, who in doubt and little faith think of themselves 'my fate is hidden from God' (40: 27; 49: 14). In this context we have 'prophecy's most comprehensive statement about the word of Yahweh and its effects ...; the dimensions are extended to the furthest limits of thought and even right into theological radicality' (G. von Rad, *Old Testament Theology*, vol. 2, Edinburgh, 1965, p. 93):

As the rain and the snow come down from heaven,
    and return not thither but water the earth,
making it bring forth and sprout,
    giving seed to the sower and bread to the eater,
so shall my word be that goes forth from my mouth;

> it shall not return to me empty,
> but it shall accomplish that which I purpose,
> and prosper in the thing for which I sent it. (Isa. 55: 10f.)

Although the mention of the rain's fertilizing power reminds us of the myth of father sky who impregnates mother earth through the rain, which is thought of as seed, the thought is nonetheless only an image. The distinction between the two events in nature and history is maintained, while the common ground is discovered in the unconditional reliability of the event. Like the quotation from Jeremiah ('my word like fire' 23: 29), but now in more detailed form, the comparison in the form of 'as ... so' is intended to illustrate the reality of the word. An almost creative force, though not natural, nor yet magical, is ascribed to the word. What is meant is neither a vague and contentless word nor an objectified one, but the word of promise uttered through the prophet (cf. Isa. 44: 26; 45: 23). As already in Isa. 9: 7, 'The Lord sent a word' the term 'send', which is borrowed from the commissioning of the prophet (6: 8; 61: 1; Jer. 1: 7 et al.) is transferred to the word: 'It shall succeed in that for which I sent it' (cf. Ps. 107: 20; 147: 15, 18). Thereby something of the character of the prophet himself is transferred to the word. It appears 'in the function of a messenger of God' (L. Dürr, *Die Wertung des göttlichen Wortes im Alten Testament und im antiken Orient*, Leipzig, 1938), is authorized, but remains in his service. As subject of the sentence it becomes the tradent of an action of its own, but not (yet) a hypostasis, a being thought of as having substance, or a personally independent mediator figure appearing alongside God or even in his place.

Is there a danger that the word in such passages will be over-exalted to become a mythological entity? Certainly they express the dynamic character and so the significance of the word very emphatically. The real-life situation, and with it both the content and the substance of the word, recede in significance, but are by no means lost, so long as the passages are not separated from their context. The character of the word as address is then surely preserved.

'In Israel the ancient Near Eastern concepts of the creative power of the divine word have been transferred to Yahweh' (H.-J. Kraus, on Ps. 147: 15ff.). But is this opinion true without qualification? Certainly in Israel's surroundings there are strikingly similar statements.

Ancient Near Eastern attestations praise the loftiness and power, but also the endurance and reliability of the divine word: 'the word, which tears open the heavens above ... and shatters the earth below', or 'Your word lets justice and righteousness arise' (L. Dürr, *Die Wertung des göttlichen Wortes*, pp. 9, 17).

So in this respect too an ancient Near Eastern influence upon Israel is possible, or even probable. It remains however striking that passages which follow most closely the ancient Near Eastern models within the prophetic literature, and indeed in the Old Testament as a whole, appear only at the late period, after a long journey of faith and thought. Are statements about an, as it were, independently effective word of God with a mythical and objective sound to them only possible after it has been made clear by the historical setting and the context of the passage that its relationship to man has not been lost?

§15 Wisdom

1   The wisdom literature (primarily Proverbs, then Ecclesiastes (Koheleth) and the book of Job) is the area of the Old Testament which displays the closest contacts with the ancient Near East. Unlike its historical experience, Israel's wisdom seems to rest upon an already given knowledge, into which the Yahwistic faith only gradually penetrated to give it new form. The Old Testament can not only compare Solomon's wisdom with foreign wisdom (1 Kgs. 5: 10), but borrow smaller collections of proverbs from foreigners (Prov. 30: 1; 31: 1; cf. Job 1: 1). Even a long section of Proverbs (22: 17–23: 11) runs parallel to a large degree to the Egyptian wisdom teaching of Amenemope (before 1000 BC).

Egypt was the country in which wisdom thinking was especially cultivated, and a rich wisdom literature developed. Imhotep, architect of the first pyramid (the step-pyramid of Sakkara, c.2600 BC), was regarded as the oldest wisdom teacher and the model of the class of scribes. In fact this literature was predominantly intended for the schools of the scribes or officials, in which the pupil was addressed as 'son' of the teacher. The situation was similar in Mesopotamia.

The books preserved in the Old Testament with a wisdom character – Proverbs, Ecclesiastes and Job – are late in date, and were brought together only in the 'writings', the third part of the Hebrew canon. Nevertheless the wisdom of Israel is not necessarily a late, post-exilic phenomenon, for it could have received many sorts of influences from the ancient Near East, especially from Egypt. Furthermore the first writing prophets already presuppose wisdom thinking (Isa. 5: 20f.; 31: 2; cf. Amos 6: 12 et al.). So in the period of the monarchy there must have been at least individual proverbs, and probably collections of proverbs were soon put together in the court (Prov. 25: 1). Prov. 10–22: 16 and 25–9 are generally regarded as the oldest collections. Solomon is regarded even at a late date as the originator and embodiment of wisdom (1 Kgs. 3; 5, Prov. 1: 1; 10: 1; 25: 1; cf. Eccles. 1: 1, 12; S. of S. 1: 1). It finds literary expression however in extremely different forms; a long road of thinking and of experience had to be travelled before in the later post-exilic period extensive and theologically reflective compositions like the dialogue of Job and Ecclesiastes could be formed.

2   The term 'wise', which characterizes these particular books of the Old Testament and unites them, appears little in the corresponding ancient Near Eastern literature, or is absent altogether. Egyptologists therefore speak more generally of 'instructions for life'; the occasion and the main content of this literature are well expressed by this term. The wise man reflects upon human

behaviour (in the world as well as towards one's neighbour) and its consequences, and passes on traditional and well-tried experience of life as well as his own. In it practical knowledge (such as, for instance, the craftsman has, Isa. 40: 20; Exod. 31: 3 et al.) is united with more theoretical knowledge and expressed in poetic language. Wisdom grows out of a concern for the understanding of the natural, the social, the material and the personal environment, and thereby helps man to find his way in the world, to be aware of dangers and to avoid harm. The man who listens to the insights of wisdom and follows them understands how to find his place in given situations; he supports goodness and right, is not presumptuous, uses his tongue reflectively (Prov. 18: 21), etc., has good fortune, respect, success and wins life (12: 28; 13: 14; 15: 24 et al.). However experiences are not always unambiguous, and in changing situations can be contradictory (26: 4f.; 11: 24; 17: 27f.; 18: 25 et al.). So what is important is recognition of the right time (15: 23; cf. 25: 11; Eccles. 3: 1ff.).

Conversely the Old Testament has no equivalent for the concept of *maat* which in Egypt is central. It represents the right balance and the correct order in society and world, and is also personified as a goddess.

Israel does not know a single basic order which runs through world, history and human behaviour, but rather seeks to discover different and varying relationships of order. So the many comparisons between the natural and the human world (Prov. 25: 3, 14; 26: 1ff., 11 et al.), into which a dash of humour is infused (26: 14; cf. 22: 13), are the more understandable. These are related to man, as also nature wisdom, which is only found in an allusion in the Old Testament (1 Kgs. 4: 33; Heb. 5: 13), is related to man (cf. the number proverbs in Prov. 30: 15ff.; also Ps. 104; Job 38ff. et al.)

It follows from the origin and purpose of wisdom that it is related less to the nation (Prov. 11: 14; 4: 28; 28: 15; 29: 2, 18) than to the individual, and reflects not so much upon the behaviour of the true Israelite as upon that of man as such. By contrast with the Egyptian 'instructions for life' a specifically civil-servant ethos is of less significance; the proverbs are not tied to a particular class or a group; they are intended to address every man. Is this difference to be explained from the fact that Old Testament wisdom is at home not only at the court (cf. 23: 1ff.; 31: 1; also the royal proverbs 16: 10ff.; 20: 2, 8, 26; 25: 22 et al.) and in the school, but also in the family, and that its origins reach not only back to the advanced cultures but also to Israel's nomadic past?

The wisdom of the nomadic 'sons of the east' (1 Kgs. 5: 10f.; Job 1: 3; 2: 11; Jer. 49: 7; Obad. 8 et al.) is famous. The Old Testament tells occasionally of wise women (2 Sam. 14: 2; 20: 16, 22), Upbringing and relationship to father and also mother are important themes in Proverbs (10: 1; 15: 5, 20; 17: 25; 22: 6, 15; 23: 13f., 24, 26; 29: 15 et al.). However behind the address 'son' the relationship of teacher to pupil may stand, as in the ancient Near East (so 4: 1 et al.?). Was there an actual profession of wise men who had 'counsel' to impart (Jer. 18: 18)? The wise giver of counsel was highly respected at the royal court (2 Sam. 16: 23; cf. Prov. 14: 35; 20: 18; 24: 6; also the messianic expectation of Isa. 11: 2).

3   The realization that in human life action and consequence, behaviour and fate, are related is not found only in wisdom thought, but is nevertheless fundamental to it:

> As you have done, it shall be done to you,
>> your deeds shall return on your own head. (Obad. 15; cf. Prov. 12: 14)

> He who digs a pit will fall into it,
>> and a stone will come back upon him who starts it rolling.
>>> (Prov. 26: 27; cf. Ps. 7: 15f. [Heb. 7: 16f.]; Eccles. 10: 8f.).

> He who walks in integrity walks securely,
>> but he who perverts his ways will be found out. (Prov. 10: 9)

As laziness leads to poverty, diligence to wealth (Prov. 10: 4; 11: 16; 28: 19; but 11: 24), so malice brings disaster, but good actions salvation and life (10: 2, 16; 11: 2, 18ff.; 22: 8f. et al.). Therefore 'a man who is kind (ultimately) benefits himself' (11: 17, 25). Many of the proverbs speak not of a once-for-all action but of a lasting, unchanging attitude of man, which can be expressed in different actions. In fact the contrast of righteous and wicked, wise and foolish, etc., distinguishes 'Israelite wisdom from that of its environment; what was found there only entirely on the margin, here becomes the main element' (H. H. Schmid, *Wesen und Geschichte der Weisheit*, 1966, p. 155). By their contrasting concepts such utterances (especially 10: 1ff.) include not only observation of situations but also evaluation. Is there a concealed demand in them to fight on the side of the wise, the righteous or the industrious? Its character as address to a particular person comes out explicitly only in the exhortations, which can call men to forgiving behaviour with reference to the action-consequence context:

> If your enemy is hungry, give him bread to eat;
>> and if he is thirsty, give him water to drink;
> for you will heap coals of fire on his head,
>> and the Lord will reward you.
>>> (Prov. 25: 21f.; quoted in Rom. 12: 20; cf. Prov. 24: 17f., 19f.; Ps. 37: 1f.)

Is a consciousness of God also presupposed in those proverbs which simply state the connection between action and consequence as human experience (like 22: 8f.; 26: 27)? Is God here understood as guardian of law-governed order, or did the creator give it in the course of the world? With a belief in God there comes into the action and consequence correlation, whether this is known beforehand and expressed or not, not only a personal element but also a note of freedom (cf. 16: 1, 9; 19: 21; 21: 1, 31 et al.). It is in any case clear within the message of the prophets that God himself reveals destiny and brings it in in the future as punishment for men's deeds (Amos 4: 1f.; Isa. 5: 8f.; Jer. 22: 17f. et al.).

Already in the ancient Near East the correlation of action and consequence, which has also been described as 'a synthetic understanding of life' or as a 'realm of action which effects men's destiny,' appeared not only as the automatic ordering given by nature, but at least also as the working of a god – connected perhaps with exhortations to social behaviour:

> Exercise no violence among men;
>> for God punishes with the same. (Ptahhotep, 6th Instruction)
> Bend not thy bow
> and shoot not thine arrow at a righteous man,
> lest God come to his help
>> and turn it back upon thee. (Sayings of Ahikar 126; *ANET*, p. 429)

> Give bread to eat, give wind to drink!
> Who begs for alms, him clothe and honour!
>> His God rejoices over him for it,
>> this pleases (the sun god) Shamash,
>> He rewards him for it with good. (*AOT*, p. 292)

Similarly the Old Testament draws ethical consequences from the belief that God 'requites man according to his work' (Prov. 24: 12), or 'turns back' the action upon the doer (Ps. 28: 4; 94: 2):

> He who is kind to the poor lends to the Lord,
>> and he will repay him for his (good) deed.
>>> (Prov. 19: 17; cf. above on 25: 21f.)

The belief that the poor can trust in God is so important to the Old Testament that it inserts this confession (22: 23; 23: 11; also 22: 19) into the proverbs taken over from the Egyptian wisdom instruction of Amenemope (22: 17ff.), and frequently expresses a similar belief (14: 21, 31; 17: 5; 21: 13; 22: 9; 24: 11f.; also Exod. 22: 22f., 26f, et al.).

> Retaliation is God's concern alone:

> Do not say, 'I will repay evil';
>> wait for the Lord, and he will help you. (Prov. 20: 22; cf. 24: 29)

> In many exhortations and warnings the proverbs remind us of the Decalogue (28: 24; 6: 20ff.; 19: 5 et al.), but they seek to awaken understanding, while the Decalogue demands it unconditionally and without reservations.

4   In its concern to determine the position of man in relation to his environment, wisdom is conscious of the limits of human understanding. Man, even the king, is concealed from himself:

The king's heart is a stream of water in the hand of Yahweh;
   he turns it wherever he will. (Prov. 21: 1; cf. 25: 2)

A man's mind plans his way,
   but Yahweh directs his steps.
                (Prov. 16: 9; cf. 19: 21; 21: 30f.; Gen. 50: 20)

The plans of the mind belong to man,
   but the answer of the tongue is from Yahweh. (Prov. 16: 1)

If the connection of thought and action, indeed of thought and speech remains
unknowable and uncontrollable, 'how then can man understand his way?' (20: 24)
Therefore it is right for man to be modest and to practice humility:

Every one who is arrogant is an abomination to Yahweh.
                (16: 5; cf. 16: 18f.; 18: 12; 22: 4; 29: 23 et al.)

Do you see a man who is wise in his own eyes?
   There is more hope for a fool than for him.
                (26: 12; cf. 3: 5ff.; 21: 30; Jer. 9: 23f.)

Elsewhere too the proverbs reach beyond direct experience, in speaking in varied
ways of Yahweh, and so introducing an element in the fate of man which is
incalculable, and indeed unfathomable:

The blessing of Yahweh makes rich,
   and he adds no sorrow with it. (Prov. 10: 22; cf. 16: 3; Ps. 127: 2)

Sheol and Abaddon lie open before Yahweh –
   how much more the hearts of men!
                (Prov. 15: 11; cf. 15: 3, 1 Sam. 16: 7 et al.)

All the ways of a man are pure in his own eyes,
   but he who weighs the spirit is Yahweh.
                (Prov. 16: 2; 21: 2; cf. 17: 3; Jer. 17: 10)

God's judgement helps man to decide between justice and injustice; for false
balances, a corrupt heart or a lying tongue are 'an abomination to Yahweh' (Prov.
11: 1, 20; 12: 22; 17: 15 et al.). He is the protector as well as creator of the poor
(14: 31; 17: 5; above, §11f, 5). The rich man too owes his life to him however, so
that for all the social antitheses a basic ground common to man is found:

The rich and the poor meet together;
for Yahweh is the maker of them all.
(Prov. 22: 2; cf. 16: 4, 11; 20: 12; 29: 13)

In spite of such weighty (though as a whole isolated) statements, wisdom thought cannot without qualification be assigned to a 'theology of creation' unless the concept is so enlarged that it embraces the whole of man's experience of reality.

Just one single proverb refers to God's mercy towards the man who acknowledges his sin. Does not faith then break up the connection of action and consequence, even if it expresses itself in this language?

He who conceals his transgressions will not prosper,
but he who confesses and forsakes them will obtain mercy.
(Prov. 28: 13; cf. Ps. 32: 3ff)

So wisdom is aware of love and forgiveness (also Prov. 10: 12; 16: 6 et al.), although it feels a quite unmistakable reserve towards the cult, at least the sacrificial cult (above, Excursus 6, 6).

5   While wisdom appears in the originally probably independent song in Job 28 as something comparable to ore, material but inaccessible to man, in the supposedly latest collection in the book of Proverbs, in which the units of sayings are much longer (ch. 1–9), it is personified. It may be that ancient Near Eastern concepts of a female deity have some influence here. Wisdom commends itself (Prov. 1: 20ff.) and delimits itself over against Lady Folly (9: 1ff.), but is not yet, or is only incipiently, an independent hypostasis alongside God. If according to Prov. 3: 19f. 'Yahweh has founded the earth in wisdom', it is still regarded as a property of God (cf. Ps. 104: 24), but in Prov. 8: 22ff. it is the first of the works of creation. Although wisdom introduces himself, she refers at once to God; he remains (as in Prov. 3: 19) decidedly the subject of the introductory sentence:

Yahweh created me at the beginning of his work,
the first of his acts of old . . .
When there were no depths I was brought forth;
When he established the heavens, I was there,
When he drew a circle on the face of the deep,
when he made firm the skies above,
when he established the fountains of the deep,
when he assigned to the sea its limit . . .
then I was beside him, like a master workman,
and I was daily his delight,
rejoicing before him always. (Prov. 8: 22–30)

Wisdom is neither divine nor everlasting. It is created, but before all other creatures. Its venerable antiquity, its presence at the creation of the world and its closeness to God show its preeminence. Its significance, and indeed necessity for man (vv. 31ff.), is the climax of the utterance: 'he who finds me finds life, and obtains favour from Yahweh' (v. 35).

An insight that is already found in the older wisdom, 'the fear of Yahweh is a fountain of life' (14: 26f.; cf. 15: 16 et al.) leads beyond it, and becomes the basic concept of the collection in ch. 1–9, and at the same time the motto of the whole book:

> The fear of Yahweh is the beginning of knowledge.
> (Prov. 1: 7; cf. 9: 10; 15: 33; Ps. 111: 10; Job 28: 28)

When the fear of Yahweh is the entrance to or the main part of wisdom, this is definitively incorporated into the faith of the Old Testament (cf. Jer. 9: 22f.).

6 It remains connected with this faith, while far-reaching doubts about the correctness of its perception appear. According to the proverbs the attitude of man decides his future:

> The hope of the righteous ends in gladness,
>   but the expectation of the wicked comes to nought.
> (Prov. 10: 28; cf. 11: 7, 23)

The distinction according to which 'the evil man has no future' (24: 20) is dubious to Ecclesiastes:

> There are righteous men to whom it happens according to the deeds of the wicked, and there are wicked men to whom it happens according to the deeds of the righteous. (Eccles. 8: 14; cf. 7: 15; 9: 2)

This Preacher (as the term Koheleth is translated) wrote his reflections or aphorisms probably in the third century BC, and may have been influenced not only by ancient Near Eastern precedents, but also by early Hellenistic popular philosophy, especially scepticism. Like the psalmist occasionally ('I have been young, and now am old; yet I have not seen the righteous forsaken, Ps. 37: 25; cf. Prov. 24: 30ff.) Ecclesiastes writes in the first person (1: 12ff.), but has contradictory experiences: injustice reigns 'under the sun', that is, upon earth (3: 16; 4: 1; 5: 7; 8: 9), the natural order of things is upside down (10: 6f.), man is evil (8: 6, 11), and 'there is no righteous man upon earth . . . who has not sinned' (7: 20). But in the last resort the crisis of wisdom arises from doubts about the action-consequence connection, and from thoughts about death. Koheleth does indeed concede that wisdom is of more advantage than folly (2: 12ff.; 4: 5f, 13: 8: 1; 9: 17ff. et al.), but this advantage has no permanence (1: 17; 2: 16; 7: 11f., 23ff.).

For the fate of the sons of men and the fate of beasts is the same.
As one dies, so dies the other.
They all have the same breath . . .
All go to one place;
all are from the dust,
and all turn to dust again. (3: 19f.; cf. 9: 2ff.; below, Excursus 8, 3)

In the face of death Koheleth can find no right answer to the question 'What is good for man while he lives?' (6: 12; cf. 1: 3; 3: 9). 'There is nothing better than that a man should enjoy his work' (3: 22). But even the invitation 'eat, drink, enjoy life!' (9: 7ff.; 5: 17ff.; 8: 15; 11: 9 et al.) is accompanied by the insight, 'this also is vanity' (2: 1; 3: 22; 11: 10). If 'all is vanity' (1: 2, 4; 12: 8 et al.) is not death preferable (2: 17; 4: 2f.)?

In spite of all his scepticism Koheleth takes the course of the world, as well as the ups and downs of life, as being from God's hand (2: 24f.; 3: 13; 5: 17f.; 9: 1; 12: 7 et al.): 'God has made it so, in order that men should fear before him' (3: 14; cf. 5: 6; but without excess: so 7: 16f.). History with its acknowledgement of God's guidance and saving action as well as the (prophetic) hope in God's future are very much in the background in Koheleth, but he holds fast to the exclusiveness of faith, and so the first commandment (esp. 7: 14). What God has determined, man may not alter (3: 14; 6: 10; 7: 13). So Koheleth holds onto faith in God's good ordering of the world, but it remains unfathomable to man (3: 11; cf. 7: 24, 29). He cannot even rightly know himself and his future (9: 1, 12; 3: 2; 8: 7). It might seem that Koheleth knows only of God's providence, and not of God's love. Do we have here a faith without trust?

7   The position is quite different in Job, which was formed a little earlier, growing from its origin in the story of Job (chs. 1–2; 42: 7ff.) through the formation of the dialogue, down to the insertion of additions (e.g. ch. 28; 32–37), but over a longer period (roughly fifth to third centuries). Koheleth (6: 10) shares with Job (especially 9: 12ff., 19, 32f.) the realization that man may not dispute with God. But in spite of his admission of his helplessness Job in his wrestling with God does not ultimately give up hope and trust. He appeals against the God who persecutes him for no reason (7: 12ff.; 9: 21ff.; 16: 9ff. et al.) to the God who will do him justice and help him (16: 19ff.; 19: 25f.; 31: 35; cf. below, Excursus 8, 6). It is presupposed that Job is suffering innocently (1: 1; 9: 21; 23: 10ff.; 27; 31) – a problem which has already been reflected upon in the ancient Near East in various texts (cf. NERT, pp. 133ff.). So the connection of action and consequence, of guilt and suffering, to which the 'friends' hold rigidly in spite of Job's objections (4: 7ff. to 22: 5ff.) is broken. God's answer (ch. 38ff.) teaches Job about God's government of the world, and makes him aware of the limitations of man. Job 'revokes' his laments and accusations, returns to humility before God (42: 5f.; 2: 8) and accordingly receives his lot again (1: 21; 2: 10) from the hand of

God. In view of the change which richly restores to Job what he has lost (42: 10ff.) the narrative seems to demonstrate through the fate of an individual and his behaviour the confession that 'Yahweh makes poor and makes rich, brings low and exalts' (1 Sam. 2: 6ff.; Deut. 32: 39).

The man who prays Ps. 73, who is also oppressed by the discrepancy between action and consequence for a man, goes one step further than Job. God 'holds' the believer even in death (vv. 23ff.; below Excursus 8, 6). Wisdom material is found not only in the psalter (also Ps. 37 et al.) but elsewhere too far beyond the wisdom literature as such. The prophets for instance incorporate wisdom material (Isa. 1: 2f.; 11: 2; 40: 12ff. et al.) or point out in reply to their contemporaries who think themselves wise (5: 20; cf. 29: 14ff.; 44: 25; 47: 10ff.) that 'yet he, Yahweh, is wise' (31: 2).

IV THE LATE PERIOD

1   While the period of the Israelite monarchy, lasting roughly four centuries, can be surveyed really well, our historical information about the exilic and post-exilic periods is much more restricted. The final conquest of Jerusalem by Nebuchadnezzar in 587 BC broke in three respects the visible foundations of the Yahwistic faith – temple, Davidic dynasty and possession of the land.

> Thy holy cities have become a wilderness,
>   Zion has become a wilderness,
> Jerusalem a desolation.
> Our holy and beautiful house,
>   where our fathers praised thee,
> has been burned by fire. (Isa. 64: 9f.)

History undid the realization of centuries-old promises, or the promises proved to be overtaken by history. On the other hand the prophetic threats which said that God's power would be revealed in the suffering of the nation were fulfilled:

> The Lord has done what he purposed,
>   has carried out his threat;
> as he ordained long ago,
>   he has demolished without pity;
> he has made the enemy rejoice over you,
>   and exalted the might of your foes. (Lam. 2: 17)

Such a decisive turning point led necessarily to profound alterations in Israel's understanding of God, but despite the losses faith nevertheless increased. There was however no complete break, for the Babylonians in the main deported only the upper strata of society, and apparently the greater part of the population remained in the land (cf. 2 Kgs. 25: 12; Jer. 39: 10; 40: 6). These remaining Judahites continued worship on the site of the temple even after the destruction of the sanctuary; it is only the later history of the Chronicler (with Ezra and Nehemiah as its conclusion) that assumes a break in the cult in Jerusalem, because it saw the true line of faith in the exiles (cf. Ezra 1). So there was some measure of continuity even in Palestine; here too traditions were preserved and passed on. But from now on the people was divided. Those still resident in the land had to reconsider their position; but it was the Gola, those deported in 597 and 587 (2 Kgs. 24: 14–16; 25: 11; Jer. 52: 28–30) who took theological thinking further. We have to consider to which of these two sides new developments have to be ascribed. In any case from the exile on certain features come increasingly sharply to the fore which are not so much rooted in the past as pointing forward to the future. So in certain respects it is right to see the beginnings of Judaism precisely in the exilic period; the former league of tribes now becomes the Jewish community.

Little is known of the fate of the Judahites who were resettled in Babylon. Although forced to go there, they were not (in spite of Isa. 42: 7, 22; 45: 2) shut up as captives, but lived in nearby villages (Ezek. 3: 15; Ezra 2: 59) as a subject population, which could provide cheap labour. According to Jer. 29: 5f. it was possible for them to build houses, to lay out gardens and to live off the produce. The elders could gather together (Ezek. 8: 1; 14: 1; 20: 1), when someone was telling a story or singing (33: 30–33). But those who had stayed behind in Jerusalem held that 'they are far from Yahweh' (11: 15; cf. 33: 24). The land was 'foreign' (Ps. 137: 4), 'unclean' (Ezek. 4: 13), not a land in which one could legitimately worship God (cf. 1 Sam. 26: 19; Hos. 9: 3f.; Amos 7: 17; Jer. 16: 13). Only lamentations were allowed (cf. apart from Lamentations, Zech. 7: 3, 5; 8: 19; also Ezek. 11: 16 et al.; above, §9b, 4). For these services of prayer, as for circumcision and the observance of the sabbath rest, there was no need of the temple. So the longing for Zion remained strong (Ps. 137; Jer. 51: 50).

Nevertheless the exiles did not return to their homeland as a group when it became possible for them to do so under Persian rule, after the conquest of Babylon by Cyrus in 539 BC. Although there were several groups of returning exiles (cf. Ezra 2; 7) many stayed on voluntarily in Babylon; the Gola, deported under compulsion, became the diaspora. Business documents of the banking house of Murashu and sons from the fifth century, in which the names of Jews too are found, show how good living conditions could be in the Persian period. So of necessity the social structure changed; the Jews became traders. But the diaspora did not consist by any means only of the community in exile in Babylon. The banishment of the Israelites of the northern kingdom to Assyria and Media had taken place almost a century and a half earlier (2 Kgs. 15: 29; 17: 6). Then the conquerors had pursued even harsher tactics of scattering the conquered Israelites among foreign nations, so that they were gradually absorbed by them and lost their individuality. Finally the disturbances after 587 were followed by an emigration of Judahites to Egypt, in flight before the vengeance of the Babylonians (2 Kgs. 25: 26; Jer. 43: 7; 44: 1; 24: 8; cf. also Deut. 17: 16; Zech. 10: 10). A diaspora in Egypt is also attested by the Elephantine papyri, which come from a military colony on an island on the Nile. Jewish mercenaries served there in the sixth and fifth centuries BC, and had a temple of their own with a syncretistic form of worship, in which the deities Anat-Bet-El or Anat-Yahu and Asham-Bet-El ('name of Beth-el', cf. 2 Kgs. 17: 30) were worshipped alongside Yahweh, perhaps as hypostases of him.

It has been conjectured that there were also Jewish settlements in Arabia from the time of the last Babylonian king, Nabonidus. Jewish slaves were sold even as far as Greece (Amos 1: 6, 9; Joel 3: 6–8; Ezek. 27: 13; cf. 2 Chr. 32: 16f.). It was not only warfare (with its mercenaries, deportation, flight and slavery) that provided the occasion for the emergence of the Jewish diaspora; trade was no less important. Trading colonies increased both close to and further from Palestine (cf. already 1 Kgs. 20: 34; 10: 28f.) and developed into firm settlements. As the world was increasingly opened up under the Persian empire and especially after the time of Alexander in the Hellenistic and Roman periods, emigration was attractive. In the end there were substantial Jewish communities not only in the smaller neighbouring lands (Jer. 40: 11), in Egypt (Isa. 19: 18–20) and Mesopotamia, but in the whole of the Mediterranean, indeed in the whole world then known (11: 11f.; 1 Macc. 15: 16–24; Acts 2: 9–11). Among the famous centres of the Greek-speaking diaspora were Alexandria in Lower Egypt, where the Septuagint was formed, and Antioch in Syria; here the Old Testament traditions and the spirit of Hellenism met and mingled.

After the victory of Cyrus (cf. Isa. 44: 28f.; Ezra 1: 1) the homeland of Judah also changed from being a Babylonian to a Persian province. Contrary to the promises of Deutero-Isaiah (Isa. 40ff.) the return of the exiles was not a single movement, still less a miraculous one, but took place gradually in separate thrusts and under wretched conditions. 'Israelites can live again in the land of promise, but under foreign dominion, and the temple is rebuilt, but it is not the centre of a people united in its own land' (O. H. Steck, 'Das Problem theologischer Strömungen in nachexilischer Zeit', *EvTh* 28 (1968), p. 455). Ezra 3 tells us of a rebuilding of the altar and of the laying of the foundation stone of the temple, but the rebuilding did not take place in the reign of Cyrus, who had given permission for it (Ezra 6: 3–5), but about two decades later, in the years 520 to 515 BC at the instance of the prophets Haggai and Zechariah (Ezra 5: 1f.; 6: 14f.). But the messianic expectations which both these prophets (Hag. 2: 21–3; Zech. 4; 6: 9–15; cf. above, §12d, 6) directed towards the Davidide Zerubbabel, remained unfulfilled; the monarchy was not restored.

Later Nehemiah and Ezra, the one externally with the building of the wall around Jerusalem (Neh. 1–7; 12: 27–43), the other internally with the commitment to the law (Neh. 8) provided for the consolidation and separation of the community (prohibition of mixed marriages, Ezra 9f.; Neh. 13: 3, 23ff.; cf. Mal. 2: 11f.). It is disputed whether the 'law of the God of heaven', which Ezra brings with him in the company of a group of returning exiles from Babylon (Ezra 7: 12ff.), is Deuteronomy, the Priestly writing (including the Code of Holiness, Lev. 17–26) or even the Pentateuch as a whole.

In the course of these arguments (Neh. 2: 10, 19; 4: 1ff. [Heb. 3: 33ff.]; already Hag. 2: 14?) the separation of the Samaritans began, and then became irrevocable in the fourth or third century (Zech. 11: 14; John 4: 20). At this time the Pentateuch was already in existence as a given canon and binding law, and was taken over as such by the Samaritans. It was only later that the final formation of the prophetic canon took place (perhaps in the third century) and finally that of the Old Testament as a whole (*c.* AD 100).

Alexander the Great took over the inheritance of the Persian empire in 332; then when the empire was divided up into the kingdoms of the Diadochi, Palestine fell for a century (301–198 BC) under the suzerainty of the Ptolemies of Egypt, and then of the Seleucids of Syria. When Antiochus IV Epiphanes in the course of his policy of Hellenization even attacked the Jewish cult, the Maccabees rose in a war of liberation. In memory of the new dedication of the temple in 164 BC the feast of Hanukkah was later celebrated. At this time of persecution the Book of Daniel was developed out of older material, and this was the beginning of apocalyptic literature.

The diaspora was assisted in mainintaining its faith in a foreign milieu by the development of the synagogue. It is attested with certainty from the third century BC; its origins are not known in detail. It made possible a regular gathering on the sabbath, in which readings were made from the law, which was canonized by then, and the prophets, far away from the Jerusalem temple (cf. Neh. 8, esp. v. 8). In consequence in Jewish worship as a whole sacrifice declined in importance compared with the exposition of scripture and prayer. But the emigrants maintained their link with the homeland (2 Macc. 2: 18 et al.). Jerusalem was regularly visited at the great pilgrimage festivals like Passover (cf. Zech. 14: 16ff. of the nations); gifts to the temple are also attested from a later period. When these links were violently broken off after the destruction of the temple and city by the Romans in AD 70 and 135, the Jewish faith survived even this savage attack with the help of the synagogue. Palestine itself then accepted the form of worship of the diaspora.

2   Life in exile compelled Israel more and more to emphasize the exclusiveness of its faith. If it did not wish to disappear abroad, it had to reflect upon its own distinctiveness; it preserved the tradition and let its distinctive features come to the fore. Old cultic usages which were formerly not fundamental came to have a new and exclusive sense: circumcision, which was probably customary in Egypt and among Israel's eastern neighbours (Jer. 9: 24f.) but not in Mesopotamia, became now a distinguishing feature and 'sign of the covenant' (Gen. 17P). The strict observance of the sabbath commandment too became constitutive for adherence to the Yahwistic faith (the work of seven days in Gen. 1; Exod. 16; 31; Isa. 56: 2ff.; 58: 13f.; Jer. 17; Neh. 10: 32 et al.; cf. above, Excursus 2). The food laws emerged as a third feature, which in particular forbade the consumption of blood and unclean food including pig-meat, which was important in the Adonis and mystery cults, cf. Isa. 65: 4f., 66: 17 (Gen. 9: 4; Lev. 11; 17: 10ff.; Ezek. 33: 25; Zech. 9: 7; Dan. 1: 5ff.; 2 Macc. 6: 18ff.; 7; Acts 10: 14; 15: 28f.; on washing before meals Matt. 15: 2; Mark 7: 3f.; John 2: 6).

Because only the Torah guaranteed the demarcation of the people of God as a pledge of his presence, the law, which originally only affected individual acts of disobedience, in the end came to be the basis of the relationship to God himself. Only then did it become possible to gain membership of the people of God by acceptance of the commandments. Here was 'a certain people scattered abroad and dispersed among the peoples in all the provinces of your kingdom; their laws are different from those of every other people' (Esther 3: 8). This distinction could, from the later part of the Persian period, lead to conflict (cf. Zeph. 3: 19; Esther 2: 9f., 20; 3: 2ff.; Dan. 3; 6).

Nevertheless even in the post-exilic period the worship of idols could be a danger (Zech. 10: 2; 13: 2; of the worship of trees, Isa. 1: 29; 57: 5; 65: 3f.; 66: 17). So the first commandment remained necessary.

3   Apart from the writing down and expansion of the laws, and also the redaction of the prophetic books, the greater part of the literature of the Old Testament came into existence precisely during the exile and in the following period. A look back at the past helped men to understand their present position. Lamentations and some of the psalms bewailed what was lost: 'O God, why dost thou cast us off for ever? . . . There is no longer any prophet, and there is none among us who knows how long' (Ps. 74: 1, 9). The Deuteronomistic history developed a comprehensive picture from the time of Moses to the present (Deut.-2 Kgs.). The Deuteronomist used as a standard for the evaluation of events the first and second commandments, and the demand for centralization of the cult which was made by Deuteronomy (the reform of Josiah, 621 BC); disaster was understood as a realization of the threats of the prophets. On the other hand the Priestly work with its theological approach began with the creation (Gen. 1) and gave a pattern to the early history of the nation before the entry into Palestine.

While these two history works are without an eschatological hope in the strict sense, and at best leave open obliquely the possibility of a new future, the prophets Ezekiel and Deutero-Isaiah promise a change. In the preaching of Ezekiel we see achieved the change from the message of judgement to the message of salvation (Ezek. 34ff., esp. 37). Deutero-Isaiah, at a time at which the communion between God and nation seems to be broken (Ezek. 37: 11; Isa. 40: 27; 49: 14), begins with the call 'Comfort, comfort my people, says your God' (40: 1). His message reduced to the simplest terms is one of eschatological imminent expectation: a new period has begun; 'now it springs forth, do you not perceive it?' (43: 19; cf. 46: 13). The prophet sees the coming of God and his kingship being proclaimed: 'Behold your God!' (40: 9), 'Your God has become king' (52: 7; above, §11a, 6). The contrast between the new age that is coming and the past age is so strong that Deutero-Isaiah even expresses it conceptually by the contrast 'the former' and 'the new'. Because God creates something new, it is no longer right to think of the history of salvation and disaster of the past (43: 18f.; 48: 3, 6). The revelation of the 'glory of Yahweh' lies immediately in the future, all the world will see it (40: 5; 52: 10) and acknowledge God:

> To me every knee shall bow,
>> every tongue shall swear:
> Only in the Lord are righteousness and strength. (45: 23f.; cf. 45: 6)

The first commandment, which so sharply distinguishes the faith of the Old Testament from the surrounding religions, is still maintained in all its exclusiveness; for the nations take over the confession of the one God:

> God is with you only, and there is no other,
>> no god besides him. (45: 14)

Towards this goal of a universal knowledge of God the people of God itself is to act as 'messenger' (42: 19) and 'witness' (43: 10, 12; 44: 8):

> Behold, you shall call nations that you know not,
>> and nations that knew you not shall run to you,
> because of Yahweh your God, and of the Holy One of Israel. (55: 5)

Israel does not yet go out to the nations in missionary zeal, but in the expectation of Deutero-Isaiah can be perceived a surprising change, which has taken place since the exile. As the foundations of faith break apart, the body of adherents of the faith is expanded to an unprecedented degree by the accession of foreigners (cf. Isa. 56: 3ff.; Zech. 8: 20ff.; Neh. 10: 29; Judith 14: 10). Unity in one place is exchanged for increase in many places. The double hope of Deutero-Isaiah is taken further: in the gathering of the people of God scattered throughout the world (Isa. 43: 5–7; 49: 22; 27: 12f.; 62: 11f.; Zech. 10: 6ff. et al.) and the confession of the one God by all (2: 11 [Heb. 2: 15]; 8; 20ff.; Isa. 25: 6; Ps. 22: 27f. [Heb. 22: 28f.]; 1 Kgs. 8: 43, 60 et al.). Occasionally this universalism even yearns for a time in which God is near to every place. The nations do not need (as in the tradition of a pilgrimage to Zion, Isa. 2: 2ff. et al.) to come on pilgrimage to Zion, but can remain in their own homelands:

> Yahweh appears over them;
>> for he makes all the gods of the earth vanish.
> And to him all the islands of the nations bow down,
>> everyone in his place. (Zeph. 2: 11; cf. Mal. 1: 11; Isa. 66: 18ff.)

With the change of the people of God into the diaspora community therefore, a development comes about which in the end makes the Jews in other countries several times more numerous than those resident in Palestine. The exclusive and imageless worship of God is the main attraction of joining the Jewish community. Faith and enlightenment here become linked; for over against the human deities of the myths faith in the unportrayable God who is over the whole world succeeds in asserting itself (cf. below, §17, 1). The significance of history is reduced, and continuity with the past is represented primarily by the first and second commandments.

But alongside the growth externally there is a gradual dissolution of the people of God internally. The hope of unity has no basis in the present-day reality. On the contrary, at a time which hopes for the gathering together of the scattered peoples, the community itself falls apart. Already in prophetic preaching a division is anticipated in the expectation of a 'remnant' (since 1 Kgs. 19: 17f.). This division within the nation took place in the post-exilic period, and became increasingly deeper and more obvious (cf. e.g. Isa. 65; Mal. 3: 14ff.). Different theological tendencies come to be opposed to one another, and finally in the New Testament period harden into particular groups and parties.

Ps. 1 explicitly contrasts the one archetypally righteous man to the majority of ungodly men; and here the tension of minority and majority within the people of God itself appears. Does the 'assembly of the faithful' (Ps. 149: 1 et al.) no longer consist of all the people? Such a possibility was unknown in ancient Israel. It is no longer membership of the nation but the behaviour of the individual that decides his relationship to God. While earlier the nation as a whole made up a fellowship, now the community was constituted increasingly of its individual members (cf. Isa. 44: 5; Ezek. 18 et al.); it is their common faith that makes a unity of them. Ps. 1 removes altogether any fellowship with the ungodly; although the distinction made does not produce a static contrast of two groups its intention is pedagogical, to lead men on to the right way by a contrast of black and white.

This incipient dissolution of the community is reflected in many ways in the psalter, although often less sharply. While for instance terms like 'pious' or 'god-fearing' were once used of every Israelite, and 'poor' or 'humble' indicated poverty or sickness, these expressions later serve as honorific titles for a part of the people as a whole which is being demarcated from the other part. Because the actual point of dispute is the understanding of God, the distinction comes to a head with on the one side the pious or god-fearing, and on the other side the godless who oppress the poor (cf. psalms of thanksgiving and wisdom psalms like Ps. 34: 16ff. [Heb. 34: 17ff.]; 37: 28f.; 49; 73; Mal. 3: 16). If both groups perhaps already form a community proper, they do not yet appear here, as they do from the Maccabaean period (1 Macc. 2: 42; 7: 13) as fixed classes or parties sharply separated from one another. The 'pious' are still generally those who seek God (Ps. 22: 26 [Heb. 22: 27]), love him (145: 19f.), hope for his goodness (147: 11) and so praise him (52: 9 [Heb. 52: 11]; 145: 10). They are dependent on God because they themselves are 'broken' (34: 18f. [Heb. 34: 19f.]; 51: 16f. [Heb. 51: 18f.]); and just because they are in need of help they are assured of it (37: 39f.). From these cases we are shown what man's position is. Yet not everyone understands himself in this manner.

The rift which in the present runs through the community also determines one part of their future expectations. Judgement can still be proclaimed also to the generations after the exile. Israel as it actually is is not simply the hoped-for 'remnant' (so Hag. 1: 14; 2: 2); purification is still needed (Zech. 13: 8f.; 14: 2, cf. Isa. 65: 6f. et al.). Even at the end of this life the division does not cease. Dan. 12: 2 (below Excursus 8, 6) proclaims a double resurrection, the one to life, the other to shame. The long-hidden tension between the *ecclesia visibilis* and *invisibilis* at last becomes clearly visible here.

§16 Apocalyptic

The law is intended to preserve the purity of the people of God, and to this extent is specially concerned for a particularistic exclusiveness. In contrast apocalyptic has a cosmic and universal purpose: its hope is that the God of the nation will reveal himself as the God of the world. While the community as a whole sees the prophetic expectations already fulfilled in its present life, and so understands its present reality as the manner of life that corresponds to God's will, a part of it emphasizes that the prophetic expectations are still future. This apocalyptic faith then no longer embraces the totality of the nation, but lives rather in smaller groups inside the community. 'The law is for all, secret knowledge is for the elect' (P. Volz, *Die Eschatologie der judischen Gemeinde im neutestamentlichen Zeitalter*, 2nd edn., Tübingen, 1934, p. 5). So law and apocalyptic are not mutually exclusive, but the two do not form a unity; they can exist alongside one another, but also be opposed to one another, until finally orthodox Judaism more or less entirely rejects apocalyptic thought forms after the failure of the Bar-Kochba revolt (AD 135).

That God is a God who will come is a prophetic message, which apocalyptic only takes up and carries further, though at the same time it changes it. The sayings of the post-exilic prophets, who inherit the mantle of their great predecessors, make it clear that prophecy in its late period (especially Ezek. 38f.; Joel (ch 3: Heb. chs. 3f.); Zech. 12–14; Isa. 24–27) at least prepares the way for apocalyptic themes, and that conversely apocalyptic in many ways takes over traditional prophetic material (the reign of God and of the Messiah, judgement on Israel and the nations, the destruction or deliverance of Jerusalem, etc.) and reinterprets it.

Common features are also seen in the form of proclamation. Like the prophets (Amos 7f.; Ezek. 8–11; 40ff.; especially Zech. 1–6) the apocalyptists receive and narrate their revelations in visions and auditions (Dan. 7–12). While prophetic sayings originally had a concise and rhythmic form, later they become more wordy, and finally can pass into an elevated prose. In apocalyptic this process has reached its climax; it scarcely proclaims its message at all orally, but only in writing. This is a significant difference, but it did not come in suddenly, but developed gradually. In spite of the great gulf which divides prophecy and apocalyptic in their main forms, there are substantial connections, which do not apply only to details. The distinctive features of apocalyptic, which (to give the usual terms used) are dualism with a strong contrast of God and world, the doctrine of ages of the world with a division of time into periods, determinism in history, the transcendence of the reign of God and pseudonymity of the actual works, only gradually developed.

a PAST AND FUTURE

1 The apocalypses, like the words of the prophets, are addressed to contemporaries, and so contain both address and demand. Both forms of preaching are rooted in their own situation, with the difference that the apocalyptic visions of the future no longer make the connection with their own time explicit, but conceal it under the device of pseudonymity. Famous people from the history of Israel appear as the authors, prophets, teachers of the law or wise men, like Ezra, Baruch, Isaiah, Elijah, Moses or Abraham; but sometimes both nearer and more distant history are passed over and figures from primeval history like Adam or Enoch are brought in. This too is not completely new; Israel had historicized the feasts and laws, and ascribed Deuteronomy and Ps. 90 to Moses.

To the prophets the place and time of the reception and transmission of the message were so important that they sometimes stated both (Isa. 6: 1; 7: 1–3 et al.). Even in the post-exilic period sayings in Haggai and Zechariah are dated by the exact day (Hag. 1: 1; Zech. 1: 7; 7: 1 et al.). But this contrast, that the prophets let their words appear under their names (Amos 1: 1), while the apocalyptists make use of the names of others, is not an unqualified one. Probably no prophetic book has remained without additions, in which unknown writers seek the authority of the prophet for their hopes for the future. From the time that the author of the message 'Comfort, comfort my people' (Isa. 40–55) remained silent about his name, not only individual sayings but whole sections or books (Isa. 56–66; 24–7; Zech. 9–14; Mal.) remained anonymous. Even the first narrative part of Daniel (ch. 1–6) spoke of Daniel in the third person, without an indication of authorship, and only the second visionary section (ch. 7–12) abandoned anonymity, and went over to pseudonymity, being attributed to Daniel, a wise man at the court of Nebuchadnezzar.

This change was not accidental, but determined by the situation; it depends on an alteration in the understanding of tradition (cf. Isa. 34: 16; Dan. 9: 2). Instances can be found very early of prophets taking over the message of their predecessors (cf. above, §14a, 2, 4). Micah with his demands for justice, love and humility (6: 8) was summing up the messages of Amos, Hosea and Isaiah. Trito-Isaiah quotes sentences of Deutero-Isaiah word for word in Isa. 60–62, but gives them a new meaning; in later prophets like Joel quotations from the prophetic literature are frequently found. Zechariah (1: 4ff.; 7: 7) explicitly holds up to its hearers or readers as an example the call to repentance of the 'earlier prophets'. So the prophet supports his authority by reference to earlier preaching; he utters his own word through interpreting that of others. This relationship to tradition becomes even closer in the course of time, until finally the canon is formed, and makes possible a constant reference back to the word of God in its written form. Because the interpretation of the present is done by means of texts from the past, the apocalyptic visions must be understood as predictions from earlier, and even very early times, and therefore must appear pseudonymously. The secrets of the future are still hidden from the people at large, and only revealed to certain specific people in the present. After the demand 'but you, Daniel, shut up the words, and seal the book, until the time of the end', comes the assurance 'the words are shut up and sealed until the time of the end' (Dan. 12: 4, 9; cf. 8: 26). The decisive course of events has long been prophesied, and now it is revealed to a few, because the events of the end, which affect everyone, are now imminent.

2   Knowledge from the past affects the future. 'The vision is for the time of the end' (Dan. 8: 17; cf. 2: 20ff.). The seer Enoch introduces his address about the coming day of judgement by saying 'it was not for the present generation that I was concerned, but for the future one' (1: 2). The apocalyptic vision reveals the secrets of the course of this world, and specially the date and the manner of them. Its subject is the course of this world and of history, and the hope of the future. 'For the world has lost its youth, and the times begin to grow old' (4 Ezra 14: 10). The decisive question is 'what has the future to bring, what is God doing at the end of time?'

The answer is given by visions, which paint a picture of coming events to a much higher degree than the prophetic predictions. The images are linked less (as in e.g. Amos 7; Jer. 1) to everyday occurrences, but rather portray the imaginary (Dan. 2: 31ff.) and include mythical material to a much greater extent. But the images often take the form of comparisons, which are already found in prophetic preaching (like symbols of animals and trees). Dreams or visions need interpretation, which is given by wise men or angels (Dan. 1: 17; 5: 11f.; 8: 15ff.; cf. Zech. 1: 9, 13ff.; and already Gen. 40f. et al.). Daniel 'can reveal mysteries' (2: 47) because 'the spirit of the holy gods' dwells in him (4: 6) and the God of heaven is able to reveal secrets (2: 28ff.; cf. Gen. 41: 38f.).

The images often fade away into ineffability: 'something that looked like' (Dan. 7: 13 et al.; cf. already Ezek. 1). While this brings out the impossibility of speaking precisely about the future, apocalyptic is in fact intended precisely to foresee the future, and even to fix its dates (Dan. 7: 25; 8: 14; 12: 7; esp. 9: 24ff.); for wickedness has its measure which will be full at the end (8: 23). On this later view world history runs its course from the beginning in fixed periods to its goal; every event has its place in the succession of ages (Enoch 85ff.; 93), so that events still in the future can be calculated. This thought of a world plan of God takes the prophetic proclamation further, that God has a plan in history (cf. Isa. 14: 27; 28: 29; 46: 11; also Eccles. 3: 14f.; 6: 10 et al.). Now the future is no longer given the character of the new (as in Isa. 43: 19, 'Behold, I am doing a new thing'), but of that which is already known; it can be known in just the same way that the past can.

Nevertheless the ways in which the future is conceived remain varied. There are more strongly this-worldly or other-worldly, national or universal expectations, hopes of the future both with and without a messianic kingdom, etc. Individual statements can diverge so much that they contradict one another and are mutually exclusive. It comes out at this point that they are built on different traditional materials. In particular, statements about the duration of the world vary. But the basic attitude with which history is encountered is uniform. The hope that a radical change is coming is common to all writers; it is only the exact form that is given different representations.

b DUALISM

One constant basic attitude is provided by a dualism of divine and human power, of future and present, of good and evil.

1   While the prophets originally threatened disaster to Israel and to its neighbouring nations (Amos 1f. et al) the judgement is later extended to all nations. Zechariah (1: 18–21 [Heb. 2: 1–14]) in his vision of the four horns which are destroyed by four smiths foresees that all nations who have destroyed the people of God will be cast down by God. The number four indicates the totality of the world; specific hostile powers are no longer in view. In the eschatological images of Zech. 12 and 14, which portray a war of the nations 'on that day' before Jerusalem, no names are given, and no reason is offered for the attack of the enemies and the end of distress. (But the coming action of God can be rescued from the reproach of arbitrariness by appeal to the guilt of man, so Isa. 24: 5f., 20; 26: 21.) So the transition from prophecy to apocalyptic brings with it a loss of history: future expectations more and more abandon their link with history. In losing their historical particularity, however, the events obtain a significance which goes far beyond that which they had as individual events. The historical is generalized, and the individual becomes universal. The proud city in the songs of the so-called Apocalypse of Isaiah (Isa. 25: 1ff.; 26: 1ff.) no longer has a name, but thereby becomes a symbol of the world city; or the covenant meal of the elders on Sinai (Exod. 24: 11) is expanded into a festal meal in which all the nations take part (Isa. 25: 6).

The expectations of a coming judgement, which take up the prophetic predictions of the future, heighten them and stretch them to cover a worldwide framework, fit into this context. While the prophets interpret the world history of their time, in which the great powers of the ancient Near East appear in Palestine, the apocalyptic view reaches beyond such particular details. Not only all living beings (Zeph. 1: 2f.) but also heaven itself (Isa. 24: 4, 21); cf. Ezek. 32: 7 et al.) are brought into the judgement. Earthly and heavenly enemies are disarmed, and nothing is left unaltered. Thus while history is extended infinitely, the whole world is brought into the expectations. History and cosmos are identified. The whole universe is determined and limited by the time which brings 'a new heaven and a new earth' (Isa. 65: 17). As the world becomes a unity in the face of the creator, so history becomes a unity in the face of the coming God.

The judgement, which is extended ever further by later apocalyptic literature, is carried out (as in the threats of the prophets) by Yahweh himself. Now however it is expected exclusively as an action of God. Once the nations 'furthered the disaster' (Zech. 1: 15), by carrying out God's will, as in the case of Assyria (Isa. 10: 5ff.) and Babylon (Jer. 51: 20ff.) and also Cyrus (Isa. 41: 25; 45: 1). Now God acts alone and directly, 'by no human hand' (Dan. 2: 34, 45; 8: 25). Again therefore the loss of history goes with an intensification of the theological concept. Divine and human power become mutually exclusive:

Autonomous human world politics, recognizable already at the time of Assyrian and Babylonian suzerainty, could nevertheless be given a place within the faith of Israel through being regarded as hybris towards a commission given by Yahweh, who used these world powers to punish and to show mercy to his people. But an Israel which was politically powerless as an element in the empire of a foreign power could only heal the discrepancy between autonomous worldly power and its faith in the kingship of God with the help of a dualistic conception; and it did so increasingly. It certainly cannot be disputed that a dualistic view of the world was not characteristic of the Old Testament; but it does not seem justified by the evidence to regard the appropriation of dualistic elements as a false move or as apostasy from the faith if in the wrestling of Israel's faith with a history which was slipping out of its grasp new impulses and strengths could be brought to its confession of faith with the help of a dualistic conceptuality. (O. Plöger, *Das Buch Daniel*, 1965, p. 125)

To express the cosmic relevance of coming events, eschatological and apocalyptic expectations take over mythological motifs; for myth, while it does not have a relationship with history and the individual, is cosmically oriented. Thus the fight with the sea monster can become a symbol of the destruction of the world powers (Isa. 27: 1). Mythological concepts are generally applied less to God himself than to the foreign powers, which they are intended both to conceal and to indicate (cf. Ezek. 31; Dan. 4 of the world tree; also Ezek. 29; 32 et al.). Myth has by now long since lost its original significance, and its concepts have been hardened into a few fixed images, which can be increasingly elaborated. This growing mythology is in large measure a stylistic device, which helps to describe the future and to portray its significance more exactly.

In the sequence of four world empires the visions of Daniel attempt to survey history as a whole. 'These four empires basically cover only the period from the exile to the end (cf. Dan. 1: 1ff.), but nevertheless they form 'history'; it is the time in which Israel was brought out of its own national limits, and incorporated into the wider world' (Volz, *Die Eschatologie der jüdischen Gemeinde*, p. 141).

The unity of history is represented in Dan. 2 by an enormous human statue, which from head to foot is first gold, then silver, then bronze, then clay and iron. We find fused together in this image three basically different concepts, which have not hitherto been encountered in this form in the Old Testament, but which Israel took over, whether separately or in part at least already conjoined. The world appears in the form of a man (i.e. the macrocosm in the microcosm), the ages of the world are represented by metals, and the world empires are reckoned as four in number. Daniel is no doubt thinking specifically of the dominion of the neo-Babylonians under Nebuchadnezzar, of the Medes, Persians and of Alexander the Great, whose empire was divided up between the Ptolemaids in Egypt and the Seleucids in Syria. In any case the image is given a temporal interpretation. However mighty each empire is, its time is limited (cf. Dan. 11: 24, 27). Everything has its time (Eccles. 3: 1), and this is the basic law of apocalyptic: 'for he has weighed the age in the balance, and measured the times by measure, and numbered the times by number' (4 Ezra 4: 36f.; 13: 57f.; Enoch 92: 2). Although the four empires follow one another, the whole enormous statue of the vision is destroyed at once 'by no human hand' (cf. Dan. 8: 25) by a falling stone, which grows to be a mountain filling the whole earth. It symbolizes the kingship of God, which destroys every human form of government, and puts an end not only to the last empire but to all human dominion.

In the vision of Dan. 7 the four empires are represented by four beasts which climb out of the sea. The last beast is the most important; it represents the present (in the person of Antiocnus IV), and is therefore described in the most detail. The description of the composite beasts, which is elaborated with yet more detail in a later writer (4 Ezra 11f.) may be dependent upon ancient Near Eastern concepts. These are the origin too of the imagery of the sea of chaos, which apparently serves to survey history from primeval time to the time of the end. After a heavenly court session the fourth beast is killed, but its three predecessors too are deprived of their dominion. In place of the dominion of the beasts we have one of a man. Dominion is given to one 'who has the appearance of a man'. Just as in most messianic prophecies the future king only appears when the war is over, so that he is active only as a prince of peace, so the Son of Man only appears when the hostile powers have been conquered. But his rule is of a heavenly kind. So he corresponds to the rule of the 'saints of the Most High' (7: 13, 18ff.) – originally the heavenly court, although now Israel in included under the name. It is set out much more strongly in apocalyptic vision than was emphasized in prophetic expectations that the future does not fall within the area of historical possibilities, but comes from above, and is brought in from the next world.

In both representations (Dan. 2 and 7) anything like historical development is to be seen at most in the sequence of the different empires, but here it is accomplished according to a previously made plan of God. One kingdom succeeds another, until the end breaks in. In these images we see the deterministic view of history which is adhered to ever more strongly later on by apocalyptic. The concepts used in the two visions are not identical: the metals decline in value and strength, while the animals increase each time in violence and cruelty. Nevertheless each empire is not described in the same terms. There is still room within their schematic presentation for the distinctive character of the individual historical phenomena, and room too therefore for alteration of the situation. But what is most important for the visions is the context of history in the face of its coming end: 'What (according to apocalyptic) gives world history its final unity amidst all its variety of different phenomena, is the fact that it stands face to face with the kingdom of God' (M. Noth, 'The Understanding of History in Old Testament Apocalyptic', in *The Laws in the Pentateuch and Other Studies*, Edinburgh, 1966, p. 214).

2   The antithesis between reign of God and of man is understood not exclusively, but predominantly, from a chronological viewpoint: now is the time of the evildoers, then the time of God will break in (Dan 8: 23; 11: 36). The present is delimited, the future is eternal. The present and coming ages are contrasted as two fundamentally different eras. The antithesis appears at first unspoken (for such concepts develop only gradually), but is later made explicit: 'For this reason the Most High has made not one world but two' (4 Ezra 7: 50).

The future that has been revealed is certainly coming, even if God allows a delay (Hab. 2: 2f.; Ps. 75: 3). Although the hopes of Deutero-Isaiah for the coming of the kingdom of God were not realized, his prophetic successors held fast to an imminent expectation (cf. Isa. 60: 1). Haggai, who lives in wretched economic circumstances instead of in the promised time of salvation, announces the end of the world in connection with the rebuilding of the temple and the appointment of Zerubbabel as Messiah (Hag. 2: 6–9, 20–3). Hope is again disappointed but seeks to remain hope. In spite of recurrent experiences of non-fulfilment, the later prophets each time connect their expectations with the signs of their times (cf. Joel 1: 2). The events of the present seem to indicate an imminent end, until they pass away and the end has still not come. The imminent expectation of Daniel is not fulfilled either in spite of its adjustment of the time indication (12: 11f.), but the warmth of the expectation is by no means diminished in subsequent apocalyptic literature.

Apocalyptic has then both taken up and altered the prophetic hope. While the prophets declare a future which presses into and determines the character of the present, apocalyptic distinguishes two ages, one superseding the other. The new age now means the end of the old, not just an alteration in it. But even here there are certain transitional links between prophecy and apocalyptic. Deutero-Isaiah's declarations about the future for instance go far beyond expectations within the course of history (Isa. 40: 4; 49: 9ff et al.). In the night visions of Zechariah (1: 7–6: 8) the change is so imminent that it is already present as realized in heaven: there all opposition is already overcome, and wickedness eliminated (5: 5–11). Apocalyptic takes these ideas further. The elements brought by salvation are already present in heaven, and came down from there ready made. Best known is the image of the heavenly Jerusalem (4 Ezra 7: 26; 13: 36; Rev. 21). The contrast of present and future comes out as a spatial contrast of above and below. Here we see the influence of ancient Near Eastern concepts of the correspondence of the heavenly and earthly order (above, §6b, 4). But this inherited mythology is characteristically reshaped. Instead of a parallel existence with one alongside or above the other, we come to have a temporal succession. Heaven is the future of the earth; salvation is all the more certain because it is already 'there'. While the ancient Near Eastern mythological concept originally served to guarantee the continuation of the present situation, in its new setting this world view actually announces the supersession of the present visible reality. The contrast is now stated in a dynamic and not a static form.

3   With the end of evildoing and sin the future brings 'everlasting righteousness' (Dan. 9: 24). The change of the times fits in with the antithesis of evil and good. The traditional general view connected God simply with salvation (Mic. 3: 11); otherwise Amos (3: 6) would not have needed to lead the people to the realization 'Does evil befall a city, unless Yahweh has done it?' But from early days an 'evil intent' could also be seen as coming from Yahweh (1 Sam. 16: 14; 19: 9; 1 Kgs. 22: 22; cf. §6b, 5). Good is however increasingly reserved to Yahweh, while the evil is embodied in a distinct personal power (cf. 2 Sam. 24: 1 with 1 Chr. 21: 1), in Satan, who originally only held the position of a tempter or accuser in the heavenly court, acting according to God's will (Job 1f.; Zech. 3: 1f.). Apocalyptic extends these ideas into an antithesis of the kingdom of evil and the reign of God.

   This dualism seems to have been strengthened in Israel under the influence of the Persian religion. This explained the world by the interplay of good and evil – later represented by Ormazd or Ahura Mazda, the creator of good, and the evil spirit Ahriman. Apocalyptic is basically an Israelite movement, which derives primarily from prophecy, but wisdom and other traditions (so G. von Rad) are also found in it. Among them are foreign influences too. The Israelites of the post-exilic period were subjects of the Persians both in Palestine and in the diaspora for two whole centuries, from Cyrus to Alexander the Great. So contacts with Persian religion are easily possible; and the concepts which appear in the late period of the Old Testament, like kingdom of God, resurrection, world judgement and teaching about angels, are well known in it. It is however difficult to establish the exact antiquity of the Iranian concepts; still less can the dependence of the Old Testament material upon them be clearly demonstrated. There are however certain similarities, perhaps some influences, and no doubt also the borrowing of particular motifs.

   But Persian dualism itself could be elevated to be a form of monotheism. Ahura Mazda was regarded as the lord of the worlds, who made heaven and earth and determined the way of the stars. In the Gathas of the Avesta, which present the preaching of Zarathustra in verse form, Ahura is even described as the creator of all things, of good and of evil, of light and of darkness:

   Zarathustra asks the good god: 'I am asking, tell me honestly, O lord of life: which master created light and darkness? Which master created sleep and waking?' (Yasna 44, 5, H. Humbach, *Die Gathas des Zarathustra* I, 1959, p. 117)

Deutero-Isaiah (if we may ignore problems of dating) could be taking up this very utterance, and in any case need not be uttering polemic against Persian dualism, when he makes God say:

I am Yahweh and there is no other.
I form light and create darkness,
  I make weal and create woe,
  I am Yahweh, who do all these things. (Isa. 45: 6–7)

Probably the prophet has reached his conception, in which he contrasts God to everything else with unusual sharpness, quite independently. The pair weal and woe, like heaven and earth, denote universality: God creates everything. The Old Testament understanding of God is expressed with extreme radicalness by this distinction of God and world. In the age of Hellenism the attempt was made to preserve this utterance about God, or even to intensify it, by taking up the causal concept (nothing comes out of nothing) and negating it: God made heaven, earth and what is in it 'out of what did not exist' (2 Macc. 7: 28 et al.).

4   The realm of death is not excepted from the universal power of God. When later apocalyptic took up the hope of resurrection (Dan. 12: 1–3; cf. below Excursus 8), this increasingly acquired universality:

In those days the earth will give back those who are gathered in it and Sheol also will give back what it has received, and hell will give up what is owes. (Enoch 51:1)

Mankind is to participate in the change of the world; but the future brings both weal and woe. The prophetic expectation of a judgement, extended to an examination of mankind, is taken over to apply in the afterlife:

For after death the judgement will come, when we shall live again; and then the names of the righteous will become manifest, and the deeds of the ungodly will be disclosed. There are more who perish than those who will be saved. (4 Ezra 14: 35; 9: 15)

It remains disputed who will take part in the future life, whether all or only the righteous. There are different concepts of what the new life will be like; they are increasingly influenced by the non-Old Testament antithesis of body and soul. Because resurrection no longer represents symbolically the reawakening of the nation (Ezek. 37), but is expected to be universal, it is at the same time understood individually. There is a connection, for judgement takes place according to the deeds of the individual. The unity of the nation had to break up, perhaps, before the individual longed for life after death. So the hope of resurrection is at the same time strengthened by the problem of the righteousness of God:

does God keep faith with those who are faithful to him in life all the way to death? Faith does not rest content with the view that earthly circumstances are determined and unalterable, as the Preacher laments that they are (Eccles. 3: 19ff.; 9: 2ff.).

5   Apocalyptic hopes do not therefore simply withdraw from the present by fleeing into a glorious future, to leave the world to evil. They are meant to give consolation in time of oppression, and to give courage to persevere (cf. Dan. 3; 6). Faith can bear suffering with composure, for the oppression will not last long. Its end is already in sight: this is why we have the chronological calculations (esp. Dan. 12: 7, 11f.). Although all hope is directed to a final act of God, it is not only the future that belongs to God. The legends of the book of Daniel have as their goal the acknowledgement of God by the king of Babylon (2: 46f.; 3: 28f.; 4: 29; 5: 18ff.; 6: 26f.). His power is limited by God's almighty power (4: 14; 5: 26ff.). So the reign of God is not only in prospect after the time of wrath, but is already shown in the present.

His kingdom is an everlasting kingdom,
    and his dominion is from generation to generation.
                               (Dan. 3: 33; 4: 31ff.; 6: 27)

EXCURSUS 8: DEATH AND HOPE IN THE FACE OF DEATH

1   In the course of human life certain occasions and events, the transitions from one status to another (especially the beginning and end of life, the change from childhood to adult status, marriage, but also seedtime, harvest and the New Year) are especially liable to mythological interpretation and are surrounded by specific rites (called by A. van Gennep *rites de passage*). Death is one such zone of transition. In consequence either death or the realm of the dead has a certain power over the living in most cultures. This is attested indirectly by burial objects, and directly by literary evidence. On the other hand a strong reserve is felt in the Old Testament even towards the offering of food to the dead (cf. Deut. 26: 14) and still more towards the worship of the dead. Not even the king, who in Egyptian belief was identical with the deity after his death (Osiris), received divine honours in Israel (cf. the royal psalms 89: 48f.; 144: 3; also above §12a).

The concept of a life after death was not therefore impossible in the Old Testament period. Egyptian religion was strongly dominated by the expectation of a judgement in the next world, and there was an extensive collection of proverbial literature provided for the dead (the pyramid texts, sarcophagus texts, Book of the Dead). While the Egyptians hoped for participation by the king and later by all men in the fate of Osiris, in Mesopotamia, as in Syria-Palestine, a belief in resurrection in particular is not demonstrable, though concepts of an afterlife are by no means lacking (Gilgamesh, Inanna-Ishtar, Tammuz). The return of the dead god (e.g. Ba'al) to earth was not equated with the fate of man (cf. above, §11c, 2). If foreign influences are to be held to have had any effect in the development of a hope of the resurrection in the later Old Testament at all, they are to be looked for rather in Parseeism.

There may have been necromancy (inquiry of the dead) here and there in Israel, because the spirit of the dead man could be regarded by popular belief as a personal being with extraordinary knowledge hidden from man (1 Sam. 28: 7f., 13; cf. Isa. 8: 19; 19: 3), but conjuration of the dead, like sorcery, was prohibited and threatened with the death-penalty (Lev. 19: 31, 28; 20: 6, 27; Deut. 18: 10f.; 2 Kgs. 21: 6; 23: 24 et al.).

Accordingly Saul, who in his fear of death contravenes his own prohibition (1 Sam. 28: 3, 9) and compels the so-called Witch of Endor to call up the spirit of the dead Samuel, only learns what he suspects in any case: 'Yahweh has torn the kingdom out of your hand ... tomorrow you and your sons shall be with me (i.e. with the dead)' (vv. 17–19; cf. 15: 28).

So it can be said with G. von Rad, 'as far as we can see back into the history, Yahwism turned with a special intolerance against all forms of the cult of the dead'. 'It would still be quite wrong on the one hand to set too little store on the temptation which emanated from this sphere, or, on the other, to underestimate the power of self-restraint which Israel had to call into being in order to renounce all sacral communion with her dead'. 'Yahwism ... was particularly zealous in stripping death of the dignity allowed it in myth' (*Old Testament Theology*, Edinburgh and London, vol. 1, 1962, pp. 276f.; vol. 2, 1965, p 349).

This critical attitude undoubtedly results from faith in the God who manifests himself in history and claims exclusiveness of worship for himself (cf. Deut. 18: 9ff.). Like turning to other gods, inqury of the dead is a transgression of the first commandment. The lordship of God over the living excludes any dominion of the dead over them (whether to the detriment or to the advantage of the living), and the Old Testament declares the whole realm of death to be unclean (Num. 19: 11ff.; Lev. 11: 24ff.).

2   It was no doubt this critical reserve towards the realm of the dead tnat at first did not permit the Old Testament to integrate the problem of death in another way into its faith; a strict dissociation from the cult of the dead means reserve in respect of conceptions of the state of man after death, and so left little room for hope in the face of death.

Possibly certain concepts of resurrection, such as can perhaps be deduced from Hos. 6: 1–3 (cf. above, §11c, 3) and rather more from Ezek. 37, were known to Israel. Certainly it took over mythological concepts well known from the world around – of the tree of life, the herb of life or the water of life – only in allusions (Gen. 3: 22) or as metaphors (Prov. 3: 18; 11: 30; 13: 14; cf. Jer. 2: 13 et al.), and so did not really provide a mythological foundation to the mortality of man.

On the other hand Israel's concepts of death seem in general to have existed already in the ancient Near East, and not originally to have been much permeated by Israel's own faith. In consequence quite different ideas about the dead can exist side by side unassimilated. The expression 'lie with' or 'be gathered to one's fathers' (Gen. 47: 30; 49: 29 et al.) suggests that the dead person is united with his ancestors (in the same family grave?). But we also find the expression 'to go down to the realm of the dead, or the underworld' (37: 35 et al.), in which the dead lead a bare shadowy existence as 'spirits of the dead' (Ps. 88: 11; Isa, 26: 14, 19; cf. 8: 19; 29: 4). The individual grave and the mythological and cosmic underworld overlap as conceptions; and 'earth,' 'grave' or 'dust' are usually periphrases for the life-denying realm in the depths of the earth.

In any case the gulf between the world of the dead and that of the living is disturbingly deep. Death robs man of what he has laboriously obtained (Ps. 49: 18; Job 1: 21; 15: 29; cf. Matt. 6: 19f. et al.) and separates him from any kind of fellowship. Since in the underworld 'there is no work or thought or knowledge or wisdom' (Eccles. 9: 10), a father when he is dead does not even learn how his children fare in their subsequent life:

> His sons come to honour, and he does not know it;
> they are brought low, and he perceives it not. (Job 14: 21)

But the dead man too disappears fairly quickly from the memory of his descendants. So the underworld is called 'the land of forgetfulness' (Ps. 88: 12 [Heb. 88: 13]); cf. 31: 12 [Heb. 31: 13]). Not only fellowship with family and nation but even fellowship with God ceases:

> For Sheol cannot thank thee,
>   death cannot praise thee;
> those who go down to the pit cannot hope
>   for thy faithfulness.
> The living, only the living, he thanks thee.
> (Isa. 38: 18f.; cf. Ps. 6: 5 [Heb. 6: 6]; 30: 9 [Heb. 30: 10]; 115: 17 et al.)

God's presence is primarily in the place where men tell 'what good he has done' (Ps. 103: 2; cf. 22: 22 [Heb. 22: 23ff.] et al.). The dead cannot share the praise of the works of God:

> Dost thou work wonders for the dead?
>   Do the shades rise up to praise thee?
> Is thy steadfast love declared in the grave,
>   or thy faithfulness in Abaddon?
> Are thy wonders known in the darkness,
>   or thy saving help in the land of forgetfulness?
>   (Ps. 88: 10–12 [Heb. 88: 11–13])

3   So the Old Testament speaks in a remarkably sober way about death, without any illusions, as the 'way of all the earth' (Josh. 23: 13; 1 Kg. 2: 2), the land from

which there is no return (2 Sam. 12: 23; 14: 14; Job 7: 9f.; 16: 22 et al.). It is only with the end of life that the wearisomeness of life itself has an end:

> The years of our life are threescore and ten,
>   or even by reason of strength fourscore;
> yet their span [literally, pride] is but toil and trouble.
>
> (Ps. 90: 10; cf. Gen. 3: 19)

Therefore death brings the whole hopelessness of existence before man's eyes. Human life with its transitoriness is like the world of nature. Indeed it is even worse for man than for nature; for a tree has more grounds for hope than man:

> Man that is born of a woman
>   is of few days, and full of trouble.
> He comes forth like a flower, and withers;
>   he flees like a shadow and continues not ...
> For there is hope for a tree,
>   if it be cut down, that it will sprout again ...
> Though its root grow old in the earth,
>   and its stump die in the ground,
> yet at the scent of water it will bud
>   and put forth branches like a young plant.
> But man dies, and is laid low ...
> So man lies down and rises not again. (Job 14: 1f.. 7–12)

Not only social distinctions but even differences in ethical and religious behaviour are destroyed by death. Only in one respect do the living have an advantage; it consists for the Preacher precisely in the foreknowledge of death, namely, living with death in view:

> One fate comes to all,
> to the righteous and the wicked ...
> to the clean and the unclean,
> to him who sacrifices and him who does not sacrifice.
> As is the good man, so is the sinner;
> and he who swears is as he who shuns an oath ...
> He who is joined with all the living has hope,
> for a living dog is better than a dead lion.
> For the living know that they will die;
> but the dead know nothing,
> and they have no more reward;
> but the memory of them is lost. (Eccles. 9: 2–5; cf. 3: 19ff.)

For the Old Testament man is a unity, not an immortal soul in a transitory body: 'you are dust, and to dust you shall return' (Gen. 3: 19; cf. 18: 27; Ps. 90: 3; 103: 14 et al.). What leaves man at death is not the immortal soul, but the life-force sent by God (104: 29; cf. Gen. 2: 7 with 6: 3; Job 33: 4 with 34: 14f.).

Who knows
whether the spirit of man goes upward
and the spirit of the beast goes down to the earth?
(Eccles. 3: 21; cf. 3: 19; 12: 7)

Does this sceptical question of the Preacher remain within the bounds of the old view, or is he (like the Sadducees later, cf. Luke 20: 27) already rejecting the Hellenistic view that the 'spirit' 'goes up' to heaven after the death of a man?

Certainly the hope of the resurrection, which in the New Testament can appear as the presupposition of faith and of all talk of God (cf. 1 Cor. 15: 32) is largely alien to the Old Testament. Hebrews interprets Abraham's difficult journey to the altar to sacrifice his only son by saying 'by faith Abraham. when he was tested, offered up Isaac . . . He considered that God was able to raise men even from the dead' (Heb. 11: 17–19). But the Abraham of the Old Testament submits to the command of God because he 'fears God' (Gen. 22: 12), that is, in believing obedience without hope in a resurrection.

4 Nevertheless death is thought about from the viewpoint of faith; the Old Testament has no knowledge of an impersonal fate: 'Thou turnest man back to the dust' (Ps. 90: 3, 7f.). Even for the Preacher man remains 'in the hand of God' (Eccles. 9: 1; cf. 2: 24ff.; 3: 10ff.; above §15, 6). As life is God's creation (Gen. 1f.; Ps 36: 9 [Heb. 36: 10] et al.), so death is God's dispensation. 'Israel did not know death as in any way an independent mythical power – death's power was at bottom the power of Yahweh himself. Death was no last enemy, but Yahweh's acting upon men' (G. von Rad, *Old Testament Theology*, vol. 1, Edinburgh and London, 1962, p. 390). So even a faith which knows only of this life, and has no concept of a fellowship with God after death, does not have simply to remain silent in the face of death (Ps. 90; Job 1: 21; 2: 19 et al.).

This realization was however the result of intense debates. A number of passages still suggest that demons were regarded as the cause of sickness and death; though they are now subordinated to Yahweh and fulfil his will (Num. 21: 6ff.; Hos. 13: 14; Ps. 78: 49; 2 Sam. 24: 15f. et al.; cf. above, §6b, 5). Death too can appear occasionally as a being which acts of its own accord and is almost personal (Isa. 5: 14; Jer. 9: 20 et al.); once, drawing on ancient Near Eastern conceptions, which lived on later in the Greco-Roman world, of the Lord of the Underworld, he is even called 'the king of terrors' (Job 18: 14; cf. Ps. 94: 20). The view implicit in this title is however only developed in the post-Old Testament apocalyptic.

The psalmist can pray to God for insight into the transience of life (Ps. 39: 4 [Heb. 39: 5]; 90: 11f.), and the man who has come near to death but has escaped it gives thanks:

Yahweh, thou hast brought up my soul from Sheol,
restored me to life from among those gone down to the Pit.
(Ps. 30: 3 [Heb. 30: 4]; cf. 16: 10; 18: 4ff. [Heb. 18: 5ff.]; 33: 19; 56: 13
[Heb. 56: 14]; 103: 4; 116: 8; Jonah 2: 3 et al.)

Are such statements metaphorical and non-literal, and exaggerated perhaps as a matter of poetic style, or are they intended literally? Different answers are given by the commentators. Undoubtedly the psalmist was not in the strict sense dead; nevertheless the man praying who speaks in this way certainly does not mean only that he has escaped from the danger of death, and does not mean to speak only of ideas of death; but of the reality of it. This is possible because death is seen as a power which is at work already in life, in sickness, infirmity, persecution, in brief in loneliness and in alienation from God. The power of death is seen already when death is near (Ps. 88: 3 [Heb. 88: 4]; 107: 18 et al; cf. C. Barth, *Die Errettung vom Tode in den individuellen Klage- und Dankliedern des Alten Testamentes*, Basel, 1947). Declarations such as

Yahweh kills and brings to life;
  he brings down to Sheol and raises up.
Yahweh makes poor and makes rich;
  he brings low and also exalts. (1 Sam. 2: 6f. et al.)

are thinking primarily of deliverance from this power of death that intrudes upon life, but (as if in concrete application of the first commandment to the full breadth or even the polarity of human existence) they recognize the sole responsibility of the one God for both death and life.

5 As a whole it is characteristic of the Old Testament that this present earthly life in spite of its transitoriness is accepted with joy and thankfulness from God, and is lived in the face of God. Nevertheless this 'unity of this world and the next' is gradually lost or transcended. The confession 'thy steadfast love is better than life' (Ps. 63: 3 [Heb. 63: 4]) splits up reality between faith and experience.

Originally it was possible to be content with the knowledge that on the death of the individual the nation as a community continues, and the individual lives on in the memory of posterity (Prov. 10: 7; Ps. 112: 6; cf. 34: 16 [Heb. 34: 17]; Eccles. 9: 5), in his own descendants (Ruth 4: 10; Sir. 30: 4ff.) or upon a monument (Isa. 56: 5). But it was not possible always, especially as the close relationship of the individual to the national community began to be loosened, to remain content with such answers, which are ultimately provisional. However the new expectations develop from various different starting points.

Obedience is promised long life (Exod. 20: 12; Deut. 4: 40; Lev. 18: 5; Prov. 3: 1ff.; 10: 27 et al.). The king is greeted with the acclamation 'Long live the king' (1 Kgs. 1: 25ff.; cf. Ps. 21: 5 et al.). An early death is regarded as a punishment (1 Sam. 2: 32; cf. Gen. 38: 7; Jer. 28: 16f., Ps. 55: 23 [Heb. 55: 24] et al.), and it is said of a few especially blessed men that they died old and full of years (Gen. 25:

8; 35: 29; Job 42: 17 et al.). This remark which is only made in retrospect, certainly does not express the general or the only possible expectation in life. But the hope that is present in such utterances is later extended to everyone and vividly pictured. Thus it is said of the new future Jerusalem:

Old men and old women shall again sit
  in the streets of Jerusalem,
each with staff in hand
  for very age. (Zech. 8: 4; cf. 12: 8)
No more shall be heard in it
  the sound of weeping and the cry of distress.
No more shall there be in it
  an infant that lives but for a few days,
  or an old man who does not fill out his days;
for the child shall die a hundred years old.

(Isa. 65: 19f.; cf. 66: 7ff.; 49: 20f.)

Indeed in the future messianic kingdom peace will be so universal that even the beasts will no longer shed blood; the lamb and the wolf, the calf and the lion, the child and the snake can play with one another (Isa. 11: 6ff.; 65: 25). Death is certainly not thereby eliminated, but a hope in a life without bloodshed is expressed, in a way similar to the hope that is common to the Zion tradition and to prophecy that God will destroy all weapons (Ps. 46: 9 [Heb. 46: 10]; Hos. 2: 18 [Heb. 2: 20]; Zech. 9: 10; cf. Isa. 2: 4; 9: 5 [Heb. 9: 4] et al.).

6   The starting point and the justification for the emergent hope against death is the confession (which is in accordance with the principles of the first commandment), that even the realm of the dead is not withdrawn from the power of God: 'If I make my bed in Sheol, thou are there' (Ps. 139: 8; cf. Amos 9: 2; Hos. 13: 14; Job 11: 7f. also Isa. 7: 11). 'Sheol and Abaddon lie open before Yahweh' (Prov. 15: 11), 'naked and with no covering' (Job 26: 6).

Job on one occasion expresses this hope in a paradoxical form. In his desperate situation he cannot (as in the psalms of lamentation) long for preservation from death. Job can only pray God to hide him in the underworld; there, in the remotest corner, man seems to find rest until God's wrath has passed by. Nevertheless at this time the gracious God is asked to remember Job, in the land in which men do not remember God:

Oh that thou wouldest hide me in Sheol,
  that thou wouldest conceal me until thy wrath be past,
  that thou wouldest appoint me a set time, and remember me!

(Job 14: 13)

This utterance, which is most unusual for the Old Testament, is marked by a double paradox: God is to bring Job to the place which is not under his dominion, in order to intervene and help him there, where strictly he can no longer help. Job voluntarily wishes for death for himself, or at least a sojourn in the realm of death, but also for return from death. Certainly the boundary of death is not now finally crossed – the man thus delivered remains mortal (cf. 1 Kgs. 17: 17ff.; 2 Kgs. 4: 18ff.) – but it has lost something of its harshness and finality. Man now dares to think, to believe and ultimately also to hope in a realm which is inaccessible to the living.

It follows as a consequence of this approach that God's dominion extends also to the inhabitants of the underworld. According to Job 26: 5 they no longer live in total apathy, but feel fear of God. In a later addition to Ps. 22 (vv. 27–31 [Heb. 28–32]) the confession of the exclusive dominion of God even leads to a correction of the old idea that the dead do not praise God, and so cannot acknowledge God's might:

Yea, to him shall all the proud of the earth bow down;
before him shall bow all who go down to the dust.
(Ps. 22: 29 [Heb. 22: 30])

In consequence all the dead also are to participate in the kingdom of God, into which all the nations are drawn. Referring to the same traditio-historical context – God's reign over the whole world – the so-called Apocalypse of Isaiah promises a banquet which Yahweh as king upon Zion is preparing for all nations and with which he will bring the end of all sorrow (Isa. 24: 21–3; 25: 6–8). Here must be included too in the view of a later editor victory over death:

He will swallow up death for ever. (Isa. 25: 8; cf. 26: 19)

In this way the older hope that God will destroy all that does harm to man (be it wild beasts or weapons) in order to prevent the shedding of blood once for all, is taken over in a radically altered form: death is not only postponed in that the early death of a man is prevented, but is finally abolished, so that there is an end to the worst form of suffering upon earth. Death is no longer understood as a fate sent by God, but (with an accentuation of the old concepts which speak of the power of death) as the antithesis of God, and the statement of 1 Cor. 15: 26 that death is an enemy which is defeated by God, is not far away.

Ps. 73 goes one step further than these beliefs in that it not only expects the subjugation of the dead or of death to God's dominion, but (although only for the individual; cf. of the servant of God Isa. 53: 8ff.) also a communion with God which is retained in death:

Nevertheless I am *continually* with thee:
thou dost hold my right hand.

Thou dost guide me with thy counsel,
and *afterward* thou wilt receive me to glory.
Whom have I in heaven but thee?
And there is nothing upon earth that I desire besides thee.
My flesh and my heart may fail . . .
but God . . . is my portion for ever.
(Ps. 73: 23–6; cf. 49: 15 [Heb. 49: 16])

In this psalm faith and experience, trust in God and earthly good fortune are separated; he contrasts the true fate of the godless and of the man that trusts in God as he believes them to be with the perceptible fate as it can be seen. Even if one's personal fate contradicts this, even if 'flesh and heart', that is, individual existence and will, fail, communion with God cannot be lost (cf. Job 19: 25f.; 'even without my flesh I shall see God'). This means not as in most psalms of lamentation or thanksgiving preservation from death, but preservation in death. The 'hereafter' (in connection with the idea of a 'translation', cf. Gen. 5: 24; 2 Kgs. 2) is just hinted at, but not described. Similarly echoes are heard of the tradition of the heavenly court, robbed of its mythological form, and it serves to describe the relationship between God and the man praying the psalm as exclusive and unique. Detailed conceptions of life after death are not to be found. The expectation no doubt takes seriously an older confession like 'thy steadfast love and thy faithfulness will ever preserve me' (Ps. 40: 11 [Heb. 40: 12]; cf. 23: 6 et al.) in the face of death. In any case it is not replaced by the development of colourful pictures of afterlife, but is content with the hope in the power of God, and so comes into opposition to human experience.

In language which has a genuinely Old Testament character Dan. 12: 2 as it is universally understood announces a resurrection of the dead in the strict sense, which however is not available to all men, but remains restricted to Israel. But even the people of God will not in its totality experience glory, as the prophets have already threatened; the saved are written in the Book of Life:

And many of those who sleep in the dust of the earth shall awake, some to everlasting life, and some to shame and everlasting contempt. (Dan. 12: 2; cf. 2 Macc. 7: 9; above, §14b, 4)

Usually the roots of the hope of an afterlife that emerges in the later stages of the Old Testament are traced to belief in a recompense for the individual or in God's righteousness or faithfulness, which holds fast even in death to the man who in his life trusted in God. Undoubtedly this motif is decisive in cases where the resurrection of the individual or of groups is expected (Dan. 12: 3; 11: 33; cf. Ps. 73). But the confession of the exclusivity of the power of God which took a specific form in the first commandment must not be forgotten as a prime factor in giving rise to a hope running counter to death, since this exclusivity can tolerate no power alongside itself, and therefore on the one hand integrates death as being the work of God himself, and on the other hand incorporates the dead within the dominion of God and thereby overcomes death itself (Isa. 25: 8). Foreign (especially Iranian) influences do not need to be denied here, even though they remain very uncertain, especially since the Old Testament undoubtedly did also take over ancient Near Eastern concepts of death. In any case the Old Testament brings its faith into action against death too, and in its future expectation breaks through the barrier which has often been turned into a reproach against it, the this-worldly character of its beliefs.

§17 The Old Testament inheritance

1 'That irrational element which made the religion of Yahweh take the route from the religion of a nomadic tribe to being a world religion' (G. Fohrer, 'Das Geschick des Menschen nach dem Tode im Alten Testament', *KuD* 14 (1968)) is made intelligible by the first commandment. First it distinguishes the faith of the Old Testament from neighbouring religions, and secondly it forms the criterion by which Israel chose and recast those concepts which it made its own from among the many in the world around it. The first commandment is essentially at work even in places where it is not actually stated. It governs extensive parts of the Old Testament, if not even all of them, and thus represents in effect the common point of unity, the integrating centre. The Old Testament tries to speak in such a way of God (and also of man, cf. Ps. 16: 2; 51: 4 [Heb. 51: 6]; 73: 25 et al.) that the first commandment is upheld. This is true of debate with other religions, of the understanding of nature and its gifts, of the interpretation given of past history and of the present with its politics, and still more in the expectation of the future.

The faith of the Old Testament seeks to meet the challenge of each new situation by measuring it against the first commandment and interpreting it by this. The commandment is a sort of connecting thread or signpost in the understanding of reality, and a criterion in the interpretation of changing human experiences. In the ever varying patterns of history what is seen as vital is to preserve the exclusivity of the faith.

In consequence the significance of the first commandment can hardly be overvalued, even when its consequences are by no means obvious beforehand, nor are given and once for all, but become clearer only very gradually. The faith of the Old Testament too has its history (above, §1).

2 In the course of this history Israel saw ever more clearly the distinction between its God and the gods of the world around. The challenge of the first commandment at first excluded the worship of other gods only for believers in Yahweh; in time however the cult of all foreign gods whatsoever was mocked and condemned, even when practised by other nations. The expansion of the first (and second) commandment made other gods into 'nothings'. Hosea already attacks images of gods, because they are are made by men (8: 4, 6; 13: 2). The late period of the Old Testament describes the foreign 'gods of silver and gold' as 'the work of men's hands' (Deut. 4: 28; 2 Kgs. 19: 18; Jer. 1: 16; 25: 6f. et al.) and ironically describes the making of their images (in additions in the prophetic

books, Isa. 2: 8, 18, 20; 17: 8; 31: 7; 40: 19f.; 41: 6f.; 44: 9ff.; Jer. 10; Hab. 2: 18f. et al.). 'Can man make for himself gods? Such are no gods!' (Jer. 16: 20). In such descriptions faith in God and rational thought have joined forces to create a common front. The older period would not have been affected by this criticism; for it the image was not identical with the deity (above, §6c, 4). Later God and the world are so distinguished that nothing this-worldly can be any longer divine. So the superiority of the Israelite and Jewish faith in one single God who cannot be worshipped in an image to any sort of polytheism is proclaimed in the polemic against idols (cf. Dan. 3).

Nevertheless the Old Testament has probably never strictly denied the existence of gods in the plural. It regarded the gods not as nothing, but as good for nothing; it does not deny their existence but their power and effectiveness. The decisive question is 'what can other gods do?', not 'Are there other gods?'

> Who fashions a god
> or casts an image, that is profitable for nothing? (Isa. 44: 10)

The intercessor casts himself down before the self-made idol and beseeches him, 'Deliver me, for thou art my god!' (Isa. 44: 17). However loud he cries however 'it does not answer or save him from his trouble' (46: 7). The measure therefore by which the Old Testament tests the divinity of the gods is whether they are able to help, so that human trust in them is justified (cf. Hab. 2: 18; Jer. 2: 28; 11: 12). But the gods are not even able to do what men are capable of. It is said of the images that

> They have mouths, but do not speak;
> eyes, but do not see.
> They have ears, but do not hear;
> noses, but do not smell.
> They have hands, but do not feel;
> feet, but do not walk;
> and they do not speak a sound in their throat.
> (Ps. 115: 5–7; 135: 15ff.; Deut. 14: 28; Dan. 5: 23)

We undoubtedly hear in this utterance again the enlightened thought of the late period, which does not affect the faith of the 'Gentiles', because they believe their gods capable of precisely what is here simply denied. But the criterion which is applied to the idols is in each case the same: they are judged by their actions (Isa. 41: 24: 'your work is naught'). If they have organs of the body they cannot use them. Otherwise Hebrew thought measures material things by what they achieve; it embraces organ and function, being and action as a unity. Almost against its own will it here tears apart the connection of organ and activity. The reality remains however the standard. The images of gods have no 'spirit' (Jer. 10: 14; 51: 17; Hab. 2: 19; Ps. 135: 17), that is, neither breath nor life, and therefore no ability to achieve anything. Because they do not have the strength for action, they are 'no god', 'breath', 'deception' or even 'nothing' in comparison with the creator (Deut. 32: 21; Isa. 41: 29; Ps. 96: 5; 97: 7 et al.)

3   The Old Testament poses the same question to its own God. The actions of Yahweh and of the foreign gods can be compared (Exod. 15: 11ff.; Deut. 4: 32ff.; 32: 37ff. et al.). Hosea reports as a word of God:

> I am Yahweh your God
>   from the land of Egypt;
> you know no God but me,
>   and besides me there is not helper.   (13: 4)

The demand for exclusivity of the first commandment appears here as an assurance of God's helping presence.

In the introduction to the Decalogue too, 'I am Yahweh, your God', the emphasis rests primarily upon God's gracious assurance. The laws follow from it; they grow out of the authority to which the assurance lays claim. So the demand that the first commandment makes upon the activity of man should not be misunderstood as meaning that the Old Testament is basically legal in character.

Hosea can say simply 'helper' in parallel to God; for the Old Testament being God means precisely being able to intervene. So Deutero-Isaiah takes up this message: 'besides me there is no helper' (Isa. 43: 11; cf. 45: 21; 46: 4 et al.). The divinity of God is shown in the power which he exercises upon earth. The prophet does not however simply presuppose this, but tries to make it intelligible to his listeners in his disputation sayings (40: 12ff.) with clear arguments:

> All the nations are as nothing before him,
>   they are accounted by him as less than nothing and emptiness.
>
>   (Isa. 40: 17)

That the existence of the nations is not denied by this confession is shown by the parallel sentence in the simile, which is meant to make the negation here imaginable by the strong contrasts it draws:

> Behold, the nations are like a drop from a bucket,
>   and are accounted as the dust on the scales.   (v. 15)

Just as a drop of water does not increase the amount of water in a bucket, and as dust does not alter the balance of the scales, so the nations 'are accounted' as nothing before God; for they are not capable of doing anything. The word 'nothing' denies the capacity to act, not the very existence of its subject. 'What is real?' is answered by asking 'What is effective?'. Similarly history is the criterion of truth for Deutero-Isaiah in his lawcourt oracles: who has said the right word and by it announced what is happening (41: 2ff.; 43: 9; 48: 14)? Just as God's spirit makes the judges leaders in war, so the Persian king Cyrus is capable of world dominion because Yahweh has raised him up.

Deutero-Isaiah's precursors do not proclaim God as salvific but as the bringer of disaster, but still as effective power. Their message is that now the time for God's intervention has come (Amos. 3: 2, 6; 5: 18ff. *et saep*). Isaiah proclaims woe to his contemporaries because 'they do not regard the deeds of Yahweh, or see the work of his hand' (5: 12; cf. 5: 19).

The psalter has a similar point to make. A hymn says of God:

Bless Yahweh, O my soul,
and forget not all his benefits. (Ps. 103: 2)

The psalms of lamentation turn in prayer to God, to cry 'What are you doing?' (Ps. 13; 22), the psalms of thanksgiving tell what God has done and the psalms of confidence what he is doing that man should trust in him (Ps. 23). When their enemies make objection to the intercessor, 'Where is your God?' (42: 3 [Heb. 42: 4]), they are not inquiring where he dwells, but about the appearance of his helping power. Where doubt about God just once appears in the Old Testament ('Yahweh will not do good, nor will he do ill', Zeph. 1: 12; cf. Mal. 2: 17; 3: 14f.), it does not affect his existence, 'Is there a God?', but 'What can he do?' (Ps. 14; cf. 10: 4, 11). Finally Ps. 115: 3 (cf. 135:6; Jonah 1: 14) opposes the nations with the confession 'he does whatever he pleases'. In order to bear witness to God's freedom his activity is referred to. (So Luther's translation, 'he can do whatever he pleases' is justified; cf. Dan. 4: 29; Rom. 4: 21.)

The reality of God is discovered and confessed as being activity. God's being is action, and his action is being. Ps. 103 speaks alternately of God's epithets and of his actions:

Yahweh works vindication
and justice for all who are oppressed. (v. 6)

Yahweh is merciful and gracious,
slow to anger and abounding in steadfast love. (v. 8)

˙ In such a sentence the Old Testament speaks unusually for once of God not by describing his acts, but by describing (under wisdom influence) the essential nature of God in a fundamental way which is both generally and permanently valid (cf. Exod. 34: 6f. et al.; also above, §6b, 4). But even then God's properties are understood as being his deeds, so that the psalm can continue:

He does not deal with us according to our sins,
nor requite us according to our iniquities. (v. 9 [Heb. v. 10])

Because the Old Testament makes confession of God as effective power, it understands God through his relationship to man and to the world. Only in statements about God which directly or indirectly include man and the world can this nature of God be recognized and expressed. The first sentence of the creation narrative, 'In the beginning God created the heavens and the earth' (Gen. 1: 1), has no beginning of God to narrate, as do the theogonic myths from Israel's neighbours, but starts with the event, 'God created the world'. No previous event is touched upon. Certainly in the doxology God's everlasting character before the world can be proclaimed:

> Before the mountains were brought forth,
>   or ever thou hadst formed the earth and the world,
>   from everlasting to everlasting thou art God. (Ps. 90: 2)

But even this sentence is not really intended to state God's preexistence, how he is 'of himself', but addresses God as the enduring ground of confidence, upon whom everyone at every time can rely (cf. Ps. 102: 25ff. [Heb. 102: 26ff.]). Similarly Deutero-Isaiah (40: 12ff.) urgently emphasizes God's incomparability, so that those in despair can learn to hope again.

4   The anthropomorphisms of the Old Testament too can be understood from this didactic purpose. They make it possible to speak of God in connection with man, and so to conceive of the reality of God in connection with time, while it is said of the ineffective idols that 'they speak not, they see not, they hear not', that is, they cannot enter into particular events. So the anthropomorphisms are not only intended to confirm that God encounters men personally; they make it possible to understand God's existence as a historical one. This comes out clearly in passages which tell us that what God does and so what God is like is not eternally fixed, but alters with time. He negotiates with Abraham about his treatment of Sodom (Gen. 18: 17ff.). Because of Moses' objection and intercession he changes his mind: 'And Yahweh repented of the evil which he thought to do to his people' (Exod. 32: 14 et al.).

The election of the first king Saul or of the city of Jerusalem is later withdrawn (1 Sam. 15; 2 Kgs. 23: 27). According to the preaching of the prophets, foreign nations which Yahweh originally takes into service are later rejected by him (Isa. 10: 5ff.; Jer. 51: 20ff.).

Further through the change in the names of God in the Pentateuch the Old Testament attests on a bigger scale too a knowledge of changes in God from the time of the patriarchs to the entry, although it confesses the identity of the gods of the fathers with the God of Sinai. A similar profound change is brought by prophecy, which proclaims the relationship of God and nation (Hos. 1: 9) and expects it anew from the future (Jer. 31: 31ff.). The historical realization that Israel's understanding of God develops and has a history from the prehistoric nomadic period through the life in the land of civilization down to the Jewish period simply states more pointedly what the Old Testament itself says. People have not always thought the same of God. Nor could this be otherwise if the Old Testament were to express the reality of God in relationship to man. If then we are not content just to state the change in beliefs about God, we must conclude that God has a history in the Old Testament because he is understood historically. The confession of God's reality as activity leads to the realization of the historical character of God. It is therefore not true for the Old Testament that it is God and eternity that go together rather than God and history; for just this antithesis of eternity and time is alien to the Old Testament. 'Eternity' means rather duration and continuance in time, so to speak an intensive transitoriness.

This perhaps also hints at what is the outer limit to talk of God's historicality. Man experiences his temporality in the face of death; but the Old Testament makes the confession 'Thou art the God that dost not die' (Hab. 1: 12; above, §11c, 4); trust in him can endure. At other points too the anthropomorphisms of the Old Testament have their limits; just as sexual concepts are kept away from God, the all too human is kept distant from him as well (e.g. Ps. 50: 12f.).

5 In the course of history it can constantly be observed that the Old Testament generalizes what was originally true only of an individual. The prophetic spirit is to be available to every man (Joel 2: 28ff. [Heb. 3]), the assurances of grace to David are given to all (Isa. 55: 3), the blessings of the patriarchs are promised not only to Israel but to all nations (Gen. 12), just as every one of them is also to celebrate the new feast of the covenant (Isa. 25: 6; above, §16b, 1). So the Old Testament itself goes beyond all the limits that are given it, and finally even goes beyond the limit of human life (Ps. 73: 23f.; Isa. 25: 8 et al.; see Excursus 8, 6).

In this respect there is no ultimate limit for the God of the Old Testament either. He can loose the bond to his own place (above, §5d, 4) and break up the link to his own land (Ezek. 1), occasionally even to his own people (Isa. 66: 21; Mal. 1: 11; Zeph. 2: 11; cf. above, IV, 3). Inherited ideas can be universalized; thus the reign of God extends beyond every area and every time (Ps. 103: 19; 145: 13). To put it another way, the Old Testament expresses with increasing strength the transcendence of God.

While Sinai was regarded originally as the place of the presence of God, the Yahwist seems already to want to increase the distance between God and the place on earth when as he pictures it 'Yahweh came down upon Mount Sinai' (Exod. 19: 18, 20; above, §5d, 4). Heaven becomes God's realm from which he set out, speaks, and intervenes in human affairs (Gen. 11: 5; 21: 17; Exod. 20: 22; 1 Kgs. 22: 19ff.; Mic. 1: 3; Ps. 2: 4; Isa. 66: 1 et al.). This concept of the heavenly dwelling place of God was probably already in the pre-exilic period influenced by concepts from the religions of Israel's neighbours; for these nations had various different deities of heaven (like Ba'al Shamaim, the 'Lord of Heaven'). Foreign influence comes out more clearly in the late period, which in dependence upon Persian terminology calls Yahweh 'the God of Heaven' (Ezra 1: 2; 5: 11f.; Neh.

1: 4f.; Jonah 1: 9; cf. Eccles. 5: 2 [Heb. 5: 1] 'God is in heaven and you upon earth'). Finally heaven becomes a term for God himself (Dan. 4: 23 et saep.).

While the creation narrative (Gen. 1) looks to the past, and apocalyptic to the future, in both areas of utterance a transcendent God stands over against the world as a whole; probably for this reason declarations of creation increase in number from the exilic period on (above, §11f, 9). Because the God of Sinai becomes in his transcendence the only ruler of the world, the nations can be drawn into this faith in Yahweh; for they are themselves close to God wherever they are (Zeph. 2: 11). The belief in God's superiority to the world makes possible life abroad for the diaspora, or even drives it to missionary activity.

To express both the distance and the nearness of God, his absence and presence at the same time, the Old Testament is aware of differences in God. In the view of Deuteronomy and the Deuteronomists it is only God's name that dwells in the place chosen by him; for P it is only God's glory that is present upon earth (above, §6c, 6).

Mediating beings appear between this world and the next world, between God and man. Already in the older accounts of theophanies a messenger can represent God in human life; God is audible or visible only through an angel (Exod. 3: 2ff.; Judg. 6: 11ff.; cf. Gen. 16; 21f. et al.). He is different from God, although he appears and speaks like God (21: 17; Judg. 13: 21f.). This concept is later extended more and more. In the night-visions of Zechariah 'no one has access to the invisible and hidden God who is beyond the whole world other than the angel alone, who as mediator between the external and the internal side of heaven transmits the revelatory action of God to the world, just as he elsewhere intercepts all prayers and events in the world and brings them before the throne of God. Even the prophetic reception of revelation can only take place for Zechariah through this mediating angel; he no longer has a direct relationship to the God who thrusts forward with mighty will in his word' (F. Horst). Finally the bands of angels increase to 'thousands and thousands of thousands, even innumerable' (Dan. 7: 10); from this circle there come also particular 'princes' with names (Dan. 8: 16; 10: 13 et al.).

God's hand (Exod. 14: 8; Ezek. 37: 1; Ezra 7: 6, 9, et al.,) or divine properties like spirit, wisdom and also the word, can represent God's activity upon earth, without actually becoming hypostases, or independent beings alongside God. Even the name of God is affected by this increasing remoteness: Yahweh is replaced, because of a stricter under-standing of the third commandment (cf. Lev. 24: 16) by 'Lord' (Adonai, Kyrios) or by 'the name' (Lev. 24: 11 et al.), if use is not made of the general term 'God' (cf. 2 Sam. 6: 9 with 1 Chr. 13: 12; Job; Ecclesiastes; Ps. 42–83 et al.). Because Yahweh is understood as God of heaven and earth, as the only Lord of the world, the proper name which distinguishes the God of Israel from other gods declines in use. The word 'God' becomes a proper name (cf. Ps. 51: 1[Heb. 51: 3] et al.). Thus the difference between God and man comes to be expressed more sharply: 'How can man be righteous before God?' (Job 25: 4; cf. 9: 2, 31; Eccles. 5: 1 et al.).

The Old Testament is concerned in various ways to distinguish between God and the world. Thus according to the interpretation of the prohibition of images in Deuteronomy (4: 12ff. above, §6c, 5) nothing this-worldly may portray God, so that God is withdrawn from the possibility of representation. A question like 'To whom will you liken God?' (Isa. 40: 18; cf. §11g) gives expression to the purpose of the first and second commandments, the exclusivity and the impossibility of portraying God. By means of a distinctive technical term (*bārā*'; above, §11f, 3) the Old Testament removes God's 'creating' from comparability to human activity. Since there is nothing in the world comparable to God's activity in creation, it is deprived of concreteness. The Old Testament has here given up portraying the action of God. In other places too it has words which are reserved for talk of God, like 'forgive' or more or less exclusively used for him, like 'anger' or 'choose'. Such theological expressions can perhaps, in accordance again with the purpose of the first and second commandments, preserve the uniqueness and the impossibility of portraying God; they attempt to distinguish God's action from this-worldly events, in order to think of God as incomparable (in image: Isa. 55: 9; Ps. 103: 11f.). So we can see in very different respects how concerned the Old Testament is about the appropriateness of the concepts of God used. It struggles for the correct understanding of God.

Nevertheless the Old Testament does not succumb to the danger of making its concepts of God so abstract that human reality is lost. God's transcendence does not mean an absoluteness which allows no further relationship, his exaltedness does not mean that he has separated himself from the world and has abandoned man (cf. Ps. 73: 11; Job 22: 13f.; Lam. 3: 44). To the Old Testament God's distance means precisely that he is near to everyone (Ps. 139; Job 34: 21f.). The exalted Lord is with the humble (Ps. 33: 13ff.; 113: 5ff.; Isa. 57: 15; 66: 1f.; also 61: 1). The concept of God's dwelling in heaven means at the same time the responsibility of man to God, for heaven is the place from which the world of man is visible:

> Yahweh looks down from heaven,
> he sees all the sons of men;
> from where he sits enthroned he looks forth
> on all the inhabitants of the earth. (Ps. 33: 14; cf. 14: 2 et al.)

The distinction between above and below corresponds especially to the difference between giving and receiving; heaven gives what the earth needs (Isa. 55: 10f.). So God's transcendence does not exclude his immanence; for God is distinguished in his activity from the world. The conception of God's being outside and above this world is intended to express that God is superior in power to everything this-worldly; God's transcendence is his power (cf. Gen. 1; Isa. 66: 1f.; above, §7, 3). God gives of his omnipotence to men; it is seen in the power which he gives to those who have need of it:

> He gives power to the faint,
> and to him who has no might he increases strength.

Even youths shall faint and be weary,
   and young men shall fall exhausted;
but they who wait to Yahweh shall renew their strength . . .
   they shall run and not be weary,
      they shall walk and not faint. (Isa. 40: 29ff.)

Select Bibliography

For a much more extensive treatment, the reader is referred to the German edition of this book.

ABBREVIATIONS

AfO	*Archiv für Orientforschung*
ANET	*Ancient Near Eastern Texts relating to the Old Testament*, ed. J. B. Pritchard, 3rd edn., Princeton, N.J., 1969
ASTI	*Annual of the Swedish Theological Institute*
Bib	*Biblica*
BJRL	*Bulletin of the John Rylands Library*
BK	*Biblischer Kommentar*, Neukirchen-Vluyn
CBQ	*Catholic Biblical Quarterly*
DOTT	*Documents from Old Testament Times*, ed. D. W. Thomas, London, 1958
EvTh	*Evangelische Theologie*
HTR	*Harvard Theological Review*
HUCA	*Hebrew Union College Annual*
JBL	*Journal of Biblical Literature*
JSS	*Journal of Semitic Studies*
KAI	*Kanaanäische und aramäische Inschriften*, ed. H. Donner and W. Röllig, 2nd edn., 3 vols., Wiesbaden, 1967–9
KuD	*Kerygma und Dogma*
MThZ	*Münchener theologische Zeitschrift*
NERT	*Near Eastern Religious Texts relating to the Old Testament*, ed. W. Beyerlin, Eng. tr., London, 1978
OTS	*Oudtestamentische Studiën*
StTh	*Studia Theologica*
TDNT	*Theological Dictionary of the New Testament*, ed. G. Kittel et al., Eng. tr., Grand Rapids, Michigan, 1964–
TDOT	*Theological Dictionary of the Old Testament*, ed. G. J. Botterweck and H. Ringgren, Eng. tr., Grand Rapids, Michigan, 1974–
ThR	*Theologische Rundschau*
ThZ	*Theologische Zeitschrift*
TLZ	*Theologische Literaturzeitung*
UF	*Ugarit-Forschungen*

VT   *Vetus Testamentum*
WO   *Welt des Orients*
ZAW   *Zeitschrift für alttestamentliche Wissenschaft*
ZDMG   *Zeitschrift der Deutschen Morgenländischen Gesellschaft*
ZTK   *Zeitschrift für Theologie und Kirche*

Commentaries

References to standard commentaries are simply shown by giving the commentator's name in parentheses.

§1 The Problem

K. Koch, 'Der Tod des Religionsstifters', *KuD* 8 (1962), pp. 100–103
R. Rendtorff, 'Die Entstehung der israelitischen Religion als religions-
  geschichtliches und theologisches Problem', *TLZ* 88 (1963), cols. 735–746
See too more generally the histories of Israelite religion:
W. O. E. Oesterley and T. H. Robinson, *Hebrew Religion, its Origin and Develop-
  ment*, 2nd edn., London, 1937
T.C. Vriezen, *The Religion of Ancient Israel* (1963), London, 1967
and especially
H. Ringgren, *Israelite Religion* (1963), London, 1966
G. Fohrer, *History of Israelite Religion* (1969), London, 1973

I NOMADIC PREHISTORY

§2 The Individual Traditions

G. von Rad, 'The Form-critical Problem of the Hexateuch' (1938), in *The
  Problem of the Hexateuch and other Essays*, Edinburgh, 1966, pp. 1–78
M. Noth, *A History of Pentateuchal Traditions* (1948), Englewood Cliffs, NJ, 1972
L. Rost, 'Das kleine geschichtliche Credo', in *Das kleine Credo und andere Studien
  zum Alten Testament*, Heidelberg, 1965, pp. 11–25

§3 The God of the Fathers

A. Alt, 'The God of the Fathers' (1929), in *Essays in Old Testament History and
  Religion*, Oxford, 1966, pp. 1–77 (fundamental)
O. Eissfeldt, 'El and Yahweh', *JSS* 1 (1956), pp. 25–37
F. M. Cross, 'Yahweh and the Gods of the Patriarchs', *HTR* 55 (1962),
  pp. 225–259
F. M. Cross, *Canaanite Myth and Hebrew Epic*, Cambridge, Mass., 1973,
  pp. 1–12

J. van Seters, *Abraham in History and Tradition*, New Haven, 1975
C. Westermann, *The Promises to the Fathers* (1976), Philadelphia, 1980
W. McKane, *Studies in the Patriarchal Narratives*, Edinburgh, 1979
  On historical questions:
M. Weippert, *The Settlement of the Israelite Tribes in Palestine* (1967), London, 1971, pp. 102–126
R. de Vaux, *The Early History of Israel* (1971), London, 1978, vol. 1, pp. 161ff. and esp. 268–287

e *Appendix: The sanctuary legends*
H. Gunkel, *Genesis*, 3rd edn., Göttingen, 1910
J. Lindblom, 'Theophanies in Holy Places in Hebrew Religion', *HUCA* 32 (1961), pp. 91–106
C. Westermann, *The Promises to the Fathers* (1976), Philadelphia, 1980
  On Gen. 28:10–22 cf. the commentaries and
C. Houtman, 'What did Jacob see in his Dream at Bethel? Some Remarks on Genesis xxviii 10–22', *VT* 27 (1977), pp. 337–351
  On Gen. 32:23–32 cf. the commentaries and
T. H. Gaster, *Myth, Legend and Custom in the Old Testament*, London, 1969, pp. 205–212
R. Barthes and R. Martin-Achard in R. Barthes et al., *Structural Analysis and Biblical Exegesis* (1971), Pittsburgh, 1974
R. Coote, 'The Meaning of the Name *Israel*', *HTR* 65 (1972), pp. 137–142

§4 *The Exodus from Egypt*

S. Herrmann, *Israel in Egypt* (1970), London, 1973
R. de Vaux, *The Early History of Israel* (1971), London, 1978, vol. 1, pp. 321ff.
G. W. Coats, 'History and Theology in the Sea Tradition', *StTh* 29 (1975), pp. 53–62
W. H. Schmidt, *Exodus, Sinai und Mose*, EdF, Wissenshaftl. Buchges. z.Z., forthcoming

Excursus 1: *Redemption*
TDOT II, pp. 350–355

§5 *The Revelation at Sinai*

W. Beyerlin, *Origins and History of the Oldest Sinaitic Traditions* (1961), Oxford, 1965
L. Perlitt, *Bundestheologie im Alten Testament*, Neukirchen-Vluyn, 1969
R. de Vaux, *The Early History of Israel* (1971), London, 1978, vol. 1, pp. 393ff.
W. Zimmerli, *Old Testament Theology in Outline* (1972), Edinburgh, 1978, pp. 41ff.

E. W. Nicholson, *Exodus and Sinai in History and Tradition*, Oxford, 1973
D. J. McCarthy, *Treaty and Covenant*, 2nd edn., Rome, 1978, esp. pp. 243ff.

a *The theophany according to Exod. 19*
J. Jeremias, *Theophanie*, 2nd edn., Neukirchen-Vluyn, 1977, pp. 100ff.
G. I. Davies, 'Hagar, El-Heǧra and the Location of Mount Sinai', *VT* 22 (1972), pp. 152–163

b *The making of the covenant according to Exod. 24*
T. C. Vriezen, 'The Exegesis of Exodus XXIV 9–11', *OTS* 17 (1972), pp. 100–133
E. W. Nicholson, 'The Interpretation of Exodus XXIV 9–11', *VT* 24 (1974), pp. 77–97; 25 (1975), pp. 69–79; 26 (1976), pp. 148–160

c *The making of the covenant according to Exod. 34*
H. Kosmala, 'The So-called Ritual Decalogue', *ASTI* 1 (1962), pp. 31–61, also in H. Kosmala, *Studies, Essays and Reviews*, Leiden, 1978, vol. 1, pp. 12–42

§6 The Characteristic features of Yahwistic Faith

a *The name of Yahweh*
1 'I am Yahweh'
W. Zimmerli, *Old Testament Theology in Outline* (1972), Edinburgh, 1978, pp. 17ff., 109ff.
TDOT III, pp. 346–352
    On the Decalogue:
J. J. Stamm and M. E. Andrews, *The Ten Commandments in Recent Research* (1958), London, 1967
E. Nielsen, *The Ten Commandments in New Perspective*, London, 1968
A. C. J. Phillips, *Ancient Israel's Criminal Law*, Oxford, 1970
E. W. Nicholson, 'The Decalogue as the Direct Address of God', *VT* 27 (1977), pp. 422–433

2 The name Yahweh
R. de Vaux, *The Early History of Israel* (1971), London, 1978, vol. 1, pp. 338ff.
F. M. Cross, *Canaanite Myth and Hebrew Epic*, Cambridge, Mass., 1973, pp. 60ff.
D. J. McCarthy, 'Exod 3, 14', *CBQ* 40 (1978), pp. 311–322
H. H. Rowley, 'Moses and Monotheism' (1957), revised in *From Moses to Qumran*, London, 1963, pp. 35–63
M. Weippert, *The Settlement of the Israelite Tribes in Palestine* (1967), London, 1971, pp. 105f.

3 Was Yahweh God of the Midianites?
W. H. Schmidt, *Exodus, Sinai und Mose*, EdF, Wissenschaftl. Buchges., z.Z.,
   forthcoming

4 Was Yahweh the God of Moses?
R. J. Thompson, *Moses and the Law in a Century of Criticism*, Leiden, 1970
G. Widengren, 'What do we know about Moses?', in J. I. Durham and J. R. Porter
   (eds), *Proclamation and Presence*, London, 1970, pp. 21–47
G. W. Coats, 'Moses in Midian', *JBL* 92 (1973), pp. 1–10

b *The first commandment*
On the ancient Near East:
R. Mayer, 'Monotheistische Strömungen in der altorientalischen Umwelt
   Israels', *MThZ* 8 (1957), pp. 97–113
H. Ringgren, *TDOT* I, pp. 267–273
   For the Old Testament:
W. H. Schmidt, *Das erste Gebot*, 1969
W. Zimmerli, *Old Testament Theology in Outline* (1972), Edinburgh, 1978,
   pp. 115ff. *TDOT* I, pp. 193–197

c *The second commandment*
G. von Rad, 'Some aspects of the Old Testament world-view' (1964), in *The
   Problem of the Hexateuch and other Essays*, Edinburgh, 1966, pp. 144–165
G. von Rad, *Wisdom in Israel* (1970), London, 1974, pp. 177–185
T. Mettinger, 'The Veto on Images', in H. Biezais (ed.), *Religious Symbols and
   their Functions*, Stockholm, 1979, pp. 15–29
   On the subsequent effects:
J. Gutman (ed.), *No Graven Images: Studies in Art and the Hebrew Bible*, New York,
   1971

d *The relationship to history*
For the ancient Near East:
R. C. Dentan (ed.), *The Idea of History in the Ancient Near East*, New Haven, 1955
E. A. Speiser, *Oriental and Biblical Studies*, Philadelphia, 1967, pp. 197–212,
   270–312
B. Albrektson, *History and the Gods*, Lund, 1967
   For the Old Testament:
J. Barr, *Old and New in Interpretation*, London, 1966, pp. 65–102
J. R. Wilch, *Time and Event*, Leiden, 1969
N. W. Porteous, 'Old Testament and History', *ASTI* 8 (1970–71), pp. 21–77

Excursus 2: *The sabbath commandment*
H.-J. Kraus, *Worship in Israel* (1962), Oxford, 1966, pp. 70–88

H. H. Rowley, 'Moses and the Decalogue', in *Men of God*, Edinburgh, 1963, pp. 27–32

M. Tsevat, 'The Basic Meaning of the Biblical Sabbath', *ZAW* 84 (1972), pp. 447–459

N.-E. Andreasen, *The Old Testament Sabbath*, Missoula, Montana, 1972

H. W. Wolff, *Anthropology of the Old Testament* (1973), London, 1974, pp. 134–142

N.-E. Andreasen, 'Recent Studies of the Old Testament Sabbath: Some Observations', *ZAW* 86 (1974), pp. 453–469

II   THE EARLY PERIOD AFTER THE CONQUEST

§7   The 'Wars of Yahweh'

G. von Rad, *Der heilige Krieg im alten Israel*, Zurich, 1951, 5th edn., 1969

R. Smend, *Yahweh War and Tribal Confederation* (1963), Nashville, 1970

P. D. Miller, *The Divine Warrior in Early Israel*, Cambridge, Mass., 1973

P. C. Craigie, *The Problem of War in the Old Testament*, Grand Rapids, Mich., 1978

M. C. Lind, *Yahweh is a Warrior*, Scottdale, Pa., 1980

Excursus 3:   *The 'spirit' of God*

F. Baumgärtel, *TDNT* VI (1959) 1968, pp. 359–367

D. Lys, *'Ruach': Le souffle dans l'ancien testament*, Paris, 1963

§8   The Tribal Confederacy

M. Noth, *Das System der zwölf Stämme Israels*, Stuttgart, 1930

G. E. Mendenhall, *Law and Covenant in Israel and the Ancient Near East*, Pittsburgh, 1955

K. Baltzer, *The Covenant Formulary* (1960), Oxford, 1971

D. J. McCarthy, *Old Testament Covenant* (1966), Oxford, 1972

R. de Vaux, *Early History of Israel* (1971), London, 1978, vol. 2, pp. 695ff.

A. D. H. Mayes, *Israel in the Period of the Judges*, London, 1974

C. H. J. de Geus, *The Tribes of Israel*, Assen, 1976

D. J. McCarthy, *Treaty and Covenant*, 2nd edn., Rome, 1978

Excursus 4:   *'Covenant'*

L. Perlitt, *Bundestheologie im Alten Testament*, Neukirchen-Vluyn, 1969

W. Zimmerli, *Old Testament Theology in Outline* (1972), Edinburgh, 1978, pp. 48–58

M. Weinfeld, *TDOT* II, pp. 253–279

J. Barr, 'Some Semantic Notes on the Covenant', in H. Donner et al. (eds),
   Beiträge zur alttestamentlichen Theologie, Göttingen, 1977, pp. 23–38

Excursus 5: *Election*
T. C. Vriezen, *Die Erwählung Israels nach dem Alten Testament*, Zurich, 1953
TDOT II, pp. 73–87
W. Zimmerli, *Old Testament Theology in Outline* (1972), Edinburgh, 1978,
   pp. 43–48
B. E. Shafer, 'The Root *bḥr* and pre-exilic conceptions of chosenness in the
   Hebrew Bible', *ZAW* 89 (1977), pp. 20–42

§9 Sanctuaries and Feasts

a *Sanctuaries*
H.-J. Kraus, *Worship in Israel* (1962), Oxford, 1966, pp. 134ff.
TDOT II, pp. 139–145
P. H. Vaughan, *The Meaning of 'bama' in the Old Testament*, Cambridge, 1974
M. Haran, *Temples and Temple-service in Ancient Israel*, Oxford, 1978
   On the tent and the ark:
R. de Vaux, 'Ark of the Covenant and Tent of Reunion' (1961), in *The Bible and
   the Ancient Near East*, London, 1972, pp. 136–151
J. Gutmann, 'The History of the Ark', *ZAW* 83 (1971), pp. 22–30
TDOT I, pp. 118–130; 363, 374
A. F. Campbell, *The Ark Narrative*, Missoula, Mont., 1975
A. F. Campbell, 'Yahweh and the Ark: A Case Study in Narrative', *JBL* 98
   (1970), pp. 31–43

b *Feasts*
H.-J. Kraus, *Worship in Israel*, (1962), Oxford, 1966, pp. 45ff.
R. de Vaux, *Ancient Israel* (1958), London, 1961, pp. 484–517
M. Haran, *Temples and Temple-Service in Ancient Israel*, Oxford, 1978, pp. 289ff.

1 The Feast of Passover and Unleavened Bread
J. B. Segal, *The Hebrew Passover from the Earliest Times to AD 70*, Oxford, 1963
R. de Vaux, *Early History of Israel*, (1971), London, 1978, vol. 1, pp. 365ff.

2 The Feast of Harvest or of Weeks
E. Lohse, *TDNT* VI (1954) 1968, pp. 45–49

3 The Feast of Ingathering or of Tabernacles
J. C. de Moor, *New Year with Canaanites and Israelites*, 2 vols., Kampen, 1972

4 Other feasts
On the Feast of Purim see the commentaries on Esther.

On occasions of communal lament:
H. W. Wolff, 'Der Aufruf zur Volksklage', *ZAW* 76 (1964), pp. 48–56, also in *Gesammelte Studien zum Alten Testament*, 2nd edn., Munich, 1973, pp. 392–401

Excursus 6: *Sacrifice*
H. H. Rowley, 'The Meaning of Sacrifice in the Old Testament', in *From Moses to Qumran*, London, 1963, pp. 67–107
R. de Vaux, *Ancient Israel* (1958), London, 1961, pp. 415ff.
R. de Vaux, *Studies in Old Testament Sacrifice*, Cardiff, 1964
B. A. Levine, *In the Presence of the Lord*, Leiden, 1974
J. Milgrom, *Cult and Conscience*, Leiden, 1976
TDOT I, pp. 429–437; IV, pp. 8–29; 309–319

III THE PERIOD OF THE MONARCHY

§10 The Significance of the Canaanite Gods in the Old Testament

W. F. Albright, *Yahweh and the Gods of Canaan*, London, 1968
J. C. de Moor, 'Semitic Pantheon', *UF* 2 (1970), pp. 187–228
F. M. Cross, *Canaanite Myth and Hebrew Epic*, Cambridge, Mass., 1973

c *The god El*
M. H. Pope, *El in the Ugaritic Texts*, Leiden, 1955
O. Eissfeldt, 'El and Yahweh', *JSS* 1 (1956), pp. 25–37
R. Rendtorff, 'El, Ba'al und Yahwe', *ZAW* 78 (1966), pp. 277–292
U. Oldenburg, *The Conflict between El and Ba'al in Canaanite Religion*, Leiden, 1969
TDOT I, pp. 242–261

b *The god Ba'al*
A. S. Kapelrud, *Baal in the Ras Shamra Texts*, Copenhagen, 1952
N. C. Habel, *Yahweh versus Baal*, New York, 1964
J. C. de Moor, *The Seasonal Pattern in the Ugaritic Myth of Ba'lu*, Neukirchen-Vluyn, 1971
P. J. van Zijl, *Baal: A Study of Texts in Connexion with Baal in the Ugaritic Epics*, Neukirchen-Vluyn, 1972

§11 The New Beliefs about God

a *The kingdom of God*
M. Buber, *Kingship of God* (1932), London, 1967

W. H. Schmidt, *Königtum Gottes in Ugarit und Israel*, 2nd edn., Berlin, 1966
J. Gray, *The Biblical Doctrine of the Reign of God*, Edinburgh, 1979

b *The 'holy' God*
H. Ringgren, *The Prophetical Conception of Holiness*, Uppsala, 1948
C. J. Labuschagne, *The Incomparability of Yahweh in the Old Testament*, Leiden, 1966

c *The 'living' God*
F. F. Hvidberg, *Weeping and Laughter in the Old Testament*, Leiden and Copenhagen, 1962
H. Ringgren, *Religions of the Ancient Near East* (1967), London, 1973, pp. 14, 64f., 148–150
TDOT IV, pp. 99–104

d *Theophany*
J. Jeremias, *Theophanie: Die Geschichte einer alttestamentlicher Gattung*, Neukirchen-Vluyn, 1965, 2nd edn., 1977
TDOT II, pp. 44–49

e *The fight with the chaos monster*
M. Wakeman, *God's Battle with the Monster*, Leiden, 1973
B. Otzen, H. Gottlieb and K. Jeppesen, *Myths in the Old Testament*, London, 1980, pp. 14–20, 68f.

f *Creation*
G. von Rad, 'The Theological Problem of the Old Testament Doctrine of Creation' (1936), in *The Problem of the Hexateuch and Other Essays*, Edinburgh, 1966, pp. 131–143
L. R. Fisher, 'Creation at Ugarit and in the Old Testament', *VT* 15 (1965), pp. 313–324
J. P. Hyatt, 'Was Yahweh originally a Creator Deity?' *JBL* 86 (1967), pp. 369–377
L. I. J. Stadelmann, *The Hebrew Conception of the World*, Rome, 1970
N. C. Habel, 'Yahweh, Maker of Heaven and Earth', *JBL* 91 (1972), pp. 321–337
C. Westermann, *Creation*, London, 1974

g *Results: borrowing and appropriation – the 'incomparability' of Yahweh*
C. J. Labuschagne, *The Incomparability of Yahweh in the Old Testament*, Leiden, 1966

§12   The Monarchy

a *The king*
S. H. Hooke, (ed.), *Myth, Ritual and Kingship*, Oxford, 1958
M. Noth, 'God, King and Nation in the Old Testament' (1950), in *The Law in the Pentateuch and other Essays*, Edinburgh, 1966, pp. 145–178
A. Bentzen, *King and Messiah* (1948), 2nd edn., Oxford, 1970
S. Mowinckel, *He that Cometh* (1951), Oxford, 1956
A. R. Johnson, *Sacral Kingship in Ancient Israel*, Cardiff, 1955, 2nd edn., 1967
R. de Vaux, *Ancient Israel* (1956), London, 1961, pp. 100ff.
J. A. Soggin, *Das Königtum in Israel*, Berlin, 1967
J. H. Eaton, *Kingship and the Psalms*, London, 1976
T. Mettinger, *King and Messiah*, Lund, 1976
T. Ishida, *The Royal Dynasties in Ancient Israel*, Berlin, 1977

b *Son of God*
G. Quell, *TDNT* V (1954) 1967, pp. 959–974
G. Fohrer, *TDNT* VIII (1967) 1972, pp. 340–354
J. Jeremias, *The Prayers of Jesus*, London, 1967
TDOT I, pp. 1–19; II, pp. 145–159

c *The image of God*
J. Barr, 'The Image of God in the Book of Genesis', *BJRL* 51 (1968), pp. 11–26
J. M. Miller, 'In the "image" and "likeness" of God', *JBL* 91 (1972), pp. 289–304
TDOT III, pp. 257–260

d *The Messiah*
S. Mowinckel, *He that Cometh* (1951), Oxford, 1956
H. Ringgren, *Messiah in the Old Testament*, London, 1956
J. Becker, *Messianic Expectation in the Old Testament* (1977), Edinburgh, 1980
W. H. Schmidt and J. Becker, *Zukunft und Hoffnung*, 1981, pp. 45ff.

§13   Zion

M. Noth, 'Jerusalem and the Israelite Tradition' (1950), in *The Laws in the Pentateuch and Other Essays*, Edinburgh, 1966, pp. 132–144
R. E. Clements, *God and Temple*, Oxford, 1965
F. Stolz, *Strukturen und Figuren im Kult von Jerusalem*, Berlin, 1970
R. J. Clifford, *The Cosmic Mountain in Canaan and the Old Testament*, Cambridge, Mass., 1972, pp. 131ff.

J. J. M. Roberts, 'The Davidic Origin of the Zion Tradition', *JBL* 92 (1972), pp. 329–344

F. L. Horton, *The Melchizedek Tradition*, Cambridge, 1976

§14 Prophecy

M. Buber, *The Prophetic Faith*, New York, 1949

J. Lindblom, *Prophecy in Ancient Israel*, Oxford, 1962

G. von Rad, *Old Testament Theology*, vol. II, Edinburgh, 1965, also published as *The Message of the Prophets*, London, 1968

W. Zimmerli, *Old Testament Theology in Outline* (1972), Edinburgh, 1978, pp. 99ff., 183ff.

H. Mowvley, *Guide to Old Testament Prophecy*, Guildford, 1979

R. R. Wilson, *Prophecy and Society in Ancient Israel*, Philadelphia, 1980

a *Its prehistory*

1 Outside Israel

M. Noth, 'History and the Word of God in the Old Testament' (1949), in *Laws in the Pentateuch and Other Essays*, Edinburgh, 1966, pp. 179–193

S. D. Walters, 'Prophecy in Mari and Israel', *JBL* 89 (1970), pp. 78–81

J. F. Ross, 'Prophecy in Hamath, Israel, and Mari', *HTR* 63 (1970), pp. 1–28

W. L. Moran, 'New Evidence from Mari on the History of Prophecy', *Bib* 50 (1960), pp. 15–56

NERT pp. 122ff.

2 In Israel

R. Rendtorff, 'Reflections on the Early History of Prophecy in Israel' (1962), *Journal for Theology and Church*, 4 (1967), pp. 14–34

H. C. Schmitt, 'Prophetie und Tradition', *ZTK* 74 (1977), pp. 255–272

b *The message*

C. Westermann, *Basic Forms of Prophetic Speech* (1960), London and Philadelphia, 1967

Excursus 7: *The 'word' of God*

TDNT IV (1942), 1967 pp. 91–100

TDOT III, pp. 84–125

§15 Wisdom

M. Noth and D. W. Thomas, *Wisdom in Israel and in the Ancient Near East*, Leiden, 1955

G. von Rad, *Wisdom in Israel* (1970), London, 1972

R. B. Y. Scott, *The Way of Wisdom*, New York, 1971
R. N. Whybray, *The Intellectual Tradition in the Old Testament*, Berlin, 1974
J. L. Crenshaw (ed.), *Studies in Ancient Israelite Wisdom*, New York, 1976
J. L. Crenshaw, *Old Testament Wisdom: An Introduction*, London, 1982
D. F. Morgan, *Wisdom in the Old Testament Traditions*, Oxford, 1982

IV THE LATE PERIOD

O. Plöger, *Theocracy and Eschatology* (1959), Oxford, 1968
P. R. Ackroyd, *Exile and Restoration*, London, 1968
M. Hengel, *Judaism and Hellenism* (1969), London, 1974
P. R. Ackroyd, *Israel under Babylon and Persia*, Oxford, 1970
D. E. Gowan, *Bridge between the Testaments*, Pittsburgh, 1976, rev. edn., 1980

§16 Apocalyptic

H. H. Rowley, *The Relevance of Apocalyptic*, 3rd edn., London, 1963
O. Plöger, *Theocracy and Eschatology* (1959), Oxford, 1968
P. Vielhauer, 'Apolcalyptic in Early Christianity', in E. Hennecke and
    W. Schneemelcher, *New Testament Apocrypha*, vol. II, (1964), London, 1965,
    pp. 581–607
M. Hengel, *Judaism and Hellenism* (1969), London, 1974, vol. 1, pp. 175–218
K. Koch, *The Rediscovery of Apocalyptic* (1970), London, 1972
L. Morris, *Apocalyptic*, 2nd edn., London, 1973
W. Schmithals, *The Apocalyptic Movement* (1973), Nashville, 1975
P. D. Hanson, *The Dawn of Apocalyptic*, Philadelphia, 1975, rev. edn., 1979
J. Lebram et al., 'Apokalyptik/Apokalypsen', in *Theologische Realenzyklopädie*,
    vol. III, 1978, pp. 189–289
On dualism:
M. Noth, 'The Understanding of History in Old Testament Apocalyptic' (1954),
    in *The Laws in the Pentateuch and other Studies*, Edinburgh, 1966
K. Koch and J. M. Schmidt, 'Apokalyptik', *Wege der Forschung* CCCLXV, 1982

Excursus 8: *Death and hope in the face of death*
On the ancient Near East:
W. Baumgartner, 'Auferstehungsglaube im Alten Orient' (1933), in *Zum alten
    Testament und seiner Umwelt*, Leiden, 1959, pp. 124–146
H. Ringgren, *Religions of the Ancient Near East* (1967), London, 1973, pp. 46–48,
    121–123, 175f.
On the Old Testament:
R. Martin-Achard, *From Death to Life: A Study of the Development of the Doctrine of
    the Resurrection in the Old Testament* (1956), Edinburgh, 1960

N. J. Tromp, *Primitive Conceptions of Death and the Nether World in the Old Testament*, Rome, 1969

L. I. J. Stadelmann, *The Hebrew Conception of the World*, Rome, 1970

G. W. E. Nickelsburg, *Resurrection, Immortality, and Eternal Life in Intertestamental Judaism*, Cambridge, Mass., 1972

H. W. Wolff, *Anthropology of the Old Testament* (1973), London, 1974

J. F. A. Sawyer, 'Hebrew Terms for the Resurrection of the Dead', *VT* 23 (1973), pp. 218–234

O. Kaiser and E. Lohse, *Death and Life* (1977), Nashville, 1981

L. R. Bailey, *Biblical Perspectives on Death*, Philadelphia, 1979

Index